Postmodernism and Social Theory

B

Postmodernism and Social Theory

The Debate over General Theory

edited by
Steven Seidman
and
David G. Wagner

BLACKWELL
Cambridge MA & Oxford UK

First published 1992

Basil Blackwell, Inc.
3 Cambridge Center
Cambridge, Massachusetts 02142, USA

Basil Blackwell Ltd
108 Cowley Road, Oxford, OX4 1JF, UK

Library of Congress Cataloging in Publication Data

Postmodernism and social theory: the debate over general theory / edited by Steven Seidman and David G. Wagner.
p. cm.
  Includes bibliographical references and index.
  ISBN 1-55786-048-3 – ISBN 1-55786-284-2 (pbk.)
  1. Sociology–Methodology, 2. Postmodernism–Social aspects.
I. Seidman, Steven. II. Wagner, David G. (David George), 1949–HM24.P664 1992
301'.01–dc20   91–7750
                                                                      CIP

British Library Cataloguing in Publication Data
A CIP catalogue record for this book is available from the British Library.

Typeset in 11.5 on 13pt Garamond
by Hope Services (Abingdon) Ltd.
Printed in Great Britain by T J Press, Padstow

This book is printed on acid-free paper.

Contents

Contributors

JEFFREY ALEXANDER, Department of Sociology, University of California at Los Angeles, Los Angeles

STANLEY ARONOWITZ, Department of Sociology, Graduate Center, City University of New York

RICHARD HARVEY BROWN, Department of Sociology, University of Maryland

CRAIG CALHOUN, Department of Sociology, University of North Carolina

RANDALL COLLINS, Department of Sociology, University of California at Riverside

ROBERT D'AMICO, Department of Philosophy, University of Florida at Gainesville

CHARLES LEMERT, Department of Sociology, Wesleyan University

LINDA NICHOLSON, Departments of Women's Studies and Educational Administration and Policy Studies, State University of New York at Albany

STEVEN SEIDMAN, Department of Sociology, State University of New York at Albany

JONATHAN TURNER, Department of Sociology, University of California at Riverside

STEPHEN TURNER, Department of Philosophy, University of South Florida at St Petersburg

DAVID G. WAGNER, Department of Sociology, State University of New York at Albany

Introduction

THE POSTMODERN CHALLENGE

The social sciences have never had the luxury of feeling secure in their identity or social role. Since their inception the meaning of the social sciences has been contested. Questions about the epistemological, political, and moral status of the social sciences have persisted to this day. Are the social sciences really scientific or are they part of the humanities? Is social science different from natural science in its concept formation and explanations? Is social science necessarily ideological or is its moral and political character merely indicative of its underdeveloped state? These questions raise serious concerns about the intellectual and institutional legitimacy of the social sciences.

The 1960s and 1970s were a crucial period in the debate over the meaning of the social sciences. The dominant positivism of the social sciences was subject to a barrage of criticism. A series of philosophical movements, most notably hermeneutics, ordinary language philosophy, postempiricist philosophy of science, and poststructuralism, converged in assailing the dominant positivist orthodoxy. The critics who espoused these positions argued that the natural and social sciences involve an interpretive ordering of empirical reality; that philosophical, aesthetic, and moral considerations play a role in all empirical inquiry; and that in its resistance to empirical verification science resembles literary interpretation. Although these critics agreed on certain basic points, there was disagreement on other equally fundamental issues. For example, hermeneutically inclined social scientists favored a more contextual and descriptive approach to the generalizing analytical explanations of postempiricists.

Out of these polemics between positivism and its critics there developed a shift in the center of debate. On the one hand, the discussion now centered on arguments over the respective merits and defects of interpretive, postempiricist and critical–normative paradigms of social science. In other words, while a positivist model of social science was rejected in these theoretical debates, the epistemic privileging of science went unchallenged. Thus, social scientists advanced hermeneutics or postpostivism or critical theory as alternative foundations for social science. On the other hand, the critique of positivism, especially by poststructuralists and some feminists, challenged the scientism of positivists and their critics. Many began to emphasize the social and historical embeddedness of an inquiry, its essentially moral and political nature, and the failure and indeed undesirability of all efforts to provide a unifying social scientific paradigm. A new division was drawn between those social scientists who defended the possibility and desirability of achieving secure analytical foundations – "modernists" – and critics of this project. In the social sciences, postmodernism describes the critique of the modernist project to ground and unify the social sciences. In its critique of modernist social science, postmodernists reconsider the relationship between scientific knowledge, power, and society as well as the relation between science, critique, and narrative.

ENLIGHTENMENT AND THE MODERNIST QUEST FOR SCIENTIFIC KNOWLEDGE AND SOCIAL PROGRESS

Despite their critique of metaphysics and religion, the *philosophes* never abandoned the notion that true knowledge must be universal and grounded in some metadiscourse. Appeals to theological dogma were replaced by science as the medium of truth. Initially developed in the context of the study of nature, the scientific paradigm was extended to human nature and society. By the end of the eighteenth century there was a proliferation of proposals for a social science. They all shared two basic assumptions. First, the aim of social science was thought to be to discover general principles. The ideal was to achieve a conceptual and analytical unity by reducing the human and social domain to a limited number of general principles or laws. Scientific knowledge would be grounded in a metadiscourse that, in France and England, typically took the form of an empiricist epistemology. Second, the *philosophes* agreed that social science would function as an instrument of social progress. It would abolish long-standing prejudices and ignorance by revealing truths about human nature, society, and history. Scientific enlightenment would enable humankind to fashion a social order in accordance with the true principles of nature and history. Science would make possible humankind's rational self-creation.

From the founding years of social science to its classical age the modernist project was sustained. The major classical figures – Comte, Marx, Durkheim, Spencer, Weber, Pareto, Albion Small, or Lester Ward – endorsed, indeed propagated, the epistemological privileging of science, its quest for intellectual unity based upon discovering general principles, and its beneficial practical role. For example, although Comte and Marx disagreed on the conceptual structure and explanatory principles of a social science, they both contrasted their own scientific efforts with the pre-scientific or merely "ideological" standpoint of their predecessors and contemporary rivals. Moreover, these classic figures viewed science as contributing to social progress. Comte anticipated that his "positive philosophy" and "positive polity" would be a guide to social reconstruction in postrevolutionary France. Marx saw his critique of political economy as contributing to human emancipation by becoming a material force in transforming the working class into a revolutionary political agent.

There is, however, one way in which classical figures departed from their predecessors. Whereas the former grounded social science in a philosophical metadiscourse, the latter looked increasingly to social theory to provide foundations. We can detect the beginnings of a concept of social theory as a foundational discourse in the nineteenth century. Its aim is to set out the basic premises, concepts, and problems of social science; to provide standards in terms of which empirical and analytical disputes can be resolved; to elaborate an overarching conceptual framework that would unify inquiry. This definition of the role of theory as a grounding discourse is apparent, for example, in Marx's *German Ideology* or in his *Introduction to the Critique of Political Economy*, which purports to advance epistemic reasons defending the proposition that labor or the mode of production can serve as the foundational category of a science of society and history. No less foundational in their aims are Durkheim's *Division of Labor in Society* and *Rules of Sociological Method*, Tönnies's *Gemeinschaft and Gesellschaft*, Weber's *Economy and Society*, and Simmel's *Sociology*.

In the twentieth century, social science underwent a process of institutionalization and cultural legitimation. This has shaped social science in distinctive ways. The academicization of social science has meant the heightening of its scientistic claims. In their effort to achieve institutional legitimacy and material resources, contemporary social scientists have often felt compelled to suppress the practical-moral or political role of science. Logical positivism provided the initial intellectual rationale. As the social sciences have sought institutional autonomy they have developed their own analytical and research agendas. Intellectual disputes have tended to be handled as purely discipline-bound analytical or methodological problems. Accordingly, the role of social theory as a metadiscourse whose aim is to adjudicate disciplinary disputes has expanded. Today theory, especially sociological theory, is typically defined as a distinct "specialty" or field of expertise concerned with its own "autonomous" epistemological, analytical, and methodological problems. For example, theorists are expected to take positions on the relation between concepts and the social world, the logical structure of sociological explanation, the nature of social action, order, and change, the linkage between agency and social structure or micro- and macro-levels of analysis, and so on. Theory has assumed the role of safeguarding the rationality of social science by holding that current disagreements are, at bottom, resolvable analytical or methodological problems. In its role as a grounding discourse, social theory has become increasingly metatheoretical.

THE POSTMODERN CRITIQUE

Ironically, the very institutional success of social science may have inadvertently contributed to the critique of the modernist project. For example, the increased dependence of social science on private and public funding agencies which inevitably shapes social research raises doubts about its claims to be value-neutral. Similarly, the effort to establish a disciplinary consensus through analytical means has met with little success. Stephen Turner's essay documents the absences and inconsistencies in the various foundationalist projects pursued by sociologists in the twentieth century. However, whereas he argues that these projects often lead to fruitful research programs, they have also generated metatheoretical discourses whose sole reference point seems, at times, to be other texts and discourses on texts. This has encouraged a heightened skepticism towards the foundational aims of modernist social science. Moreover, the effort to reconfigure social inquiry into a purely analytical mode, purging it of practical, moral, and political intent, has reinforced a public perception of the obscurity of social science. This is particularly true with respect to social theory which, in its effort to ground social inquiry, has often become mired in a web of metatheoretical tangles. Postmodernism seems, in part, to be responding to this condition and to the contradictory pull of social science towards an aimless empiricism and an equally aimless theoreticism. Postmodernism, at one level, can be characterized as a movement of intellectual revitalization.

Postmodernism is not, of course, the first effort of intellectual renewal through critique and reconstruction. The history of social science reads almost like a continuous effort at revitalization. From Comte's critique of the *philosophes* or Marx's critique of Comte, to Durkheim's and Weber's critique of Marx, to the Parsonian quest to synthesize the classical tradition and the subsequent efforts to supersede structural-functionalism by neo-Marxism, exchange theory, or structural sociology, the wish to revitalize social analysis through critique and reconstruction is an abiding motif. The postmodern critique is perhaps unique in that it challenges a project of social science shared by virtually all rival schools or paradigms. Postmodernism criticizes the modernist notion that science itself, not this or that theory or paradigm, is a privileged form of reason or the medium of truth. It disputes the scientistic claim that only scientific knowledge can be securely grounded. It takes issue with the unifying, consensus-building agenda of science. It contests the modernist idea that social theory has as its chief role the securing of conceptual grounds for social research. And postmodernism criticizes the modernist notion that science is or should be value-neutral; postmodernism underlines the practical and moral meaning of science.

Central to postmodernism is its critique of the claim that scientific knowledge is universal and can be justified in a noncontextual way. Postmodernists contend that standards of truth are context-dependent. In "On the Postmodern Barricades", Linda Nicholson argues that social theories derive their coherence and compelling power because they are part of socially effective cultural traditions. The standards of European and Anglo-American social science knowledge are said to be inextricably bound up with the culturally specific presuppositions of Western modernity. For example, the separation of cognitive truths from moral and aesthetic knowledge and indeed the prioritization of cognitive truths, the emphasis upon propositional knowledge, or the rationales for what counts as evidence or facts get their coherence from Western cultural traditions. Within the social scientific disciplines, moreover, there are conflicting evaluative criteria regarding what counts as valid research or theory. For some social scientists predictability, conceptual economy, or quantifiability are the chief standards; others emphasize explanatory comprehensiveness, descriptive richness, discursive cogency, or moral political or aesthetic criteria. These heterogeneous criteria seem immune to reasoned consensus.

The postmodern critique goes beyond a general historical contextualizing of science. Steven Seidman has argued for a radical decentering of science. He proposes that social scientific knowledge bears the imprint not only of the broad civilizational and national culture of which it is a part but typically of the more specific class, race, gender, or sexual orientation of its producers. Every attempt to advance a general theoretical standpoint is deconstructed or shown to reveal, in its basic concepts and explanations, the particular social standpoint and interests of its author. For example, Seidman criticizes Marxism by showing that it not only incorporates the scientism, utilitarianism, and millenialism of the liberal bourgeois society it criticizes but that its basic conceptual framework exhibits the standpoint and bias of a white European, middle-class heterosexual male. A general theory of society and history that is centered on economically based class dynamics neglects and marginalizes social and political dynamics that revolve around gender, ethnicity, race, sexuality, or age.

A decentered view of social science underscores its practical-moral and political significance. Charles Lemert suggests that the politics of social science are inextricably tied to its epistemology. The categories and explanations of social science, he contends, unavoidably construct social reality in a way that emphasizes certain social processes and privileges specific groups and social agendas. Indeed, postmodernists view social scientific knowledge as implicated in practical projects. It is not a matter of science providing knowledge which has practical utility. Rather, social scientific knowledge is seen as a strategy by which individuals and groups promote their interests, pursue a social agenda, or struggle for power. The link between science and power goes beyond ideological politics. The social sciences are a major social power in modern societies. As Nicholson says, their practical character is fully exhibited only when we realize that science is often implicated in the institutional power of hospitals, psychiatric clinics, mental asylums, prisons, and in bureaucratic-administrative strategies to regulate our behavior and shape our body images, identities, and daily conventions. From a postmodern perspective, science stands alongside the economy, state, family, or church as a major social and political force.

Postmodernists tend to favor forms of social inquiry which incorporate an explicitly practical and moral intent, that are contextual and restricted in their focus (local stories are preferred over general ones), and that are narratively structured rather than articulating a general theory. Thus, Seidman argues for transfiguring general theory into social narratives that incorporate a moral pragmatic interest. Lemert recommends a deconstructionist mode of social inquiry that would reveal false conceptual closures and force us to attend to the socially constitutive aspects of discourse. Yet Nicholson defends a postmodern theorizing that would permit cross-cultural, generalizing conceptual strategies. Postmodernism does not necessarily reject methodologically sophisticated and analytically informed social analysis but rather invokes a suspicion regarding claims that social inquiry can be grounded in some way that gives it a privileged epistemological status. Likewise, postmodernism does not necessarily repudiate generalizing analytical moves but rejects the modernist one of a totalizing, general theory or the quest for a unified social scientific paradigm. Postmodernists are more likely to theorize in a deconstructionist mode, to substitute genealogical analysis for the theory-building efforts, to reintroduce moral and political concerns as central discursive topics.

CRITICS OF POSTMODERNISM:
IN DEFENSE OF SCIENTIFIC THEORY

The postmodern challenge to the disciplines has generated its own critics. Many modernists do not concede the impossibility of foundations in social science. Renewed efforts to frame theory as a foundational discourse have appeared, most notably in the writings of Habermas and Giddens. Others have raised practical and moral doubts about the consequences of the postmodern critique. Does postmodernism end in relativism and nihilism? Does its radical decentering call into question any rational standards of discourse? Questions have been raised about whether repudiating the project of a general theory means the abandonment of a strong program of analytical and critical theorizing. Does postmodernism's radical deconstructionism mean that all general categories become problematic or illegitimate? Does its radical historicist critique lead to a descriptivism that lacks the deep critical impulse of analytical theorizing?

One of the most basic failings of postmodernism the critics identify is its failure to distinguish the relativism of the frameworks within which sociological theorizing must proceed from the knowledge generated by employing those frameworks. The choice of a framework for investigating social phenomena is accepted as an inherently particularistic choice, subject rather directly to the deconstruction that postmodernism encourages. However, the actual investigation of social phenomena, given the adoption of a frame of reference, need not be particularlistic. Deconstruction at this level does lead directly to solipsism, the critics argue. Thus, Randall Collins, in "The Confusion of the Modes of Sociology," imagines a twenty-first-century review of a physics text, given success of the postmodernist critique throughout science. He parallels this fantasy with the analysis provided by Michael Mulkay in *The Word and the World*. In his "deconstruction" of Mulkay's postmodern "deconstruction" sociological analysis, Collins playfully suggests that Erving Goffman must have been the book's author; authorship is simply a matter of interpretation and presentation anyway. In Collins's view, postmodernism provides no means of disputing such claims.

As a consequence, the critics claim that postmodernism too readily dismisses the possibility of scientific theorizing in sociology. Most sociological critics of postmodernism argue that some sort of general (or generalizing) theory is both possible to attain and desirable to pursue. Some even argue that cumulative knowledge of fundamental social processes has already been generated in a number of areas.

This is certainly Collins's view. He believes we should focus on the investigation of fundamental social processes at an abstract level. A great deal of knowledge of this sort has been cumulated, he claims, but this success has been obscured by the confusion of practical and ideological (i.e. evaluative) frames with the scientific frame. The practical frame is applicable only within physically closed systems. The ideological frame, when treated imperially, allows us only to see what we want to see. The scientific frame, by contrast, can encompass and articulate both of the other frames; at the same time it goes beyond them to create general knowledge. Thus, despite the postmodern critique, Collins sees grounds for optimism in sociological theorizing.

Others make similar arguments, although there are some

significant differences in their images of the nature of the project involved. D'Amico briefly analyzes Carnap's notion of "framework relativism" and then more extensively considers Popper's division between the objects of world 1 (i.e. the world of physical objects and states), world 2 (i.e. the world of mental states and behavioral dispositions), and world 3 (i.e. the world of objective contents of thought). Using these ideas, he proposes how a generalizing social science might absorb much of the postmodern critique without yielding to its particularism.

One attempt to develop an understanding of the nature of these frameworks and their role in sociological theorizing has been pursued by David Wagner. Drawing on previous largely unsuccessful attempts to bridge the gap between theoretical and empirical work in sociology (especially by Robert Merton and by advocates of theory construction), he identifies several lessons to be learned from these attempts. For example, it is possible to proceed theoretically without an articulated general framework or theory. Nevertheless, general theory does serve an integrative and directive purpose we would do well to investigate in detail.

In "Daring Modesty: On Metatheory, Observation, and Theory Growth," Wagner proposes that we view general theory in terms of "orienting strategies" (i.e. metatheoretical entities somewhat similar to Kuhnian "paradigms" or Lakatosian "hard cores"). The adoption of such strategies, he argues, is necessary to do any sociological work. The truth of such strategies is not directly testable; instead, their utility is determined largely by their ability to generate more specific theories to account for social phenomena in particular explanatory domains. The success of a strategy therefore is evaluated largely on grounds internal to the strategy and is always provisional. Consequently, a single overarching general theory of society is not possible; general theories of society are necessary and important elements of sociological work. These arguments suggest to Wagner that we ought to be more modest about our claims regarding the ontological and epistemological status of general theories and more daring in our willingness to actually implement the directives of general theories.

Jonathan Turner articulates a position perhaps closer to modernism than any of the other critics, although he does introduce some significant modification to that position. In "The Promise of Positivism," Turner defends the importance of deductive rigor, prediction, and falsification as criteria for evaluating theory. However, he relaxes the application of these criteria somewhat: deductive theorizing need not be axiomatic; precise prediction is seldom possible; definitive tests are unlikely. Moreover, he thoroughly rejects the notion of theory assessment as an inductive process from neutral observations. With Collins, Turner challenges many of the criticisms of this form of positivist sociology as flowing from phemonenological solipsism and historical particularism. He suggests that these criticisms are based on a naive view of the nature of science and are in no way obstacles to a positive theory of society.

BETWEEN MODERNISM AND POSTMODERNISM: TOWARDS A CONTEXTUALIZING GENERAL THEORY

While postmodernism and general scientific theorizing are perhaps not polar opposites, they do reflect dramatically different images of the character and goals of sociological theorizing, especially in relation to political ideology. Some investigators attempt to find some middle ground between these two opposed images. Generally, these investigators take some portion of the postmodern move as given, but they also seek to go beyond that critique to recover some more general notion regarding social theorizing.

These intermediate positions between modernism and post-modernism depend on acceptance of different aspects of postmodernism, and are therefore rather idiosyncratic in character. For example, in "Social Science and Society as Discourse: Toward a Sociology for Civic Competence," Richard Harvey Brown argues for *multiple* general theories (although he comes at the issue from a point of view very different from Wagner's). Brown argues that social scientific discourse reveals a plurality of general theories, each internally consistent and each with a different root metaphor, a different intellectual telos, and a different ideological interest. Thus, positivist general theory uses organic and mechanistic metaphors which focus its ideological interest on the stability and maintenance of societal order. Such a theory cannot deal adequately with the reflexive character of individual lifeworlds.

To deal with this character Brown proposes an alternative general theory based on a metaphor of society as communicative action. Social structure is seen as a series of language structures invented through speech acts. For example, in economic analysis money constructs (i.e. signifies) value, it does not represent (i.e. communicate) the value of something else. Such an approach has several advantages for Brown. It encompasses micro-, meso-, and macro-levels of analysis; it reflexively recognizes its own moral and political functions; and it helps break down arbitrary political boundaries.

Stanley Aronowitz proposes another, very different candidate for general theory. The Frankfurt School, he argues, developed a powerful critical social theory. Its focus shifted from a critique of political economy to a critique of technical reason, mass culture, and consumerism. Critical theory provided an alternative to positivism, which was viewed as contributing to social domination.

In "The Tensions of General Theory: Is Negative Dialectics All There Is?" Aronowitz argues that critical theory is today in need of reconstruction. Its social analysis has rendered social change virtually impossible. Its standpoint has become one-dimensionally negative and rhetorical. Aronowitz calls for a reconstruction of critical theory that evolves general categories that both articulate social conflicts and assume a critical stance towards them.

Other intermediate positions are somewhat more eclectic in their choice of material to draw upon in building a more flexible notion of general theory. Craig Calhoun sees general theory as traditionally reflecting both a concern for breadth of application (universality) and for the formulation of lawlike statements. In "Culture, History and the Problem of Specificity in Social Theory," he suggests there is an alternative to both traditional concerns. He argues for a general theory that is culturally sensitive (both to the problem of difference in values and to the value of differences) and historically specific. In his view the production of theories is a historical phenomenon that yields categories adequately only in specific epochs and theories that are alternatives in a discursive field. Nevertheless, such work can be theoretically grounded more generally through continuous effort at cross-cultural and historical description.

This processual approach generates for Calhoun a "polyphonic discourse," not a single right answer to sociological questions. Local, mid-range, and general claims must always remain separate; there can be no strong deduction, reduction, or aggregation. Postmodernism, in Calhoun's understanding, is actually an internal product of modernity. Its challenge to this more general approach is flawed in two ways. First, it is unable to provide grounds for the normative judgments made in the postmodern critique. Second, its elevation of difference to absolute importance does violence to the notion of intersubjectivity. Consequently, while the postmodern critique has had much to contribute, it is ultimately only one contributor to sociological understanding.

Finally, Jeffrey Alexander challenges the dichotomization of scientific theory and relativism as false and dangerous in "General Theory in the Postpositivist Mode: The 'Epistmological Dilemma' and the Search for Present Reason." He outlines several reasons this false antagonism has been generated. For example, relativistic analysis traditionally focuses on individual perceptions, interpretations, and beliefs. But actors can be and are bound to collective standards and traditions of rationality. Theoretical analysis is relative to those collective standards, not unique and individual. Similarly, relativistic analysis treats theoretical claims as incommensurable. But incommensurability is not the same as incompatibility, which more accurately characterizes the relation between theoretical arguments.

Furthermore, there is some correspondence between our reason-created conceptual structures and reasonable observation statements. We can reach agreement about the value of at least some of our theories, even without assuming that observations exist entirely independently from them. Perhaps most important, the act of seeking consensus is the central goal. Even hermeneutical philosophy, Alexander argues, is based on the notion that lifeworlds are impersonal and assume a universal consensual form. Thus, the seeking of foundations, the attempt to create shared and binding norms of sociological activity, is central to the theoretical enterprise. Alexander concludes that if social theorizing had secure foundations, they could be put in the background and ignored. Ironically, then, it is the very absence of foundations that necessitates our pursuit of them.

THE DIALOGUE CONTINUES

The debate between postmodern social theorists and their critics is part of a broader public discussion in Western societies over the meaning and social role of science today. The optimism of the *philosophes* and their heirs that science would produce Truths that promote a good society has come under attack. The connection of science to warfare and Nazism, public discontent over scientific medicine and psychiatry, the assault on science by the black, women's, and gay movements, has rendered an unequivocal Enlightenment faith naive. Yet, science continues to have an aura and a cultural currency that is frequently appealed to by entrepreneurs, politicians, and scholars. Undoubtedly, it is science's social entanglement and its politicization initially by the left and more recently by the right that prompts much of the current debate over the meaning and social role of science.

Within the disciplines, this discussion typically takes the form of an epistemological questioning. Is science a unique, privileged form of knowledge? What kind of mode of knowing is science? How should we understand the way science is social? This questioning of science within the disciplines has been intensified by two developments. The institutional elaboration of science and its increasingly visible links to social institutions and the state have rendered it a powerful social force. From a different vantage point, as universities have opened up to hitherto excluded populations – people of color, feminists, lesbians and gay men, the differently-abled, the elderly – questions have been raised about the social role of science. The exclusions and absences of science have suggested to some that the disciplines are tied to social projects. The meaning of the social entanglement of science, the question of how science can be both a discourse claiming objective knowledge and a social force shaping social identities and normative and institutional order, we believe, lies at the root of the debates between postmodernists and their critics. These are, ultimately, debates about the meaning of science and, to recall Weber, our vocation as scholars.

PART I

Towards Postmodernism:
Reconfiguring Theory and Politics

1

General Social Theory, Irony, Postmodernism

Charles Lemert

In *The Return of Grand Theory in the Human Sciences* Quentin Skinner (1985: 5–6) characterizes the present situation in theory aptly:

> Times have certainly changed. During the past generation, Utopian social philosophies have once again been practised as well as preached; Marxism has revived and flourished in an almost bewildering variety of forms; psychoanalysis has gained a new theoretical orientation with the work of Lacan and his followers; Habermas and other members of the Frankfurt School have continued to reflect on the parallels between the theories of Marx and Freud; the Women's Movement has added a whole range of previously neglected insights and arguments; and amidst all this turmoil the empiricist citadels of English-speaking social philosophy have been threatened and undermined by successive waves of hermeneuticists, structuralists, post-empiricists, deconstructionists and other invading hordes.

Skinner is the first to admit that the impulse most common to these hordes is a "strong dislike . . . of all overarching theories and singular schemes of explanation" (1985: 12).

To describe these theories as a return of grand theory is, therefore, to use language loosely, perhaps aggressively, to call attention to the craziness of a time like the present in which, it seems, we are doing that which cannot be done. Skinner, thereby, uses irony. He perverts the famous epithet with which C. Wright Mills attacked Talcott Parsons. The "grand" in the grand theories he mentions has less to do with the scope of the theories than perhaps the attitudes and ambitions of the theorists But as theories they are not grand, in the usual sense.

Theory vexes us. This is the state of collective mind to which Skinner's irony is directed. Theory is something we do with a vengeance at the very time when theory is considered dead by many who do it. Or worse, if not dead, theory is taken – again by the majority of the theorists to whom Skinner alludes – as a final veil that must be cast aside to reveal the truth of modernity's evil.

This, of course, is only one interpretive spin put on the current status of theory. Other thinkers, while well aware of the hordes to which Skinner alludes, are less overtly troubled by the prospect of theory's mortality or its complicity in the evils of the day. If they confess objections to theory, it is to various brands of theory, not to theory itself.

Anthony Giddens and Jonathan Turner (1987), for example, have edited a book, *Social Theory Today*, which affirms, even celebrates, the vibrancy of social theory in and beyond the social sciences. Yet, when they try their hands at defining the subject matter of social theory, they retreat to old-fashioned and "bald" (their word) generalizations, admitting that "any definition of social theory is bound to be controversial" (Giddens and Turner 1987: 1). More even than Skinner's frank perversion of the idea of grand theory, the Giddens–Turner book, *Social Theory Today*, is witness to the confusion in our attempts to understand theory. What kind of a thing are we dealing with that is able to unite in a single project two men of such different convictions?

Giddens and Turner are two of the most productive, brilliant, and influential social theorists of the current generation. Yet it would be hard to name two other writers at their entirely deserved level of reputation who disagree more on the meaning and purpose of social theory. Turner, as he makes clear time and time again, is a positivist who hates the tendency of social thinkers to engage in philosophizing that goes beyond strict analytic work on testable concepts. "My bias is that philosophizing is best left to the philosophers" (Turner in this volume). Giddens, on the other hand, defends a view of social theory wherein one must think through more general matters as context to understanding the world. As such, social theory inevitably "involves the analysis of issues which spill over into philosophy" (Giddens 1984: xvii). According to Giddens, whatever social theory is, or is not, it has been and still is an endeavor that does not strongly demarcate the boundary between a social science and philosophizing. Thus, Giddens believes in social theory in its customary sense. Turner does not. What, then, brings them together in this project? Neither, surely, has need of another publication. One thing only: both believe in some sense in theory even when they cannot agree on what it is or does.

The distinctly different attitudes portrayed by Skinner in *The Return of Grand Theory in the Human Sciences* and Giddens and Turner in *Social Theory Today* are, however, united on the one general truth of theory today: *irony*. Richard Rorty (1989: 73) defines the "ironist" as:

> someone who fulfills three conditions: (1) She has radical and continuing doubts about the final vocabulary she currently uses, because she has been impressed by other vocabularies, vocabularies taken as final by people or books she has encountered; (2) she realizes that arguments phrased in her present vocabulary can neither underwrite nor dissolve these doubts; (3) insofar as she philosophizes about her situation, she does not think that her vocabulary is closer to reality than others, that it is in touch with a power not herself.

Rorty's idea of irony, though somewhat oblique to traditional interpretations of this literary trope, is directly applicable to the current situation in general theory. The sense of Rorty's idea is in the expression "final vocabularies." To speak of *final* vocabularies is to indulge the form of ideas that seek to express, convey, grasp, or define that which is ultimate or total. Grand theory, in Mill's original usage, mocked Parsons for the intent of generating a total theory of the social system. But to speak of final *vocabularies* is to concede that language has replaced truth – or, in Rorty's (1979) terms, epistemology – as the taken-for-granted substance of any such total description. Language, vocabularies, cannot be final. Thus, the very expression calls into question the finality of any statement and the ironist is that theorist who nevertheless makes grand statements, all the while recognizing they cannot be finally persuasive against other such statements.[1] Ironists, Rorty adds (1989: 73–4), are "never quite able to take themselves seriously because [they are] always aware that the terms in which they describe themselves are subject to change, always aware of the contingency and fragility of their final vocabularies, and thus of their selves."

To be sure, not every social theorist today is a pure ironist. Skinner, Giddens, and Turner, each in turn, suggest at least three ironic positions with respect to theory: aggressive, reluctant, and resistant. Skinner uses Mills's phrase "grand theory" in an intentionally ironic manner. Giddens, by contrast, could not write in such mind-boggling volume with such alluring grace if an ironist pure. He instead discusses and uses the most ironic of positions available, the poststructuralist (among others), and proceeds to write in a postironic manner. Turner hates irony as much as he hates philosophizing, yet is moved by the state of affairs in which his rugged anti-ironic positivism must suffer a "hostile intellectual environment" (Giddens and Turner 1987: 191).

Whatever social theory today is or is not, it has few choices beyond accepting, getting around, or resisting the stance of radical and continuing doubt about the final vocabulary available for use in speaking about the social world.[2] This is the salient mark of social theory today in contrast to that of a previous generation.

In 1957, in the Introduction to *Social Theory and Social Structure*, one of the most influential of all social science theory books, Robert Merton wrote:

> This announced interest in consolidating the reciprocal relations between social theory and social research is suspiciously irreproachable. Where will one find a social scientist disclaiming the desirability of the "integration" of theory and empirical research? Unless it is given some special force, this position will possess the same measure of trivial truth as the position held by Calvin Coolidge's preacher who was unexceptionally "against sin." (*Merton 1957: 4*)

Merton is one of the best sociological writers of his generation. In this passage, he uses irony skillfully. "Suspiciously irreproachable" and its illustration with reference to the wit of Calvin Coolidge puts into doubt a truism of the day. Yet, reading on, it becomes evident that Merton's doubt is very different from that of our time. Merton doubted not the possibility of consolidating theory and research but the will of sociologists to make progress toward this entirely possible and desired end. The passage quoted, accordingly, introduces the section in which he presents and defends his famous proposal of theories of the middle range. His irony was therefore not with respect to his final vocabulary, only to the apparent lack of will among sociologists to achieve the goal he presumed to be obvious and beyond doubt.[3] Whether or not everyone at the time shared Merton's adherence to this general presupposition is not so much the interesting point as is the extent to which by contrast irony in Rorty's sense, is now directed at theory as such.

IRONY

Irony is a literary trope that deals in reversal and negation (Brown 1977: ch. 5). By setting figures in odd relation to each other, irony disrupts one's sense of reality (White 1973: 37–8). When Merton uses irony he links the line attributed to Calvin Coolidge's preacher, "unexceptionably 'against sin'" to the idea that there might anywhere be "a social scientist disclaiming the desirablity of the 'integration' of theory and empirical research." The application of the former absurd notion to a plain assumption about a then prevailing opinion in social science lifts the latter beyond itself onto another, virtually cosmic, level of importance to which it does not belong. Social science, whatever it is, has nothing to do with sin. Quite the contrary, social science, especially social science that integrates theory and empirical research, is normally understood to be the very opposite of any manner of thinking that concerns itself with sin. By this move, Merton extends the ironic expression with which the passage begins, "suspiciously irreproachable."[4] Putting things that do not belong together in relation to each other creates a powerful configurative reversal. Merton's point that everyone holds (or ought to hold) a certain attitude with respect to the integration of theory and research is made by the curious move of reversing his subject's ordinary relation to, in this case, sin. The truth of his point is made by confusing the real relations among things.

Likewise, when Skinner, with a lesser literary flair, sets Mills's cynical characterization of Parsons as a grand theorizer against the current hordes of new and anything but grand theories, he forces us to think about the reality of the new theories against the old. He plays on the assumption that anyone reading his book knows *and agrees with* Mills's characterization of Parsons and, thus, will be effectively required to rethink attitudes not toward Mills and Parsons but toward the new theories. Just as Merton uses irony to call into question an earlier, insufficiently pursued belief about theory's obvious relationship to research, Skinner uses it to question the nature of theory itself.

Irony is a powerful literary device precisely because in reversing the presumably real order of things it calls everything, including the order of things, into question. It is, therefore, risky business. "Irony," according to Hayden White (1973: 37), "represents a stage of consciousness in which the problematical nature of language itself has become recognized. It points to the potential foolishness of all linguistic characterizations of reality, as much as to the absurdity of the beliefs it parodies." Irony, he adds, is metatropological. It is a general but perverse theory of tropes, of figurative language, of language itself, and of theory itself. This, then, is the sense in which irony is the necessary form to express the current attitude toward such a formerly unassailable thing as general social theory.

Irony, when applied to the idea of a general social theory, could be said to form the basis for a negative, or perverse, general theory of all things that can be represented in language, including things social. An ironic social theory is general insofar as it is a thoroughly reflexive form that calls into question the very idea of general theory, which reflection is ironically general by virtue of being perverse. The ironist position described by Rorty is one in which the theorist employs a "final vocabulary" – that is, she reaches for general statements – yet does so possessed of "radical and continuing doubts" arising from her inability to destroy or, even, resist the power of other final vocabularies.

Irony when applied to theory is, therefore, more than a literary tactic; it is a peculiar position in relation to reality. It holds that nothing is certain save language, yet that language is a safe and reasonable certitude. And, because of the certitude of language, one can, in language, make general statements about the order of things real. Yet, because language is the only certitude, there can be no definitive, general statement upon which consensus can be achieved. There is no reality, arguable or otherwise.

The ironist position, therefore, breaks with what Rorty (1989) calls the "Plato–Kant canon." It does not concern itself with the general truth, goodness, or beauty of things. Philosophy since Hegel and Nietzsche through Heidegger to Derrida is replaced by literary criticism (Rorty 1989: 79). Accordingly theoretical practice for the ironist is commentary on the texts of others, texts composed in final vocabularies one finds sympathetic to or different from one's own.

General social theory, in the hands of an ironist, makes general statements of considerable scope and ambition but puts them in an obstreperous relation to similar statements of comparable scope and ambition. The idea of an ironic general theory is more than paradox or contradiction. Irony creates confusion in order to say something that exceeds any logic. Irony is not, thereby, nonsensical. It seeks to make good sense within language. An ironic general social theory puts language first and foremost in order to get beyond the question which, since Kant, everyone asks but to which there is no conclusive answer: What is real and true?

In this sense, irony is the discursive form of postmodern social theory. Postmodernism is consistent with the claim that irony is the only and necessary attitude for theory today. This is the intent of Lyotard's (1984: [1979]) famous cliché "the decline of grand narrative." Likewise, it is the referent of poststructuralism's comparably well-known idea of decentering. Postmodernism (with which Rorty shares a direct but decentered kinship) is an ironic general social theory.[5] Its principles are:

1 Reality is discussable – not much more than this.

2 Language is primary.
3 Reality is figurative, available only within language.
4 In language one can say any and everything, including the most general of things.
5 One can never escape one's language, including all other general statements about things.
6 All the above is a historical event more than an ideological position or a logical argument.
7 Hence, postmodernism is both the end of modernity and dependent upon modernity for its language.

Can there be any such thing as an ironic general social theory derived from principles such as these? If no, then there is very little to say about the relation between social theory and postmodernism. If yes, then postmodernism can and must be considered an important resource to its construction. I believe the answer to be yes. But I hold this belief while recognizing that the alternative answers, most of them worked out in one form or another elsewhere in this book, are plausibly arguable on their own terms. I cannot hope, for example, ultimately to dissuade Jeffrey Alexander from his attempt (in chapter 12) to compose a postpositivist general theory nor Jonathan Turner from substituting an irony-free positivism for the aspirations of a general theory (chapter 6). My sole purpose can be to suggest the form of a postmodern social theory in which what is general is expressed self-consciously only within language and with a perverse, contrary relation to the ideal of a general truth about or in a real world.

THE IDEA OF A POSTMODERN (GENERAL) SOCIAL THEORY

The two most common general concepts of postmodernist social theory are decentering and difference. The third, popularly well-known term, deconstruction, is the method (if this term can be used) proper to a social theory of difference that follows from a decentering of the social world. Much has been written on, and in the spirit of, these terms. And much of that is considered obscure. I do not consider postmodernist, poststructuralist, or deconstructionist discourses irredeemably obscure, though I grant that some writing in these traditions is needlessly so. I believe the perception of obscurity derives mostly from the ironic position postmodernism has invented and cannot escape.

Irony, as I have suggested, insofar as it replaces reality with language and engages the literary devices of reversing things in order to express them, cannot help but create confusion. This is its purpose. But its purpose remains to say something – something that, in this view, can only be expressed in writing from a position in the world which recognizes that world to be fundamentally decentered and composed of differences, not essences. It is therefore more a politics than an epistemology, as many other writers, including Rorty, argue.

These being the natural conditions of a postmodernist social theory, I wish to begin at what are, in effect, the near limits of postmodernism with an illustrative text which, in being only marginally postmodern, is only relatively obscure. In their book *Anthropology as Cultural Critique* George Marcus and Michael Fischer (1986) summarize the writing of another anthropologist, Marshal Sahlins. In this text upon a text, Marcus and Fischer describe Sahlin's description (in *Historical Metaphors and Mythical Realities*) of an original text – the series of Hawaiian rituals dating from the 1830s whereby an important European, Captain James Cook, was quite literally incorporated into the indigenous Hawaiian mythic structure. Here is the Marcus Fischer text:

> By incorporating the arrival of Cook into the annual ritual enactment of their myths, the Hawaiians ensured the persistence of their cultural structures, but at the same time, brought about their transformation. The fortuitous timing of Cook's arrival and his manner of circumnavigating the islands fit exactly the Makahiki festival process of the god Lono, for whom Cook was taken. Coming ashore, Cook was escorted to the temple and made to imitate the shape of the Makahiki image while a pig was offered to him. He was anointed in the manner of Lono, and was fed by the priest associated with the ruling chief. Cook set sail at the end of the ritual, just as Lono was expected to do, but he unexpectedly returned because one of his ships had

sprung a mast. He received quite a different reception this time; tensions surrounding his return precipitated an outbreak of violence in which he was killed by a mob of Hawaiians. However, the Hawaiians treated this actual death as the annual ritual death of Lono; they returned his remains to the British and asked them if Lono would return again next year. Part of Cook's remains were to reappear in subsequent processions of Lono during the Makahiki rite, now understood as bearing the mana of Cook who came to be understood as an ancestral chief. (*Marcus and Fischer 1986: 103*)

Clearly, this text operates on no fewer than three levels. (1) The Hawaiian ritual–myth was a response to European otherness, a way of incorporating the alien culture represented by Captain Cook into their own. Over the succeeding 50 years Hawaiian culture was indeed transformed by the European presence but the ritual identification of Cook with the local god Lono permitted the local culture to a tolerable degree of ease in the transition, whatever the pain to Cook. (2) At a second level, Sahlins is offering a kind of structuralist analysis of the Hawaiian myth in which he aims to show the shifts in the culture codes of the local culture under the pressure of the historical events of which Cook was symbol. (3) At a third level, Marcus and Fischer are offering a reinterpretation of Sahlins (one he might well reject) intended to show the subtle but important changes in recent ethnographic writing in which a shift in the importance of the subject of ethnographies entails a dramatic reversal in global perspective. In this instance, the narrative focus is not so much *on* the early nineteenth-century Hawaiians as it is *from their perspective*.

Marcus and Fischer argue that when ethnographers remove themselves, and their white, European culture, from the center of attention and write from the point of view of the Other, the social world itself is transformed scientifically and politically. This result is achieved as a consequence of the operation they call a "counterethnography of subjects" (Marcus and Fischer 1986: 86). In their account the colonial invaders are incorporated, and world history – at least in the narrative – is reversed. It is not so much the Hawaiians who are examined as the Hawaiians *in a specific, described relationship to the world.* What is accounted for is the absorption of the European in the Hawaiian – not itself a remarkably new story, except insofar as it illustrates the social scientific principle Marcus and Fischer have in mind: the world is different, when seen from the point of view of those who are different.

With remarkable modesty, Marcus and Fischer have in this passage (as throughout their book) given substance to the notion of an ironic general social theory.[6] They are in fact making a general theoretical statement. The world system is comprised of social differences recognizable only from the point of view of those differences. Strictly speaking, however, this statement is not made on the basis of a direct reference to the real world system. It is an entirely discursive statement made with reference, in the example provided, to an ethnographer's text.

The relations among the three intertextual layers of their interpretation are crucial and inevitable to their theory. The primary, historical text – resulting in the incorporation of Cook – is deeply ironic. Cook is mistaken for the god Lono. This mistake results in his death and simultaneous elevation to the status of an ancestral chief, from which position his mana serves to transform the Hawaiians' cultural perception of their relations to the Europeans. Yet, it would be foolhardy to assume that this irony was played out in the real experience of the Hawaiians. It exists for us, rather, in the Marcus and Fischer text, within which it is represented in a definite rhetorical manner. At a second level, Sahlins's interpretation is almost totally lacking in irony. Even though he takes the historical and ritual experience of Hawaiians in the 1830s and converts them into something entirely alien, an anthropologist's cultural categories, Sahlins appears to be, at least here, a realist. Sahlins, insofar as he is obliquely represented by Marcus and Fischer (1986: 103–4, 108), is making interpretations of a set of historical facts which, to all intents and purposes, are representations of a real world.

At the third intertextual layer, Marcus and Fischer are engaged in an operation quite distinct from those taking place at the other two. The appearance of irony in the ritual incorporation of Cook as the god Lono is very much up for interpretative grabs until someone has the last word. The ironic force of the passage is not felt until Marcus and Fischer have their say which, as it turns out, is a general statement not only about the world system but about social theory. Their book actually argues for a revision of anthropology as cultural critique. It seeks thereby to resolve the classic dilemma of anthropology – how to read the Other – with reference to a social theory of differences. Recognition of the differences constitutive of the social world takes place, in their view, only within the narrative work of the ethnographer and it therein takes place only when the ethnography reverses the seemingly necessary relations between the local and the global.

The deepest irony in Marcus and Fischer is their proposal that interpretations of local Others entail a structural understanding of global politics.[7] Ethnography is fieldwork in alien locales; at the same time, ethnography is a politics of world differences. The anthropologist's first question is, therefore: "How to take account of a reciprocity of perspectives which requires the ethnographer to consider seriously the de facto counterethnography of subjects, who, far from being isolated from the same world system that forms the anthropologist's cosmopolitan consciousness, are often equally, if not more aware, of its operation than the anthropologist himself" (Marcus and Fischer 1986: 86). Did the Hawaiians, in the 1830s, know what they were dealing with in Cook, in the Europeans whom he represented, in the ethnographers who would soon come? From a realist point of view this is a nonsensical question. From an ironic point of view, it is not. Whatever they knew then, a century and a half ago, they are known now in the only place they exist – in texts, like that of Marcus and Fischer, in which whatever they knew when they incorporated Cook (and Europe) makes sense in an interpretation made possible by a theory of the world as differences.

This is irony. This is passable postmodernism. The question remains: Is it general social theory?

POSTMODERNISM, POLITICS, AND SOCIAL THEORY

An ironic general social theory is not just perverse. It is also political. Its irony is, moreover, closely bound to its politics. This is a readily apparent feature of postmodernism.

It is sometimes overlooked that postmodernism and post-structuralism were, from the beginning, intensely political. Before difference became the explicitly political slogan it is today (more on this later), decentering had similar political meanings. That poststructuralism, then postmodernism, appear to some to be obscure, hence anything but connected to a direct view of world change, should not blur recognition of the actual historical circumstances of their origin.

The poststructuralist movement arose directly out of the political events of May 1968 in Paris. The most important early texts of Foucault and Derrida appeared within months of these events. The early attacks of Foucault (1970 [1966]) on humanism, and of Derrida (1978a [1967]) on the idea of the center, like Lyotard's (1984 [1979]) and Rorty's (1979) later critiques of modernist rationality, though seemingly abstract and benign, were directly related to the politics of the sixties in Europe and the United States.

Foucault's *Archaeology*, for example, appeared in France in early 1969. Its famous attacks on humanist principles of subjectivity were consistent with the May Movement's direct political attack on late Gaullist political culture. Gaullism, in the manner of all modernist political regimes, used the grand traditions of French culture to mask the systematic exclusion of members of the subordinate classes from the benefits of the new welfare society, most especially France's elitist system of higher education. Similarly, Foucault's use of the term discursive practices, in the same book, could not help but be compared to aspects of the student and workers' struggle (in the United States as well as France) – a struggle in which discourse in the form of new political voices was the foremost weapon. To illustrate with reference to the American 1960s, it is no accident that the Port Huron statement in 1962 began by denouncing the silence of the students of the previous generation and that the Free Speech Movement, at Berkeley, was one of the student movement's most visible first gestures.

Postmodernism further radicalized the poststructuralist goal of rethinking the history of the West in decentered, differential, ironic terms. Insofar as poststructuralism remained (for the most part) a theory of literature, postmodernism became an even more general theory of culture – including popular culture, architecture, science, music, film, and so on – without obvious limit. Whatever it is, postmodernism is not reducible, as some would say of poststructuralism, to the idle intellectual pretenses of Left Bank literati and their followers. Indeed, a great deal of postmodernism – Philip Johnson's AT&T Headquarters building in New York City, E. L. Doctorow's or Don Delillo's novels, including *Ragtime* and *White Noise*, or a range of films, from *American Graffiti* to more recent releases like *Field of Dreams* and *Baron von Munchhausen* – could hardly be said to be inspired by Derrida or Saussure. Indeed, they are, as social practices, as different from each other as they are, collectively, from the movements inspired by the French poststructuralists.

It is necessary, therefore, at least to consider the proposition that postmodernism and poststructuralism are laid on a political foundation, that they are products of a shift of some sort in world historical structures. Consider, for example, Derrida's early deployment of what became the principle of decentering. Here are his words, delivered in 1966 at the first international conference on structuralism at Johns Hopkins University, in effect the announcement of a shift in world order:

> Until the event which I wish to mark out and define, structure – or rather the structurality of structure . . . has always been neutralized or reduced, and this by a process of giving it a center or referring it to a point of presence, a fixed origin. The function of this center was not only to orient, balance, and organize the structure . . . but above all to make sure that the organizing principle of the structure would limit what we might call the *freeplay* of the structure. (*Derrida 1978a [1967]: 247–8*)

Setting aside its philosophical claims, the passage on its own terms could as easily be a statement, in 1966, about Gaullism or even, in Wallerstein's terms, the capitalist world system. Derrida did not neglect this connection:

> Where and how does this decentering, this notion of the structurality of structure occur? It would be somewhat naive to refer to an event, a doctrine, or an author in order to designate this occurrence. *It is no doubt part of the totality of an era, our own, but still has already begun to*

proclaim itself and begun to work. (ibid.: 249–50; emphasis added)

One must consider the thesis that poststructuralism was somehow part of a shift in world social structures that began in the sixties.

The strongly political theme in early poststructuralism is maintained as the central principle of later, postmodernist aesthetics. If a politics, it is not a revolutionary politics in the customary sense. Neither poststructuralism nor postmodernism asserts a principle of historical discontinuity.[8] If, indeed, from this perspective, we are experiencing a world transformation equivalent to that which gave rise to modernity in the eigtheenth century, it will not be a transformation that enjoys a simple, linear or discontinuous, relationship to the modernity against which it takes place. This is the central idea of the Derridean deconstructive style: the old and the new are in some unusual nonlinear relationship to each other such that the very idea of old and new is altered. This is, furthermore, the point to be found in the Marcus and Fischer text on the Hawaiians – that a reduction of the role of the ethnographer as subject and an assumption of the cultural perspective of the Other is not a mere "role change" but rather the result of a radical reconfiguration of the social world – how it is understood and experienced. The world is not thrown over but rethought or, better, rewritten.

Here, precisely, is where irony and politics are joined in postmodernism. The figurative reversals basic to postmodernism's expressive style correspond to a politics, in the broader sense of the term, in which the world is envisioned to be oddly reversed. The center is deconstructed, yes; but replaced by the freeplay of discursive expression. Yet, discourse does not and cannot reinvent itself. Language is the most resistant to change of all human social things. Thus, the free discursive alternative to the Center, to structure, must employ the languages that exist. Poststructuralism must use the centered language of structuralism to effect its play. This is what Derrida does in the 1966 statement (Derrida 1978a [1967]). Deconstruction is a play against and within the language one must use. Likewise, postmodernism requires a close relationship to modernity. It is therefore, an implicit philosophy of the historical past. The past stands on its own, to be reworked in the present. The modern is material to the postmodern. Cultural, and by extension political, change involves reversals, not refusals. The politics, therefore, is ironic, as is the mode of cultural expression.

One of the most visible stylistic features of postmodernism is the absorption of the past, including the modern, into its own style. Fredric Jameson (1984a) argues that postmodernism uses the language of the past to create the experience of nostalgia but with the consequence of destroying the historicity of the past. *Ragtime, American Graffiti, White Noise,* among other post-modernist forms, rely strongly on recollection, nostalgia, or historical figures to create an experience, the aesthetic effect of which is to take both culture's consumer and the aesthetic product out of history. This effect is plainly evident in postmodern architecture. Postmodernist design uses several historical elements: gothic spires and arches, a Chippendale icon to top Philip Johnson's AT&T building, and strong modernist statements in the sheer verticality of projects. The aesthetic effect is not without pleasure, though it is jarring. Viewers and users of such buildings are, at the least, taken out of historical time by being exposed to an excess of historical icons.

One is hard put to determine whether, from any social point of view, this transformation is good or bad. Indeed one of the deepest effects, aesthetic and political, of postmodernism is to disrupt one's sense not only of the true or the false, but of the good and the bad, the present and the past, and all the other modernist dichotomies. From one point of view, postmodernist aesthetics suggests the emancipatory function of freeing the individual, the underclasses, the small social parts of society from the grip of History with a capital "H": the history of the dominant class. From another point of view (Jameson 1984a), postmodernism might be "bad" insofar as postmodernist aesthetics, most especially its architecture, are initiated and funded by the "patronage of late capitalist multinational business." Why is AT&T a patron of Philip Johnson's postmodernist aesthetic? What is its interest in dislodging, by this investment, our sense of history or an honest recollection of a real past?

Questions such as these, though difficult to answer, have a proper chastening effect. They force one to consider that postmodernism, whether "good" or "bad", must at least be considered a real event in world history – not just idle, obscure writing and talking. As such, its importance as a topic and resource of general social theory becomes more evident.

Of course, it must now be said, any prospect of a productive relationship between postmodernism and a general social theory requires a somewhat more precise understanding of the term social theory than is usually given. Clearly, having claimed that postmodernism mutually entails a political foundation for an ironic general theory, I must make the corresponding claim that such a relationship is consistent with the nature of a social theory.

It is not entirely clear what different theorists, using different vocabularies, mean by social theory. Jonathan Turner, in co-editing a book entitled *Social Theory Today* (Giddens and Turner 1987), would seem to allow social theory to mean much the same as sociological theory. Usages of this sort elide the difference between a theory proper to a science and that germane to a general view of the nature of society, which is closer to Giddens's use of the term.

What, if any, are the differences between a social theory and science-based theory, like sociological theory? It would seem natural to discuss such a distinction with reference to an epistemology of scientific truth claims. This is what Turner does elsewhere in this volume (chapter 6), where he defends the proposition that social (or, really, sociological theory) ought to obey the same rules as theory in any natural science. There are other ways to make this argument. Alexander's description, also in this volume (chapter 12), of a postpositivist foundationalism is one. Habermas's defense of modernity's ideal of emancipatory knowledge is another.

Along any continuum of differing vocabularies from Turner through Alexander and Habermas to Giddens, the distinction between an epistemologically grounded theory and social theory is eventually blurred. Habermas, quite evidently, begins not so much with a formal epistemology as with a general vision of ideal social relations from which the theory of emancipatory knowledge is garnered. Alexander, by contrast, begins more with an ideal vision of social scientific knowledge from which is developed a working epistemology. Yet, Alexander does not reduce social to sociological theory, as does Turner. Somewhere between Turner's position, on the one extreme, and Habermas's or Giddens's, on the other, the role of a formal epistemology loses its necessity and is replaced by a willingness to think first of society as such, and later (if at all) of the conditions of knowledge required for a theory of society.

The distinction between a social theory and a sociological theory is that between a readiness to place politics ahead of epistemology as the foundation for thinking and an insistence that knowledge (including a theory of knowledge) always necessarily precedes and informs statements about the social world. Thus, whether framed in the modernist vocabulary of the good society or Habermas's neomodernist ideal speech situation or Marx's vision of a specific revolutionary condition and outcome, a social theory – properly speaking – begins with a politics, of some sort, not an epistemology.

Postmodernism has radicalized this idea and, thus, enjoys a surprising if uncertain affinity to the interests and form of social theory. Postmodernism, especially in those variants described by Lyotard and Rorty, begins with a politics. Rorty, for example, says: "The idea that liberal societies are bound together by philosophical beliefs seems to me ludicrous. What binds societies together are common vocabularies and common hopes. The vocabularies are, typically, parasitic on the hopes – in the sense that the principal function of the vocabularies is to tell stories about future outcomes which compensate for present sacrifices" (Rorty 1989: 86; cf. Lyotard 1984 [1989]: 81–2). This position is readily illustrated in the Marcus and Fischer text with its distinctive political view of the world as a system of differences.

THE SOCIAL THEORETICAL IMPORTANCE OF
THE CONCEPT "*DIFFERENCE*"

The concept "*difference*" has become, at once, the most ironic and political of the terms associated with poststructuralism or postmodernism. A reconsideration of the Marcus and Fischer text will suggest how these two distinctive features combine into a theory that is truly general though by the means of an ironic reversal of world politics. Though the concept *"difference"* has endured numerous embodiments and transformations, and now is frequently used as much as a slogan as a serious theoretical concept, I would still judge it to be the most powerful social theoretical concept in the poststructuralist vocabulary, and one that is, at the same time, the most explicitly ironic and political. Examination of its development, through the course of this century, as a theoretical notion reveals just why it has this importance within poststructuralist and post-modernist thinking, and could have comparable potential as a general social theoretical concept.

The short history of *difference* begins with the linguistics of Ferdinand de Saussure, whose ideas were pretty much ignored until they were taken up in the 1940s and 1950s by the early structuralists in Paris. Since and including Saussure, *difference* has appeared in five, progressively more social, theoretical forms:

1 with Saussure, to establish the social contractarian nature of linguistic value;
2 with Lévi-Strauss, and other structuralists, to establish the autonomy of myth and of social and literary forms as indicators of structure of social meanings;
3 with Derrida, to formulate his critique of the Enlightenment, originally as a critique of the voice as the dominant form of humanistic consciousness or subjectivity;
4 with the Derrideans, and other poststructuralists including Foucault, as a critique of centered, modernist thought, and politics;
5 and, currently, as a general social theoretical concept, particularly prominent in feminist and other parasociological social theories.

I attempt only the most summary presentations of each progressive shift.

(1) With Saussure (1959), *difference* was the implicit notion that allowed him to sever linguistic signs from any direct relationship to their social world. He held that language was a complexly structured series of words and rules agreed upon by the linguistic community. The meaning of a spoken term –

"woman," for example – bears no linguistic relationship to any object in the real world, that is, any typical female of the human species. Rather, the term depends for its linguistic meaning entirely on a social contract among competent speakers of a language whose competence resides in their ability to recognize the difference between the spoken term "woman" and the absent term "man." The same applies to nondichotomous, or continuously varying terms, like "black" which when uttered makes sense because the hearer understands its crucial linguistic difference from "white," "red," "yellow," "brown."

These are not surprising today because sociologists have been trained to accept historicized or social constructionist interpretations of, for example, gender and racial distinctions. We understand very well that "woman" – the term and the concept – is a product of social process and, similarly, that "white" (as a racial designation) refers to no real object in the world. Few whites, save some albinos, have white skin. Both the gender and racial terms are social conventions. What today is not news was, early in the century, a remarkable social theoretical innovation, parallel to similar themes in the then very new schools of Durkheimian and pragmatist theories.

Though Saussure's ideas contributed, along with other linguistic traditions – those of Hjelmslev, of the Russian formalists, of Jakobson in particular, and eventually of Chomsky – to the shaping of modern linguistics, their greater importance to social theory was through structuralism, then poststructuralism.

(2) The structuralism associated most prominently with Lévi-Strauss (1967) put linguistic ideas of differences to a much broader application in the analysis of cultural forms. Lévi-Strauss's structuralist anthropology was probably as dependent on Roman Jakobson's phonetics as on Saussure's general theory of language. But, without going into these details, it should be plain that what he did was to assume cultural systems – myths, in particular – are governed by laws similar to those covering the play of differences in Saussure's language systems. His binary oppositions were the same idea of *difference*, now formalized and limited by the influence of Jakobson's phonetics, Lévi-Strauss went beyond Saussure in his speculations on the possibility of universal qualities of mind. But his specific studies

of cultural myths were consistent with Saussure insofar as they probed the formal, internal structures of myth without reference to their historical origins and transformations. The structural anthropological sense of myths lay entirely in the relationship of difference between the binary opposites.

(3) The third embodiment of the concept *difference* is Derrida's (1974 [1967], 1978a [1967]) famous play on the French words *différence* and *différance* (with an "a"). The play is between the state of "differing" and "deferring." *Differance* – with the "a" – is the deferral which is confused in speech with the straightforward concept of *difference*.

There are two interrelated themes here: The first is Derrida's attack on the privileging of the voice which he attributed to a bias in Western metaphyscis in which the voice is taken as the voice of presence – a bias that in the modern era became the basis of consciousness and subjectivity as metatheoretical axioms. The meaning "deferral" appears only when the term is written and one can see the "a" and a very different sense of the spoken term. In other words, writing contains possibilities for meaning that are hidden in speech, just as the philosophy of presence masks the play of differences in society. Speech, like Western modernist thought, suppresses the differences at play in language and society. In this respect, there is also a second implicit political theme here, though it is quite concealed in Derrida's early writings. The political idea, a corollary to the idea of the limiting structure discussed earlier, is that modernity's interest in controlling thought and political action is advantaged by its philosophical commitment to speech, to presence, to subjectivity. The ideas of an essential subjectivity or of an ideal human condition serve to limit the reality of social differences – to rule out of the present a recognition of the true differences of which social life is comprised. Accordingly, to write is to defer – to reject presence, and to affirm differences. This is the sense in which *difference* leads naturally to the more familiar poststructuralist idea of decentering.

(4) In Derrida's later thinking *difference* took on a fourth incarnation. Certainly, the political themes in the concept are clearer in the broad social theoretical claims of the poststructuralist movement, as it developed, with independent sources,

among those who followed Derrida and others. To recognize difference and differences is to decenter thought, to remove it from any form of the modernist belief that there are essential, single truths to history. If there is an essential truth, of any kind, then there is only one truth – and virtually certainly that is the controlling truth of the dominant class.

This same idea appears in Foucault's writings, which can be characterized as a history of the modern subject's subjugation (Lemert and Gillan 1982). He attacks the metaphysical idea of a universal subjectivity, in order to write a series of histories of the ways in which people, especially in the modern era, have been subjugated – in mental hospitals, in clinics, in prisons, in confessionals, by means of public health instructions on sexual conduct, by the teachings of the social sciences.

At the most superficial level, his famous concept, *power/knowledge*, is simultaneously a critique of modernity, and an assertion that there is no such thing as subjectivity – only subjects (plural). Any claim, Foucault argued, that knowledge can be produced and appropriated apart from power is a claim that sides with those in power. The ideal of enlightened rationality, therefore, was the instrument of oppression of those in whose interest it was, in the early stages of capitalism, to conceal the violence hidden behind the calm exteriors of the shop room floor, to borrow Marx's classic phrase.

Foucault's critique of modernity, however, is not philosophical – at least not after his false start in *The Archaeology of Knowledge* (1972 [1969]). He sets aside such modernist concepts as the subject-object distinction in order to clear the table for his histories of subjugation. As long as *subjectivity* remains as a primary concept, we shall never understand its use in the formation of subjects under capitalism. Subjectivity is the code word of modernism which masks the truth of modernity that subjects are subjugated to the dominant cultural and economic interests of capitalism.

I have admittedly skewed this characterization of Foucault in the direction of a more familiar Marxist vocabulary, but this remains a tolerably accurate representation. Though Foucault does not use the Derridean term, difference, he is mounting a very similar argument. The intellectual and political world must be decentered in order to free us to experience and understand the differences of social reality – differences experienced most acutely by those in the excluded positions in Western society: women, homosexuals, the poor, the working class, nonwhites, the third world.

(5) Recall that the written form *"différance,"* with the "a," reveals the missing, lacking, element in speech. Writing, the politics of *difference*, is the politics of those who, on a daily basis, experience the pain of social exclusion, of lack, of loss. This is why the concept has been taken up by representatives of social groups most acutely aware of social pain. There is an impressive and growing literature exploring the social theoretical importance of postmodernism and the concept of *difference* – with respect to African-American experience (Henry Louis Gates 1988 and Hazel Carby 1987), third world literature (Edward Said 1979, Fredric Jameson 1986), and working-class culture (Paul Willis, and others associated with the school of Cultural Studies in Great Britain; see Hall et al. 1980). But the most fully developed exploration of these themes is by feminist theorists.

Theorists most prominently associated with, or at least sympathetic to, postmodernism are Jane Flax (1987), Donna Haraway (1985), Nancy Fraser and Linda Nicholson (1990) and Sandra Harding (1986). One of the discussions in this literature of greatest general social theoretical interest is that over feminist standpoint theories. In the simplest of terms, a feminist standpoint theory critiques male-dominated Western thought by countering with the assertion of a feminist theory of knowledge. If, to use the most commonplace of assumptions, Western thought is dominated by male rationality, then the feminist standpoint would be to substitute a less rational, more intuitive mode of reasoning as an epistemological basis for scientific knowledge. Those – including Fraser and Nicholson, Jane Flax, and perhaps most notably Donna Haraway – who dispute the feminist standpoint theory do so because it remains essentialist, simply substituting for the critiqued cultural models of masculinity equally universal feminist ideals for knowledge, social relations, and moral development. Jane Flax (1987: 633) summarizes the contradiction in this point of view: "We cannot simultaneously claim (1) that the mind, the self, and knowledge are socially constituted and that what we can know depends upon our social practices and context *and* (2) that feminist theory can uncover the Truth of the whole once and for all."

In other words, a feminist standpoint theory insofar as it seeks to assert an essentialist, centered, and universal cultural model remains modernist. Such a perspective, no less than male-dominated modernism, obliterates the true social differences that mark and shape the lives of concrete individuals. There is no essential Woman, anymore than there is an essential, humanist Man. As an alternative to feminist standpoint theories Donna Haraway and Sandra Harding (in a more ambivalent way) propose the concept of "fractured identities." Feminists must think of themselves (and they must act) in reference to identities fractured not only by gender but by race, class, and world position as well. There is no abstract total woman, only black-African or white – working-class or white – American . . . women.

> Once "woman" is deconstructed into "women," and "gender" is recognized to have no fixed referents, feminism itself dissolves as a fundamental part of our political identities, as a motivation for developing political solidarities – how could it in a world where we can now name the plethora of moral outrages designed exactly to contain us, to coerce us, within each of our culturally specific womanly activities? But because of this historical specificity of sexism's structures, this strain of feminist thought encourages us to cherish and defend our "hyphens" – those theoretical expressions of our multiple struggles. (*Harding 1986: 146*)

The value of the concept-fractured identities is apparent, and it is no coincidence that it arises at the very time when social theorists are re-evaluating hitherto segregated theoretical categories such as race, class, and gender. It stands today as one of the most compelling advances in the complex, yet short, history of the concept *difference*.

Difference, in its most recent form, is a radically ironic concept. One could say, however, that its extension into a motion like fractured identities so reduces theoretical analysis into smaller and more local unities as to be nihilistic. Where does the hyphenization stop? Can it stop short of the pure, isolated individual? Is the social world thus atomized? If, for example, such essentialist notions as the feminist standpoint are given up to fractured identities (to differences in the extreme), then what becomes of the oppositional consciousness necessary for thinking through or acting with respect to the position of women in the world? How does one generate either a theory or a politics of exclusion without a total concept of the excluded?[9]

The ironic resolution of questions such as these involves the recognition that, however radical their political purposes, all such totalizing concerns are synonymous with a realist epistemology. The ironic position accepts that theories and politics are real only and insofar as they are expressed in concrete and actual locales. Neither is the proper business of universal categories. People do not suffer as members of categories, but in specific times and places. This is the virtual equivalent to the ironist and postmodernist claims that reality is figurative, that one can never escape language in which everything can be said, however general.

To remain within an essentialist, totalizing vocabulary is to enjoy the passing methodological satisfaction of conceptual leverage at the tremendous expense of a diminished access to the only persuasive reality there is – what people, in concrete settings, learn to say, and do say, about their conditions. When they speak, they do, indeed, make very general statements. But they do so in spite of the fact that because they recognize their difference from others they do not and cannot believe in a world that is whole or real outside of what they experience and express. What after all was the reality of the Hawaiians outside that which came to be expressed, in a series of texts, from their own ritual form to the Marcus and Fischer interpretation which affirmed their difference by turning the world around?

An ironic general social theory, a postmodern social theory, requires the easy sacrifice of a modernist commitment to a reality that cannot be confirmed. Does that make it any less general? Does that make it any less responsive to the truth of things which, after all, exist only in what we are able to say?

CONCLUSION

There is some good reason to believe that the 1960s represented the end of the long reign of the modern, liberal consensus which reached its zenith and held its own throughout the 1940s, 1950s, and early 1960s. The years around 1968 were, as in the familiar line from Yeats, truly a time when the center did not hold. Tet, Columbia, Kent State, Chicago, Paris, Prague, Mexico City – are the names for epicenters of the disintegration many experienced in relative youth. No one can say even now, 20 years and more later, whether that collapse of the Center was a moment or movement. But surely we can agree that, whatever permanent happened then, thereafter the world was more decisively marked by the differences that divide black and white, women and men, rich and poor, first and third world, and on and on. The new terms of our vocabulary – "black," "third world," "feminization of poverty," even – as Donna Haraway suggests – "woman" (and certainly "women") have changed our way of speaking and thinking about the world in which we live.

Social theory and sociology – two different but related endeavors – understand this reality of *difference*. And post-modernism is important to us as a tradition of social thought that has taken seriously – intellectually and politically – the ironic centrality of differences in a decentred world.

NOTES

1 Rorty (1989) puts the idea of irony to the specific purpose of describing that which remains once totalizing truths, including modernity's commitments to epistemology, are rejected (Rorty 1979). This is the postmodernist element in Rorty's thinking, on the basis of which he seeks to describe irony as the appropriate private attitude corollary to the reconstruction of liberalism he proposes in *Contingency, Irony, and Solidarity*. This latter element is, of course, that which places him in an eccentric relation to postmodernism and, ironically, somewhat closer to Habermas (see Rorty 1985).

The use of irony, and other tropes, in current social theory is widespread. The earliest usages were the importance of the distinction between metaphor and metonomy in Lévi-Strauss, Jakobson, and Lacan (see White 1978: 31). Hayden White (1973) uses a theory of tropes, including irony, to analyze 19th-century historiography. Richard Harvey Brown (1977) develops irony as a central element in his reconstruction of a logic of social scientific discovery. Brown (1977: 197–205) discusses the importance of irony in Goffman's style. More recently, Marcus and Fischer (1986: 14–16) build on White's ideas, suggesting that in social theory emerging from the sixties irony has become a dominant force, though in a sort of dialectic relation to a continuing quest for realism. Important though these sources are, none has yet developed a full and explicit meta theory of theory as irony, though Brown comes close.

2 "All human beings carry about a set of words which they employ to justify their actions, their beliefs, and their lives. These are the words in which we formulate praise of our friends and contempt for our enemies, our long-term projects, our deepest self-doubts and our highest hopes. They are the words in which we tell, sometimes prospectively and sometimes retrospectively, the story of our lives. I shall call these words a person's 'final vocabulary.' It is 'final' in the sense that if doubt is cast on the worth of these words, their user has no noncircular argumentative recourse" (Rorty 1989: 73).

3 Richard Harvey Brown (1977: 178–90) astutely identifies Merton's explicit and substantive use of theoretical irony in the famous distinction between manifest and latent functions, the topic of the lead essay in *Social Theory and Social Structure*.

4 "Suspiciously irreproachable" works ironically in a manner different from Skinner's "grand theory" and Rorty's "final vocabulary." Whereas the reversals are obvious in the latter two (that is, calling grand theories that set out to be anything but grand), the reversal in Merton's expression is the effect of a redundancy. Anything irreproachable is by its nature suspicious. Thus, Merton mocks the "announced intention" to consolidate theory and research, which merits suspicion because it is an unattained irreproachable intent.

5 For a discussion of the relations and differences between structuralism, poststructuralism, and postmodernism, see Lemert (1991).

6 Marcus and Fischer (1986: 13–16) discuss irony with explicit reference to Hayden White (1973). They seek to keep the ironic perspective in relation to a robust realism (see 1986: 15). In this respect they shrink from a thoroughly postmodern position, even though it would seem that their actual interpretations of ethnographers' texts is thoroughly ironic.

7 Marcus and Fischer use Immanuel Wallerstein's world system theory appreciatively in their interpretation of the Cook ritual narrative. They take it, quite correctly, to be a supple but essentially realist theoretical perspective. It is interesting to note the differences between Wallerstein and Marcus and Fischer in the use of secondary texts. Wallerstein refers virtually without exception to secondary historical sources, but does so in a realist fashion (e.g. Wallerstein 1974). His secondary sources are taken as real data. Marcus and Fischer, by contrast, use their secondary sources (e.g. Sahlins) as rhetorical opportunities.

8 The mistaken notion that they do derives, no doubt, from Foucault's (1970 [1966]) extreme use of discontinuity in *The Order of Things*, a usage he soon recanted.

9 Harding (1986) proposes to combine elements of the fractured identities and standpoint perspectives.

REFERENCES

Abel, Elizabeth (ed.) 1980: *Writing and Sexual Difference*. Chicago: University of Chicago Press.

Alexander, Jeffrey 1989: "General theory in the postpositivist mode: the 'epistemological dilemma' and the search for present meaning." See chapter 12 of this volume.

Althusser, Louis 1970: *For Marx*. New York: Vintage Books.

Barthes, Roland 1970: *Writing Degree Zero and Elements of Semiology*. Boston: Beacon Press.

Bernstein, Richard 1985: *Habermas and Modernity*. Cambridge, Mass.: MIT Press.

Brown, Richard Harvey 1977: *A Poetic for Sociology*. Cambridge: Cambridge University Press.

Brown, Richard Harvey 1987: *Society as Text*. Chicago: University of Chicago Press.

Carby, Hazel 1987: *Reconstructing Womanhood: The emergence of Afro-American Woman Novelist*. New York: Oxford University Press.

Deleuze, Gilles and Felix Guattari 1977 [1972]: *Anti-Oepipus: Capitalism and Schizophrenia*. New York: Viking Press.

Derrida, Jacques 1974 [1967]: *Of Grammatology*, tr. G. C. Spivak. Baltimore: Johns Hopkins University Press.

Derrida, Jacques 1978a [1967]: *Writing and Difference*. Chicago: University of Chicago Press.

Derrida, Jacques 1978b [1967]: "Structure, sign and play in the discourse of the human sciences," in Derrida (1978a), pp. 278–94.

Derrida, Jacques 1985: "Racism's last word," in Henry Louis Gates (ed.), *"Race," Writing and Difference*. Chicago: University of Chicago Press, pp. 329–38.

Flax, Jane 1987: "Postmodernism and gender relations in feminist theory," *Signs*, 12/4 (Summer).

Foucault, Michel 1970 [1966]: *The Order of Things: An Archaeology of the Human Sciences*, New York: Pantheon.

Foucault, Michel 1972 [1969]: *The Archaeology of Knowledge*, tr. A. M. Sheridan Smith. New York: Pantheon.

Foucault, Michel 1978 [1976]: *The History of Sexuality*, vol. 1: *An Introduction*. New York: Pantheon.

Foucault, Michel 1979: "What is an author?" in *Textual Strategies: Perspectives in Post-Structuralist Criticism*. Ithaca NY: Cornell University Press, pp. 141–60.

Fraser, Nancy, and Linda Nicholson 1990 [1988]: "Social criticism without philosophy: an encounter between feminism and postmodernism," in Linda Nicholson (ed.), *Feminism/Postmodernism*. New York and London: Routledge and Chapman & Hall.

Gates, Henry Louis (ed.) 1985: *"Race," Writing and Difference*. Chicago: University of Chicago Press.

Gates, Henry Louis 1988: *The Signifying Monkey: A Theory of Afro-American Literary Criticism*. New York: Oxford University Press.

Giddens, Anthony 1984: *The Constitution of Society*. Berkeley: University of California Press.

Giddens, Anthony, and Jonathan Turner (eds) 1987: *Social Theory Today*. Palo Alto, Calif.: Stanford University Press.

Hall, Stuart et al. 1980: *Culture, Media, and Language: Working Papers in Cultural Studies, 1972–79*. London: Hutchinson.

Haraway, Donna 1985: "A manifesto for Cyborgs: science, technology, and feminism in the 1980s," *Socialist Review*, 15/2 (March–April); 65–107.

Harding, Sandra 1986: *The Science Question in Feminism*. Ithaca, NY: Cornell University Press.

Jacoby, Russell 1987: *The Last Intellectuals*. New York: Basic Books.

Jameson, Fredric 1984a. Forword pp. vii–xxii to Jean-François Lyotard, *The Postmodern Condition*. Minneapolis: University of Minnesota Press, pp. vii–xxii.

Jameson, Fredric 1984b: "Postmodernism and the cultural logic of late capitalism," *New Left Review*, 146 (June).

Jameson, Fredric 1986: "Third world literature in the era of multinational capitalism," *Social Text*, 15 (Fall).

Jencks, Charles 1977: *The Language of Post-modern Architecture*. New York: Rizzoli Publications.

Kristeva, Julia 1974: *La révolution du langage poétique*. Paris: Editions du Seuil.

Lacan, Jacques 1968: *The Language of the Self*. New York: Delta Books.
Lacan, Jacques 1977: *Ecrits: A Selection*. New York: Norton.
Lemert, Charles 1991: "The uses of French structuralisms in sociology," in George Ritzer (ed.), *The Frontiers of Social Theory*. New York: Columbia University Press.
Lemert, Charles, and Garth Gillan 1982: *Michel Foucault: Social Theory and Transgression*. New York: Columbia University Press.
Lévi-Strauss, Claude 1967: "The structural study of myth," *Structural Anthropoplogy*. New York: Anchor Books, pp. 202–28.
Lévi-Strauss, Claude 1970: "Overture to *Le cru et le cuit*," in Jacques Ehrmann (ed.), *Structuralism*. New York: Anchor Books, pp. 31–55.
Lyotard, Jean-François 1984 [1979]: *The Postmodern Condition: A Report on Knowledge*, tr. G. Bennington and B. Massumi. Minneapolis: University of Minnesota Press.
Marcus, George, and Michael M. J. Fischer 1986: *Anthropology as Cultural Critique*. Chicago: University of Chicago Press.
Merton, Robert 1957: *Social Theory and Social Structure*. Glencoe, Ill.: Free Press.
Moi, Toril (ed.) 1987: *French Feminist Thought: Politics, Patriarchy, and Sexual Difference*. New York: Basil Blackwell.
Portoghesi, Paolo 1982: *After Modern Architecture*. New York: Rizzoli.
Rorty, Richard 1979: *Philosophy and the Mirror of Nature*. Princeton, NJ.: Princeton University Press.
Rorty, Richard 1985: "Habermas and Lyotard on postmodernity," in Richard Bernstein (ed.), *Habermas and Modernity*. Cambridge, Mass.: MIT Press, pp. 161–76.
Rorty, Richard 1989: *Contingency, Irony, and Solidarity*. Cambridge: Cambridge University Press.
Said, Edward 1979: *Orientalism*. New York: Random House.
Saussure, Ferdinand de 1959: *Course in General Linguistics*. New York: McGraw Hill.
Skinner, Quentin (ed.) 1985: *The Return of Grand Theory in the Human Sciences*. Cambridge: Cambridge University Press.
Turner, Jonathan 1990: "The Promise of Positivism," chapter 6 in this volume.
Wallerstein, Immanuel 1974: *The Modern World System: Capitalist Agriculture and the Origins of the European World-System in the Sixteenth Century*. New York: Academic Press.
White, Hayden 1973: *Metahistory: The Historical Imagination in the Nineteenth Century*. Baltimore: Johns Hopkins University Press.
White, Hayden 1978: *Tropics of Discourse*. Baltimore: Johns Hopkins University Press.

2

Postmodern Social Theory as Narrative with a Moral Intent

Steven Seidman

This chapter is prompted by my belief that sociological theory – though not necessarily sociology or social theory – has gone astray. Much sociological theory is unconnected to current research programs, divorced from current social movements and political struggles, and either ignorant of major political and moral public debates or unable to address them in ways that are compelling or even understandable by nontheorists. Sociological theory has become the domain of theory specialists, with its own technical problems and vocabularies. Only sociologists who specialize in theory acquire sufficient fluency in its language and discursive strategies to be able to do theory in a way that confers credibility, social status, and material reward. Needless to say, few people except for theorists read sociological theory texts.

What accounts for this distressing state? Certainly as Russell Jacoby has argued (1987), a tendency in academia for intellectual life to drift towards disciplinary inwardness and closure is pertinent. As theorists take their own specialty problems and conventions as their reference point, their work becomes technical and obscure. Disciplinary insularity seems less detrimental to the natural sciences but, it promotes intellectual obscurity and sterility in sociology. Perhaps this is the case because the value of sociology lies ultimately in its contributions to clarifying current social affairs or otherwise shaping public life.

The explanation I wish to offer regarding the regrettable state of sociological theory focuses on certain assumptions that theorists have held about sociology as a science and about the role assigned to theory. Many sociological theorists believe that science is an epistemologically privileged type of knowledge. Its defense is necessary, moreover, in order to preserve rationality and a society that guarantees freedom and social progress. They assume that the defense of sociology as a science must take the form of theory providing foundations or grounds for sociological analysis. Providing foundations entails explaining why sociology should adopt a specific set of premises, concepts, and explanatory models. In a word, theorists assume that the task of resolving disciplinary disputes or paradigm conflicts requires proposing general criteria and ideals for a correct or valid sociology.[1] Sociological theorists step forward as virtual police of the sociological mind, creating order and disciplinary coherence in the name of rationality and progress.[2] They have not been successful. Their efforts have yielded not a defense of reason but a bewildering proliferation of texts, discourses, and disputes that render sociological theory intellectually obscure and make it irrelevant to broader public concerns. Ironically, this effort also has elicited a suspicion of the nonrational character of sociology. This quest for foundations, for providing proofs or principles of justification, causes much of the malaise of sociological theory.

In the past decade these assumptions about science and theory have been challenged by a discursive clamoring that frequently goes under the name of postmodernism.[3] The postmodern intervention is not merely another rehashing of debates between positivists and their critics or between scientific and humanistic sociologists. Indeed, these seemingly endless discussions may be taken as sympotomatic of the current impasse of sociological theory and of its stultifying insularity. Postmodernism raises questions about this very configuration of debate. The postmodern intercession aims to revitalize sociology by reforming its disciplinary code. Accordingly, under the banner of postmodernism I will offer a series of reservations about sociological theory. I will urge a shift in the role of theorists from building general theory or providing epistemic warrants for sociology to serving as moral and political analysts, narrators of stories of social development, producers of genealogies, and social critics. I advocate a change from a discipline-centered social inquiry whose reference point is debates in specialty areas to contextualized local narratives that address public conflicts.

THE NEW SOCIAL MOVEMENTS, POST MODERNISM, AND THE POLITICS OF EPISTEMOLOGY

I will not offer a theory or an extended discussion of the meaning of postmodernism; the meaning will be clarified in the context of my discussion. I wish, however, to identify some social underpinnings of postmodernism and at least to allude to its social and ideological importance. I intend to explore what I regard as a close link between postmodernism and the new social movements. I hope this approach dispels the misleading view that the discourse of postmodernism is itself a symptom of the academicization of intellectual life.

Let me make one point concerning the practical-moral or broad social significance of postmodernism. Postmodernism as a movement of cultural and discursive innovation emerged from the new social movements of the 1970s and 1980s (Huyssen 1984). The major creators and carriers of postmodern social thought have been connected to these movements. In France, the most prominent names are François Lyotard (1984), Jean Baudrillard (1983a, b), and Michel Foucault (1978, 1980). Central to their poststructuralist/postmodern turn in the 1970s was the break from the Communist Party and Marxism as the center of leftist politics, signaled by the student movements and by numerous local struggles (e.g. those of women, gays, ecologists, the mentally ill, prisoners) that surfaced as oppositional movements.[4] Similarly, in Britain and in the United States, it is striking that the main carriers of a postmodern discourse have been aligned closely to these movements. For example, the pioneers of a "social constructionist" approach to sexuality and homosexuality – Katz (1976), Jeffrey Weeks (1977), Gayle Rubin (1984), and Foucault himself (1978) – have been influenced deeply by the gay movement.[5] Similarly, American feminists like Jane Flax (1987), Sandra Harding (1986), Donna Haraway (1985), or

Nancy Fraser and Linda Nicholson (1990) have been in the forefront of promoting a postmodern social criticism.[6] In short, the shift of leftist politics in the 1970s from the politics of labor to the new social movements and to a post-Marxian social criticism forms an important social matrix for the rise of a postmodern social discourse.

Marxism lost its pivotal ideological role in leftist politics with the rise of the new social movements. In the United States, where the social base of Marxism was significantly narrower than in Europe, these movements were almost immediately at odds with Marxism and with the concentration of leftist politics on labor and class conflict. They had to struggle against Marxism to establish the legitimacy of their own oppositional claims and practices. Although Marxism facilitated social criticism among gays, feminists, and blacks, the privilege it accorded class politics rendered racial, gender, and sexual struggles secondary and marginal. These movements broke away from Marxism. By the mid-seventies, the left, in Europe and in the United States, was socially and ideologically decentered. It was composed of a plurality of movements, each focused on its own local or particular struggles to build autonomous communities, to evolve its own language of social analysis and to forge its own oppositional politic.

This social reconfiguration of leftist politics was accompanied by a theoretical decentering. The new social movements had to confront the epistemological privileging of Marxism as the language of radical social criticism. Marxism had to be debunked as a local project tied to the particular interests of labor, a project that was not always compatible with the struggles of women, gays, people of color, students, or the differently-abled. Movement intellectuals created new perspectives on the past and present that disputed the Marxian claim to universality and totalization. For example, feminists challenged the validity of applying Marxian economic and class analysis to pre-modern kinship-based societies (Rubin 1975; Rosaldo and Lamphere 1974; Ortner and Whitehead 1981). Indeed, feminists raised serious doubts about the validity of the Marxian analysis of modern societies, because its concept of production excluded sexual and household reproduction and failed to analyze how gender is involved in economic production.[7] The feminist critique had the effect of narrowing Marxism to a local conceptual and political strategy centered on labor and class politics. No post-Marxian social theory has emerged to unify and center these oppositional communities and discourses. Indeed, during the 1970s, social criticism split into myriad local critical analyses mirroring the social fragmentation of the left.

Viewing Marxism as a conceptual and practical local project contributed to a general questioning of science as a universal type of knowledge that necessarily promotes social progress. This epistemological doubt is heightened insofar as the struggle of these movements for autonomy and justice has brought them into direct conflict with science as an authoritative discourse and an institutional order. Unlike the oppression of wage labor, which is linked directly to political economic dynamics, the ways in which women, gays, people of color, and the differently-abled are socially disempowered is linked closely to public representations that are stigmatizing or otherwise devaluing and marginalizing. Quite frequently these constructions of identity carry the authority of science. In the course of their struggles for autonomy and affirmative identities, these movements have had to challenge the right of science to create symbolic and normative conventions which often have functioned to oppress the diverse populations that the movements represent. As they contested the authority of science, these minority communities evolved a postmodern criticism of science. The claims of science to value-neutrality and objectivity have been debunked; science now figures as a local conceptual practice bearing the mark of the sociohistorical embeddedness of its producers. This critique of science, which emerged from the practical struggles of these movements, is now at the center of public and academic discussions of postmodernism.

My point can be clarified by recalling some central features of the women's and gay movements. Women and gays, of course, are subject to political and economic oppression in the form of economic discrimination, denial of certain civil and political rights, political under-representation, inadequate enforcement of their rights, and so on. Accordingly the struggle for social, political, and economic equality remains integral to feminism and to gay liberation. Yet, unlike the situation in labor movements, a key agenda of feminists and gay liberationists is the struggle to create affirmative identities and communites, to gain social legitimation for their feelings, desires, and lifestyles. This struggle often has set them against science and its institutional powers. Thus feminists attack the medical and scientific disciplines – psychiatry, psychoanalysis, and the social sciences – for constructing concepts of womanhood that carry normative and behavioral directives which disempower women. Feminists have challenged scientific-medical constructions of women as biologically destined to be wives and mothers (e.g. Weisstein 1973; Millet 1969; Ehrenreich and English 1979); they attack representations of women as emotional, nurturing, and other-directed because this characterization makes women responsible for caretaking functions. Feminist critics have documented the deeply androcentric values and interests of science and challenge its authority as a privileged, enlightening discourse. Feminists have highlighted the practical power of science to construct a concept of womanhood that carries norms of appropriate female desire and behavior; they have underscored the power of science as a force of domination. Although some feminists have sought to transcend an androcentric science with a truly universal science that could be used for feminist ends, many feminists repudiate the very claim of science to epistemic privilege. Some feminists have substituted a frankly gynocentric science; others have relativized science by evolving alternative feminist social discourses. For example, the writings of Adrienne Rich (1977), Andrea Dworkin (1976), Susan Griffin (1978), Susan Brownmiller, Mary Daly (1978), Alex Schulman, and Kate Millet (1969) suggest a nonscientific mode of social analysis that frequently combines autobiographical, literary, social-scientific, and journalistic styles. In the main, their discourses function as local interventions addressing the "woman question." They provide women with a language of social criticism as well as the cultural building blocks for forging an alternative – woman-centred – culture that entails a postscientific epistemology and that at times is frankly relativistic and pragmatic.

In the gay movement we can observe a similar movement towards a postmodern position. Although legislative reform is integral to the gay community, the heart and soul of its politics center on the struggle for self-affirmation and the effort to expand the range of acceptable social differences by legitimating gay subcultural lifestyles (Altman 1977, 1983). Indeed, the struggle for civil rights is connected inextricably with the politics of identity inasmuch as the denial of rights is justified on the grounds that homosexuality is viewed as unnatural, abnormal, or socially deviant. The fight for affirmative identities is essentially a matter of cultural politics, i.e. a struggle over public representations of homosexuality. At the heart of this identity politics is a critical analysis of science and its institutional bearers (e.g. hospitals, psychiatric clinics, mental institutions, prisons, schools, scientific associations). Gays approach science as a key social force implicated in relations of sexual domination. Specifically, gays and lesbians have documented the ways in which science oppresses homosexuals by authorizing concepts of same-gender desire or intimacy as symptomatic of a psychological malady, a state of moral inferiority, or a social pathology. Individuals who have same-gender longings are transfigured scientifically into a psychologically abnormal, morally inferior, socially dangerous human type: the homosexual (Foucault 1978; Weeks 1977). The public authority of science, anchored in its presumed epistemic privileging, makes these scientific-medical constructions socially credible and influential (Katz 1983; Greenberg 1988; Weeks 1985; Faderman 1981). Many individuals who have intimate same-gender longings internalize a "homosexual" self-identification and suffer the grave psychological and social costs of bearing a stigmatized identity. The gay movement has fought against this homosexual label in part by confronting the authoritative claims of science. A critical debunking process is ensuing along the lines found in the black and women's movements. First, the objectivity of science is challenged as its heterosexism is uncovered in its basic premises, concepts, and explanations. Second, the view of science as a privileged representation gives way to defining science as a social force that shapes humanity and history in ways no less significant than the economy, kinship groups, or political institutions. Finally, the assumption that science necessarily contributes to enlightenment and social progress is disputed as its historic role in undermining same-gender intimacy and in producing stigmatizing identities is uncovered, (Smith-Rosenberg 1985a; Duggan 1983).

The critique of science by feminists and gay liberationists has challenged the modernist claim to epistemically privileged status. Similarly, the modernist assumption that science promotes enlightenment and progress, and that its epistemic defense is necessary to safeguard Reason and a good society, has been shaken severely. Science appears more and more to be a discursive and institutional strategy to impose and maintain a hierarchical order. The claim to epistemic privilege seems to be a tactic to exclude, silence, or otherwise disempower socially threatening or marginal groups. In short, science appears as a social practice that is part of the ongoing struggle among groups to impose and legitimate their conflicting interests. These new social movements and their politics of inclusion and diversity form a social backdrop to the current debate over postmodernism inside and outside academia. In the remainder of this chapter, I intend to make a case for postmodernism as a social discourse.

THE MALAISE OF THEORY
IN ITS DISCIPLINARY MODE

Marx and Engels' *German Ideology*, a classic text in sociological theory, will serve as a case study of the problems of foundationalism. As is well known, this text marked the decisive break of Marx and Engels from German Idealism in both its orthodox (Kant, Fichte, Schelling, and Hegel) and its heterodox version, i.e. the Young Hegelians. Marx and Engels sought to provide an alternative perspective on society, history, and modernity. Moreover, they sought to provide an epistemological warrant for that perspective. Their aim, in other words, was note merely to propose a different approach to human studies but also to silence their rivals by claiming to have furnished "foundations" or epistemologically sound reasons for their approach.

Marx and Engels did not have to take the foundationalist approach; they could have recommended their approach on pragmatic grounds. For example, they might have reasoned that in view of their interests in economic and political reform and in improving the lot of laborers, a "materialist" analysis is strategically advantageous. They might have suggested that a materialist-scientific social critique is more likely to contribute to the politicization of wage labor than is a critique in the language of philosophical idealism. Instead, however, Marx and Engels claimed epistemological privilege for their conceptual strategy. They proposed that their "materialist" theory articulates social realities more closely than other theories, which express the personal and social prejudices of their producers.

The claim to have discovered the language of society, achieving the breakthrough to science in the human studies, simultaneously involves the delegitimation of rival paradigms as mere precursors or ideologies. It carries a demand for the social marginalization of these rival paradigms and their supporters. By claiming an epistemologically privileged status for their ideas, Marx and Engels rationalized their own aspirations for social authority. To invoke an epistemic warrant for one's ideas, in other words, is tied to an interest in shaping society. By taking the foundationalist approach, Marx and Engels intended to silence or challenge the authority of their rivals and the social agenda and efficacy of their rivals' discourse. They wished to authorize one story of the past and present (history as the story of class conflict), one moral drama (human alienation and the recovery of freedom through revolution), and one heroic subject (the working class) as well as a political strategy to achieve a social state that would redeem past suffering (socialism).

Aside from their epistemological claim to have furnished a breakthrough language, Marx and Engels were engaged in a practical-moral or social project. They aimed to shape history by authorizing a particular social discourse that carried a particular social and political agenda. Marx and Engels did not understand their own discourse as a social and moral project in this sense. Accordingly they were not compelled to offer pragmatic reasons or a moral defense for their epistemological and ontological assumptions. They believed that there were epistemic, not merely pragmatic, grounds for deciding between conceptual strategies. Hence their critique of idealism proceeded entirely on an empistemological level.

It is instructive to recall briefly the epistemic rationales of Marx and Engels, not only because they appear repeatedly in sociological theory but also because even a cursory examination shows them to be little more than ethnocentric appeals or rhetorical strategies. I will comment on three key epistemic claims that Marx and Engels make in order to recommend "Historical Materialism."

First, in contrast to idealism, which explains social order and change by recourse to the internal logic of ideological abstractions, Marx and Engels analyze ideological formations in relation to the behavior of real individuals:

> In direct contrast to German philosophy which descends from heaven to earth, here it is a matter of ascending from earth to heaven. That is to say, not of setting out from what men say, imagine, conceive . . . but setting out from real, active men, and on the basis of their real life-process demonstrating the development of the ideological reflexes and echoes of their life-process.(*1976: 36*)

Marx and Engels appeal to realism or to grounding theory in the reality of living and acting individuals as a basis for their claim of the epistemic superiority of materialism over idealism. They do not, however, provide additional clarification as to the meaning of real individuals, nor do they explain how they know what is real. Indeed, it is as if they are saying that real, active individuals exist objectively to be observed, if only our perceptions were not clouded by idealist mystification.

This empiricism is hardly credible. Real individuals who shape their world and themselves are not observable. What is considered real is a function of social and linguistic conventions. What is empirically observable is inseparable from the language in use – and from the conceptual resources available. The "individual" is a concept that some, though not all, groups use to create or shape intellectual, moral, and social order. It has the same status as categories such as the family, the tribe, or the nation. Indeed, the notion of the individual as an autonomous agent who is the source of order and change is at best a fiction or an analytical construct. As sociologists – and Marx himself – have argued congently individuals are constituted by society and therefore are penetrated by society in an infinite number of ways that make it impossible, except for analytical or ideological purposes, to distinguish the individual from society. Marx and Engels' claim to realism to authorize their discourse turns out to be little more than an appeal to the individualistic prejudices of modern, middle-class Westerners.

Second, in contrast to idealism, which advises us to analyze the internal conflicts of ideological or symbolic systems in order to recover the formative processes of human history, Marx and Engels urge us to focus on individuals' material productive activity. Their epistemic rationale is fairly straightforward. Before individuals can think and produce symbolic or cultural order, they first must reproduce their natural material existence. Humans, after all, are part of a natural organic order. An interchange with the external natural environment is necessary in order to reproduce human life. Thus productive activity or labor becomes the foundational category upon which Marx and Engels build a materialist theory of society and history. "Men can be distinguished from animals by consciousness, by religion or anything else you like. They themselves begin to distinguish themselves from animals as soon as they begin to *produce* their means of subsistence . . . By producing their means of subsistence men are indirectly producing their material life . . . What they are, therefore, coincides with their production . . . Hence what individuals are depends on the material conditions of their production" (ibid.: 31).

Unfortunately, the category of labor is quite ambiguous. In the end it cannot support the conceptual edifice that Marx and Engels build upon it (see Habermas 1971, 1973). The category of "productive" activity either expands to include virtually all human practices, in which case it is useless as a conceptual strategy, or it narrows arbitrarily to economic laboring activity (Nicholson 1986). The latter may provide a useful conceptual strategy but it is unjustified. Why should economic labor be privileged as a formative practice over (say) reproductive, domestic, cultural, political, or legal practices? Surely the need to reproduce our material life through labor is no more urgent than the need to reproduce our lives through sexual reproduction and domestic activity. Similarly, economic laboring practices always are embedded in a sociocultural and political context that involves normative and legal regulation and structures of institutional and political authority as well as gendered identities and relations. What makes any one moment of this configuration epistemologically privileged? Marx and Engels provide no answers to these questions. Their claim to ground the epistemic authority of materialism by assuming the ontological primacy of the category of productive activity appears to be little more than an ethnocentric and perhaps androcentric prejudice (Baudrillard 1975, 1981).

Third, Marx and Engels claim epistemic superiority for materialism on the grounds that it conceptualizes consciousness only as the consciousness of particular living individuals rather than as obeying a logic of reason or symbolic order. They accuse the idealists of reification and of being ideological, while they themselves invoke the presumed authority of realism. We do not need to rehearse the limits of epistemic claims to realism. Indeed, the idealists need to be interpreted as saying only that symbolic production is shaped by existing cultural traditions and conventions in order to render the claim of an internal cultural logic at least credible. Moreover, Marx and Engels' own conceptual strategy is notoriously ambiguous. They oscillate between two strategies of relationg "consciousness" to "being." In one of these formulations, "being" determines "consciousness." Consciousness is little more than the product of physiological processes. "The phantoms formed in the brains of men are also, necessarily, sublimates of their material life-process" (Marx and Engels 1976: 36).

Yet even in less mechanical formulations, it is difficult to uphold this thesis. After all, being is always conscious being, and seemingly it is as reasonable to speak of consciousness structuring being as the reverse. In fact, Marx and Engels opt at times for a more dialectical version of this relation. "Being" shapes "consciousness," but the latter, in turn, can form "being."

> This conception of history [starts] from the material production of life itself – and comprehending the form of intercourse connected with and created by this mode of production . . . also explaining how all the different theoretical products and forms of consciousness . . . arise from it . . . [T]hus the whole thing can, of course, be depicted in its totality (and therefore, too, the reciprocal actionof these various sides on one another). (*ibid.: 53*)

Yet if structures of consciousness can shape material life, it seems arbitrary to assign categorical or epistemological primacy to the latter. The relationship between "being" and "consciousness," it seems, should be an empirical or a pragmatic decision.

Marx and Engels' attempt to provide an epistemic warrant for their conceptual strategy does not stand up to critical scrutiny. Their foundationalist rationales amount to little more than appeals to certain modern Western, often androcentric, cultural preferences. To their credit, they virtually abandoned metatheory after *The German Ideology* in favor of analyzing current developments from their materialist vantage point. It is reasonable to ask why they felt the need to provide an epistemic rationale for their conceptual strategy, especially in light of their political interests.

Marx and Engels, like their rivals, subscribed to the "modernist" dogma of scientism. They believed in the epistemological superiority of science as a mode of knowledge. Nonscientific modes, such as philosophy, theology, religion, aesthetics, literature, and art, were demoted to the status of subjective belief or ideology. Marx and Engels viewed themselves as doing for the study of history what they believed Newton and Darwin had accomplished for the study of nature.

Marx and Engels were not alone in aspiring to achieve a science of history. They had some credible rivals (e.g. Adam Smith, John Stuart Mill, Auguste Comte, Herbert Spencer, Lorenz von Stein), each of whom asserted that his own work inaugurated a true science of society and history. Faced with this theoretical conflict, Marx and Engels apparently felt compelled, by virtue of their scientistic ideology, to provide epistemic reasons for the superiority of their conceptual strategy. There was more at stake than maintaining intellectual credibility or aspiring to conceptual dominance. To claim epistemic privilege is to demand social authority for a discourse and its carriers. Claiming an epistemic warrant for a conceptual strategy discredits the social projects of rivals. To describe a discourse as ideological de-legitimates its social agenda; it challenges the authority of those social elites and institutions which obtain their legitimacy from some presumably true discourse. In contrast, to assert that a social agenda is legitimated by a discourse which speaks the language of truth confers legitimacy on that agenda and its supporters.

The discursive conflicts of Marx and Engels' were connected to at least two practical struggles. First, they were in conflict with social and cultural elites (clergy, landed nobility, and humanistic elites) who drew on the epistemic warrant that philosophy, religion, or aesthetics provided for their legitimation. The ideology of scientism was intended to undercut the epistemic warrant for the social power of these elites. Second, Marx and Engels were in a struggle with "modernist" rivals over the shape of the emerging new epoch that they described and evaluated in conflicting ways. Thus the battle that Marx and Engels waged with classical economics over the right to claim a breakthrough to a social science was simultaneously a struggle over which social agenda and which social groups should be empowered. In short, the politics of epistemology was bound up with practical-ideological struggles over the right to shape history.

Are there any costs to Marx and Engles's adopting a foundationalist approach? What, if anything, is lost in trying to offer epistemic support for a discourse? Does this effort not promote reflexivity and consensus strategies of conflict resolution? Indeed, there are advantages to foundationalism – but there are considerable costs as well. I wish to comment on two of these costs.

First, the quest to uncover epistemic principles of justification has led to a failure to grasp discourse as a practical-moral project. Dazed by their scientistic self-understanding, Marx and Engels were unable to reflect on the moral meaning of their discourse. They acknowledged the practical intent of their discourse, but this intent itself was given an epistemic warrant by their theory of history. If Marx and Engels had admitted that there was no epistemic warrant for their discourse, they would have understood it simply as a conceptual strategy that carried a practical-moral and a social agenda. They would have been compelled to give reasons for their discourse as a practical and moral project. Indeed, if they had concluded that foundational rationales are never more than local ethnocentric prejudices and that epistemic closure is very likely an illusory hope, they would have been provoked to argue for their conceptual approach on pragmatic grounds. Their disputes with rival theories would not have been over epistemic first principles – individualism versus holism, materialism versus idealism, rationalism versus historicism – but over the practical-moral consequences of choosing one or another conceptual strategy.

A pragmatic turn has distinct social benefits: it expands the number of parties who may participate in the debate as equals. Where a discourse is redeemed by metatheory, experts step forward as authorities. This situation contributes to the depoliticization of the public sphere because ordinary citizens lack the expertise to participate as equals in social discourse. By contrast, as a discourse is judged by its practical consequences or its moral implications citizen participation expands. All citizens are qualified to assess social norms and to advocate ideals of social life. A pragmatic move, in principle, implies an active, politically engaged citizenry participating in a democratic public realm.

A second cost of taking a foundationalist view is the danger that a discourse will become socially obscure because its primary reference is other metadiscourses. As texts pile up, with their own coherence resting in this intertextuality, the arcane and technical character of theoretical vocabularies and disputes renders them socially marginal and meaningful only to theory specialists. If we have learned anything from the history of philosophy or the history of sociology, it is that foundational disputes permit very little, if any, consensus. The reasons are not difficult to find: the criteria that allow for possible closure or consent seem heterogeneous and ultimately incommensurable. How do "we" judge or assign priorities to epistemic standards that include empirical adequacy, explanatory comprehensiveness, quantitative precision, predictability, logical coherence, conceptual economy, intellectual scope, aesthetic appeal, practical efficacy, and moral acceptability? How do we agree on what intellectual closure might or should look like? What would need to be included in a valid theory? What, after all, should serve as a standard of validity? Further, what criteria should be invoked to justify this standard? Finally, who is to make these decisions? Who, in other words, are the "we" that legislates justificatory strategies? The conclusion seems inevitable: foundationalist arguments are circular and seem unable to avoid being local and ethnocentric.

Marx and Engels largely avoided the drift into metatheoretical obscurity and social irrelevance. Their involvement in class politics, along with their social positions outside academia, compelled them as intellectuals to relate their work to their practical engagements. Their social thought remained anchored in and responsive to the major social and political developments of their time.

As for intellectual life in the contemporary United States, we find the social circumstances of the intellectual, especially the sociological theorist, are dramatically different. Sociological theory occurs exclusively in academe; it is a disciplinary creature. Indeed, it has become a specialty area with its own problems and disputes, its own languages and rhetorical conventions. It has its own status hierarchy. Sociological theorists are oriented primarily to internal disputes in their specialties. This drift towards the insularity of sociological theory is reinforced by a scientistic ideology that legitimates science by claiming to promote the growth of knowledge and human rationality. Sociological theory appears more and more as an expert culture, split off from the practical moral concerns of everyday life and the major public disputes of our time. Theorists struggle around dominance in their area of specialty and achieving status in their discipline. The standards of social hierarchy among theorists have become increasingly formal – they consist of mastery and innovation of a technical language and the sheer quantity of published work. The successful theorist, in addition, builds networks and coalitions and promotes himself or herself by fostering the right alliances with powerful persons, journals, universities, and presses.

Because the codes of the discipline dominate theoretical practices, theorists are less able than in the past to resist the move from disciplinary dispute or paradigm rivalry to metatheory. This tendency is reinforced by the increasing autonomy of empirical area specialties (demography, crime, organization, religion, family); these areas have evolved their own theories and conceptual strategies, which rely less and less strongly on the general theories and metadiscourses produced by sociological theorists. The latter may respond to this status anxiety by seizing upon metatheory or disputes over the foundations of sociology as their own autonomous subject matter.[8] Indeed, sociological theorists, like any other status group, may invest their metatheoretical role with exaggerated importance – as the defenders, say, of disciplinary coherence and rationality.

By the mid-1970s, if not earlier, sociological theorists had stepped forward as area specialists whose expertise lay in foundationalist problems or disputes. Theorists in effect have declared themselves experts in a metatheoretical discourse that addresses foundationalist issues such as the nature of social action and order, the relationship between agency and structure, culture and social structure, micro and macro social analysis, the link between concept and reality, and the logic of explanation. The value of this discourse lies less and less in clarifying major public developments or debates, and not at all in its contribution to current research programs. Indeed, much current innovative sociological theory, such as the writings of Alexander (1983), Giddens (1984), Runciman (1983), Elster, or Münich, has little or no link to empirical disputes or ongoing research concerns. These scholars' metadiscourses do not address the specific conceptual and research issues of area specialty sociologists.

Although metadiscourse claims legitimacy on the basis of preserving order and rationality in the discipline, this development seems increasingly like a self-serving ideology masking a struggle for dominance in a specialty. Not only do theorists have diminishing impact on researchers whose work is shaped primarily by internal considerations of area specialty; the field of "theory" itself seems incoherent and holds little realistic promise for future consensus. In truth, theorists have reached nothing even approximating consensus about how disciplinary foundations ought to look or what they might be. Instead of a concentrated, centered discourse focused on a series of limited problems or issues, one finds a near-infinite number of local, heterogeneous, and changing disputes occurring in a dazzling diversity of languages that often imply divergent (if not incommensurable) philosophical, moral, and ideological standpoints. There is virtually no standardization of language, no agreement on central problems or on standards to evaluate our discursive production. Instead there is a babble of vocabularies addressing a variety of local, changing disputes. Indeed, much of this discourse involves struggles to authorize a particular dispute or problem or a particular theoretical language.

Typically, a text backed by a socially powerful network briefly captures the attention of some of the principal figures in the field. A discussion ensues; certain problems and disputes or a particular vocabulary may acquire prominence among sociological theorists. Such coherence is short-lived at best because the field is always divided. Other rival theorists with their own texts, vocabularies, and networks clamor for recognition and area specialty status. Some are heard, but many others may gain the attention of very few; still others clamor and are heard by no one, but still may win tenure and promotion. Very little in these discourses is settled, if indeed that is the purpose. Foundational problems seem basically to be philosophical, moral, ideological, and practical – and therefore irresolvable. Moreover, although the conversation of theorists does little direct harm, it has become excessively elitist, obscure, and socially marginal. In my view, there are few compelling reasons to keep it going. The time has come for theorists to begin a different conversation.

SOCIOLOGY AND THEORY IN A POSTMODERN MODE

I have not offered any arguments ruling out success in the quest for foundations in sociology. Until now my doubt has been merely pragmatic. Foundationalism ought to be abandoned because of its unfortunate consequences: it promotes the intellectual obscurity and social irrelevance of theory, contributes to the decline of public moral and political discourse, and furthers the enfeeblement of an active citizenry. I would like to introduce an epistemic doubt, although still I will not argue for the impossibility of success in the foundational quest. Instead I will raise a pervasive doubt, on which I elaborate a critique of "modernist" sociology that goes beyond a critique of foundationalism. I will pursue this critique into a positive proposal for a "postmodern" concept of social inquiry and theory.

Modern human studies never have been able to avoid the suspicion that their products – concepts, explanations, and theories – are imprinted with the particular prejudices and interests of their creators. The suspicion may be posed as follows: How can an individual, knowing subject who has particular interests and biases by virtue of living in a specific society at a particular historical juncture and occupying a specific social position defined by his or her class, gender, race, sexual orientation, ethnicity, and religious status, produce concepts, explanations, and standards of truth that are universally valid? How can we assert that humans are constituted by their particular sociohistorical circumstances and also claim that they can escape their embeddedness by creating nonlocal, noncontextually valid concepts and standards? How can we escape the suspicion that every move by culturally bounded agents to generalize or universalize their conceptual strategy is simply an effort to impose a local, particular prejudice on others who do not share that prejudice?

As this doubt becomes firmer and more pervasive, the very project of science is questioned. The suspicion arises that science is tied to the project of Western modernity and, indeed, that it is tied inextricably to more concrete social dynamics and struggles. Once the veil of epistemic privilege is torn away, science appears to be enmeshed in networks of social practices and power relations. The postmodern unmasking of science as a practical-moral force aims to bring public accountability to a powerful social element that at present is almost unaccountable by virtue of the ideology that accompanies it and its disciplinary autonomy. We are moving ahead of ourselves, however; let us return to the great suspicion that plagues the human studies.

This suspicion seems to be elicited by the very claim of science to epistemic privilege. When the *philosophes* challenged the authority of the Church and the landed nobility, they did so by contesting the religious or metaphysical epistemological grounds of their secular power. By proposing that the ideas gained by religious or philosophical methods do not count as true knowledge but only amount to subjective opinion or prejudice, they challenged the authority of the clerical and aristocratic hierarchy. The *philosophes* claimed in effect that the appeal to religious tradition or divine revelation to authorize clerical secular power was illegitimate and fraudulent. The appeal to religious tradition, they argued, was a self-interested strategy on the part of the clergy to justify their claims to social prestige and power. The *philosophes'* own appeal to science as a privileged medium of truth was intended, of course, to legitimate the social project entailed in their own discourse as well as their claim to social authority. Although the *philosophes* helped to establish science as the dominant epistemology of Western modernity, their programs of human studies were contested. They fell victim to the very rhetorical strategy that they used against their nonscientific rivals.

It was Marx who postulated the interested or ideological character of human studies. Interpreting rival conceptual approaches through the prism of social class analysis, he made epistemic doubt systematic. No human studies program could escape the suspicion that its scientific pretensions masked class interest. Marxism itself fell prey to this suspicion. Not only have "bourgeois" sociologists turned Marxism's class analysis against itself, but recent post-Marxian social critics have attacked the claim of Marxism to epistemic privilege by revealing its modern Eurocentric and androcentric bias. The history of human studies exhibits a parade of pretenders to having achieved a true science of society; in turn, their claims to value-neutrality, objectivity, and universality have been invalidated by revealing their particular social interests, value commitments, and social agendas.

The development of post-Marxian oppositional communities and politics in the 1970s and 1980s, I believe is a pivotal point in the politics of epistemology. As feminists, people of color, gays and lesbians, ecologists, and the differently-abled, among others, responded to the social science disciplines, they produced an impressive critique that highlighted the practical-moral or interested character of disciplinary discourses. Through innumerable case studies, for example, feminists have documented the androcentric bias of the modern disciplines, especially the social sciences. They have revealed a masculine bias in the decisions about what problems are worthy of study, in definitions of the key topics of analysis (e.g., the neglect of the study of emotions, intimacy, domesticity), in the design and methodology of research (e.g. quantitative in preference to more ethnographic approaches), and in the basic guiding categories or concepts of analysis (e.g. the emphasis on categories relating to paid labor, organized politics, public organizations and bureaucracies, or class movements).[9] Furthermore, many feminists contend that the guiding epistemological and ontological assumptions in the disciplines indicate a masculine standpoint. The dualisms that are pervasive in the modern sciences – for example culture versus nature, mind versus body, objectivity versus subjectivity, public sphere versus private sphere, reason versus emotion – seem to be connected to a specifically modern Western and masculine experience (see e.g. Bordo 1986; Keller 1985; Jagger and Bordo 1989; Harding and Hintikka 1983).

Although some feminists believe that a truly objective human science can be achieved by correcting the social sources of masculine bias, the logic of the feminist critique makes it implausible that feminists' own standpoint will not be open to criticism from the perspective (say) of a person of color, or a gay or lesbian, or a member of the working-class. Similarly, this critique would apply to feminists who argue that a gynocentric standpoint provides a privileged epistemic vantage point. We need only ask whose gynocentric standpoint or whose feminism provides the privileged epistemic standpoint, because versions of "women's experience" or true womanhood are heterogeneous and often conflicting. Theories from a feminist-standpoint seem inevitably to lean towards a feminist postmodernism because the unity of the subject – woman – is fragmented and diversified by the clamor of different women's voices contesting orthodoxy and demanding recognition for their unique experience of womanhood (see Harding 1986; Riley 1988; Spelman 1988).

With the rise of minority communities (e.g. blacks, women, gays) and discourses, there has arisen a widespread critique of modernist legitimations of science on the grounds of the growth of knowledge, the defense of reason, or public enlightenment, and the social progress that is presumed to follow automatically from scientific advance. The knowing subject or producer of knowledge now is viewed as insinuated so deeply into the product – the human sciences – that one hardly can believe the claim by any knowing subject to have created general categories and explanations which are universally valid representations rather than reflections of a particular standpoint. Discourses cannot escape the suspicion that they bear the mark of their producers; the producers, in turn, bear the mark of their particular social identity and interests. Just as the knowing subject is constituted by his or her gender, race, nationality, class, sexual orientation, and so on, so too are the products of thought. Because this relentless epistemological suspicion is turned by feminists, against disciplinary discourses, and then against itself, and because this trope is repeated among African-Americans, Hispanics, Asians, gays, lesbians, conservatives, liberals, and leftists, no social discourse can escape the doubt that its epistemic claims are tied to (and yet mask) an ongoing social will to shape the course of history. The claim to truth, as

Foucault suggested, is inextricably an act of power – a will to form humanity.

I believe that this epistemic suspicion is at the core of postmodernism. It challenges the basic aim of disciplinary discourses to create general – indeed universally valid – conceptions of society, history, and modernity. Postmodernism contests the representational view of science that is dominant in the disciplines. It disputes the belief that there is a close if not necessary connection between science, public enlightenment, and social progress. Postmodernism underscores the practical-moral or socially constitutive character of science; it sees the disciplines as implicated in heterogeneous struggles to shape humanity. Postmodernism does not favour the end of social enquiry but only the end of "modernist" legitimations and some of its conceptual strategies. Invoking epistemic privilege, knowledge for its own sake, the growth of knowledge, public enlightenment, and social progress to justify human studies should not be sufficient to legitimate disciplinary discourses. This is especially the case in light of the enormous national resources that the disciplines command today and the serious questions raised about their intellectual and social value.

If the dominant concept of human studies is objectionable for all the reasons I have stated above, what would a postmodern alternative look like? I offer a sketch of one concept of postmodern social analysis and social theory.

I recommend abandoning the project of developing general theories such as historical materialism, structural-functionalism, or French or American structuralism. I also have doubts about the value of more narrowly focused general theories of (say) the state, social movements, modernization, or crime. It seems to me that general theories cannot escape being culture-bound or ethnocentric because of their sociohistorical embeddedness. Inevitably they bear the mark of their producers' sociohistorical constitution or identity. Generations of theoretical efforts to evolve premises, concepts, and explanations that are valid across different groups and societies, to establish a master language of society, history, and modernity, have been shown repeatedly to be ethnocentric. Moreover, general theories are more likely than local, contextual social analyses to promote essentializing, reified identities, to promote and legitimate social hierarchies, to repress social differences and particularities, and to ignore the interests of marginalized populations or simply to be irrelevant to their struggles and aims. Finally, general theories mask their will to shape history. They contribute to the de-politicization of the public sphere by trying to transfigure moral and practical struggles into analytical or metatheoretical struggles.

The postmodern suspicion of generalizing extends to the unreflective use of general categories. For example, postmodern feminists criticize the essentialist discourse of gender – both androcentric and gynocentric – that posits a bipolar gender order composed of a fixed, universal "man" and "woman." Within a feminist postmodernism, these concepts are understood as social constructions in which the discourse of gender itself is a part of the will to shape gender. The discourse about gender is tied to the ongoing struggle to assign gender identities, social roles, and statuses to males and to females. "Womanhood" and "manhood" are seen neither as natural facts nor as settled social facts but as a ceaseless, contested struggle among various groups, institutions, and discourses to establish an ordering of individual and social lives along the dimension of gender.

Similarly, recent gay and lesbian scholars have criticized the essentialist discourse of sexuality – in both a heterosexual and a homosexual context – that assumes a natural sexuality which divides people into heterosexuals and homosexuals. Rather than defining individuals as heterosexuals and as homosexuals, as if these were fixed, universal categories of sexual identity, the writings of Foucault (1978) Jeffrey Weeks (1977), Jonathan Katz (1976), Caroll Smith-Rosenberg (1985), among others, view these social identities as historical constructions (see n. 6). Although a discourse of natural sexuality that divides humans into two major sexual/human types – heterosexual and homosexual – may take on a social efficacy (e.g. people adopt these labels as either negative or affirmative self-identities), they remain a fiction or a normative construction. In short, the discourse that frames desire as fixing sexual and self-identity is seen not as describing a natural reality but as an effort to shape a hierarchical sexual order that assigns meaning, value, and a social location to certain desires and acts defined as "sexual."

The postmodern problematization of general categories raises a serious challenge to the possibility of human studies in the modernist mode. If generalizing discourses contribute to the social construction of identities, cultural conventions and institutional orders, then the very object of study is itself in part a product of the discourse. This understanding of social discourse as a powerful social force, making social reality and yet naturalizing it and concealing its own practical power, disposes postmoderns towards genealogical social analysis. Genealogies aim to uncover the social processes concealed by hegemonic essentialist discourses and to implicate these discourses in those formative social processes. Genealogies account for the social production of identities and institutional orders that frequently are assumed to be natural; they aim to free individuals from essentialist identities that constrain behavior; they strive to unearth submerged alternative languages to describe experiences and open up new possibilities for social identification and behavior.

In addition to genealogical social analysis, I urge substituting for standard, modernist generalizing conceptual strategies more local narratives that respond to national disputes and current social conflicts. Local narratives would analyze a circumscribed social phenomenon in a densely contextual way. This procedure entails analyzing an event (e.g. homelessness, the underclass, AIDS, divorce) in its particular social setting (e.g. in a particular city in a specific country at a specific time), while attending to its heterogeneous meanings for different populations. For example, a postmodern analysis of the homeless might begin by situating this population in its concrete social locale – e.g. in Albany, New York, in 1990. This step entails more than locating this phenomenon spatially and temporally; it involves viewing it in relation to the social and political structure of that locale. Thus a study of homelessness in Albany could not be separated from the socially distinctive fact of a political culture and a social order that have been controlled by a city machine for most of the twentieth century. The meaning and the structure of homelessness are inseparable from the social locale of which it is a part. Furthermore, the homeless would not be viewed as a homogeneous population whose experience is essentially the same. Instead they would be understood as consisting of people of diverse, heterogeneous experiences and exhibiting social patterns that vary according to gender, race, religion, age, sexual orientation, occupational history and skills, familial status, and so on.

As general or global analyses of homlessness give way to densely contextual, local narratives, it would be likely that such studies would be respectful of the complex experiences of the people under study. Discourses of victimization or heroism would give way to more morally ambiguous accounts. Local narratives are more likely to articulate the viewpoints and concerns of their subjects. In this way, social analysis could function as an important vehicle by which socially marginal or disempowered people gain a public voice. Thus, by staying close to the experiences of those it studies, human studies could contest the very categories of identification of public discourses that may be tied to administrative, legal, or political concerns which in turn may conflict with the interests of those implicated in the discourse. Do not the terms "the homeless," or the "underclass," create public identities or self-identifying labels? These not only homogenize and reify a changing, heterogeneous phenomenon but perhaps unintentionally create new forms of state and medical-scientific systems of social control.

I do not discount completely the value of generalizing social analyses. Studies of the "homeless," the "underclass," "black Americans," "divorced women," or "homosexuals" can be instrumental in making a previously invisible phenomenon a topic of public concern, moral debate, or political interest. Thus, generalizing studies such as Michael Harrington's *Other America* (1962), William Wilson's *Truly Disadvantaged* (1987), Lenore Weitzman's *Divorce Revolution* (1985) or Kathleen Barry's *Female Sexual Slavery* (1984) are quite useful in this regard. Similarly valuable are generalizing studies that try to change public perception on an issue of general public interest. Thus, synthetic generalizing studies are important; examples are Linda Gordon's *Woman's Body, Woman's Right* (1977), Barbara Ehrenreich and Deirdre English's *For Her Own Good* (1979), Lillian Faderman's *Surpassing the Love of Men* (1981), Simon Watney's *Policing Desire* (1987), or Alfonso Pinkney's *The Myth of Black Progress* (1984), which reconfigure public understandings of abortion, lesbianism, AIDS, or blacks in America. Yet I believe that these generalizing analyses should give way to local narratives. Generalizing discourses inevitably become essentializing discourses and create new categories of self-identity – "the poor," the "underclass," the "lesbian," the "black," the "woman" – which suppress differences, create new social hierarchies, and may be stigmatizing as well.

The meaning of theory in a postmodern mode would change too. The quest for general theories, models, principles, or laws would be either abandoned or relegated to a minor role. This does not mean that postmodern human studies would relinquish general reflection or broad social perspectives in favor of exclusively local analysis. I can imagine one form that theory might assume in a postmodern mode (Seidman 1991).

Theory might entail developing synthetic analyses of contemporary social developments. These narratives would not necessarily respond to specific policy or political events, but to some general development or social configuration. They might cover large areas of time and space, and would aim at clarifying current affairs or redescribing the present in ways that reveal new practical-moral or political possibilities. Although these major stories inevitably would involve generalizations, they would not be general theories, nor would they be like the grand narratives of Comte, Marx, Spencer, Durkheim, or Parsons.

Unlike these evolutionary theories, postmodern narratives would neither claim to be grounded in a metadiscourse nor be transnational in their focus. Instead, postmodern stories of development would be centered on a particular nation or social unit; their narratives would be more historically contextualized and more event-centered than the classical grand narratives. Robert Bellah's *Broken Covenant* (1975) is exemplary. Bellah offers a redescription of America's past and present. He relates a tale of the current cultural crisis of the US by embedding the present in a historical narrative of America's cultural origins and development. His narrative aims to bring the reader into a dialogue about the social and moral meaning and future of the US. Similarly, in *The Habits of the Heart* (1985), Bellah and his colleagues provide a historically anchored diagnosis of America's moral culture that draws on this historical understanding as they assume the role of moral advocates. Other texts that illustrate the notion of theory as narrative synthesis or redescription include C. Wright Mills, *White Collar*(1951); Christopher Lasch, *Haven in a Heartless World* (1977), David

Riesman, *The Lonely Crowd* (1953), and Tocqueville's *Democracy in America*.

Developing broad narrative redescriptions of contemporary affairs is a task for which sociological theorists are somewhat prepared by their training. At least until recently, the last few generations of American sociological theorists have had to master texts that offered broad perspectives on history and modernity. To shift into theory in a postmodern mode would require relinquishing the general analytical project of constructing a universally valid sociological language that presumably grounded these big stories. In addition, the grand narrative would be discarded in favor of more historically anchored, nation-centered stories. In other words, unlike the global stories of world-historical change of (say) Marx or Durkheim, the ultimate value of the postmodernists' narratives would lie in contributing to current national conflicts and in shaping their outcome. This quality would encourage sociological theorists to become fluent in moral analysis.

Moral inquiry, as I see it, would not entail constructing a metadiscourse in the tradition of Kant's *Groundwork of the Metaphysic of Morals*. It would abandon the quest for a transcendent moral reason or, for that matter, for any appeal to universal ethical principles or values. Such metadiscourse is vulnerable to the same reservations as metatheory. Moral inquiry can be socially compelling only in a historicist, pragmatic mode. If offering universal principles carries no epistemic authority or (to put it differently) if the invocation of those principles has little or no social efficacy, moral inquiry must take the form of appeals to cultural tradition or current social conventions and ideals to justify social practices or norms.

Specifically, the moral claims of a discourse – its social agenda and social judgment – would be assessed by analyzing its personal and social consequences in light of the traditions, conventions, and ideals of that society. For example, whereas a Marxian critic would merely appeal to a link between capitalism and social inequalities to provide a moral warrant for socialism, the postmodern critic would be compelled to make the moral case for change. This process would entail more than appealing to abstract values (e.g. equality, freedom, individualism) or advancing general proposals for reform (e.g. to socialize property). A postmodern critic of capitalism would need to appeal to social norms and conventions embodied in current social practices to make his or her critique more socially compelling – for example, to refer to recent legislation, current laws, or institutional practices affirming norms of equality or democracy that are contradicted by the particular rules or practices under capitalism. Similarly, the postmodern critic would need to go beyond abstract proposals for reforms (e.g. to socialize property) and instead outline specific changes and policy proposals as well as considering the varied consequences of such changes. Social criticism in a postmodern mode would lose its current rhetorical and often socially obscure character, because it would be forced to articulate its critique in a way that would be useful to social movements, legislators, and policy makers.

As social criticism became more local and more pragmatic, perhaps it would become more relevant to the larger public. At this moment, academic outsiders, journalists, and independent intellectuals dominate public moral and political discussion. Public intellectuals such as Michael Harrington, Barbara Ehrenreich, George Gilder, Irving Kristol, Irving Howe, Midge Decter, Betty Friedan, and Charles Krauthammer shape many of the major moral and political debates of the day. Sociologists trained in the study of institutional dynamics and encouraged to be reflective about conceptual strategies are well suited to assume the role of public intellectuals.

A FINAL WORD ON RELATIVISM

This sketch of postmodern human studies is meant to be suggestive – and provocative. Many issues remain unaddressed and many questions unanswered. In particular, the abandonment of foundationalism raises the specter of relativism – and, some would say, of nihilism. The abandonment of epistemic and moral certainty does entail relativism, if by that we mean a heterogeneity of standards of truth and moral rightness. We can only appeal, as Rorty argues persuasively (1979, 1982) to cultural traditions or social conventions and ideals to gain credibility for our cognitive claims and our claims to moral validity. This type of relativism does not, I think, amount to surrendering to nihilism, although it may imply a degree of social flux and conflict that some may judge unacceptable. This course is preferable, in my view, to the repression of difference and diversity that is implied in the quest for foundations and disciplinary order.

In any event, I think the attempt to connect relativism to nihilism is misleading. Nihilism would follow only if our social behavior and institutional order depended on epistemic and moral concensus, in some essential way for its stability and coherence. To make this claim credible it would have to be shown that foundationalist discourses (e.g. epistemology, sociological metatheory, moral philosophy) have even the slightest social impact. As Rorty remarked, however, the existence of modern science and modern culture does not depend on the legitimating function of epistemology, the philosophy of science, or aesthetics. These discussions could disappear without any noticeable effect on our culture.

As Linda Nicholson has written in this volume (chapter 3), relativism is a practical or social problem, not a stance that one adopts or does not. It involves a breakdown in communication, typically temporarily, between individuals, groups, or communities. In the main, however, individuals and communities with divergent interests and world views find ways to negotiate a common life without necessarily agreeing on standards of truth or morality and even without subscribing to world views that overlap significantly. I can maintain both that the epistemology of postmodernism projects ceaseless social heterogeneity and conflict and that in practice heterogeneous interests, values, world views, and lifestyles negotiate a coexistence which does not depend on the metadiscursive efforts of a moral and intellectual elite. Of course, relinquishing the specter of relativism means that intellectuals, especially academics, must give up a key strategy for claiming social authority. At a certain level, the claim that intellectuals have a duty to discover epistemic and moral order as a necessary condition of social and moral progress may be seen as a power strategy that gives social authority to their own discourse and social role.

NOTES

I wish to thank Linda Nicholson for her comments on this chapter.

1 See Stephen Turner's essay in this volume (chapter 4).
2 See Seidman 1989. Discontent over the state of social theory, especially sociological theory, for its metatheoretical centering is becoming widespread. See e.g. remarks by Clifford Geertz (1983: 4–5) and Theda Skocpol (1986: 10–12).
3 Key discussions of postmodernism as it relates to social theory include the special issues of *Theory, Culture and Society* (1988) and *Cultural Critique* (1986–7); Kellner 1988; Foster 1983; Lash 1985.
4 Foucault, for example, makes this link between his own work in the 1970s and the new social movements. See esp. "Two lectures," in *Power/Knowledge* (1980).
5 Also important are the writings of Caroll Smith-Rosenberg (1985b); John D'Emilio (1983); and Mary McIntosh (1968).
6 The rise of postmodernism in feminism, especially in the early 1980s, seems to be a response to developments within feminism towards a gynocentric essentialism. Feminist postmodernism, in other words, is a reaction to the closure and exclusionary currents within feminism as it has assumed a gynocentric standpoint. This gynocentric essentialism, with its reified notion of womanhood, is evident in cultural feminism but is also to be found in the socialist-feminism of Nancy Chodorow (1978) or the liberal feminism of Carol Gilligan (1982). On cultural feminism, see Alice Echols (1983, 1984).
7 Cf. Young 1981; Flax 1981, 1990; Balbus 1982. See also the essays in Trebilcot 1984. From a nonfeminist perspective, see the critique of Marx's concept of labor by Jürgen Habermas; the relevant essays are collected in Habermas 1989.
8 See the attempt to defend metatheory as a specialty area of sociological theory by George Ritzer (1988).
9 Among those studies which document an androcentric bias in social science, see e.g. Smith 1979, 1989; Millman and Kanter 1975; Westkott 1979; Anderson 1983.

REFERENCES

Alexander, Jeffrey 1983: *Theoretical Logic in Sociology*, vol. 1: *Positivism, Presuppositions, and Current Controversies*. Berkeley and Los Angeles: University of California Press.

Altman, Dennis 1983: *The Homosexualization of America*. Boston: Beacon Press.

Anderson, Margaret 1983: *Thinking about Women*. New York: Macmillan.

Balbus, Isaac 1982: *Marxism and Domination*. Princeton, NJ: Princeton University Press.

Barry, Kathleen 1984: *Female Sexual Slavery*. New York: New York University Press.

Bellah, Robert 1975: *The Broken Covenant*. New York: Seabury Press.

Bellah, Robert, et al. 1985: *Habits of the Heart*. Berkeley: University of California Press.

Bordo, Susan 1986: "The Cartesian masculinization of thought," *Signs*, 11 (Spring).

Baudrillard, Jean 1975: *The Mirror of Production*. St Louis: Telos Press.

Baudrillard, Jean 1981: *For a Critique of the Political Economy of the Sign*. St Louis: Telos Press.

Baudrillard, Jean 1983a: *In the Shadow of the Silent Minorities*. New York: Semiotext (e).

Baudrillard, Jean 1983b: *Simulations*. New York: Semiotext (e).

Chodorow, Nancy 1978: *The Reproduction of Mothering: Psychoanalysis and the Sociology of Gender*: Berkeley: University of California Press.

Cultural Critique 1986–7: "Modernity and modernism, postmodernity and postmodernism," special issue, 5 (Winter).

Dale, Mary 1978: *Gyn/Ecology*. Boston: Beacon Press.

Duggan, Lisa 1983: "The social enforcement of heterosexuality and lesbian resistance in the 1920s," in Amy Swerdlow and Hanna Lessinger (eds), *Class, Race and Sex*. Boston: G. K. Hall.

Dworkin, Andrea 1976: *Our Blood*. New York: Harper & Row.

Echols, Alice 1983: "The new feminism of yin and yang," in Ann Snitow et al. (eds), *Powers of Desire*. New York: Monthly Review Press.

Echols, Alice 1984: "The taming of the id: feminist sexual politics, 1968–83," in Carole Vance (ed.), *Pleasure and Danger*. Boston: Routledge.

Ehrenreich, Barbara, and Deirdre English 1979: *For Her Own Good*. New York: Doubleday.

Emilio, John D' 1983: *Sexual Politics: The Making of a Homosexual Minority in the United States, 1940–1970*. Chicago: University of Chicago Press.

Faderman, Lillian 1981: *Surpassing the Love of Men*. New York: William Morrow.

Flax, Jane 1981: "Do feminists need Marxism?", in Jane Flax (ed.), *Building Feminist Theory*. New York: Longman Quest Staff.

Flax, Jane 1990: "Postmodernism and gender relations in feminist theory," in Linda Nicholson (ed.), *Feminism/Postmodernism*. New York: Routledge and Chapman & Hall.

Foster, Hal 1983: *The Anti-Aesthetic: Essays in Postmodern Culture*. Port Townsend, Wash.: Bay Press.

Foucault, Michel 1978: *The History of Sexuality*, vol. 1: *An Introduction*. New York: Pantheon.

Foucault, Michel 1980: *Power/Knowledge: Selected Interviews and Other Writings, 1972–1977*, ed. Colin Gordon. New York: Pantheon.

Fraser, Nancy, and Linda Nicholson 1990: "Social criticism without philosophy: an encounter between feminism and postmodernism," in Nicholson (ed.), *Feminism/Postmodernism*. New York and London: Routledge and Chapman & Hall.

Geert, Clifford 1983: *Local Knowledge*. New York: Basic Books.

Giddens, Anthony 1984: *The Constitution of Society*. Berkeley: University of California Press.

Gilligan, Carol 1982: *In a Different Voice*. Cambridge, Mass.: Harvard University Press.

Gordon, Linda 1977: *Woman's Body, Woman's Right*. New York: Penguin.

Greenberg, David 1988: *The Construction of Homosexuality*. Chicago: University of Chicago Press.

Griffin, Susan 1978: *Woman and Nature*. New York: Harper & Row.

Habermas, Jürgen 1971: *Knowledge and Human Interests*, tr. Jeremy Shapiro, Boston: Beacon Press.

Habermas, Jürgen 1973: *Theory and Practice*. Boston: Beacon Press.

Habermas, Jürgen 1989: *On Society and Politics*, ed. Steven Seidman. Boston: Beacon Press.

Haraway, Donna 1985: "A manifesto for Cyborgs: science, technology, and socialist feminism in the 1980s," *Socialist Review*, 15.

Harding, Sandra 1986: *The Science Question in Feminism*. Ithaca, NY: Cornell University Press.

Harding, Sandra, and Merrill Hintikka (eds) 1983: *Discovering Reality*. London: Reidel.

Harrington, Michael 1962: *The Other America*. New York: Macmillan.

Huyssen, Andreas 1984: "Mapping the postmodern," *New German Critique*, 33.

Jacoby, Russell 1987: *The Last Intellectuals*. New York: Basic Books.

Jagger, Alison, and Susan Bordo (eds) 1989: *Gender/Body/Knowledge*. New Brunswick, NJ: Rutgers University Press.

Katz, Jonathan 1976: *Gay American History*. New York: Thomas Crowell.

Katz, Jonathan 1983: *Gay/Lesbian Almanac*. New York: Harper & Row.

Keller, Evelyn Fox 1985: *Science and Gender*. New Haven, Conn.: Yale University Press.

Kellner, Douglas 1988: *Jean Baudrillard: From Marxism to Postmodernism and Beyond*. Cambridge: Polity Press.

Lasch, Christopher 1977: *Haven in a Heartless World*. New York: Basic Books.

Lash, Scott 1985: "Postmodernity and desire," *Theory and Society*, 14.

Lyotard, Jean-François 1984 [1979]: *The Postmodern Condition: A Report on Knowledge*, tr. G. Bennington and B. Massumi. Minneapolis: University of Minnesota Press.

McIntosh, Mary 1968: "The homosexual role," *Social Problems*, 16 (Fall).

Marx, Karl, and Friedrich Engels 1976: *The German Ideology*, in *Collected Works*, vol. 5. New York: International.

Millet, Kate 1969: *Sexual Politics*. New York: Ballantine.

Millman, Marcia, and Rosabeth Moss Kanter (eds) 1975: *Another Voice: Feminist Perspectives on Social Life and Social Science*. New York: Anchor Books.

Mills, C. Wright 1951: *White Collar: The American Middle Classes*. New York: Oxford University Press.

Nicholson, Linda 1986: *Gender and History: The Limits of Social Theory in the Age of the Family*. New York: Columbia University Press.

Ortner, Sherry, and Harriet Whitehead (eds) 1981: *Sexual Meanings*. Cambridge, Cambridge University Press.

Pinckney, Alfonso 1984: *The Myth of Black Progress*. Cambridge: Cambridge University Press.

Reisman, David 1953: *The Lonely Crowd*. New York: Doubleday.

Riley, Denise 1988: *Am I that Name?: Feminism and the Category of "Women" in History*. Minneapolis: University of Minnesota Press.

Ritzer, George 1988: "Sociological metatheory: a defense of a subfield by a delineation of its parameters," *Sociological Theory*, 6 (Fall).

Rorty, Richard 1979: *Philosophy and the Mirror of Nature*. Princeton, NJ: Princeton University Press.

Rorty, Richard 1982: *The Consequences of Pragmatism*. Minneapolis: University of Minnesota Press.

Rosaldo, Michelle, and Louise Lamphere (eds) 1974: *Women, Culture and Society*. Stanford, Calif.: Stanford University Press.

Rubin, Gayle 1975: "The traffic in women," in Rayna R. Reiter (ed.), *Towards an Anthropology of Women*. New York: Monthly Review Press.

Rubin, Gayle 1984: "Thinking sex: notes for a radical theory of the politics of sexuality," in Carole Vance (ed.), *Pleasure and Danger*. Boston: Routledge.

Runciman, W. G. 1983: *A Treatise on Social Theory*. Cambridge: Cambridge University Press.

Seidman, Steven 1988: "Transfiguring sexual identity: AIDS and the contemporary construction of homosexuality," *Social Text*, 19–20 (Fall).

Seidman, Steven 1989: "The tedium of general theory," *Contemporary Sociology*, 18 (July).

Seidman, Steven 1991. "The end of sociological theory: the postmodern hope," *Sociological Theory*, 8 (Fall).

Skocpol, Theda 1986: "The dead end of metatheory," *contemporary Sociology*, 16.

Smith, Dorothy 1979: "A sociology for women," in Julia Sherman and Evelyn Torton Beck (eds), *The Prism of Sex*. Madison: University of Wisconsin Press.

Smith, Dorothy 1989: "Sociological theory: methods of writing patriarchy," in Ruth Wallace (ed.), *Feminism and Sociological Theory*. Newbury Park, Calif.: Sage.

Smith-Rosenberg, Caroll 1985a: *Disorderly Conduct*. New York: Knopf.

Smith-Rosenberg 1985b: "The female world of love and rituals: relations between women in nineteenth-century America," in Smith-Rosenberg 1985a.

Spelman, Elizabeth 1988: *Inessential Women*. Boston: Beacon Press.

Theory, Culture and Society 1988: "Postmodernism," special issue, 5 (June).

Tocqueville, Alexis de 1835; Eng. tr. 1838: *Democracy in America*. Many edns.

Trebilcot, Joyce (ed.) 1984: *Mothering: Essays in Feminist Theory*. Totowa, NJ: Rowman & Allanheld.

Watney, Simon 1987: *Policing Desire*. Minneapolis: University of Minnesota Press.

Weeks, Jeffrey 1977: *Coming Out: Homosexual Politics in Britain from the Nineteenth Century to the Present*. London: Quartet Books.

Weeks, Jeffrey 1985: *Sexuality and Its Discontents*. London: Routledge.

Weisstein, Naomi 1973: "Psychology constructs the female," in Anne Koedt, Ellen Levine, and Anita Rapone (eds), *Radical Feminism*. New York: New York Times Book.

Weitzman, Lenore 1985: *The Divorce Revolution*. New York: Free Press.
Westkott, Marcia 1979: "Feminist criticism of the social sciences," *Harvard Educational Review*, 49.
Wilson, William 1987: *The Truly Disadvantaged*. Chicago: University of Chicago Press.
Young, Iris 1981: "Beyond the unhappy marriage: a critique of dual systems theory," in Lydia Sargent (ed.), *Women and Revolution*. Boston: South End Press.

3

On the Postmodern Barricades:
Feminism, Politics, and Theory

Linda Nicholson

In the last ten years, postmodernism has emerged as a significant intellectual movement. However, to use the term "movement" may be somewhat misleading, since postmodernism, as cross-disciplinary, has come to possess different meanings in the diverse disciplines which it has affected. Thus, for example, in architecture the "modernism" to which postmodernism is "post" includes a period from approximately the 1920s until about the 1970s. For philosophers and social theorists, the "post" more often refers to the period after "modernity," the latter usually signifying the period from approximately the seventeenth century to the present.

My focus will be on the meaning of postmodernism in social theory. I intend to argue the utility of a somewhat stipulative version of postmodernism for social theory. To make my case, I shall use feminist theory as an example. I shall show that it is possible to develop a type of postmodern feminist theory which is both politically and philosophically preferable to feminist theory uninfluenced by postmodern concerns. And what can be said about feminist theory has relevance for other types of social theory.

Even within the specific domain of social theory, postmodernism has come to signify a wide range of positions. At the risk of overly simplifying this range, three major themes can be identified: (1) a rejection of the all-encompassing and frequently teleological theories of human history and social change associated with Enlightenment ideas about reason and progress, and with Hegelianism and Marxism; (2) a linking of claims about social life, human nature, and criteria of truth and validity with strategies of power; and (3) a replacement of the emphasis on the individual subject and the contents of the consciousness of that subject by an emphasis on language as intersubjective.

My concern will be with the first two of these themes and their relevance for contemporary social theory. When postmodernists criticize the Enlightenment view of history as reason's advance against superstition, the Hegelian idea of spirit coming to know itself, and the Marxist vision of history as the steady working out of class conflict, their criticisms are not primarily about the specific truth or falsity of these views. Rather their rejection is of the premise underlying all of these positions: that human history can be captured in one grand story. This hope that the social theorist can, in one illuminating stroke, solve the basic puzzles of human existence or social change has been pervasive throughout modernity, manifesting itself not only in such narrative, teleological views as these three examples represent, but also in much of non-narrative modern social theory. But from a postmodern perspective, this kind of hope is suspect. Consequently, one prominent contemporary postmodernist, Jean François Lyotard (1984 [1979]), has proposed the abandonment of such attempts, replacing such grand narratives as the above with what he describes as "mini-narratives."

There are certain difficulties with Lyotard's notion of mini-narratives which I shall discuss shortly. But, for now, I wish to note what is legitimate in Lyotard's move. Grand social theory, in either narrative or non-narrative form, tends to suffer from one serious weakness: key categories within it are frequently ambiguous in meaning. This problem results from the fact that such theory must satisfy two incompatible tasks. It must be both large enough to incorporate all possible human activities, encounters, and projects while specific enough to encompass this range in a non-trivial way. The attempt to do both invariably results in an ambiguity in the meaning of key terms, that is, between one meaning which is broad and somewhat vague in reference and another which is more specific but also less able to incorporate a wide range of cases. Moreover, the more specific meaning tends to reflect the assumptions and perspectives of the theorist's own culture or subgroup within the culture.

An example of this point is the category of production within Marxism. The meaning of this category slides between two possible readings. First, there is the highly common interpretation in which production is understood as referring to activities concerned with the making of food and objects, that is, equivalent to its predominant meaning in capitalist societies. It is this interpretation of the term which is most frequently used by Marxists in illustrating a specifically Marxist analysis of a particular social phenomenon. This reading of "production" has been subject to a variety of challenges centering on its narrowness, for example, by feminists who argue that it ignores activities commonly performed by women, such as childrearing. In response, Marxists frequently turn to a second reading in which this term incorporates all activities conducive to the reproduction of the human species. While this reading precludes such challenges, it also provides little practical guidance for analyzing any given society or form of social change. Thus, to the extent the theory provides practical guidance, it does so by being andro- and ethnocentric. Both the andro/ethnocentrism and the more general ambiguity over the correct interpretation are consequences of the attempt to construct a theoretical category which is both broad enough to explain all of human history, yet specific enough to give that explanation a non-trivial content.[1]

In sum, a tendency of general theory is to move between triviality and ethnocentric projection. But, the objection goes, if we give up the project of general theory altogether, do we not have to accept the inevitable conclusion of relativism? This jump is made because of a widespread belief that the abandonment of general theory must lead to the development of a plethora of claims about social life and social change and no decision-making procedures to decide amongst those which are in conflict.

To this response, one needs to insist on a few distinctions. The abandonment of general social theory only poses the possibility of relativism in so far as it is accompanied by the abandonment of the idea of a belief in cross-cultural, mediating criteria of truth and validity. A plethora of claims about social life becomes problematic only when there are no means to decide among those which are in conflict. Thus, one could reject the idea of general social theory without becoming a relativist by maintaining the idea of cross-cultural criteria of truth.

However, since many postmodernists tend to accompany their rejection of general social theory with a rejection of the notion of cross-cultural criteria of truth, relativism becomes an issue with which any defender of postmodernism must deal.

For my own response to this issue, let me suggest, as others have done, that relativism is parasitic on an objective perspective. It is only in relation to the idea of a grounding position external to and encompassing all possible positions that an absolute claim about the lack of such a final grounding makes sense. And certainly, relativism has frequently been interpreted as making such an absolute claim about the lack of any final grounding. As many have noted, this absolute claim renders relativism contradictory. One cannot both assert the limits of all claims to truth while disputing the unqualified truth of that very assertion. However, both the argument for grounding and the denial of the possibility of grounding are symbiotic and share a common ideal: fundamental proof. From the perspective of the relativist, the anti-relativist holds onto this ideal from a fundamental anxiety; from the perspective of the anti-relativist, the relativist abandons it out of a fundamental carelessness. Both charges are well taken. But both charge and counter-charge can be avoided by bypassing the ideal altogether. This move does not entail the abandonment of much of what those who are in the grip of this anxiety claim it entails. For one, it does not entail the abandonment of criteria of truth immanent to the practices which generate them, a position supported by both Lyotard and Richard Rorty. Nor does it even entail the denial of the possibility of cross-cultural tools of adjudication, such as a commitment to dialogue or the law of non-contradiction. It merely entails denying the claim that such tools can always serve as sufficient means for adjudicating contested claims. And, as I shall discuss shortly, it does not even entail the abandonment of general values, general categories, and *contra* Lyotard, large theories, provided these all are conceptualized in ways I shall elaborate.[2] It only brings with it the admission that it is unlikely we will ever be able to identify one value, one category, one theory, or one tool of adjudication both big enough and specific enough to resolve all possible conflicts.

To speak of criteria of truth immanent to the practices which generate them is to focus on the situational elements which make proof possible or not. This approach suggests an alternative mode for interpreting relativism: relativism becomes the situation which results when communication breaks down. Thus, relativism becomes a life possibility rather than a theoretical position. And in viewing it as a life possibility, we can begin to speculate about the conditions which lead to difficulties in maintaining communication: when participants lack common beliefs able to mediate conflicting ones; when they possess terms which cannot be translated into the vocabulary of the other; when conflicting interests motivate the construction of conflicting beliefs and vocabularies.

But the response then continues: this mode of analyzing truth claims quickly translates the topic of truth into the topic of power. Is not Lyotard being consistent in rapidly moving from talking about truth claims to talking about agonistics? But certainly from the perspective of many philosophers and even from the perspective of some political activists, this is a very problematic jump. According to many philosophers, it is imperative to keep questions of truth separate from questions of power. And even from the perspective of the political activist who admits of the interconnection of truth and power, the jump is problematic. From the correct observation that truth contains a dimension of power cannot be deduced the claim that truth *is* power. Before we make *that* move, we need to legitimate the identification of the two and not just their connection. At stake is the very important political distinction between 'legitimate and illegitimate claims to power.

Thus we need to examine a bit more closely the interconnection of knowledge and power advanced by many in the postmodern camp. A central point to recognize in understanding the postmodern move is that power takes a variety of forms. Thus, to claim that knowledge is a kind of power is not to claim that it is identical to that power which is exhibited by access to guns or possession of superior physical force. And even "knowledge/power" can assume a variety of forms, some of which may be *more legitimate than others*, given the rules for legitimating truth claims within a culture. Therefore to admit of the interconnection of knowledge and power is not to abandon the distinction between legitimate and illegitimate claims to power. For example, in a Western culture where adherence to certain rules of discourse gives legitimacy to claims, one can both admit of a distinction between legitimate and illegitimate claims and recognize that the ability to adhere to such rules itself represents a type of power. Moreover, one can also see how the claim of the separation of knowledge and power itself represents a power move, that is, the type of power move which enhances power by denying it.

Another way to elaborate these points is to employ Foucault's point that power is not always repressive; it can also be productive. For example, specific regimes of "knowledge/power" produce certain distinctions, criteria of legitimation, acceptable procedural rules as they also deny others. Thus, insofar as such regimes make possible certain forms of discourse, as for example among natural scientists, they also make possible forms of communication which otherwise would not exist. Therefore, the power exhibited by natural scientific discourse is very different from the one we associate with physical violence, which insofar as it is associated with claims to knowledge, often shuts communication down.

Thus the postmodernist need not abandon the distinction between legitimate and illegitimate claims to power as she or he need not abandon the more encompassing idea of criteria of truth. The difference between the postmodernist and the modernist on these issues is rather that the former and not the latter denies the possibility of such criteria external to any specific historical tradition. From within any given tradition, we always have means for allowing certain discursive moves and not others, of admitting of the legitimacy or not of specific claims. Of course, there may arise circumstances where those from different traditions, or those abiding by different rules from within the same tradition, come together and clash, and where communication breaks down. This possibility, however, describes a possible life situation and not a theoretical position one either adheres to or not.

But, says the modernist, suppose I accept your description of what I call relativism as a breakdown in communication. Is not the difference between us that I and not you believe there are means for overcoming the problem?

The postmodernist has available several forms of response to this move. The first is to point out that the means advocated by theorists of modernity have been problematic for similar reasons to those noted in the earlier discussion of general theory: they tend to be ethnocentric. Moreover, since the ethnocentrism is often implicit rather than explicit and carries with it the demand that all organize their modes of communication in accord with the theorist articulating the proposal, such proposed means of adjudication invariably are politically authoritarian. If it were possible to develop means which did not give priority to culturally specific forms of communication and which were also specific enough to resolve real conflicts, the attempt to locate cross-cultural means of adjudication would indeed be worthwhile.

The postmodernist has available a second means of response. He or she can claim that it is not as though the abandonment of the search for foundational means of adjudication entails the admission of no means of adjudication. Particularly when the communicative conflict occurs among participants who share a common history, one can frequently find some common belief, value, or criterion of adjudication to resolve the conflict. Thus, one important resource in mitigating relativism as a life situation is the existence of shared aspects of a common tradition.

This last point also has relevance against the arguments of the politically motivated social theorist who would claim that the turn to postmodernism leaves us with too few tools to wage politically necessary struggles. As the above indicates, there is no reason why a postmodernist could not appeal, for example, to the very same values of equality or liberty that a modernist might appeal to in defending his or her political stance. The difference is that while the modernist would believe such values to be grounded outside of human history, in the human condition or society as such, the postmodernist has given up on that belief.

To be sure, lest the appeal to common beliefs, values, and criteria of adjudication be interpreted as signalling any necessary alliance between postmodernism and a conservative stance, it must also be stressed that common beliefs, values, etc. can be appealed to only as *possible* resources. When these are not available as means of mediation, the only resources left might be human ingenuity or luck, and these by their very nature offer no guarantees of success. Thus, a postmodern stance must admit of the possibility of breakdowns in communication. But to admit this is not to deny the many means by which humans do maintain communication, even in the context of differences.

And as the postmodern turn does not entail abandoning the use of common values, beliefs, etc. as means of mediating conflicts, so also does it not entail abandoning other politically useful tools available to the modernist, such as big categories like gender, race, or oppression. Rather, I would claim that what is required only is a shift in how we understand and use such categories.

As I earlier noted, one frequent pitfall attendant upon the use of big categories is ambiguity in meaning. Modern social theorists frequently have stretched the meanings of categories of their societies in order to incorporate large stretches of human history, while also retaining the more particular meaning to retain needed specificity. Thus, not only have they attributed ambiguous meanings to key categories of their theories, but they have also used categories helpful for picking out phenomena of their own societies in analyzing other societies where the analytical helpfulness of such categories becomes more problematic. Again, this problem is exemplified in the Marxist category of class. But if the social theorist can be reflective about such changes, looking to identify shifts in meaning and/or a decline in the usefulness of his or her analytical categories, there appears no reason why she or he need abandon big categories *per se*.

The attentiveness which I am suggesting demands more than flexibility and open-mindedness. As Nancy Fraser and I have argued, at issue are the kinds of categories the postmodern theorist would seek out. Because of the problems which have accompanied the use of big categories, the careful postmodernist ought to be wary of those which lend themselves to such abuse. For example, categories which implicitly or explicitly gain their credibility through appeal to biological qualities of human beings or assumed necessary aspects of the human condition are those the postmodernist would wisely avoid. For the same reason, when postmodernists did use big categories, they would be attentive to shifts in their appropriate interpretation and situate their applicability in the persistence of empirically identifiable structures of social life (see Fraser and Nicholson 1988: 362).

Similar points might be made about theory itself, i.e. there is nothing *ipso facto* contradictory about the idea of a postmodern theory. Again, more relevant than the question of the acceptance or rejection of theory is the question of how such theory should be understood. Most important is the pragmatic understanding of theory as tool. From a postmodern perspective, theories gain their legitimacy through their usefulness, a value itself acknowledged as immanent to a specific historical tradition. It is because of this pragmatic bent of postmodernism that science loses its privileged position as "the mirror of nature" and takes its place with other modes of discourse, such as history and poetry, as legitimate in proportion to its usefulness. Moreover, those features which tend to characterize postmodern social theory, such as a high sensitivity to issues of historicity, again follow from the very contingent evidence of what constitutes illuminating social theory.

Of course, this pragmatic interpretation of theory is not entirely absent from modern social theory. Indeed, on my reading of what is valid in the postmodern stance, there is not the absolute break with modernity others might suggest.[3] Instead I am formulating a stance which is legitimately continuous with aspects of modernity. I can admit this while also claiming that there are aspects of modernism with which it decisively breaks, apsects which have serious political ramifications.

Key here is the universalizing thrust of modern social theory. Certainly, one might say that the universalizing impulse of the Enlightenment represented a forward move away from the particularistic elements of more medieval social principles. One might even say that the Marxist description of the proletariat as a universal class was necessary for the times and had emancipatory aspects. But, by the mid-twentieth century, this element of modernism was being widely used to justify reactive stances, at least in the US and western Europe. For example, Enlightenment humanism has been used against affirmative action and against many proposals which employ race and gender as criteria in providing educational and economic opportunities. Similarly, late twentieth-century Marxism has frequently employed the general categories of production and class to legitimate the foreclosure of what has been genuinely disruptive in such movements as feminism, the struggles against imperialism and racism, and the gay rights movement. Thus, to reject the universalizing impulse of modernity now is to open spaces for those movements closed off by Enlightenment humanism and by Marxism.

In sum, I am suggesting that we think of postmodernism as linked in both continuous and reactive ways to modernism and evaluate it in light of the political needs of our time. But such a historical characterization seems also most consistent with many of the theoretical claims of postmodernism. Certainly, some postmodernists have at times been moved to generalize the meaning of postmodernism, so that it becomes, like theories of modernism, a position outside of history, waiting only for the appropriate historical moment for its truth to be grasped. Thus statements that history is discontinuous or that speech is agonistic float amidst postmodern rhetoric.[4] Such universalizing claims, however, are obviously problematic and can be avoided by more consistently conceptualizing postmodernism as a stance which arises out of modernism. What follows, however, is that it might, not surprisingly, participate in elements of modernism while also getting its critical force from the critique of modernism. Such a perspective, therefore, provides us with the tools to develop a complex analysis of its politics and its relation to other political and theoretical movements.

FEMINISM AS CASE STUDY

I wish to give these very general and preliminary remarks greater specificity through focusing on feminist theory. Feminist theory serves as a useful example for my purposes because it contains tendencies to endorse the kinds of arguments I have been making so far while also recreating the very problems of general theory I have also begun to describe. Moreover, feminist theorists, like other feminist scholars, see their work as tied to a political movement. Thus, to the extent that feminist theorists move in a postmodern direction, they must deal with the charge of postmodernism's lack of political strength.

Many of the arguments feminists have made about Western philosophy and social theory might be described as postmodern. Because feminists have had to take on the dominating assumption within the academy that prevailing positions were encompassing and "objective" in contrast to the limited and biased nature of their own pronouncements, feminists have been forced to deal directly with the methodological issues of objectivity and universalism. In pointing out the partial and biased nature of much of traditional and contemporary scholarship, feminists have quite frequently become suspicious of all claims to impartiality and generality.

However, because this methodological suspicion arose in the context of a specific academic/political struggle, feminist methodological claims have not been quite identical to those of postmodernists. While feminists have argued that traditional and contemporary scholarship has been biased and limited, they have also argued that it has been biased and limited in quite specific ways, that is, in masculine ways. Feminists have pointed to the fact that interesting and important texts written by women invariably have been overlooked in favor of those written by white, Western men. They have argued that the issues which have dominated the disciplines – such as, in history, wars and governments – have been issues which have most concerned men. And they have claimed that even the styles of thinking and writing which have dominated many disciplines, such as an emphasis on clarity, dispassion, and the abstract over the imaginative, the passionate, and the concrete, have also reflected masculine modes of thinking and writing. So while feminist criticisms of the academy have overlapped in many significant ways with those of postmodernists, they have also differed in their association with specific political allegations.

But as the above brief summary of the feminist critique reveals, the political dimension of the critique involved a partial retreat to some of the strategies of modernism. Thus, as Nancy Fraser and I have argued, in the process of pointing out the partiality of modern social theories, feminists frequently employed generalizing categories like "masculinity" and "femininity" in problematic ways. Consequently, the feminist position became ambiguous. On the one hand, feminism has been quite explicit about the historical embeddedness of all theoretical perspectives, including its own. It was hardly possible to denounce the false universality of its adversaries through an appeal to the situatedness of theory within history, while denying the same charge about its own claims. On the other hand, feminist theorists too frequently have displayed a decided casualness about the specific historical content of their claims. Few raised the question of the possible inappropriateness of using categories like "men," "women," or "the family" across grand sweeps of history, and it was often primarily Marxists and anthropologists who made the even more minimal point that such terms needed different interpretations in different cultures.

There were varied reasons for this casualness. Many prominent feminist theorists came out of traditions and were taught by teachers accustomed to the universalizing moves of modernism. Indeed, one often sees the very same types of universalizing strategies in some prominent feminist theorists as in the position of the teachers they are revolting against.[5] Moreover, over the course of the past several decades feminists, including feminist theorists, have been pushed to stress the depth and pervasiveness of sexism in the face of a widespread cultural tendency to de-emphasize and trivialize it. Similarly, a dominant tendency within the culture has been to deny the relevance of gender even while using gender against women in oppressive and exclusionary ways. To counteract such oppressive silence about gender and to stress the seriousness of the problem of sexism, feminists have often felt pressed to speak in broad general terms. A related strategy, prominent amongst feminists since the early seventies, has been to revalue gender-coded attributes, to underline what is positive about those modes of thinking and acting which have been associated with women. However, this gynocentric turn, prominent in much feminist writing over the seventies and eighties, also brought with it much essentializing talk about women.

I wish to claim that these essentializing moves, while understandable, are both theoretically and politically problematic. Feminists can produce better theory – and politically stronger theory – by more consistently abiding by their postmodern inclinations.[6]

Let me begin by focusing on the theoretical problems which have attended feminism's generalizing moves. I argued in the preceding section that a problem accompanying the encompassing aims of modern social theory was the tendency to use categories in ambiguous and ultimately ethnocentric ways. And when we look at the variety of explanations which have been offered by feminists from the late sixties through the early eighties to account for sexism as a cross-cultural phenomenon, this is exactly the problem which continually surfaces.

Take for example the use of the category of "the family" in radical feminist writings of the late sixties and early seventies. Early radical feminists (e.g. NY Radical Feminists 1973: 379, 381) often pointed to the family as the locus of female oppression. This theoretical move was important insofar as it directly challenged the prevailing liberal and Marxist tendency to look to political and economic interactions outside of the family as the source of all social inequity and oppression. However, because this explanation was not accompanied by historical analyses of the origins of "family" in modern, western contexts, the meaning of "family" remained ambiguous, often taking on a significance specific to that of the contemporary white, middle-class, Western, family. Therefore, it was not surprising that many black women felt alienated from this explanation, seeing within their own history a more positive meaning of "family."

Similar problems arose even on the part of theorists more clearly sensitive to the problem of cultural variation. For example, many of the contributors to the highly influential anthropology collection *Women, Culture and Society* (Rosaldo and Lamphere 1974), developed an ultimately problematic general category, "domestic/public" to try to explain female devaluation in many different societies. While these theorists, most of whom were anthropologists, and many of whom were also sympathetic to Marxism, were highly conscious of the need for any social theory to allow for cultural diversity, they hoped to find in this category a means to also account for the apparent ubiquity of sexism. The argument was that while the separation between domestic and public spheres took on a variety of different forms in different societies, the existence of some version of this separation in many societies could account for the authority men frequently have over women.

However, as one of the exponents of this position, Michelle Zimbalist Rosaldo, later came to recognize, even this very general explanatory category was ultimately problematic. Rosaldo (1980) asserted that a putative cross-cultural domestic/public separation represented a post-Victorian projection. Since the nineteenth century, Western theorists have falsely projected the isolation of home from politics and work, an isolation specific to the last two centuries, onto earlier societies where it is not applicable. And, as Rosaldo also questioned (ibid.: 399–400), even when there is an apparent similarity between post-Victorian and other cultures (as, for example, in the powerlessness of both Pygmy women hiding in huts and American women confined to the home), how much about the causes of this powerlessness for either is illuminated by appeal to a cross-cultural "domestic/public separation"? Rosaldo's comments recall a problem of general categories I have previously remarked on: that they vacillate between a concreteness too tied to our own cultural meanings and a generality too vague to illuminate specific cases.

As a final example of the problematic nature of generalizing moves in feminist theory, we can point to Chodorow's (1978) use of the term "mothering." Chodorow, to use "mothering" as the link which unites widely disparate cultures, defined the term broadly as basic female caretaking of infants and young children. Yet in specific analyses of the differences female caretaking generates for boys and girls, she often gave it a meaning more limited to specific cultures, most notably Western culture. For example, Chodorow speaks of the development of psychic traits in young boys following from the fact that the male figures they must come to identify with are distant and abstract. But this claim makes sense only for cultures where mothering is a relatively privatized activity. Chodorow recognizes that the degree to which mothering is privatized varies amongst cultures and she notes that her analysis is most applicable to those cultures where this holds. But she claims, nonetheless, to be describing a universal, cross-cultural phenomenon. Thus, in a reply to her critics, Chodorow states:

I think that there are important cross-cultural continuities that feminists ignore at our peril. First, *women* mother (. . . not only in our society . . .) and second, women's capacities for relationship and nurturance – as opposed to men's creating of a more separate and more distanced ego that treats women as objects – do seem to develop in many different societies and are *internal* and *psychological*. These psychological qualities vary in degree and content and in relation to other aspects of personality. They also have varying effects on women's gratifications from mothering and desires to mother, and therefore their overall significance changes in different times and places. *Nonetheless, these qualities retain some qualities of sameness and help to form* male dominance. (*Lorber et al, 1981: 508–9*; emphasis added)

The problem in this response is that the phrase "some qualities of sameness" leaves too many questions unanswered. If we say that a greater female capacity for relationship (a vague and cross-culturally suspect claim) is a consequence only of the fact that female beings have primary responsibility for early childcare, we are left with the task of explaining how psychic phenomena follow from this merely biological universal. On the other hand, to the degree to which we associate social meaning with this fact, and give the argument needed specificity, we also postulate generalities relatively easy to disprove. Thus again we run into the problem of an ambiguity between a generality empty of meaning and a specificity tied to modern forms.

But most problematic about all of these explanations are their political consequences. All of these explanations contain at least the tendency to read all of history and culture in terms of modern Western social forms. All tend to treat the modern Western privatized and separated family as privileged. Thus, they enact the same type of exclusionary theoretical moves that can be found in the generalizing theories of modern Western men. The difference is that such moves, in the feminist case, stand in contradiction to the widely ascribed aim of creating theory which *does not* falsely generalize the perspective of dominant groups.

But is there a way to avoid these exclusionary moves and still produce politically powerful theory? I believe there is, but it entails abandoning the kind of cross-cultural, causal models exemplified in the above accounts. All of the theories I have discussed are committed to the premises that male dominance can be similarly described across cultures and that we can locate one phenomenon as its cause. But I would argue that neither premise is warranted. As most feminist anthropologists now claim, the forms male dominance assume are widely disparate. And all of the explanations which have been created to identify an ultimate cause are highly suspect.

Moreover, a causal model is not the only means we can use for depicting and explaining cross-culturally pervasive phenomena. Thus, abandoning a causal model does not entail thinking about sexism as an *ad hoc* and thus relatively trivial social fact. We also can employ the mode of narrative which can be as lengthy and as multi-stranded as the phenomena to be analysed demand. In other words, to explain a phenomenon such as sexism, which is large in its historical scope, but also diverse in its forms, we might create either one large or many overlapping and intersecting stories. The explanatory force and comprehensiveness of our account can as easily attest to the extent and seriousness of sexism as one grandiose explanation aimed to do.[7]

In the telling of such stories, we might even legitimately use big categories to focus on structural features of social organization over time. For example, in my own book *Gender and History* (1986: 69–130), I focused on the institution of kinship, particularly its early importance and subsequent decline, in order to account for changes in gender relations over large stretches of Western history. I argued that, in the modern period, changes in kinship relations led to the emergence of separate public and private spheres, whose later dynamics led in turn to important changes in gender relations. So, to repeat a point made in my opening remarks: I am not arguing against the use of carefully selected categories to provide narrative synthesis when that is appropriate. The use of such categories becomes suspect only when we treat what such categories pick out as endemic to human existence *per se*, do not focus on the possible need to reinterpret their meanings to adequately deal with changing phenomena, and inadequately allow for their possible inapplicability.

Moreover, we need not even assume that narrative is the only genre of politically powerful social theory legitimate from a postmodern perspective. As I suggested, by admitting big categories into narrative accounts we can acknowledge the possibility of structural features of societies remaining relatively static over long periods of time. Again, it is only when the categories which are used to describe such structures are employed without a sense of possible historical inapplicability that such analysis becomes problematic (Fraser and Nicholson 1988: 362).

Finally, what is most important about pursuing these types of research directions is that they do not violate recognized political mandates of feminist research. Because such approaches make explicit their historical and cultural boundaries, their integration into grander accounts does not run the risk of exclusion that is present for general theory. Thus, there is no reason why the different stories of contemporary women from diverse ethnic, racial, and class backgrounds cannot be conjoined into accounts which tell complex tales. Such tales would be as politically powerful as those based on one grand theme but, unlike the latter, would draw their strength from their diverse components, rather than from the suppression of such diversity. Indeed, if we look at the direction women's studies have been moving in the past ten years, this is the very strategy which has become dominant. Feminist scholarship has, more and more, abandoned the attempt, common in its first ten years, to solve the puzzle of sexism in one insightful account. Rather, it has taken the very different route of encouraging attention to a multitude of problems, topics, cultures, and time periods, integrating the results when possible, but merely describing difference when not. It is a strategy conducive to both political and scholarly strength and one other politically concerned social theorists might very well emulate.

NOTES
===

This chapter was written shortly after Nancy Fraser and I had co-authored "Social criticism without philosophy" (Fraser and Nicholson 1988, reprinted in *Theory, Culture and Society*, 10/3, 4 (1988), pp. 345–66; and again in Andrew Roth 1988: 373–94). Since Nancy and I had worked together in formulating the relation of feminism and postmodernism in "Social criticism without philosophy," it is often difficult separating our work together in that paper from many of the arguments I make here, particularly in the second section. I will indicate the places where this is the case. I also wish to thank her and Mark Berger for their suggestions for this paper. In addition, I want to thank Steve Seidman for his comments and continued support.

1 For a more extensive discussion of this ambiguity in Marx, see Nicholson 1986.
2 The claim that a postmodern position can be articulated which does not entail the abandonment of theory is one made in "Social criticism without philosophy" (Fraser and Nicholson 1988).
3 Fredric Jameson makes a similar point about the continuity between modernism and postmodernism, claiming that "radical breaks between periods do not generally involve complete changes of content but rather the restructuring of a certain number of elements already given: features that in an earlier period or system were subordinate now become dominant and features that had been dominant again become secondary" (Jameson 1983: 123).
4 As an example of the latter point, consider Lyotard's remark: "This last observation brings us to the first principle underlying our method as a whole: to speak is to fight, in the sense of playing, and speech acts fall within the domain of a general agonistics" (1984 [1979]: 10).
5 For example, the universalism inherent in the female developmental model suggested by Carol Gilligan directly parallels the universalism inherent in the developmental model of Lawrence Kohlberg, against whom Carol Gilligan's argument is directed. See Gilligan 1982.
6 The position of these last few paragraphs is elaborated in Fraser and Nicholson 1988.
7 A similar position is articulated by Fraser and Nicholson 1988: 362. A more extensive elaboration of it can be found in Nicholson 1986: 89–91.

REFERENCES

Chodorow, Nancy 1978: *The Reproduction of Mothering: Psychoanalysis and the Sociology of Gender*. Berkeley: University of California Press.

Fraser, Nancy, and Linda Nicholson 1988: "Social criticism without philosophy: an encounter between feminism and postmodernism," *Communication*, 10/3, 4: 345–94.

Gilligan, Carol 1982: *In a Different Voice: Psychological Theory and Women's Development*. Cambridge, Mass.: Harvard University Press.

Jameson, Fredric 1983: "Postmodernism and consumer society," in Hal Foster (ed.), *The Anti-Aesthetic: Essays on Postmodern Culture*. Port Townsend, Wash.: Bay Press.

Lorber, Judith, Rose Laub Coser, Alice S. Rossi, and Nancy Chodorow 1981: "On the reproduction of mothering: a methodological debate," *Signs*, 6/3 (Spring).

Lyotard, Jean-François 1984 [1979]: *The Postmodern Condition: A Report on Knowledge*, tr. G. Bennington and B. Massumi. Minneapolis: University of Minnesota Press.

Nicholson, Linda 1986: *Gender and History: The Limits of Social Theory in the Age of the Family*. New York: Columbia University Press.

NY Radical Feminists 1973: "Politics of the ego: a manifesto for NY Radical Feminists," in Anne Koedt, Ellen Levine, and Anita Rapone (eds), *Radical Feminism*. New York: New York Times Book.

Rosaldo, Michelle Zimbalist 1980: "The use and abuse of anthropology: reflections on feminism and cross-cultural understanding," *Signs*, 5/3.

Rosaldo, Michelle Zimbalist, and Louise Lamphere (eds), *Women, Culture and Society*. Stanford, Calif.: Stanford University Press.

Roth, Andrew (ed.) 1988: *Universal Abandon?* Minneapolis: University of Minnesota Press.

4

The Strange Life and Hard Times of the Concept of General Theory in Sociology: A Short History of Hope

Stephen Turner

Richard Rorty's *Philosophy and the Mirror of Nature* (1979) showed that Heidegger, Dewey, and Wittgenstein had each been groping toward a rejection of "foundationalism," the attempt to find some sort of grounding for our ultimate presuppositions. Modern social theorists from Hobbes to the present have employed foundationalist appeals. Paradigmatically, these have been appeals to criteria of cognitive validity: behaviorist attempts to exclude explanations with mental predicates, neo-Marxian charges that given theories are "unhistorical," and Alexander's claims that various formulations of Durkheim or Weber are insufficiently "multidimensional" may all be given as instances. But all these arguments have been inconclusive. Each step in the argument proceeds as though, by raising the matter in theoretical dispute to the next level of abstraction to the level of criteria for theory-choice, we will arrive at an unequivocal victory for one of the solutions to the problem under dispute. But what occurs is something different: at each level there prove to be a variety of possible criteria. And when we try to resolve the conflict between them by going to the next level of abstraction, that is, to construct criteria of adequacy for these answers, we find the same thing.

In this chapter, I will simply assume the rejection of foundationalism and concern myself with a problem that comes into view only once we separate out foundationalism from some of the issues with which foundationalism appeals are usually entangled. The theme of this contribution is hope. The hopes with which I will be concerned are the hopes that have been part of the various projects for a scientific sociology, though I suspect that an analogous paper could be written about other conceptions of "theory" and their aims. As Polanyi has stressed (1964), there is an element of hope in all science: the hope that the investigator can fill in the lacunae that remain in his or her attempts at solving some scientific problem. The history of the hopes which have been part of the various projects for general sociological theory is a conspicuously dismal one. There is nevertheless something to be gained by assembling some historical examples: we can more readily identify some of the more persistent and important lacunae, and perhaps conclude with a more reasonable sense of what hopes we should have.

BEYOND THE CRITIQUE OF FOUNDATIONALISM

It is easy enough to appropriate Rorty's point that the foundationalist arguments that are conceived as a cure to relativism and subjectivity merely reproduce these diseases in a more virulent form at the meta-level, and apply this point to the history of social theory. The history one would get would be a history of the various philosophical foundations of sociological programs, or a history of "positivism" and its enemies. But this is bad history, for reasons that will become evident, and unhelpful in explaining the present appeal of various research programs in sociology. The presently convincing forms of sociological argument do not depend solely or even largely on anything so simple as a foundationalist philosophy such as "positivism." They also depend on hope, hope which is often based on initial successes. Not surprisingly, arguments against "positivism" have had little effect on their appeal. But the appeal of "positivist" social science, or for that matter of ethnomethodology or Weberianism, is nevertheless not wholly separable from the foundationalist elements of their various programs.

Weber's methodological writings are a good place to begin to differentiate some of these forms of appeal. In his famous essay inaugurating his editorship of the *Archiv*, Weber was among the first to attempt to systematically distinguish the various aims of social theory. One question he asks, and attempts to resolve, is the question of how the various goals of social science relate (1949: 74–6). One of his polemical targets was the Millian goal of a sociology made up of causal generalizations or laws and located within the hierarchy of the sciences such that its laws would be ultimately explained by the laws of chemistry or physics. This kind of science, he argued, even were it to be created, would not serve the cognitive aims that are primary for us, namely to explain the present as it is meaningful to us, because the language of chemistry and physics, however suitable for constructing laws, cannot be translated into the language in which we describe the things we want explained (ibid.: 75). Weber's argument here is a specimen of "foundationalism," though Weber does not present it as such. As Weber's critics pointed out (cf. Turner and Factor 1984: 115–20), the argument presupposes a picture of the ultimate character of the knowable objects of the social and physical world, and divides the kinds of scientific understandings we can have of these objects accordingly, into nomic sciences for the objects (such as molecules) which are no more than tokens of a type, and "meaning" or value-related sciences for those objects that are historical "individuals" and therefore cannot be adequately treated as tokens of a type.[1] But the analysis is an *explication* of what he takes to be successful historical explanations – a philosophical account of their conceptual properties – rather than an expression of hope. For Weber, there is no millennium: our explanatory problems can be solved, at least as well as they can be solved, by means that are already at hand.

In Durkheim's *Rules* (1982), which is thoroughly foundationalist in its realist image of the problem of word–world relations, we see something else: the idea of what I will call a "breakthrough vocabulary." For him as for Weber, the vocabulary of common persons represented an ideology or *Weltanschauung*: unlike Weber, he believed that the sociologist, like the natural scientist, could and should free description from this ideological starting-point, and discover strict laws, and a vocabulary appropriate to them, behind the confusing veneer of misleading concepts that society currently uses to represent itself (Durkheim 1982: 60–70). When Durkheim contrasts the vocabulary of the marketplace, the *idola fori*, to the language of the real social facts they conceal, he thinks of his contrast in a foundational way, although he is a realist rather than a positivist. But he does not believe that the breakthrough to the new vocabulary has been fully realized. In contrast to Weber, his strictures on sociological concepts are meant to be aids in bringing the millennium about. So there is a large element of hope which is essential to this methodological self-conception.

For Durkheim, the millennium would occur at the moment when the words of our theories corresponded to the order of real social facts. But we do not need to think of the possibility of a new vocabulary for social science in this metaphysical way: we may simply hear in Durkheim the promise of a radical revision of our capacity to predict and quantitatively describe the social processes of interest to us, without being concerned at all with the metaphysical question of the relation of this vocabulary to ultimate reality.

For historical reasons, the hope and the metaphysics usually have come bound together. The desire to predict and control, it is often said, has its origins in a particular metaphysical world picture, the "modern project," and the project itself depends on a claim to authoritative or privileged correspondence to reality. As a historical matter this is doubtless true. But the practical successes of the modern project in relation to technology have enabled it to root itself in the tacit expectations and way of thinking of modern peoples, and the necessity of these metaphysical roots has thus disappeared. Indeed, in the discourse of science itself they have withered, and far more completely than did the "state" to which Lenin's famous prediction attached. In social science they have perhaps not withered. But it is important to see that transformations and differentiations of social science practice, many of which had begun before the time of Durkheim and Weber, have vastly complicated and altered the role of foundationalist arguments and their relation to the claims of the social scientist. Many social science ideas have become part of the everyday expectations of modern people, and thus do not call for "grounding"; some bodies of social science practice have evolved in such a way that they are largely autonomous from the levels of arguments that foundationalist appeals might have to resolve.

This suggests that it would probably be a fruitless task to try to distinguish and separate all of the various non-foundationalist intellectual, cultural, and perhaps even emotional appeals on which the acceptance of various methodological ideas about "general theory" have been based. But it is certainly possible to identify some of the places where these appeals have departed from reasoned argument and rested on hope. In this paper I will be primarily concerned with the long legacy of hope surrounding the problem of the status of statistics and sociological measurement, and incidentally concerned with such conceptions of general theory as the Parsonian project.

THE PROBLEM OF STATISTICS

The early modern social theorists supposed that the appearances of social life, or history, could be reduced to "laws" that were fundamentally the same in logical form as the laws of natural science. At least until Mill, who was a practicing economist as well as the philosopher of social science who originated much of the conventional idea of what a completed structure of laws in the social sciences would be, the dominant idea was that statistics were at most a kind of weak preliminary to a nomic social science which would have as its task the construction of laws. By such devices as the composition of forces, these laws were to explain the appearances cataloged by statisticians. Mill himself thought the two tasks (of cataloging statistical results and constructing laws) had to go hand in hand, and insisted (though even in his own time this was not plausible) that the task of the construction of laws "stand sentinel" over the task of collection (Turner 1986: 56–9). Comte was overtly hostile to statistics, believing that what contemporary statisticians called "laws" (typically curves fit to rates, such as death rates by age) were not laws at all, but a stopping-point before genuine scientific knowledge (ibid.: 28).

The problem of the relation between law, cause, and statistical results was to become a major theme in the nineteenth-century tradition of *Moralstatistik*, and many of the arguments developed during the high period of this movement were to reappear as part of the critique of statistical positivism in twentieth-century sociology (Porter 1986). The history of

Moralstatistik is a curious one, for it is the first dramatic example of the intellectual failure of an academic social science discipline. The myriad results established by the moral statisticians proved to be largely uninterpretable at any level beyond that of the tables themselves. The dispute over the status of the "laws" exhibited in the tables revolved for the most part around the problem of free will: the question was "in what sense do these statistical 'laws' determine the outcomes they describe?" The complex ramifications of this issue as it was discussed at the time need not concern us here, but some of the arguments have relevance to contemporary claims.

One such argument is this: causal laws, as understood by Mill, are statements of "unconditional invariant succession." One can loosen this requirement by allowing for the possibility of probabilistic causation. As we shall see, Mill does this in a certain way, and it is done more radically later. But this resolves only the difficulty with the requirement of "invariance." None of the supposed statistical "laws" in fact *held* unconditionally"; in Mill's terminology, they were at best "empirical generalizations" which held under specified conditions. Mill's own discussion of the problem of the status of the results of "the method of agreement" dealt with the example of Kepler's laws, which described the circular motions of a limited set of objects, the planets. These motions were unlike those of other physical objects, so there was no suggestion that these laws were themselves general or explanatory (Mill 1973; 293–4, 432; cf. Turner 1986: 32–3). One could make them explanatory, however, by deriving them from some higher laws of motion which unconditionally applied to all physical objects of a particular kind, and this Newton achieved. Mill thought of statistical results as having the flaws of the mere generalizations produced by the method of agreement, namely that they might be no more than extended coincidences or "accidental" generalizations (Mill 1973: 547; cf. Turner 1986: 37).

In Mill's case, the difficulty was compounded by the recognition that the actual empirical materials on which the social sciences were forced to practice when they attempted to generalize included, in large and ever increasing part, statistical results, such as tables of rates, rather than strict generalizations. Mill accommodated this by an equivocation which at one stroke salvages the idea of generalization and holds off the problem of probabilistic causation: he construed the results of statistics as "approximate generalizations" (Mill 1973: 591; cf. Turner 1986: 40–59). The probabilistic character of the generalizations was thus held to be an infantile disorder that would vanish as the social sciences advanced under the "sentinel" of the task of theorizing by proposing deductively linked laws that could be made even more precise.

But no account of how this process of moving from rates to "approximate generalizations," to strict generalizations, on to causal laws is to occur can be found in Mill, and none was available to him. Mill had, strictly speaking, no reason to believe that statistical results could be converted into generalizations. So while the term "approximate generalization" is promissory, the promise is empty. Indeed, his own discussion of the difficulties of the last stage in the process in the face of the kind of complexity one finds in social sciences, a discussion rehearsed by Durkheim, warranted quite pessimistic conclusions, as Durkheim certainly understood (1982). The trajectory of Mill's own work bore out the pessimism. At one point he expected to write a volume creating the science of character, ethology, which his larger model demanded (and which was the subject from which many of his examples of approximate generalizations were drawn). The going was more difficult than he expected, and the project was soon abandoned. But Mill never used this unhappy experience to revise his views, nor did he acknowledge that the difficulties undermined his vision.

In Mill, then, the lacuna, and thus the point at which hope is needed, was concealed. Quetelet was more direct: he admitted that it would take a Newton (Quetelet 1848: 301) to formulate the explanatory laws governing the various laws governing the properties of the "*homme moyen*" that he had discovered, which were tables of rates (such as age-specific crime rates). The mathematical properties of the *homme moyen* were hideously complex, and no Newton could be found to reduce them. And in spite of the endless repetition of the claim that statistics were to lead to genuine laws, no other solution was to be found. Principled skeptical arguments of various kinds subsequently developed, in particular the claim that statistical laws *could* be no more than descriptions, that is, empirical laws which held under particular historical conditions which themselves changed or evolved in ways which could not be subject to "laws," statistical or otherwise. This was the historical school's critique of "Manchester" economic principles extended to the claims of *Moralstatistik*.

Arguments like these, combined with the failure of *Moralstatistik* to lead to the promised deeper laws, led to a curious reaction, which set in during the 1880s in Europe. Statisticians, many of whom had been reluctant to mix claims about cause with the compilation of statistical results in the first place, turned away from causal questions. The younger generation devoted their attention to a series of problems in the mathematics of dispersion, and similar problems that had been neglected in the era of Quetelet's greatest influence. Statistics, which had been an empirical social science often prosecuted by statisticians with very limited mathematical background, became a formal discipline, mathematical statistics.

THE ABANDONMENT OF THE DEDUCTIVE MODEL

The failure of the moral statistics tradition, and the failure of Mill's model, cleared the stage for a radical departure, which went back to Comte but rejected virtually the whole of the nineteenth-century inheritance of ideas about cause and law. The key figure in this new development was Karl Pearson, a Marxist at the time of these writings and a reformer who had been influenced as a student at Cambridge by a Comtist librarian. Pearson's departure had two strands: his renovation of Comte, which was a restatement of the law of three stages as a progression from the ideological, to the observational, and then to the metrical; and his rejection of the nineteenth-century identification of laws with perfect mathematical relationships, on the ground that all scientific theories were idealizations to which empirical truth never corresponded. He combined the two ideas by rejecting such concepts as cause and explanation as "animistic" residues of the pre-scientific stages of thought (1911: 121n), and arguing that their replacement at the metrical stage would consist in metrical descriptions of the empirical distributions of sequences. The same goal held for social science: its own sequential relations could be precisely described metrically by means of regression lines and correlation coefficients, techniques that had been recently developed. Among the many implications of this argument was a denial of any difference in kind between the laws of physics and those of a correlational social science.

Virtually no one accepted this radical philosophy of science completely. But it had extraordinary and wide impact. In New York, a circle around Morris Raphael Cohen studied *The Grammar of Science*, as did Jerzy Neyman in Warsaw, and as did the salon of quantitative sociologists and other social scientists run by Franklin H. Giddings, who became Pearson's major popularizer in American sociology.

Giddings's adaptation of Pearson had two curious implications in relation to "theory." On the one hand, by accepting Pearson's idea that statistical results should be regarded as the end point of scientific inquiry, it legitimated speculative social theory as a necessary beginning point of social science. The business of sociology was to be the metricization of the kind of speculative social theory that had successfully been transformed into claims supported by "observation." By the term "observational," Giddings himself usually meant "validated by reference to known facts of history": Spencer's central insight that human nature evolved was his pet example of a sociological truth verified by observation. On the other hand, Pearson's conception had no room for the nomic social science envisioned by Mill, and indeed any deductive theory in social science would, in Pearsonian terms, be inappropriate to the final stage of science. A premise in a theoretical argument would have to hold invariably for some class for anything much to follow *deductively* from it: probabilistic arguments are deductively feeble. But Pearson believed that the invariable laws of science were idealizations and therefore literally false, and this entailed the abandonment of deductive theory as an ideal. Giddings was more willing than Pearson to accept the use of such concepts as explanation and cause, even at the final stage of science. But his own formulation of the goals of metrical sociology had no role for deductive theory.

Consequently, Giddings's own image of the future of sociology was a radical departure from the ideas of Mill and

Quetelet. Like Mill, he used the concept of approximation, but he did so in a quite different way, expecting it to lead to quite different conclusions. He treated the laws of nature as constants:

A constant is an unchanging ratio of one variable quantity to another; for example, the unchanging ratio of the circumference of a circle to its diameter. When we have discovered and made sure of a constant we have attained the supreme end of scientific study in one domain or part of a domain, and have equipped ourselves with perhaps the most powerful tool that man can own and use. In electrophysics, chemistry, thermo-dynamics, and other inorganic sciences many constants have been found and verified. In the organic sciences the phenomena studied are so complicated that only approximations to constants have been obtained, and not many of them. (*Giddings 1924: 24–5*)

He extrapolated this to psychology and sociology, and came to some rather modest expectations:

It is probable that in psychology a number of useful approximations will be achieved. That we shall work out many very close approximations in the social sciences is doubtful. For a long time to come we shall hardly do more than discover such general relations as that of the approximately inverse ratio of a meeting of minds to an increasing heterogeneity of population, or as that of the increase of lawlessness with the multiplication of laws. (*ibid.: 25*).

This formulation leaves open the possibility of greater precision but holds out little hope. When he asked, "What then is possible" for us to achieve, his answer was:

We can discriminate and identify variables and discover ways to measure amounts and rates of variability. We can ascertain the conditions under which variation occurs and (a closely related research, when not in fact the same one) we can ascertain how variables consort with one another; that is to say, we can determine their concurrences, associations, and correlations. For the present our most serious work consists in obtaining correlations. These are by no means perfect substitutes for constants, but they are the next best thing. (*ibid.: 25–6*)

By interpreting these correlations as "uncontrolled experiments" we would learn which variables and which relations are important in *many* settings: these would be to sociology what constants would be to the natural sciences. The role of deductive theory in this was to be nil: Mill's idea that social science had to be deductive, Giddings believed, was "fatal, if true, to sociology." Fortunately, he thought it was not true: the statistical inductive method produced conclusions quite as valid (ibid.: 172–81), because, as Giddings also insisted (confusing objective and subjective probability), the premises of deductive social science were themselves only probable.

Hope and practice

One point in telling this shaggy dog story is that the various alterations of cognitive purposes which lie between Comte and Giddings have little to do with foundationalism as such. Pearson had his metaphysical slogans, notably "variation is the law of nature." But Giddings's use of Pearson was to make a science of sociology possible by scaling down expectations and diminishing the need for hope. A better way to tell the story of twentieth-century American quantitative sociology might be as follows: Giddings and his students were reformers, who were well aware of the rhetorical power of statistics in politics. One suspects they would have been attracted to this rhetorical tool apart from its place in a revised "law of the three stages" and, indeed, it was during his career as a journalist that Giddings first became enamored of the products of the Massachusetts Bureau of Labor Statistics, which included survey research and studies of multiple cases on social topics of many kinds, from divorce and alcoholism to profit-sharing. Giddings himself contributed the first systematic study of profit-sharing. When the Rockefeller almoners chose to promote a "realistic" approach to social problems in the twenties and thirties, statistical sociology was the beneficiary, just as fifty years earlier the Massachusetts Bureau of Labor Statistics had been created under political pressure by labor groups seeking authoritative backing for their own reformist aims. Even in 1870, these statisticians were concerned with the causes of such things as the high price of provisions. When the use of the analogy with experiment popularized by Yule (1896) and promoted by Giddings (as "uncontrolled experiments") (1924: 25–6) and his students (as the *ex post facto* design) enabled later writers to apply statistical data to these causal questions, it is not surprising that they did. At no stage did their choice of the methods depend exclusively on their ideas about the ultimate character of a social science.

The ways of applying statistical methods went through a kind of trial and error evolution and elaboration in which objections to practical interpretations – for example, questions about "assumptions" – were dealt with by *ad hoc* improvements designed to make the methods more "robust" and the specific inferences less questionable. The improvement of methods of causal inference was discontinuous, or, more accurately, the methods which were shared with the proto-econometricians in the teens and twenties were developed in econometrics and have been borrowed back by sociologists in various forms since the mid-sixties. In the intervening years, especially the forties and fifties, quantitative sociology concentrated on measurement, sampling, and designs inspired by psychology.

The rise of the opinion survey, which had a long but fitful history reaching back to the 1840s, led many sociologists to focus on the problem of attitudes and their measurement. Giddings had preferred behavioral indices, though he devised clever paper and pencil tests himself. Attitude measures gained ground, in part because they represented an improvement on behavioral indices and on Giddings's own tests, an improvement on Giddings's own terms – namely better fit with what was known (1924) – and an improvement because of the alliance with psychology they enabled. Contrary to Giddings's belief that the outcome of statistical methods for the foreseeable future would be correlations, these "by no means perfect substitutes for constants" (1924: 26),[2] the new statistical sociology of Lazarsfeld and Stouffer aspired to improvements in the precision of measurement. The possibility of this substitution depended on the fact that the goals Giddings had advanced had become increasingly marginal to the practice, which no longer needed their justification.

In short, then, we may say that throughout this period there was a significant demand for social statistics which did not depend on any notion of its ultimate scientific purposes, and which grew as new buyers entered the marketplace, such as foundations and, later, corporations interested in polling and market research and, still later, the federal government, through its various schemes of research subsidy. Throughout this period there were step-by-step improvements in technique, that is, improvements which overcame practical limitations or problems with methods previously accepted as legitimate but recognized to be crude, or improvements which defined mechanical procedures for what had previously been data-based judgment calls, such as the acceptance of certain kinds of hypotheses. Such improvements were valuable apart from any relevance to the goal of general theory. They were rarely discussed in reference to these goals until the late forties and early fifties, when it took the form of hopes that were in retrospect totally unwarranted, but which still prowl about in our lives like the ghosts of dead religious beliefs.

THE RETURN OF DEDUCTION

Samuel Stouffer (the best student of Giddings's own best student, Ogburn), writing in the late forties and early fifties, presented one of the major modern versions of the new image of the state and future of sociology, one that was directly informed by the idea that the moment to make sociology a "real science" had arrived. The effect of opinion polling on the development of sociology as a science was, he argued, analogous to the aid lent to science by engineering discoveries: practical public opinion polling helped improve measurement. The possibility of improving measurement seems to have led Stouffer to contemplate improvements in the precision of social science formulations far beyond those Giddings had envisioned. In a debate with Percy Bridgman, the Harvard physicist who had coined the term "operationalism," and who resolutely denied that "significant measurement" presently existed in the social sciences (and seems to have believed that it could not), Stouffer stressed the need for better "gadgets," e.g. better questionnaires and better test concepts. But he placed this need in the framework of the idea that sociology could progress on the model of medicine, where "not one grand conceptual scheme, but many limited generalizations were to mark the conquest of mankind's scourges" (Bridgman debate file, Stouffer Papers).

The limited generalizations needed now, he said elsewhere, were the sort that could be stated in terms of, and tested using, the tools we now have. The larger aim is to make sociology into a science, meaning "a body of theory, of theoretical propositions, general in character, which have the power of generating propositions which can be stated operationally and verified empirically" (1951 speech at the University of Minnesota, Stouffer Papers). One may note that the vocabulary here is far closer to logical positivism than Giddings's and Ogburn's Pearsonian skepticism, and that Stouffer's strategy for achieving these aims was similar to Merton's strategy of "theories of the middle range." The element of hope in this conception is very large, much larger than the element of hope in Giddings.

The appeal of this model could not rest on either its present applicability or the fact that the many difficulties faced by any model which involves deductive relations between generalizations had somehow been resolved. Rather they were papered over with attractive slogans.[3] Both the optimism, and the troubles, are analogous to Mill's.[4] Stouffer's phrase, "limited generalizations," is in a sense even more disingenuous than Mill's "approximate generalizations," in that the statistical material which was the main product of Stouffer's efforts consisted not of generalizations at all, but of tests of the existence of effects or attempts to disentangle real effects from spurious ones. They were certainly "limited," and not only in the sense Stouffer had in mind; it was a characteristic discovery and source of frustration that even these very modest demonstrations of significant differences of means or significant chi-squares did not travel very well (cf. Cronback 1986).

The key difficulty is this: deductive relations such that one generalization can be derived from another cannot hold unless the generalizations take a very stringent logical form, paradigmatically "all a's are b's." While deductive arguments may be constructed that entail probabilistic claims, such as "40 percent of a's are b's," these claims are themselves difficult to use in conjunction with other probabilistic claims to deduce other claims without introducing such problematic notions as "independence." Worse, if we are to suppose that the underlying relations of interest to sociology are themselves probabilistic, the laws expressing these relations would have little value in deduction. The sociological methods of the time, however, did nothing to establish claims which were "general" and only rarely involved models which were stochastic in the strict sense of specifying actual proportions of outcomes. Typically the claim was that such and such variable x was not independent of such and such variable y for such and such population, at the 0.5 level.

On occasion the most sophisticated methodologists conceded that their constructions were not "theories." In 1959, when the young Patrick Suppes commented that a model of Lazarsfeld's (in this case one of the rare attempts at a stochastic construction) was not a theory and did not seem to lead to a theory "in the accepted sense of the word," Lazarsfeld replied with the feebly optimistic assertion that "the term 'theory' may be too ambitious for the type of analysis presented in the introduction. On the other hand it should be recognized that this type of work is necessary at the present stage of development and may well lead to more basic and refined concepts" (International Sociological Association 1961: 350–1). Needless to say, he did not explain how this could occur, or whether these concepts would contribute to the goal of theory "in the accepted sense of the word": the "present stage of development," like the phrase "approximate generalization," is a promise or a hope, in this case one with extraordinarily little substance.

Giddings, who knew his Pearson (1911), his Mill (1973), his Venn (1962), and his Jevons (1878), understood the underlying difficulties here, and this was why he rejected Mill's insistence that social science be deductive. Ogburn, who kept intact his mentor's Pearsonian scruples, perhaps without fully grasping their basis, never went beyond treating statistics as a sometime, pragmatic substitute for experimentation. Their successors lost these scruples and embraced the new model without understanding the formal difficulty raised by the innocent term "deductive." This became the great lacuna in their conception of the goal of a scientific sociology. As with Mill when he ran into troubles with the approximate generalizations of ethology, they simply did not attend to the difficulties: the fact that for them, in contrast to Giddings, discussions of the ultimate aims of social science knowledge had become incidental to the practical (and successful) business of survey research made this failure to attend possible. But the moment of high optimism and minimal attention to these problems was extremely brief.[5]

In due time, the difficulties came home to roost. In the late fifties and sixties Hans Zetterberg, a fellow traveler, published a series of editions of his *On Theory and Verification in Sociology* (1966). A long series of books and articles on "theory construction" followed, each confused, but each describing a kind of theory visibly distant from present empirical sociology. The exceptions, notably Stinchcombe's *Constructing Social Theory* (1968), managed to evade the issue of deductivity entirely, in this case by resorting to question-begging graphic devices, particularly arrows. Discussions of "theory" became almost completely detached from the methodological literature,[6] and Stouffer's idea of theoretical propositions from which hypotheses testable by present methods could be deduced vanished into a thicket of *ad hoc* confusions, equivocations, and evasions. The occasional forays of methodologists into the theory construction literature (e.g. Blalock 1969) were riddled with elementary errors, as were attempts, such as Blau's (1964), to formulate empirical theories on the model of deductive theory.[7] The critics of scientistic social science found formulations like Zetterberg's to be an easy mark, and largely ignored the forms of causal statistical reasoning being practiced in substantive domains. In any case, their criticisms had little effect: actual statistical practice was improving, and these long-range issues could be ignored.

Parsons's vision

Parsons's optimisim was an even more extreme variation on Stouffer's and Merton's: in 1945, Parsons writes that

> sociology is just in the process of emerging into the status of a mature science. Heretofore it has not enjoyed the kind of integration and directed activity which only the availability and common acceptance and employment of a well-articulated generalized theoretical system can give to a science. The main framework of such a system is, however, now available, though this fact is not as yet very generally

appreciated and much in the way of development and refinement remains to be done on the purely theoretical level, as well as its systematic use and revision in actual research. It may therefore be held that we stand on the threshold of a definitely new era in sociology and the neighboring social science fields. (*1954: 212*)

If this was not sufficiently clear, he adds that "what we need is not a science purified of theoretical infection – but one with the nearest possible approach to an *equivalent* of the role of mathematical analysis in physics" (ibid.: 224).[8] Shortly afterwards, Parsons led a spectacular, tone-setting attempt to lay the groundwork for a "General Theory of Action" (Parsons and Shils 1962).

Yet in Parsons, as in Stouffer, optimism went together with the equivocal use, or outright misuse, of key terms, such as "theory" and "deduction." Homans recounts an instance of this which he coyly says he believes to be true.

In a lecture which he gave at Cambridge, England, of all places, where John Maynard Keynes was then the God of economics, Talcott asserted that Keynes's theory was "an interesting special case" of Talcott's own theory of action. In real theories, a special case is one in which the general propositions are applied to only a few of the given conditions to which they may be applied. Thus the theory of the tides is a special case of Newtonian mechanics. To argue that a phenomenon is a special case of a theory is certainly to argue that it can be deduced from the general propositions of the theory. But Parsons had not deduced Keynes's theory from his own. What he had done was something quite different. As we have seen, Parsons's conceptual scheme contained four categories at every level. He thought he had found in Keynes's theory four categories that corresponded in some way to the four of his own but were less comprehensive in scope. This is not deduction, for Talcott stated no propositions relating the categories to one another. The finding of correspondence between categories is something anyone with a little imagination can always succeed in doing. I was told that when Talcott made his statement a member of the audience shouted, "Shit!" (*Homans 1984: 328*)

Sociologists come to this conclusion far more slowly.

If we are to use the vocabulary of logic in something other than a spurious figurative sense, the cognitive justification for the usage, as Homans suggests, was nil. Parsons himself later admitted this: his efforts

> starting with the subject–object distinction or differentiation or however it is characterized, running through pattern variables and ending up with the four-function paradigm, do not constitute in the usual sense *theory*. They do not constitute, as it has often been put, "if–then" propositions such as propositions stating the relation between increases and/or decreases of mass or velocity in a system of Newtonian mechanics. They stand on a different level. (*1979–80: 15*)

He called this level "metatheory"; ordinarily he characterized his construction as a "frame of reference" (ibid.), a conveniently vague term with Whiteheadian and neo-Kantian resonances.

The task of constructing a frame of reference was conceived by Parsons in a fashion which owed something to Kant's project of identifying the presuppositions of Newtonian physics. His *Structure of Social Action* (1937) was an attempt to identify the valid presuppositions of the action theory underlying no fewer than four Newtons – Marshall, Pareto, Durkheim, and Weber – a task which was implicitly constructive in intent, given the differences of opinions between his Newtons. Parsons's own formulations on these topics are peculiar but revealing. Parsons believed, in contrast to neo-Kantianism, and indeed to Kant, that there was something like a positive task of creating a frame of reference or conceptual scheme that could be performed prior to the construction of a theory in the usual sense; that one could, so to speak, do the work of Kant before the work of Newton. He obviously did not regard what he was doing as simply a philosophical enterprise, and was generally unwilling to address philosophical criticisms. In 1941, Parsons wrote to Erich Voegelin describing his correspondence with Schutz, and reflected that

Possibly one of my troubles in my discussion with Schutz lies in the fact that by cultural heritage I am a Calvinist. I do not want to be a philosopher – I shy away from the philosophical problems underlying my scientific work. By the same token I don't think he wants to be a scientist as I understand the term until he has settled all the underlying philosophical difficulties. If the physicists of the 17th century had been Schutzes there might well have been no Newtonian system. (*Parsons to Voegelin, Aug. 18, 1941, quoted in Rehorick and Buxton 1986: 13*)

By the same token, one might say, if there had been Kants or Parsonses who succeeded in giving a persuasive conceptual formulation that appeared to overcome the incoherencies of contemporary physics, there might have been no Newtonian system. Parsons did not see this because he believed that his "conceptual framework" was not just a synthetic tidying up of dead theorists' vocabularies of action, but represented a "breakthrough," to use one of his favorite terms (see Homans 1984: 324). But his results were at best breakthroughs in a prospective sense: only if one was extremely optimistic about the prospects of social science, as Parsons was, could one ignore all the limitations of present concepts and techniques and focus on the pace of improvement, or like Parsons, of the refining and elaboration of his scheme.[9]

THE IDEA OF PIECEMEAL PROGRESS

A fair formulation of the 35 years after Stouffer and Parsons made their original claims might be this: the postwar picture of sociology as a theoretical science, painted differently in its details by each of its leading figures, broke up into different compromises, few of which abandoned the program entirely, but each of which put the expected realization of a very large part of the program into the distant future or quietly abandoned it. Sometimes the act of abandonment was not quiet. Philip Converse recalls

a lengthy evening's conversation I once had during a chance encounter in a small town in France with a well-known American social scientist in 1959. To my surprise, he was in considerable depression at the state of social science. Being but a year beyond finishing my own doctorate and still feeling high, I spent much of the conversation trying to weed out where such a dismal depression could be coming from. I finally boiled it down in my mind to these propositions, which he made more or less explicit: Here it was 1959; social science had been seriously underway for thirty years, or fifty years, or one-hundred years, depending upon how you wanted to count, and we still had not had Sir Isaac Newton yet. (*1986: 43*)

Much of sociology returned, in practice, to the Giddingsian aim of identifying important variables and their correlations (cf. Lieberson 1985). Several programs not only survived, but prospered precisely by ignoring, or putting off into the very distant future, the larger ambitions that are central to Parsons and the Mertonian view of science.

One case of this is the tradition described by David Wagner in *The Growth of Sociological Theories* (1984) as the expectation states theoretical research program. We can use this as a case study of the piecemeal approach as a strategy. One of Wagner's points in his discussion is that this is a success story in a way that the larger and familiar story of competition between "paradigms" or approaches is not. Such competition, he argues, degenerates into unfruitful "metatheoretical" debate that inhibits the growth of theories. In our terms, because they are "foundational," the debates are irresolvable and lead to relativism at the metatheoretical level. To make his case, which is itself metatheoretical, Wagner must redefine success, and he does so by borrowing Imre Lakatos's concept of research programs, and claiming that expectation states work has "progressed" and is therefore a "progressive" theoretical research program such as those Lakatos supposed to be characteristic of living areas of natural science and mathematics.

Lakatos's point in creating this historiographic category was to revise Popper's falsificationism by giving some rationale for the kind of willingness to accept anomalies for the time being and to ignore criticism that has historically characterized living areas of science. His solution is, roughly, that as long as the core ideas of a given program continue to be fruitful, it is rational to continue to accept them. This idea rationalizes the dogmatism Kuhn observed, without accepting dogmatism as such in science, and salvaged the Popperian notion of criticism by locating it at the level of science "as a battleground of research programmes rather than isolated theories" (Lakatos 1970: 175), a battleground in which programs fail by failing to predict novel facts.

It may be noted that Lakatos was a famous opponent of sociology, given to writing letters to *The Times* against its acceptance at Cambridge. So this is *prima facie* a surprising philosophical authority for Wagner to invoke. What the choice perhaps suggests is that there is a serious incongruency here. No one nowadays denies, because no one thinks it is an issue, that experiments on people placed in highly artificial environments and set at various tasks might very well behave in a sufficiently predictable fashion that clever measurement and clever statistical analysis might detect "effects" of one variable or another. Nor do they deny that, with a great deal of effort, people could show new relations between various effects and improve on their underlying understanding of, and vocabulary for describing, the relations between these measurable effects. No one thinks this is an issue because no one thinks of this kind of work as an end in itself. The point of experiment is thought to be to find strict and highly generalizable principles, and, especially, to establish a vocabulary in terms of which one could redescribe the world outside the laboratory in such a way that it could be brought under control or predicted substantially more effectively than could be done under "pre-scientific" descriptions. Hence Pasteur's famous slogan, "give me a laboratory and I will raise the world." The expectation states program fulfills part of this strategy of temporary retreat into the artificial world of the laboratory. But is it intelligibly construed as an attempt to establish something more fundamental? Perhaps it need not be so construed. But does it make sense to treat it as solely a laboratory tradition?

The answers to these questions take us beyond the framework of Wagner's argument, but not, as we shall see, beyond Lakatos's. If we ask what the ultimate aim of the research program is, the obvious answer is that it aims to construct a theory that does account for the processes by which judgments of justice, prestige, and so forth are produced in social interaction outside the laboratory and in such consequential areas of social life as politics. This aim involves hopes whose reasonableness and coherence may be assessed. The aim also provides grounds for experimenters expanding the list of variables to include in their analyses. The fact that the theories as presently formulated apply only to artifical situations in which experimental subjects are deprived of the usual information, context, and so forth that we know pre-scientifically to bear on such judgments is understood to be a defect. But we hope to remedy the defect once the strategy of beginning with rigorously established laboratory results and improving and elaborating our concepts and formalizations has brought us to the point where these topics can be accounted for in a way that does improve on common sense. In its own way, then, expectation states theory has substantial ambitions; and one can readily identify conceptual, formal, and measurement problems that it will need to overcome. One might also reasonably say that we have been through hopes of similar kinds before, with figures like Stouffer, and learned that the problems are intractable.

Wagner does not construe the program in this way, or at least he does not attempt to deal with these kinds of issues. He argues simply that the program is progressive or cumulative. Unfortunately, the technical terminology of the philosophy of science is not very helpful in sorting out the implications of this claim: terms like "theory" and "prediction" as used in the expectation states tradition do not correspond to the uses found in Lakatos, and this turns out to be especially troublesome for his key thesis. Lakatos's central claim is that progressive research programs are those with theories with the following property: they anticipate results *other than and in addition to* those the theory was designed to explain (Lakatos 1970: 123–5).[10] Lakatos provides some examples of this, but these examples are too technical to explicate here. Whewell's original examples are perhaps somewhat more accessible. Whewell says that

> when Newton had collected from Kepler's Laws the Central Force of the sun, and from these, combined with other facts, the Universal Force of all the heavenly bodies,

he suddenly turned round to include in his generalization the Precession of the Equinoxes, which he declared to arise from the attraction of the sun and moon upon the protuberant part of the terrestrial spheroid. The apparent remoteness of this fact, in its nature, from the others which which he thus associated it, causes this part of his reasoning to strike us as a remarkable example of *Consilience*. Accordingly, in the Table of Astronomy we find that the columns which contain the facts and theories relative to the *sun* and *planets*, after exhibiting several stages of induction within themselves, are at length suddenly connected with a column till then quite distinct, containing the *precession of the equinoxes*. (Whewell 1967: 77–8)

The criterion makes sense in the case of highly formalized theories with precise predictions, and highly precise independently observed results, such as the table containing the precession of the equinoxes. Whether it can be extended to such less formal, statistical contexts as expectation states research is highly questionable. It is clear, however, that Lakatos himself would have claimed that expectation states theory flunked the test.

Lakatos believed that his major achievement in formulating his conception of "research programs" was to supply "*a new criterion of demarcation between 'mature science,' consisting of a mere patched-up pattern of trial and error.*" The criterion was that theories in a progressive tradition have "unexpected excess content." He acknowledged that "one may achieve . . . 'progress' with a patched-up, arbitrary series of disconnected theories." But he insisted that "Good scientists will not find such makeshift progress satisfactory; they may even reject it as not genuinely scientific. They will call such auxiliary hypotheses merely 'formal,' 'arbitrary,' 'empirical,' 'semi-empirical,' or even '*ad hoc*'" (Lakatos 1970: 175). When he looked around for examples of such "degenerating problem shifts," he produced two old standbys, Marxism and Freudianism, which he included in the category on the grounds that their *ad hoc* revisions fail to anticipate new facts. He then claimed that his "requirement of continuous development" (ibid.: 175)

hits patched-up, unimaginative series of pedestrian "empirical" adjustments which are so frequent, for instance, in

modern social psychology. Such adjustments may, with
the help of so-called "statistical techniques," make some
"novel" predictions and may even conjure up some
irrelevant grains of truth in them. But this theorizing has
no unifying idea, no heuristic power, no continuity. They
do not add up to a genuine research programme and are, on
the whole, worthless. (*ibid.: 176*)

Lakatos expands this in a footnote by citing a paper by Meehl
which argued that while the effect of methodological advances
in the physical sciences was to make corroboration more
difficult, in the behavioral sciences it was the reverse, meaning
statistical significance, or the rejection of the null hypothesis,
was made easier to achieve. He speculates that the "theorizing"
condemned by Meehl may be *ad hoc* in the sense of involving
purely empirical or formal auxiliary revisions (ibid.: 176). The
statistical methods in question are akin to those used in the
expectation states program.

  Whether expectation states theory has a "unifying idea" which
rises above the empirical, and whether the revisions are *ad hoc* in
Lakatos's bad sense is perhaps itself not a very fruitful question.
As I have suggested, at the state of formalization of expectation
states theory and at the present state of predictive imprecision,
clear unanticipated empirical implications of the appropriate
sort, such as the precession of the equinoxes, are hard to imagine.
A better question might be whether the story Wagner tells about
"progress" in expectation states theory could not also be told by
looking at, say, the citations over the last 50 years to Weber's
Protestant Ethic thesis. Does this thesis, after all, not serve
heuristic purposes and prove itself in new contexts, such as Japan
(Bellah 1985) and the third world (cf. Berger 1986); and do its
auxiliary theories, such as those involving Protestant and
Protestant-like behavior in the third world, predict novel facts,
meaning facts other than those on which the auxiliary theory was
based? *Pace* Lakatos as formulated by Wagner, the same may
perhaps be said of the many auxiliary theories devised in the wake
of the failure of the proletariat to live up to its historical mission.
For that matter, it could be applied to uses of the concept of
anomie, or any of a host of the sociological theories still used in
research and as aids to analysis.

What this suggests is that Lakatos as formulated by Wagner has provided an extremely *weak* criterion for distinguishing progressive from degenerative problem shifts. If we accept as corroboration the kinds of statistical evidence on which the expectation states program rests or the kinds of corroboration taken to be intrinsic to other scholarly traditions in the social sciences, it is difficult to see what "patched-up pattern of trial and error" would not qualify: virtually all academic traditions are progressive in the sense of continuous expansion to new problem domains and topics.[11]

Other research traditions, such as Conversational Analysis, have also settled for the claim that they are "progressive," so Wagner's defense of expectation states theories raises a general issue. Is "progressiveness" in this weak sense enough? Wagner's desire to distinguish the expectation states program from other modes of sociology on the grounds of its fulfillment of criteria deriving from the problems of demarcation in the philosophy of natural science suggests that he at least believes that the actual "successes" of the program are not enough to impress anyone with its "scientific" merit. So it seems that even if we abandon the suggestion that our efforts at improving our ideas will contribute to a radical break with common sense or lead to a comprehensive, Newton-like synthesis, we are still in need of some kind of warrant for our ideas that is external to the tradition or program itself. To the extent that this is true, Wagner's thesis falls prey to the usual difficulties of foundational arguments.

Hope today

Are hopes of the sort I have attributed to the expectation states program in some sense essential? If so, what can be said about the coherence of such hopes today? Wagner's formulation leaves out hope, but it seems evident that the "problems" the program attempts to solve cannot even be formulated without at least implicit reference to some larger aims. These may be tacit, and may not be well defined or even a matter of complete consent. Similarly for such enterprises as conversational analysis or for that matter critical theory or neofunctionalism: to the extent that they are living programs and not calcinated dogmas, they have aims that have not yet been fulfilled.

But there are hopes and hopes. The historical thesis of this discussion has been that the grand program of a comprehensive social theory with the authority or validity, if perhaps not the form, of theories in natural science, is a program that has had no satisfactory expression since the early editions of Mill's *System of Logic*, at which time the rise of statistics made the goal increasingly irrelevant to what was known of the social world in the numerical forms of description in which an increasing portion of this knowledge was being formulated. With the exception of such anti-deductivist writers as Giddings, each later version of the ideal either failed to accommodate the reality of the mass of statistical results or equivocated on such topics as the character of the deductive links of the "theories" it aspired to. To recount this history is not to provide yet another foundationalist argument to the effect that such a theory is an impossibility; indeed, understanding that the visions of a social science that these arguments attempt to evoke are in large part fantasies reminds us why such critical arguments typically fail to be fully persuasive. They are arguments against utopian dreams, with the utopian aspects hidden under equivocations and lacunae. Understanding the project of expectation states theory only as a progressive tradition, for example, obscures its extra-laboratory explanatory purposes, and the utopianism of its hopes to explain the domain of politics. These visions are not, however, immune from all forms of rational assessment. But we can come to see that some programs rely on unreasonable hopes. And we may find that the hopes are concealed in ways which prevent this unreasonableness from being apparent.

The brunt of this discussion should not, however, fall on those social theorists who have articulated their hopes or, like Wagner, attempted to explicate the aims of their programs or give a coherent rationale for them. A more important point is this: much of what passes for metatheoretical criticism in sociology relies on insincere or mindless appeals to standards of theoretical adequacy that would, if they were sincerely meant and fully formulated, be easily seen to be utopian or hopelessly vague. The history of hope, and especially the legacy of Parsons, makes criticism of this sort possible: the critics unironically use the standards implicit in the programmatic claims of the moments of great optimism as a source of terms to abuse theories and forms of analysis for their incompleteness, unhistoricalness, failure "to account for power," or to deal with the psychological, or symbolic, or interpretive aspects of some matter, or to integrate micro and macro, or to serve this that or the other cognitive aim whose fulfillment was promised by past programs. These unironic uses are insincere, at least in this sense: the ideal of complete, integrative, historical "theory" that is presupposed by the criticisms is not an ideal which they seriously suppose can be fulfilled by existing or reasonably anticipatable "theories." But to demand that a theory "account for power" or "account for change" is to speak as though these were practically actualizable considerations, as though it was evident what it is to "account" for such things, and as though some adequate account was readily at hand.

Considered apart from the excessive optimism chronicled here and apart from the foundationalist claims made on behalf of various specific forms of theory, the substantive successes of social theory and of social explanation in many of its forms are genuine and defensible. Our problem is to have the one, the successes, without the other, the discourse-destructive fantasies. Social inquiry *needs* aims in order to constitute "problems." But the ideal of general theory has too often served as a utopia whose utopianism is concealed. To live the theoretical life under the banner of this utopia is intellectual Micawberism, which invites a deserved marginalization to intelligent discussion about social life. To the extent that our categories of criticism and praise presuppose hopes that we do not acknowledge as such, we act in bad faith. And by failing to appreciate differences in the reasonableness of hopes, we risk denigrating or failing to appreciate achievements.

NOTES

1 Hence the concept of ideal-type and Weber's constant reminders that these, however necessary as tools, are not to be treated as real (1949: 80).

2 The idea that some set of more basic and enduring relations will or can be specified is an enduring yet *sotto voce* feature in present quantitative sociology (cf. Lieberson 1985).

3 In spite of the logical positivist ring to the formulation, it is clear that Stouffer had no interest in the issues of formalization and symbolic logic that were the technical core of logical positivism. So if he believed that these techniques would serve as a solution to the problems, he did nothing to act on the belief.

4 Mill used the term *axiomata media* to describe the deductive principles of the sciences located in the hierarchy of the sciences between general sociology, i.e. laws of historical development of the overarching Comtean level, and the genuinely explanatory laws he believed psychology would supply. Merton's notion of middle-range theory and Stouffer's idea of limited generalizations both resemble Mill's usage, and share its problems. The usage does have the effect of displacing the need for optimism onto the possibility of constructing such theories. It appeared to Merton and Stouffer, as it had to Mill, that this was a task which could be more readily accomplished with present means; like Mill, they discovered otherwise.

5 Exemplified by Lazarsfeld's 1950s collaboration with Ernest Nagel in teaching a course on the philosophy of social science and developing training materials.

6 An exception is Land (1971), who is plainly utopian, and perhaps Berger et al. 1962, who never deal directly with problems of the logical form of theories *per se*. Another apparent exception is Jasso (1988), but see Turner (1989). In her reply to this comment, Jasso showed that she did not grasp the concept of a deductive argument. On one page, she quoted a standard definition of mathematical proof which stressed that all theorems must be derivable from the original axiom set alone. On the same page she admitted, though in a concealed way, that her own arguments did not fit this model but were, as I had suggested, cases where "a particular derivation requires introduction of an additional assumption." She managed to claim that this "does not weaken the derivation" (1988: 156). In fact, the number of "additional assumptions" required is so large and the information in them must be so rich that it is questionable whether they would not be sufficient for making the predictions *without* the addition of empirical claims about "the distributive justice force." This is a crucial question for Jasso and for others in her tradition, because the only warrant for claims about the existence of such a "force" is a *post hoc ergo propter hoc* argument which is only persuasive if there is no other way to explain the results. In the cases she presents, as I had suggested, it is likely that the "results" can be "derived" without

reference to her "principle," from purely formal considerations; but as she has not herself produced genuinely deductive arguments, it is difficult to demonstrate this point: she has provided very vague sketches of arguments; all that one can do in reply is to supply alternative sketches, which I did.

7 Arguments for all these claims could be provided, with little difficulty, and less profit (cf. Meehl 1970, 1986; Turner and Wilcox 1974; Turner 1977). It is perhaps useful to know that the most sophisticated recent attempts to defend "causal analysis" from its many critics in statistics (Freedman 1985) and elsewhere (Baumrind 1983) have generally abandoned the claim that these analyses yield physics-like "theory," and treated the methods as eliminative techniques (Glymour 1983; Glymour et al. 1987; 7–8, 12–13) which give empirical grounds for distinguishing a subset of models from between a finite set of plausible hypotheses. Indeed, part of the aim of the literature is to make the point that it is "not nearly enough" merely to "test" a model. As Glymour notes, "often the tests applied to causal models are of low power given the sample size, meaning that for all anyone knows there may exist many, many alternative models that would also pass whatever test has been applied" (Glymour et al. 1987: 31).

Glymour explicitly argues that "the result is not a system of laws that hold in every circumstance, or even a list or weighting of causal factors that hold in every possible circumstance." He defends the approach on the grounds of utility (1983: 128). He cautions social scientists that "critics who demand of the social sciences a full-fledged theory may be asking for too much," and commends the enterprise of designing multivariate *ex post facto* experiments as a *substitute* (1983: 134).

8 On some occasions he formulated his image of theory in a way that appears to be highly congenial to the vocabulary of logical positivism. "The theory of concern to the present paper in the first place constitutes a 'system' and thereby differs from discrete 'theories,' that is, particular generalizations about particular phenomena or classes of them. A theoretical system in the present sense is a body of logically interdependent generalized concepts of empirical reference. Such a system tends, ideally, to become 'logically closed,' to reach such a state of logical integration that every logical implication of any combination of propositions in the system is explicitly stated in some other proposition in the same system" (Parsons 1954: 212–13).

9 Nico Stehr suggests that Merton had his own version of the idea of a breakthrough vocabulary. Nevertheless, the effect of the concept of "middle-range theory" was to reduce expectations. Lazarsfeld never regarded "general theory" in sociology as a reasonable goal, on the grounds of the complexity of the subject matter. At best, he thought,

some kind of theory consisting of psychological principles might be possible. He characterized the concept of middle-range theory as a verbal trick, in that it suggested that big-range theory could be built out of middle-range theories. This skepticism was perhaps shared *de facto* by many sociologists. One may reasonably ask some pointed questions about who believed in the goal of general theory, in what sense; and to what extent they regarded it as the sort of activity to which their own time and their own departmental resources might be committed.

10 The thought, Lakatos says, is akin to Whewell's notion of the consilience of inductions, with the difference that Whewell mistakenly thought consilience to be relevant to proof, whereas Lakatos did not. Wagner's formulations indicate that he is not using this crucial criterion at all, at least not in the sense Lakatos intended, which, one suspects, would exclude any social science or psychological research – perhaps by design.

11 If Lakatos's criterion is applied strictly, the expectation states program is not "progressive" in the appropriate sense, for no novel predictions have been made by the program's theories beyond those the theories were designed to explain, or at least Wagner does not give any examples of such anticipations.

REFERENCES

Baumrind, Diana 1983: "Specious causal attributions in the social sciences," *Journal of Personality and Social Psychology*, 45: 1289–98.

Bellah, Robert N. 1985: *Tokugawa Religion: The Cultural Roots of Modern Japan*. New York: Free Press.

Berger, Joseph, Bernard P. Cohen, J. Laurie Snell, and Morris Zelditch, Jr 1962: *Types of Formalization in Small-Group Research*. Boston: Houghton Mifflin.

Berger, Peter 1986: *The Capitalist Revolution: Fifty Propositions about Prosperity, Equality, and Liberty*. New York: Basic Books.

Blalock, Hubert M. Jr 1969: *Theory Construction: From Verbal to Mathematical Formulations*. Englewood Cliffs. NJ: Prentice-Hall.

Blau, Peter M. 1964: *Exchange and Power in Social Life*. New York: Wiley.

Converse, Philip E. 1986: "Generalization and the social psychology of 'other worlds,'" in Donald W. Fiske and Richard A. Shweder (eds),

Metatheory in Social Science: Pluralisms and Subjectivities, Chicago: University of Chicago Press, pp. 442–60.

Cronbach, Lee, J. 1986: "Social inquiry by and for earthlings," in Donald W. Fiske and Richard A. Shweder, (eds), *Metatheory in Social Science: Pluralisms and Subjectivities*, Chicago: University of Chicago Press, pp. 83–107.

Durkheim, Emile 1982: *The Rules of Sociological Method*, ed. and intro. Steven Lukes; tr. W. D. Halls. New York: Free Press.

Freedman, D. 1985: "Statistics and the scientific method," in W. Mason and S. Feinberg (eds), *Cohort Analysis in Social Research: Beyond the Indentification Problem*. New York: Springer, pp. 343–66.

Giddings, Franklin H. 1924: *The Scientific Study of Human Society*. Chapel Hill: University of North Carolina Press.

Glymour, Clark 1983: "Social science and social physics," *Behavioral Science*, 28: 126–34.

Glymour, Clark, Richard Scheines, Peter Spirtes, and Kevin Kelly 1987: *Discovering Causal Structure: Artificial Intelligence, Philosophy of Science, and Statistical Modeling*. Orlando, Fla.: Academic Press.

Homans, George C. 1984: *Coming to My Senses: The Autobiography of a Sociologist*. New Brunswick, NJ: Transaction Books.

International Sociological Association 1961: *Transactions of the Fourth World Congress of Sociology (1959)*, 350–1.

Jasso, Guillermina 1988; "Principles of theoretical analysis," *Sociological Theory*, 7/1: 154–63.

Jevons, William S. 1878: *Elementary Lessons in Logic: Deductive and Inductive*. London: Macmillan.

Lakatos, Imre 1970: "Falsification and the methodology of scientific research programmes," in Imre Lakatos and Alan Musgrave (eds), *Criticism and the Growth of Knowledge*, Cambridge: Cambridge University Press, pp. 91–196.

Land, Kenneth C. 1971: "Formal theory," in Herbert Costner (ed.), *Sociological Methodology*. san Francisco: Jossey-Bass, pp. 175–220.

Lieberson, Stanley 1985: *Making It Count: The Improvement of Social Research and Theory*. Berkeley: University of California Press.

Meehl, Paul 1970: "Nuisance variables and the ex post facto design," in Michael Radner and Stephen Winokur (eds), *Analyses of Theories and Methods of Physics on Psychology*, vol. 4. Minnesota Studies in the Philosophy of Science. Minneapolis: University of Minnesota Press, pp. 373–402.

Meehl, Paul 1986: "What social scientists don't understand," in Donald W. Fiske and Richard A. Shweder (eds), *Methodology in Social Science: Pluralisms and Subjectivities*. Chicago: University of Chicago Press, pp. 315–38.

Mill, John Stuart 1973: *A System of Logic: Ratiocinative and Inductive*, Books I–III, ed. J. M. Robson. Toronto: University of Toronto Press.

Parsons, Talcott: Papers. Harvard University Archives, Cambridge. Mass.

Parsons, Talcott 1937: *The Structure of Social Action*. Glencoe, Ill.: Free Press.

Parsons, Talcott 1954: *Essays in Sociological Theory*, rev. edn. Glencoe, Ill.: Free Press.

Parsons, Talcott 1979–80. "On theory and meta-theory," *Humboldt Journal of Social Relations*, 7: 5–16.

Parsons, Talcott, and Edward A. Shils (eds), 1962: *Towards a General Theory of Action: Theoretical Foundations for the Social Sciences*. New York: Harper Torchbooks.

Pearson, Karl 1911: *The Grammar of Science*, 3rd rev. and enl. edn. London: A. & C. Black.

Polyani, Michael 1964: *Science, Faith and Society*. Chicago: University of Chicago Press.

Porter, Theodore M. 1986: *The Rise of Statistical Thinking, 1820–1900*. Princeton, NJ: Princeton University Press.

Quetelet, L.A. 1848: *Du système social et des lois qui le régissent*. Paris: Guillaumin.

Rehorick, David, and William Buxton 1986: "Recasting the Parsons–Schutz dialogue: the hidden participation of Eric Voegelin," paper presented at International Society for the Sociology of Knowledge meetings, New Delhi, August.

Rorty, Richard, 1979: *Philosophy and the Mirror of Nature*. Princeton, NJ: Princeton University Press.

Stinchcombe, Arthur L. 1968: *Constructing Social Theories*. New York: Harcourt, Brace & World.

Stouffer, Samuel: Papers. Harvard University Archives. Cambridge, Mass.

Turner, Stephen P. 1977: "Blau's theory of differentiation: is it explanatory?", *Sociological Quarterly*, 18: 17–32.

Turner, Stephen P. 1986: *The Search for a Methodology of Social Science: Durkheim, Weber, and the Nineteenth-Century Problem of Cause, Probability and Action*. Boston Studies in the Philosophy of Science, 92. Dordrecht: D. Reidel.

Turner, Stephen 1988: "Jasso's principle," *Sociological Theory* 7/1: 149–53.

Turner, Stephen P., and Regis A. Factor 1984: *Max Weber and the Dispute over Reason and Value: A Study of Philosophy, Ethics, and Politics*. London: Routledge.

Turner, Stephen, and William Wilcox 1974: "Getting clear about the sign rule," *Sociological Quarterly*, 15: 571–88.

Venn, John 1962: *The Logic of Chance*, 4th edn. New York: Chelsea.

Wagner, David G. 1984: *The Growth of Sociological Theories*. Beverly Hills, Calif.: Sage.

Weber, Max 1949: " 'Objectivity' in social science and social policy," in E. A. Shils and H. A. Finch (eds), *The Methodology of the Social Sciences*. Glencoe, Ill.: Free Press, pp. 44–112.

Whewell, William. 1967: *The Philosophy of the Inductive Sciences*, Part 2, selected and ed. G. Buchdahl and L. L. Laudan. London and Edinburgh: Cass.

Yule, G. U. 1896: "On the correlation of total pauperism with proportion of out-relief. II: Males over sixty-five," *Economic Journal*, 6: 613–23.

Zetterberg, Hans L. 1966: *On theory and Verification in Sociology*, 3rd enl. edn. Totowa, NJ: Bedminster Press.

PART II

Critics of Postmodernism: In Defense of Scientific Theory

5

Defending Social Science against the Postmodern Doubt

Robert D'Amico

Freud turns to a companion in his railway car as it heads toward a station in Herzegovina (Freud 1960: 3f). He wants to ask his companion if he has seen the frescoes at Orvieto but suddenly realizes that he has forgotten the name of the artist Signorelli and can only remember the names Botticelli and Boltraffio, which he knows are not correct. He is embarrassed since he now appears to know less about art and Italy than he intended by starting the conversation. Also in halting this casual conversation Freud is in turn reminded of some very disturbing thoughts he had wished to avoid by turning the conversation toward Italy and art. He had been telling his travelling companion a story about Turkish customs, as reported by one of Freud's medical colleagues, but stopped because the report dealt with matters of sexuality and death which Freud thought inappropriate for such a casual conversation with a stranger.

Freud goes on to give a complex and controversial explanation of his memory lapse, discomfort, and embarrassment. It is the kind of explanation that, in both its limitations and yet attraction to many thinkers, characterizes the problematic status of the social sciences. Even though Freud maintains that the name Signorelli was forgotten for a "reason," he also holds that these reasons function just like causes for behavior, and thus can be treated scientifically. Forgetting and mistaken recollection result from mechanisms which unconsciously censor speech.

In Freud's case he reports that prior to the remarks about

Italy he was telling his companion of the response of Turks to a fatal medical diagnosis. They say to the doctor, "Sir, what can I say? I know that if he could be saved you would save him." As Freud rationally reconstructs the event, he changed the topic of conversation because the context of the story included details about Turkish sexual practices (that part was conscious), but then he suggests that questions of death and sexuality, central to the Turkish reminiscence, had become repressed because earlier in his travels, at Trafoi, he was notified of a former patient's suicide.

The mechanism of systematic forgetting runs as follows. Thoughts of sexuality and death are censored or repressed (both consciously and unconsciously apparently). In this case the censoring is linked unconsciously to the phrase "Sir (Herr), what can I say . . . " representing the Turkish custom of resignation before death and Freud's own resignation before his patient's death. The word "Herr" is linked to "Herzegovina" (the train's destination) and in translation as "Signor" removes part of the now inaccessible name Signorelli. But this same chain of association, by letters and meanings, serves to explain why Freud *can* recall Botticelli and Boltraffio. The fuzzy account is that in the name Signorelli the removal of "Signor" allows the "elli" to become attached to the "Bo" in "Bosnia" (where the Truks discussed in the medical report lived) to produce the false recollection "Botticelli." Since the bad news of his patient's suicide was learned of in "Trafoi," that place name connects with the same "Bo" of Bosnia to produce the second substitute name "Boltraffio."

Now whatever else one thinks of such an explanation, there appears to be something so arbitrary about it, so curious, that it ceases in any fundamental sense to be an explanation. Rather than clearing up the memory lapse it leaves it even more mysterious. First, the associative chain works sometimes by similarity of letters, irrespective of meaning; the "Bo" from "Bosnia," "Botticelli," and "Boltraffio" (and the equally meaningless place name "Trafoi"). But other parts of the chain are by translation of meaning as from "Herr" to "Signor," irrespective of any similarity in the letters. Parts of words are sometimes retained as the "Bo" from "Bosnia" but sometimes not as in the "nia" from "Bosnia."

Also, Freud shows that a certain "chain" of terms makes him forget a name because of associations with death and sexuality. But he then uses the same chain to explain why he remembers two names also associated with death and sexuality. Boltraffio and Botticelli are "substitutions" for the forgotten and repressed name "Signorelli." Thus the explanation works by saying that whenever there is repression there is *both* a forgetting of a name and a substitution of a name. But if both the forgetting and the substitution work by the same mechanism of word association (sometimes by letters and sometimes by meaning), how has the forgetting been explained? Is not Freud's story an entertaining narrative rather than a serious explanation?

Traditionally Freud's effort has been dismissed for reasons revealed by this small example. Freud seems to offer two inconsistent generalizations implicit within his model of explanation (repression produces remembering and it produces forgetting). Freud's account excludes falsifying evidence since the associative chain is so flexible that virtually any word could fit it as a false recollection. Finally, Freud's explanation ignores simpler, plausible accounts.[1]

Recently, however, some social scientists have had Freud recommended as a model, not because of psychoanalysis *per se*, but because the social sciences should learn from precisely these *kinds of examples* (Taylor 1985: 15–57; Habermas 1971). Freud's failure is not a weakness of his theory but of all the human sciences. Certain problems are peculiar and fundamental to the social sciences; the role of translation and meaning, the role of narratives in explanations, and the reflexivity and circularity of inquiry. Freud was on the right track, it is suggested, but he was misled by expectations he inherited from his natural scientific training, and which the social sciences must abandon.

Consider for a moment a fascinating passage from Hume. Hume argues that the "constancy of human nature" is the required presupposition of all social science. "Would you know the sentiments, inclinations and course of life of the Greeks and Romans? Study well the temper and actions of the French and English: you cannot be much mistaken in transferring to the former *most* of the observations which you have made with regard to the latter" (Hume 1977: 55). Hume defends this assumption because it allows the political theorist to "fix the principles of his science in the same manner as the physician or natural philosopher." What the social scientist does is become "acquainted with the *regular springs of human action and behavior.*" Without such uniformities of behavior no general observations would be possible and "no experience, however accurately digested by reflection, would serve to any purpose." In Hume's view, social science is the study of what connects human action with its motives and reasons, i.e. the causes of behavior. There is no significant difference, Hume holds, between physical necessity and what he calls "moral necessity." In harmony with Freud, Hume even suggests that "the most irregular and unexpected resolutions of men may frequently be accounted for by those who know every particular circumstance of their character and situation" (ibid.: 58–60).

Hume continues with a vivid description of a prisoner being led to the scaffold. The kind of necessity that the prisoner feels, Hume argues, is a "train of ideas in his mind" – his foreseeing death, the impossibility of escape, etc. – and it is no different from nor less certain than the "train of causes" of physical necessity, namely the physiological effects of bleeding due to execution. Hume's overall point is that causation is not some inner unobservable force within things or nature that brings about effects. Cause is nothing more than the kind of constant conjunction of events found by empirical inquiry. Therefore human motives or thoughts, such as fidelity or fear, are just as much "causes" as are knife blades and ropes. Thus the social sciences are just as capable of lawful inquiry as the natural sciences.

Though Freud and Hume might appear as odd philosophical bedfellows, they share an optimism about the social sciences. Freud claims to "have elucidated the mechanism of false recollection [paramnesia]" and, like Hume, treats this mechanism as parallel to physical necessity. Both believed the social scientist could replicate the success of the natural scientist in discovering causal connections, expressing them in laws and making predictions. Both hoped that empirical evidence would provide the lawlike explanations of human life and society by such inferred mechanisms of causality.

In the late nineteenth century in German philosophy and

sociology a series of arguments were put forward to separate the social and natural sciences and counter the naturalism inherent in both Hume and Freud. This approach was linked with a creative period of social science in Germany, specifically in the work of Max Weber (1949), Heinrich Rickert (1986), and Georg Simmel (1980). Many of these positions and arguments made a surprising return later in the twentieth century in historicist Marxism and, following Wittgenstein, the interest of philosophy of language in social anthropology and theories of interpretation (Lukács 1971; Sartre 1960; Winch 1958; Apel 1967). In all these cases the impulse came from a dissatisfaction with accounts of explanation, cause, and lawfulness in the natural sciences. I have discussed in more detail the philosophical issues that arose around the idea of historicism, which is a vital case within this larger debate (D'Amico 1988). But for purposes of this chapter I will follow the theme of the volume and take the position of postmodernism as the latest version of suspicion toward naturalism and its optimistic view of the social sciences, as that is found in modern adaptations of Freud's physiological realism or Hume's empiricism. I have no idea if there really is such a position as "postmodernism" but I have culled certain conclusions from Jean-François Lyotard's *The Postmodern Condition* (1984). There appear to be three characteristic themes or postulates which are meant to defeat naturalism and the identification of the natural and social sciences.

First, there is what might be called the anti-Platonist view of classification. In more than one dialogue Plato has Socrates contrast the skilled butcher who cuts the meat along the articulation of the bone with those who hack at random. The point appears to be that there *is* a proper way to "carve up" reality, and not just any system of distinctions will do. Classifications are inherent, intrinsic, and natural. In rejecting such a view in the name of the conventional, arbitrary, and perhaps pragmatic schemes of concepts and classifications, postmodernists share the spirit of the very sophism Plato hoped to stamp out. Specifically Lyotard implies that we separate "narrative and scientific knowledge," because the instrumental or practical success of the sciences provides a basis for agreement and consensus that cannot occur in the narrative accounts, for which Lyotard offers the relativity of "language games."[2]

Second, postmodernism appears to be an anti-realist account of knowledge and science because it treats representation, correspondence, and reference as dependent on a conceptual framework or scheme. The notion that scientific theories strive to faithfully "picture" the world requires an account of representation which is theoretically neutral. But the ontological categories are embedded in the very accounts of reference in such a way that accounts of "likeness" shift historically and culturally and these shifts are not themselves ruled by convergence toward the most faithful replica of reality (Barnes 1982: Bloor 1983).

Third, postmodernsm also shares with ancient sophism a deep distrust of philosophy. There are, it is held, no foundational arguments, no justifications or grounds for knowledge, and thus no principles or guides for theory other than heuristics. Fundamental distinctions between a narrative and an explanation, or rhetoric and logic, are as relative to categorical frameworks as ontology. Thus the function of philosophy to legitimate knowledge through reflection *must* fail. Lyotard expresses this final point by saying that postmodernism is "incredulity toward metanarratives."

Do these arguments justify a separation of the natural and social sciences? It is not my aim to simply show that these concerns were anticipated in the past. What does seem to me a confusion is that these arguments are often taken as good reasons for abandoning certain research strategies in the social sciences. Apparently these arguments, or ones like it, are given as "justifications" for dismissing the collection of data, for dismissing certain heuristic guides for theory, for abandoning quantitative techniques, or dismissing attempts at formulating convering-law explanations. I think these conclusions are mistaken, even without debating the case for each particular theoretical strategy or technique.

Before explaining why I do not think these arguments have the impact that some think they have on the social sciences, and quite appart from the fact that they continue to play a role in philosophical disputes, I want to try to make clearer what is behind the postmodern attack. Oddly enough, many of these moves can be found in Rudolf Carnap's late and influential restatement of positivist doctrine, "Empiricism, semantics and ontology" (1956). Carnap's central argument is that to believe in the existence of theoretical entities is nothing more than to use a "linguistic framework." Carnap shows how conventionalism and empiricism are compatible, and why the arguments for the conventional dimension of knowledge (which one finds echoed in postmodernism) are fully integrated within a thoroughgoing empiricism.

Conventionalism holds that necessary truths, and specifically mathematical and logical propositions, are true in virtue of conventions about symbolic systems. As an extension, Carnap holds that any set of entities or ontology is a "way of speaking," a provisional and revisable set of ontological commitments. Language makes the representation of its world possible and there is no one correct representation.

Any sufficiently rich theory in the natural or social sciences uses theoretical terms, or postulates unobservable entities and mechanisms. Some have assumed, like Freud, that some procedure for experimentation and confirmation of such "posits" is all that is needed to conclude that in fact they do exist. But such evidence is frequently challenged or rejected because empirical evidence is compatible with different theoretical devices and rarely resolves deep disputes about which theoretical picture is correct. How should such questions be resolved?

Carnap suggests that there are actually two questions here concealed in the syntax of our natural languages. First, there is an "internal question" which is relatively trivial. It is answered by following whatever rules and procedures are of necessity part of the linguistic framework in use. But second, there is what Carnap calls an "external question" concerning whether that given linquistic framework is the correct one for representing the world. Carnap considers the second question illicit.

Consider, for example, people coming to doubt their belief in the commonsense objects of everyday life after studying some modern physics. They would experience what Wilfrid Sellars calls a clash between the "manifest image" of everyday life and the "scientific image" of the world. Which account is correct? What they would wonder is whether such everyday objects as chairs or trees are real. They would wonder if the macro-objects of their everyday life were *really* just fuzzy blurs of wave-particle dualities.

According to Carnap's analysis we can understand this questioning of representation in two ways. The "thing language" of everyday life has clear guidelines and procedures for determining whether something exists. Thus if a child asks, "do unicorns exist?" you understand the question as meaning do they exist in the way horses exist. Like any linguistic framework, there will be rules for not only correctly formulating statements but for semantically linking statements with what constitutes a good or reliable observation of a normal-size object, and how to use these reports to confirm or disconfirm hypotheses about such objects. With modern physics we shift to another language, designed for wholly different purposes, and with quite different rules, criteria, or procedures for determining whether the entities it designates exist or not. But these languages, while designed for the purposes they serve, cannot be used in each other's contexts and for each other's purposes. For Carnap, then, postulating the existence of entities is a rather trivial act, and is certainly not a mysterious achievement. Conflicting ontologies should not cause problems, since the domain of existents follows from and alters with linguistic practice.

> The concept of reality occurring in these internal questions is an empirical, scientific, non-metaphysical concept. To recognize something as a real thing or event means to succeed in incorporating it into the system of things at a particular space–time position so that it fits together with other things recognized as real, according to the rules of the framework.   (*Carnap 1956: 207*)

Only philosophers, suggests Carnap, ask whether there is a way to fix existence prior to or independent of any such linguistic frameworks. The philosopher asks whether this entire framework is correct. Does it *really* correspond to reality? In Carnap's very "set-up" of the problem one senses his strategy. The second question is predicated on denying Carnap's conventionalist strategy about ontology and linguistic frameworks. It assumes that there are criteria for determining the correctness of reference and designation apart from the syntax and semantics of a language. In other words, the external question assumes representational realism and rejects empiricism. If we argue about ontology we are granting legitimacy to the external question. But Carnap's point is to show that the external question is not answerable.

> It [the external question] cannot be resolved because it is framed in the wrong way. To be real in the scientific sense means to be an element of the system; hence this concept cannot be meaningfully applied to the system itself. Those who raise the question of the reality of the thing world itself have perhaps in mind not a theoretical question, as their formulation seems to suggest, but rather a practical question, a matter of a practical decision concerning the structure of our language. We have to make the choice whether or not to accept and use the forms of expression in the framework in question. (*ibid.*)

If we call the external question "metaphysical" and the internal question "empirical, scientific," then Carnap's point is that the metaphysical question is either reformulated into an empirical, scientific question or not. The metaphysical questions that cannot be reformulated into empirical, decidable questions (the relatively trivial internal questions) are not theoretical or cognitive claims at all. They are not true or false claims about the world but are constitutive claims; they express a practical preference for a certain ontological framework, or in a pedagogical way support the use of a certain framework.

Frameworks, for Carnap, encompass everything from astrology to quantum mechanics and humors to viruses. One can see how Kuhnian historicism, in which science is the history of frameworks which change for no internal reason, and Feyerabend's recent epistemological anarchism concerning all judgments about ontology or methodology are direct outgrowths of Carnap's framework relativism. In calling these frameworks "linguistic" Carnap raised, however, some difficult questions that have spawned a large and complex philosophical debate.[3] I will ignore that for now, since I am using Carnap's clearer formulation, even if it fails ultimately to separate these questions, simply to show why the postmodern postulates do not constitute unique problems for the social sciences.

Carnap understands language to be a "tool" which we replace or reinvent as our needs and purposes change and therefore opposes any "naturalism" in which categories or concepts are treated as inherently fixed and determinate.

> In my view, a language, whether artificial or natural, is an instrument that may be replaced or modified according to our needs, like another other instrument. For the naturalists, ordinary language seems to have an essentially fixed character and therefore to be basically indispensable, just like our body with its ordans, to which we may add accessories like eyeglasses, hearing aids . . . However, a natural language is not an unchangeable function of our body, but something we have learned; therefore we can replace it by another language
>
> (*Carnap 1963: 938–9*)

The conventionalist stratagem is linked to the sophistic position that philosophers can ultimately provide no argument for or against frameworks. All philosophy can do is recommend or counsel on practical, aesthetic, heuristic, or pedagogical grounds the adoption or rejection of some constitutive framework (psycho-physical dualism, for example). Only residual Platonism questions whether ontological commitments should be so treated as mere conventional agreements. While "turn right on red" seems safely treated as a cultural rule or prohibition of the conventional sort (since the color or side of the road are a matter of agreement), the statement "a human pregnancy takes nine months" is a matter of fact no matter what numbering system, dating system, or theory of human physiology and sexuality. It is that kind of "matter of fact" that the realist wants as a "natural kind" to which all categories must conform.

In this debate Carnap is like Hume since he wants to demonstrate that we need not worry about whether our "conjunctions" are natural and thus somehow inherent in the world. We cannot distinguish by evidence whether concepts are in the world or in the framework. Thus there is no point in wondering if there is a matter of fact which transcends all theories and frameworks. For our purposes, then, Carnapian framework relativism is characteristic of all knowledge, not just knowledge of cultural conventions.

The social sciences would have to consider an alternative model of explanation if it could be shown that certain theoretical categories in the natural sciences converged on a standard of truth or replication in the external, realist sense. But if those expectations or standards are illicit, then we change frameworks in just the same way as we change from a pocketknife to a table saw, to use Carnap's analogy, when our standards of cutting change. But there is no single standard of "cutting" and thus no need for social science to counter its failure to live up to this standard. Beyond cultural and practical preferences, there is no correct tool of all inquiry.

How can this approach be helpful? I will turn to some well-known arguments for the separation of the social and natural sciences. First, it is held that the social sciences are unique because their object of study is not a "matter of fact" but some humanly constituted regularity. The social sciences study cultural artifacts, rules, prohibitions, institutions, economies, constitutions, customs, and decision procedures. But these "objects" do not fall within the methods of the natural sciences. Further, the social sciences produce explanations of these structures which of necessity include citing human purposes, intentions, motives, and understandings and which once again distinguish these narrative-type explanations from those in the natural sciences.

Karl Popper (1972) has defended a three-level ontology that helps clarify this kind of issue. He divides "things" in the world into what he calls "worlds 1, 2, and 3." World 1 encompasses all states of material things and objects which would range from trees to neutrinos. Popper's classification does not resolve questions of scientific change, nor does it defend scientific ontologies against commonsense ones, so the entities that inhabit world 1 are not rigidly defined. Popper's point is to distinguish these object-states from world 2, which includes all mental states such as beliefs, intentions, fears, motives, and feelings. At this point Popper sounds like a traditional dualist separating mental and physical phenomena, but Popper's controversial recommendation is to distinguish both worlds 1 and 2 from a world 3 of what he calls the content of libraries, theories, narratives, computer tapes, or records of all sorts but also the kind of abstract objectivity of constitutions, legal systems, and problem situations; not as these contents are thought in world 2, but as this content exists objectively and independently of all mental states and all material records. Popper argues that we should maintain the autonomy of each world and not reduce the abstract world 3 to either world 1 or world 2. Numbers, for example, are neither physical objects nor are they merely mental states; they are, even as the products of human beings, autonomous objectivities. Worlds 1, 2, and 3 do interact because subjective mental states, such as intention, can become "embodied" in world 3 objects as the content of letters, agendas, or propositions, all of which in their status as material records are world 1 physical objects. Finally world 3 objectivities can materially change world 1 and, in proof of their autonomy, they may produce changes neither expected nor intended by a world 2 beliefs, expectations, or desires.

We see now the problem with creating a distinctive status for the social sciences because they study world 3 objects. Popper has shown the unreliability of two naturalist or realist assumptions. First, that if something is not a physical object then it must be a mental state. Second, that whatever is not material or physical is not objective. It is possible in his view to make objective statements about abstract objects. Further, there can be objective knowledge about quite abstract and non-material objectivities which is not merely an expression of private thoughts or feelings. Therefore social scientists are in no more a compromised or unique position than a physicist studying a hypothetical, theoretical construction such as a gamma particle, or a biologist moving between a complex problem situation and the cellular material under the microscope (in which both the use of the microscope and the preparation of the material under the slide require theoretical decisions and a framework). The point is not that there is no difference between world 3 objects, but that all inquiry involves worlds 1, 2, and 3, so that there are no grounds for treating the study of cultural objects as a special problem.

World 3 objectivity has led to a fascination with interpretation theory. The reason is that when an anthropologist wants to "explain" some cultural object, what the anthropologist is expected to do is first interpret or understand the whole cultural context. In effect the anthropologist views the artifact as the embodiment of a world 2 mental state, such as a purpose, intention, or value, and then must somehow determine whether or not the society studied also gives that meaning or interpretation to the object. Of course this heuristic is controversial. Many social scientists would hold that the explanation of face-painting or suicide is autonomous from the subjective reasons or thoughts members of the society may or may not have about these practices. While there may be good reasons for stressing that like any inquiry this kind of research takes skill, experience, and the theoretical equivalent of a "green thumb," that in no way shows that the anthropologist is theoretically incapable of making objective and decidable claims about the cultural object. If we recall Carnap's advice on "bracketing" our ontological assumptions we will remember that our inquiry has not become indeterminate just because the object studied is unlike a rock or chemical reaction. In other words, we can distinguish between the descriptive statements that we are investigating from the recommendations or prescription about which heuristic to follow. If Carnap is right, the social scientists are in the same boat as everyone else in having no guarantee about prescriptive or constitutive recommendations for empirical inquiry.

The world 3 distinction also shows how social processes can be "lawful" in the sense that, as Hume and Freud tried to show, human behavior can exhibit a necessity and "compulsiveness" as materially embodied. Of course Popper's ontology is meant as a rejection of Hume's reduction of reasons to physical necessities, but both views agree that in neither society nor nature do we freely constitute our world out of our mental states. Some social scientists and philosophers have been tempted to take literally the notion derived from Vico that humans "make" their culture and can know it from the inside, whereas nature, which is not made by "man," can be known only as it appears. But we do experience the inability to control the objectivity of social action as the unintended consequences of our actions just as we experience the externality of physical nature. The social world is a fabric of unplanned and unforeseen consequences and therefore has just the same kind of independence from individual thought and will as the physiology of cells. It seems to me that Durkheim's argument about "social facts" was precisely that they be treated as "thing-like" for the social sciences because social facts are not simply the result of individual intentions and decisions.

The old Windelband, Rickert, and Simmel idea of a distinction between the nomothetic and idiographic sciences can also be handled in this manner. The original idea is that the natural sciences deal in lawlike generalities that do not apply to individual cases, whereas the social sciences are only interested in singular, particular events. The point is obscure because these authors usually had very naive views about natural laws, and because they do not make clear if the difference is merely a matter of access to information. In other words, the natural sciences achieve what they call nomothetic accounts by the use of, for example, *ceteris paribus* clauses or limits on initial conditions. Popper, in accepting this view that the laws of the sciences are hypothetical conjectures, argued that the problem in the social sciences is that the laws turn out to be trivial and relatively uninteresting. But to argue, against the traditional view, that the social sciences are fundamentally incapable of discovering laws is to say something about the nature of the object studied. I have already covered part of that problem above, but in addition this objection is wrong about what information the social scientist seeks. If a sociologist studies unemployment rates and explores hypotheses about its relationship to social policy decisions, voting, and population movements, at no point does she or he care about having this knowledge about Norman Skolimowski of Chicago, Illinois, if that is what the original authors meant by a "particular." Popper could be correct that the laws will prove trivial in that they will all amount to nothing more than "all things being equal, battles are won by the more powerful opponent." But that does not establish an *a priori*, conceptual limit to the idea of unlawfulness, prediction, or explanation in the social sciences. Further, it does not show that another model of explanation is necessary. Even a narrative contains implicit lawful claims and generalizations. If the idiographic position were taken seriously, each occurrence would be unique and unreproducible so that it could neither be represented nor restated. All one could do is silently point at the event as it goes on.

Some social scientists, and their philosophical fellow travelers, actually say that the job of the social scientist is not description of social processes but the recommendation, evaluation, or prescription of some framework. In effect, they identify the function of the social sciences with what Carnap considered the practical questions of traditional philosophy. They perceive social science as a kind of praxis or advocacy either of some theoretical approach or of some policy. Some are even prepared to embrace the view that such advocacy is non-cognitive and therefore rhetorical and pedagogical. It follows from all this that the social sciences are not genuinely sciences at all.

I think Peter Winch leans toward this idea and he views evaluative statements as inherently undecidable (Winch 1972: 151–70). Lyotard seems to agree, since he holds that narratives cannot be universalized. Without going into this equally large issue it can be pointed out that even if there is an irreducibly prescriptive element in the social sciences (which would also be present in the natural sciences, according to Carnap's picture of framework relativism), and even if the prescription partly defines what is to count as empirical, that still leaves decidable problems for the social sciences. Again the undecidable status of grounds and reasons is not a problem solely of the social sciences, even if social scientists try to tackle these questions directly.

Also prescriptions can always be reformulated in such way as to be conditional and therefore empirically investigated. As Carl Hempel argued (1980), you can test values by formulating them as means–ends judgments. "*If* our children are to be happy, emotionally secure, creative individuals rather than guilt ridden and troubled souls *then* it is better to raise them in a permissive than in a restrictive fashion." In this way the prescription is restated as a universal or probable means–ends relationship, which is capable of an empirical test. Of course that test would not prove that we should raise those kinds of children. The ultimate or categorical value is clearly not testable, since it does not describe a state of affairs but asserts an unconditional standard. Therfore, even the introduction of an evaluative or prescriptive dimension into the social sciences, which the medical sciences share, for example, does not bar empirical inquiry, though once again the prescriptive standard is not itself empirical.

Perhaps a more famous and complex expression of some of the above points is found in Jürgen Habermas's now famous account of "human interests" at the base of knowledge. The natural and social sciences are "transcendentally constituted" by different interests; the interest for technical control in the case of the physical sciences and the interest for communicative understanding in the case of the social sciences. These contrastive constitutive frameworks bring about correspondingly different object-domains, modes of inquiry, and cognitive standards. There is a good deal of questionable philosophical baggage in this account that social scientists need not immediately concern themselves with, except to realize that even Habermas is now doubtful about the feasibility of this version of transcendentalism. Also one should note that it bears some similarity to Carnap's framework model but with a more mysterious guarantee about the "correctness" of specific frameworks for specific types of inquiry.

The point is that for purposes of determining the character of social science research Habermas's more sophisticated account of a distinctive status for those sciences is rather innocuous. Habermas does not clarify why "empirical, analytic" inquiry is exclusive to the natural sciences. Since the framework supervenes over what is defined as the domain of empirical evidence, this allows for a shift in the object-domains and empirical procedures. Habermas (1971) seems to adopt, without much argument, an instrumentalist view that constrains research in the physical sciences to what is operationally defined and useful. But the domain of empirical research can be more broadly conceived and need not be tied so closely to instrumental criteria. In effect, the methodological heuristics that emerge from seeking communicative understanding in the social sciences allow for claims that are empirical. Of course this weaker argument does not demonstrate which framework's empirical domain is correct, but Habermas's transcendental argument does not seem likely to supply such a proof either.

The most interesting problem, which I have left for last, is whether the social theories themselves enter into inquiry in the social sciences in a way that they do not in the natural sciences. Does this self-reflexivity constitute the crucial and purely conceptual difference between these sciences? In this view the point is that theoretical change in the natural sciences leaves the object of inquiry, such as a chemical reaction, indifferent and unaffected by the new theoretical categories. But in the social sciences different theories literally change the reality of social life. The notion is that by successfully studying criminals with "labeling theory" one is doing more than describing pre-existing "natural kinds," called criminals, but changing our very conception of that social reality. Though I think this is an important insight, again I think Carnap allows us to handle this point. We should distinguish the constituting of the domain of "objects" from the descriptive success, utility, or applicability of the theoretical framework. What a social scientist is noting with this point is the need to defend labeling theory against alternative accounts of criminality. That will often involve pedagogical, rhetorical, and practical appeals, but we should not think that in having the flexibility to change such fundamental categories we change our reality, such that it means the social sciences study a unique and mysterious ontological instability.

NOTES

1 For the argument against psychoanalysis as a non-falsifiable theory, the classic statement is in Popper 1973. The argument for choosing a simpler explanation is outlined in Timpanaro 1976.
2 Michel Foucault (1972) suggests the link between these arguments and ancient sophism's anti-Platonism. See also Nussbaum 1985: 129–39.
3 The attack on this view was launched with Quine's "On Carnap's views on ontology" (1966) and his *Ontological Relativity* (1969).

REFERENCES

Apel, Karl-Otto 1967: *Analytic Philosophy of Language and the Geisteswissenschaften*. Dordrecht: Reidel.

Barnes, Barry 1982: *T. S. Kuhn and Social Science*. New York: Columbia University Press.

Bloor, David 1983: *Wittgenstein: A Social Theory of Knowledge*. New York: Columbia University Press.

Carnap, Rudolf 1956: "Empiricism, semantics and ontology," in *Meaning and Necessity*. Chicago: University of Chicago Press.

Carnap, Rudolf 1963: *Philosophy of Rudolf Carnap*, ed. Paul Arthur Schilpp. La Salle, Ill.: Open Court.

D'Amico, Robert 1988: *Historicism and Knowledge*. New York: Routledge.

Foucault, Michel 1972 [1969]: *The Archaeology of Knowledge*, tr. A. M. Sheridan Smith. New York: Pantheon.

Freud, Sigmund 1960: *Psychopathology of Everyday Life*. tr. Alan Tyson. New York: Norton.

Habermas, Jürgen 1971: *Knowledge and Human Interests*, tr. Jeremy Shapiro. Boston: Beacon Press.

Hempel, Carl 1980: "Science and human values," in E. D. Klemke, Robert Hollinger and A. David Kline (eds), *Readings in Philosophy of Science*. Buffalo, NY: Prometheus Books.

Hume, David 1977: *An Enquiry Concerning Human Understanding*. Indianapolis: Hackett Publishing.

Lukács, Georg 1971: *History and Class Consciousness*, tr. Rodney Livingstone. Cambridge, Mass.: MIT Press.

Lyotard, Jean-François 1984 [1979]: *The Postmodern Condition: A Report on Knowledge*, tr. G. Bennington and B. Massumi. Minneapolis: University of Minnesota Press.

Nussbaum, Martha 1985: "Sophistry about conventions," *New Literary History*, 17/1 (Autumn).

Popper, Karl 1972: "Epistomology without a knowing subject" and "On the theory of objective mind," in *Objective Mind: An Evolutionary Epistemology*. Oxford: Clarendon Press.

Popper, Karl 1973: *Conjectures and Refutations*. London: Routledge.

Quine, W. V. O. 1966: *The Ways of Paradox*. New York: Random House.

Quine, W. V. O. 1969: *Ontological Relativity*. New York: Columbia University Press.

Rickert, Heinrich 1986: *The Limits of Concept Formation in Natural Science*, tr. Guy Oakes. Cambridge: Cambridge University Press.

Sartre, Jean-Paul 1960: *Critique de la raison dialectique*. Paris: Gallimard.

Simmel, Georg 1980: *Essays on Interpretation in Social Science*, ed. Guy Oakes. Totowa, NJ: Rowman & Littlefield.

Taylor, Charles 1985: "Interpretation and the sciences of man," in *Philosophy and the Human Sciences*. New York: Cambridge University Press.

Timpanaro, Sebastiano 1976: *Freudian Slip: Psychoanalysis and Textual Criticism*, tr. Kate Soper. London: New Left Books.

Weber, Max 1949: "'Objectivity' in social science and social policy" and "Critical studies in the logic of the cultural sciences," in E. Shils (ed.), *The Methodology of the Social Sciences*. Glencoe, Ill.: Free Press.

Winch, Peter 1958: *The Idea of a Social Science and its Relation to Philosophy*. London: Routledge.
Winch, Peter, 1972: *Ethics and Action*. London: Routledge.

6

The Promise of Positivism

Jonathan Turner

It is somewhat unfashionable these days to proclaim oneself a positivist, especially in social theory circles where we have been inundated with European "sophistication" – phenomenology, hermeneutics, structuralism, critical theory, and the like. Indeed, social theory is now a kind of philosophical debating society where knowledgeable and erudite scholars discuss just about everything except the operative dynamics of the social universe. Indeed, this book on the viability of general theory would seem preposterous in the natural sciences and even in the more mature social sciences.

As one who sees himself as a natural scientist, therefore, I am uncomfortable with the necessarily philosophical nature of this volume. My bias is that philosophizing is best left to the philosophers – they are certainly better trained for it and they certainly need the work. Thus, as I address the prospects of positivism, I confess my philosophical naivety. I am not embarrassed by this fact, since I would hypothesize an inverse relationship between philosophical sophistication and capacity to explain how the social world works. Practicing scientists have a very different agenda than the philosophers and historians of ideas who currently dominate theory circles. Nonetheless, in my own simple way, let me outline what positivism is, what its critics seem to find so objectionable, and what positivistic theory proposes as an alternative to the smug cynicism, relativism, and solipsism that has infected sociological theorizing in recent decades.

WHAT IS POSITIVISM?

Auguste Comte's vision of positivism was to regard "all phenomena as subject to invariable natural *Laws*" (1830: 5; italics in original). His ideal was, of course, the physics of his time; and he argued that the best illustration of a scientific law is "the case of the doctrine of Gravitation" (ibid.: 6). Moreover, he was extremely wary of causal and functional (final cause) analysis, because these tended to direct attention to either the empirical sequence of events leading to a phenomenon of interest or to its empirical consequences in a particular situation. For Comte, concern with causality pushes one to historical or empirical description, whereas positivism seeks to uncover the "relations of succession and resemblance" of invariant, as opposed to unique, properties of the universe.

Comte did not always follow his own advice, and later he abandoned much of the detached value-neutrality advocated in his early work. Moreover, while he is clear about the need to "pursue the discovery . . . of Laws, with a view to reducing them to the smallest possible number," he was never very clear about what these laws should look like. Phrases like "natural relations of succession and resemblance" are notably vague, with the result that subsequent interpreters of positivism have portrayed it in somewhat different terms. Some (e.g. Carnap 1966; Hempel 1965) have advocated a "logical" positivism in which the vehicle of explanation is "logical deductions" from the law (*explanans*) to a set of empirical phenomena (*explanandum*). Others (e.g. Popper 1959, 1969) have added the criterion of "falsifiability," arguing that explanation involves repeated efforts to disprove a general law with empirical data. Still others would impose the criterion of "predictability," viewing explanation as laws which predict what will be found in empirical tests. And more recently, positivism has been associated with "raw empiricism" and "induction" in which mounds of data are first collected, regularities observed, and laws extracted. Comte would turn over in his grave on this last use of the label "positivism" for, as he emphasized, data without theory are a "great hindrance" to the development of science (Comte 1830: 242).

What, then, is positivism? My views relax, somewhat, the criteria of deductive rigor, prediction, and falsification, while rejecting any assumption that positivism is an inductive enterprise. Moreover, contrary to Comte's concerns over causality and David Hume's assertion that the cause of phenomena can never really be known, I think that we must come to grips with the question of causality, even over the objections of the philosophers. Let me elaborate on each of these points.

First, most advocates of "axiomatic" theory are imposing an unrealistic criterion on positivism. Much of what constitutes a "deductive system" in science is, in reality, "folk-reasoning" in which verbally stated laws are used to interpret a set of empirical events. For example, the synthetic theory of evolution is, for the most part, a verbally stated set of ideas which are invoked to explain a wide range of phenomena. Thus, it is unlikely that the deductions in sociological theory will be like those in physics, where the mathematics can be used as the calculus for deductive activity. At times, we may be able to state relations mathematically, but our deductions will rarely be in terms of the calculus of mathematics, or some other system of formal logic. We should, therefore, be content with laws that are stated precisely and with juxtapositions of the law with data in a way that seems reasonable and justified. Obviously, what is "reasonable and justified" will be subject to negotiation and organizational politics, but this is true for even the most precise formulations in physics. So we should not get terribly upset about the issue (more on this later).

Second, the criterion of prediction is also unrealistic for any science which cannot test most of its laws in experimental situations, or under circumstances where extraneous forces can be eliminated or, alternatively, known and measured. I am not advocating retreat into the *ceteris paribus* clause, but rather, a simple recognition that, most of the time, tests of theories will come in natural empirical systems where many unknown, countervailing, and intersecting forces are at work, making precise predictions difficult. Such is often the case in science –

geology and earthquake predictions being one example – and the failure of precise prediction does not obviate the scientific nature of theory-testing. The real question is this: does a theory increase understanding of how and why (note, not necessarily "when") empirical phenomena operate? Again, there is always organizational and personal politics involved in what is defined and accepted as "understanding," but, as noted above, sociology and the social sciences in general are not different from the hard sciences on this score.

Third, the criterion of falsification assumes that theories are stated with a high degree of precision, that the calculus from *explanans* to *explanandum* is exact, and that extraneous factors can be controlled. Otherwise, it would be hard to know if a law is really refuted, since imprecision in formulating the law, informal use of a deductive calculus, or effects from extraneous variables can all be used as justifications to "save" a law from refutation. Moreover, as Kuhn (1970) argues, the politics of a science often work to explain away anomalies and efforts at the falsification of laws, at least for a time. The criterion of falsification is not irrelevant, however, for data must be used to assess the plausibility of laws; and in the end, those laws that lose plausibility in the face of the data will be jettisoned. But this process of falsification is not a mechanical lock-step procedure, as some appear to imply, but rather a more fluid process of negotiating and assessing plausibility. Of course, at times one can make definitive tests, but this is much more rarely possible in the social sciences than in the hard sciences.

Fourth, positivism is concerned with assessing theory with data, but assessment is not an inductive process. The goal is to generate theory first, and then assess its empirical merits. Naturally, knowledge of empirical events can often help generate theory, but theories rarely just emerge from data sets. Once immersed in data, one rarely rises above them to see the invariant properties of the universe that they illustrate. Abduction, or the simultaneous use of abstract concepts and data, is often involved in generating the creative ideas of theory (Willer and Webster 1970), but the goal of positivism is to use this creative synergy to posit abstract theoretical principles that are, in theory at least, testable. And by "testable," I do not advocate only the use of quantitative methods; at times, ethnographic or historical methods will be more appropriate or, alternatively, all that is possible. Positivism is thus extremely hostile to data collection for its own sake, to quantitative versus qualitative oppositions, and to any activity that assumes "the data speak for themselves." For as Comte observed (1830: 242), "no real observation of any kind of phenomenon is possible, except as far as it is first directed, and finally interpreted, by some theory."

Finally, the question of causality cannot be ignored, if only because Western thought in general, as well as specific engineering applications of theoretical ideas, encourage thinking in terms of cause and effect. In some ultimate philosophical sense, perhaps, cause cannot be known, but we can nonetheless conceptualize forces in the universe as affecting each other in patterned and, where possible to assess, causally connected ways. For properties of the universe are "connected" – no matter how mysterious in some ultimate sense these connections are for the philosophers. And we can conveniently see these connections as causal, leaving the agonizing over the issue to the philosophers. More importantly, if we entertain the existence of "cause," it becomes possible to model more complex configurations of forces in the universe which, otherwise, could not be parsimoniously stated as a theoretical law. Indeed, as I will argue later, the construction of robust causal models can facilitate the development of abstract laws.

Although my remarks thus far could be construed as a critique of positivism, I am arguing more directly that much of the criticism of positivism and the possibilities for a natural science of society is based upon a highly caricatured vision of the "hard" sciences. At times, as is the case in physics, there is a high degree of mathematical precision involved; indeed, the logic of mathematics *per se* can become a theory-generating force. But most natural science consists of a mixture of very precise (mathematical) laws, looser verbal formulations, exact experimental tests, field assessments of plausibility, and efforts at practical application of theoretical ideas. Such can be the case for social science. That is, we can generate precise laws, mixed with less precise formulations; we can assess the empirical plausibility of our laws, although not with the same capacity for controls as in some (though not all) natural sciences; and we can use our laws in projects involving (and let me say the tabooed words here) "social engineering." If this seems like only a metaphor of natural science, I would suggest that those making the charge have a profound misunderstanding of the substance and organization of the "hard" sciences.

I have argued only in general terms, but I will return with more specific suggestions for what positivistic theory should look like, and be about. Before doing so, however, let me briefly review some of the criticisms of the position that I am advocating.

CRITICISMS OF POSITIVISTIC SOCIOLOGY

In a sense, I view philosophical "discourse," to use the currently fashionable term, as a waste of time. Such discourse pulls us into philosophical controversies, while rarely providing insight into how people behave, interact, and organize. Nonetheless, my position can be better understood by addressing some of the questions raised by the critics. I will catalog these criticisms under the labels (1) phenomenological solipsism, (2) hermeneutical dualism, (3) historical particularism, (4) critical discourse, and (5) scientific politics. There are more points of attack, of course, and various versions and elaborations of these five positions. But this listing is sufficient for my purposes, especially since others in this volume will devote their energies along these lines.

Phenomenological solipsism   The crude version of this criticism is that all conceptualizations of the world "out there" are filtered through acts of human consciousness and are, therefore, reifications. The extreme form of this argument is that nothing really "exists out there," independent of consciousness. Hence, exact knowledge of "nature" is not possible or, at the very least, understanding of the dynamics of consciousness should precede analysis of the external world. This line of criticism is equally true for the hard sciences; and while there is a legitimate point to be made here, where does it get us? It takes us to a corner to contemplate our navel, I would suggest. And more significantly, since the natural sciences seem to know a lot about the physical and biological universe "out there" without undue agonizing over the distorting effects of cognitions, we would do well to ignore this criticism and avoid the excessively contemplative program it suggests.

Hermeneutical dualisms   The old issues of the *Methodenstreit* have been resurrected in the assertion that there is a fundamental dualism between the natural and social sciences. The social world is symbolic in that actors engage in representations and interpretations of their situations, whereas the natural world is not. Indeed, as Giddens (1984) has emphasizes, social sciences evidence a "double hermeneutic" in that the topics and subjects of social science inquiry can use the findings of science to restructure the nature of their universe, thereby obviating the "timeless" character of social scientific laws. Hence, all that is possible for theorists is to construct broad sensitizing schemes that will, in the end, become irrelevant as active agents reconstruct the fundamental nature of the social universe.

While the capacity of agents in the social world to use social science laws cannot be denied, my sense is that this would not obviate sociological laws. Rather, the use of laws will help validate and confirm them. In fact, the criterion of a plausible law would be that no matter how much agents may try, the fundamental processes denoted by the law cannot be altered. Critics of positivism like Giddens mount their critique on a basic confusion between empirical generalization (a summary of specific empirical events at a particular time and place) and law (a statement of relation between invariant processes that transcend a particular time and historical setting). By viewing empirical generalizations as laws, they can then confidently assert that laws are not immutable, since empirical events described by the "law" are always changing and in flux by acts of human agency. I would argue that these changes and fluctuations can be understood by more abstract laws, but as long as critics can mix the empirical with the theoretical, they can mount their hermeneutic soap box and proclaim that general positivistic theory is impossible. Such a position takes us nowhere; it reduces sociology to trivial empirical descriptions, philosophical scheme-building, and transitory interpretations of this or that empirical event.

In my view, the symbolic dimensions of the social universe

are no less "natural" than the properties of the physical and biological universes; and there is no reason why active agents' use of knowledge about these symbolic dimensions should be any more successful in altering the fundamental properties of the social universe than they have been in changing the basic properties of the physical and biological realms. True, theoretical knowledge can be used to change empirical settings – from bombing a city with nuclear weapons to reorganizing a bureaucracy – but the laws of physics and sociology are not thereby obviated. If anything, their plausibility is supported (however tragically in the first case).

Historical particularism The historicist argument is often couched in the hermeneutical terms described above, but it has unique elements that should be addressed separately. The extreme hermeneutical version of this position is that humans are constantly remaking their history, and hence, it is not possible to have laws that are universal across time and context. Analyses of historical and empirical events must, therefore, be couched in the particular terms of the time. At the other extreme is the argument that historical periods may evidence processes which can suggest laws for the epoch. Marx's analysis of capitalism might represent one version of this argument, since he isolates laws that can be used to describe its internal contradictions that would lead to its transformation. Somewhere between these extremes falls much of the current revival of historical sociology, which seems a curious mixture of dense empirical description, conceptual interpretations (the generality and universality of which are rarely specified), and conceptual scheme-building (e.g. Mann 1986; Wallerstein 1974), where it is unclear again whether or not invariant processes are being postulated.

I am far less hostile to historical analysis than either phenomenological and hermeneutic critics, because in most historical approaches there is an effort to say something about how the social universe operates, at least for some (typically unspecified) area and/or period of time. Yet, we must recognize that positivistic and historical explanations are fundamentally different modes of understanding the universe, making criticisms of one by the other somewhat inappropriate. Historical explanations are causal descriptions of sequences of empirical events (or classes of such events), whereas positivistic explanations are deductive, seeking to explain empirical events with abstract laws. The two kinds of explanation simply yield different kinds of knowledge; and while science usually seeks deductively organized theory, historical analysis serves other useful purposes. But, when historical sociologists insist that positivism is an inappropirate approach to sociological analysis because deductive explanation and scientific sociology are impossible, they have condemned sociology to a descriptive role – tracing sequences of events at particular times and places. Thus, they have made sociology redundant with history.

The descriptions of historians are, in my view, data that require further explanations with laws; and in fact, most of the laws of positivism will need to be assessed in light of longer-term historical data. Historical sociology can thus prove to be a valuable resource for positivism, even in the face of historians' hostility to a natural science of society. This hostility is based, I think, on a chauvinism about historical explanations that prevents historical sociologists from appreciating the difference between what they do and what science does. Thus, it is difficult to take too seriously criticism by those imposing an inappropriate criterion of explanation on positivism.

Critical discourse   Theorists such as Jürgen Habermas (1970) argue that the creation of knowledge reflects certain interests – in the case of positivism, interest in control and reproduction of the current status quo. For Habermas and other critical theorists, efforts to generalize from existing empirical conditions lead to the formulation of "laws" that implicitly assert the inevitability of such conditions. Positivism thus operates as a legitimating ideology in support of all those who have an interest in the status quo. For critical theorists, social science should expose the oppressive features of existing conditions, while encouraging discourse over less restrictive alternatives.

This line of argument misrepresents positivism as a science of induction in which generalizations are always made from existing empirical conditions, while rejecting Comte's view that sociological laws can be used to reconstruct society. In contrast to critical theorists' charges, the goal of positivism is not to abstract from what exists, but to understand empirical situations in terms of laws. These situations are not always current, for concepts of the historical past are often topics of investigation (presumably the critical theorist would then assert that positivism also legitimates the past). In any case, laws of positivist sociology need not support the present status quo (or the past); indeed, they could be used by critical theorists, or anyone, to reconstruct society, as Comte himself advocated. Moreover, as Comte argued, critique without knowledge about the operative dynamics of the universe can easily become an empty ideology for the impossible or, as is certainly the case with Habermas, present us with a hopelessly naive picture of society as a kind of academic debating society.

Much critical theory, in my view, is discourse among isolated and out-of-touch academics that bears very little relation to the operative dynamics of the universe (in fact, critical theory rather nicely legitimates the role of academics). Indeed, I suspect that if critical theorists ever had the power to impose their program, a new generation of critical theorists and revolutionaries would emerge to undo the damage wrought by the public debating society created by ivory-tower academics. I find it difficult, therefore, to accept criticism from a group of scholars whose interests are so well served by an academic system that lets them be safe and critical, never confronting for themselves sources of power and oppression in the real world. The goal of positivism is to understand the dynamics of power, inequality, and other basic properties of human organization (not to preach for their maintenance or elimination); for this reason I suspect that positivism might be the critical theorists' best friend, since it would provide them what they currently lack – an understanding of the operative dynamics of human organization – in pursuing their critique and program for reconstructing society.

Scientific politics   Thomas Kuhn's (1970) work initiated, or reinvigorated, the sociology of knowledge in which the organizational, professional, and political processes influencing the production of scientific knowledge are examined. Many others have joined this line of analysis (e.g. Fuchs 1986; Whitley 1984) and have, I think, produced interesting works. Indeed, such works usually employ, at least implicitly, many laws of human organization, and as a consequence these studies of science represent a good source of data to assess the plausibility of laws on human organization. But this discovery that science is like any other human endeavor – that is, it is subject to the same laws as other patterns of human organization – has often adopted a rather extreme critique of science: if scientific knowledge is subject to political, professional, and organizational forces, the "objectivity" of such knowledge is questionable; and, what is more, the self-correcting character of this knowledge (through conjectures and refutations) is highly suspect.

This critique makes a good point, and then carries it too far. It should hardly be surprising to a positivist, who views all action and organization as subject to invariant laws, that science enjoys no privileged position. However, what the critics ignore is the fact that, in the long run and despite the political, organizational, and professional constraints involved, the knowledge produced by science is the most isomorphic representation of the "world out there." The engineering applications of abstract principles should be sufficient to indicate that scientific knowledge is not all negotiated politics.

It is true, no doubt, that the research problems, methods, and, at times, the theories of science are circumscribed by the professional structure of scientific organizations (Whitley 1984; Fuchs and Turner 1986); but over the long run, theories are subject to tests that increase or decrease their plausibility as explanations. No other idea system has this same capacity; and as the sociological version of science, positivism is our best hope for generating knowledge that would not only be most representative of the "world out there," but also the most useful (for whatever purposes, such as realizing the project of critical theory to mitigate forms of inequality, discrimination, and over-use of power).

These five criticisms of positivism, as well as the many variants of them, are based on either a profound misunderstanding of what positivism is or a set of assumptions which would yield very little that is interesting, important (by all standards except those of ivory-tower academics), and useful. Positivism is, of course, not the only important intellectual activity in which sociologists can be engaged, but to the extent that the goal of sociology is to understand the operative dynamics of the social universe, positivism represents our best choice. And it is certainly superior to the alternatives implied by critics. For if the programs of the critics were followed, sociology would be a mixed bag of rather pedestrian philosophizing, historical and empirical description, ideological debate and commentary, vague scheme-building, commentary on current (and past) events, extreme relativism, and a general doubt that we can know or do anything. Thus, I do not see the critics as presenting a very interesting or creative alternative to positivism. But among those committed to a view of sociology as a scientific activity, theory means somewhat different things to various scholars, and so, to frame my particular strategy, let me briefly review various approaches, outlining the problems and prospects of each. In this way, I can place my positivistic approach into the context of varying strategies currently employed by sociological theorists.

VARIETIES OF SOCIOLOGICAL THEORY

As I have argued elsewhere (Turner 1985, 1986, 1987a), there are four basic approaches to building sociological theory: meta-theoretical schemes; analytical schemes; propositional schemes; and modeling schemes. Each of these is summarized below.

Metatheorizing schemes Many in sociology argue that for theory to be productive, it is essential to block out the basic presuppositions that should guide theoretical activity. Before adequate theorizing can occur, it is necessary to address a number of fundamental questions. What is the nature of human activity, human interaction, human organization? What is the most appropriate set of procedures for developing theory and what kind of theory is possible? What are the central issues or critical problems on which sociological theory should concentrate? And so on. Such questions and the rather long treatises (e.g. Alexander 1982–3) that they often pull theory into the old and unresolvable philosophical debates – idealism versus material-ism, induction versus deduction, subjectivism versus objectivism, and the like.

What makes these treatises "meta" – that is, coming after or subsequent to, as the dictionary informs us – is that these philosophical issues are raised in the context of yet another re-analysis of the great theorists, such as Karl Marx, Max Weber, Emile Durkheim, and Talcott Parsons. Although these works are always scholarly, filled with long footnotes and relevant quotations, my sense is that they often suffocate theoretical activity. They embroil theory in unresolvable philosophical issues and they easily become scholastic treatises that lose sight of the goal of all theory: to explain how the social universe works. Thus, metatheorizing is interesting philosophy and, at times, a fascinating history of ideas, but it is not theory and it is not easily used in actual theorizing.

Analytical schemes   A great deal of theorizing in sociology involves the construction of abstract systems of categories that presumably denote key properties of the universe and crucial relations among these properties. In essence, such schemes are typologies that map the important dynamics of the universe. Abstract concepts dissect the basic properties of the universe and then order these properties in a way that is presumed to offer insight into the structure and dynamics of the social world. Explanation of empirical events is achieved when the scheme can be used to interpret some specific empirical process. Such interpretations are of two basic kinds: when the place or niche of an empirical event in the category system is found, then the empirical event is considered to be explained; or, when the scheme can be used to construct a descriptive scenario of why and how events in an empirical situation transpired, then these events are seen as explained.

These somewhat different views of explanation by analytical schemes reflect two basic approaches: naturalistic analytical schemes and sensitizing analytical schemes. The first assumes that the ordering of concepts in the scheme represents an "analytical accentuation" of the ordering of the universe (Parsons 1937); as a consequence of this isomorphism, explanation is usually seen as involving the discovery of the place of an empirical event in the scheme. The second approach often rejects positivism as well as naturalism, but even its more positivistic versions argue that the system of concepts can only be sensitizing and, at best, can only provide general guidelines for interpreting empirical events.

Those following the naturalistic variant often argue in a vein similar to metatheorists: the analytical scheme is a necessary prerequisite for other kinds of theoretical activity (e.g. Münch 1982). For until one has a scheme which denotes and orders at an analytical level the properties of the universe, it is difficult to know what to theorize about. Thus, for some, naturalistic analytical schemes are a necessary preliminary to further theorizing. In contrast, those employing sensitizing analytical schemes often reject the search for universal laws as fruitless, since these laws will be obviated as the fundamental nature of the world changes (Giddens 1977, 1984), but among those who accept positivism, the sensitizing scheme is seen as a necessary prerequisite to theory because it denotes the important classes of events to be explained.

Propositional schemes Propositional schemes revolve around statements that connect variables to one another. That is, propositions state the form of the relation between two or more variable properties of the social universe. Propositional schemes vary widely and can be grouped into several types: axiomatic, formal, and empirical.

Axiomatic theorizing involves deductions, in terms of a precise calculus, from abstract axioms that contain precisely defined concepts to an empirical event. Explanation consists of determining if an empirical event is "covered" by one or more axioms. As I emphasized earlier, however, axiomatic theory is rarely possible in those sciences that cannot exert laboratory controls, define concepts in terms of "exact classes," and use a formal calculus such as logic or mathematics (Freese 1980). While sociologists (e.g. Emerson 1972a, b; Homans 1974) often use the vocabulary of axiomatic theory – axioms, theorems, corollaries, etc. – they are rarely in a position to meet the requirements of true axiomatic theory. Instead, they engage in formal theorizing (Freese 1980).

Formal theorizing is watered-down axiomatic theorizing. Abstract laws are articulated and, in what is often a rough and discursive manner, "deductions" to empirical events are made. Explanation consists of visualizing an empirical event as an instance or manifestation of the more abstract law. The goal of theorizing is thus to develop elementary laws or principles about basic properties of the universe. Formal theorizing is what most of those using the vocabulary of axiomatic theorizing actually do in practice.

The third type of propositional scheme – the empirical – is not really theory at all. But many theorists and researchers consider it to be so. Indeed, as I stressed above, many critics of positivism use examples of empirical propositional schemes to indict positivism. For instance, I have already alluded to the tendency of the critics of positivism to confuse abstract law about a generic phenomenon and generalization about a set of empirical events. This assertion that empirical generalizations are laws is then used to mount a rejection of positivism: there are no timeless laws because empirical events always change. Such a conclusion is based upon the inability of critics to recognize the difference between an empirical generalization and an abstract law; but even among those sympathetic to positivism, there is a tendency to confuse what is to be explained (the empirical generalization) with what is to explain (the abstract law). This confusion takes several forms.

As noted above, one is to elevate the humble empirical generalization to the status of a "law." Another is to accept Robert Merton's (1957: 85–120) famous advocacy for "theories of the middle range" where the goal is to develop some generalizations for a substantive area – say, urbanization, organizational control, deviance, socialization, or some other substantive topic. Such "theories" are, in fact, empirical generalizations whose regularities require a more abstract formulation to explain them. Yet a good many sociologists believe that these middle-range propositions are theories, despite their empirical character.

Modeling schemes The use of the term "model" is highly ambiguous in the social sciences. In the more mature sciences, a model is a way to represent visually a phenomenon in a way that exposes its underlying properties and their interconnections. In social theory, modeling involves a variety of activities, ranging from the construction of formal equations and computer simulations to graphic representations of relations among phenomena. I will restrict my usage of the term to theorizing in which concepts and their relations are presented as a visual picture that maps properties of the social universe and their interrelations.

A model, then, is a diagrammatic representation of events that includes: concepts that denote and highlight certain features of the universe; the arrangement of these concepts in visual space so as to reflect the ordering of events in the universe; symbols that mark the nature of connections among concepts. In sociological theory, two types of models are generally constructed: abstract-analytical models and empirical-causal models.

Abstract-analytical models develop context-free concepts – for example, concepts pertaining to production, centralization of power, differentiation, and the like – and then represent their relations in a visual picture. Such relations are usually expressed in causal terms, but these causal connections are complex, involving varying weights and patterns (such as feedback loops, cycles, mutual effects, and other non-linear connective representations).

In contrast, empirical-causal models are usually statements of correlation among measured variables, ordered in a linear and temporal sequence. The object is "to explain variance" in a dependent variable in terms of a series of independent and intervening variables (Blalock 1964; Duncan 1966). Such exercises are, in reality, empirical descriptions because the concepts in the model are measured variables for a particular empirical case. Yet, despite their lack of abstraction, they are often considered "theoretical." Thus, as with empirical propositional schemes, these more empirical models will be less useful in theory-building than the analytical ones. Much like their propositional counterparts, causal models are regularities in data that require a more abstract theory to explain them.

This completes my review of various strategies for building sociological theory. As is evident, I see only some of these as appropriate for positivistic theorizing and for theorizing in general. A brief review of the relative merits of these strategies will produce a clear conception of how I think positivistic theory should be constructed.

A STRATEGY FOR BUILDING POSITIVIST THEORY

Theory should, first of all, be abstract and not tied to the particulars of a historical/empirical case. Hence, empirical modeling and empirical propositional schemes are not theory, but regularities in the data that require a theory to explain them. They are an *explanandum* in search of an *explanans*. Second, positivism emphasizes that theories must be tested against the facts, and thus metatheoretical schemes and elaborate naturalistic analytical schemes are not theory proper. Sensitizing analytical schemes, however, can be used as starting-points for building testable theory. If the anti-positivist tenets among some practitioners can be ignored, such sensitizing analytical schemes provide a sound place to *begin* conceptualizing basic classes of variables that can be incorporated into testable propositions and analytical models. This could also be possible with naturalistic analytical schemes, but more difficult in actual practice because such schemes tend to become excessively concerned with their own architectural majesty, thereby making it awkward to transform them into more precise models and propositions. Finally, in contrast to Comte's early advocacy, theory must involve more than abstract statements of regularities; it must also stress the issue of causality, but not the simple causality of empirical models. My view is that analytical models provide an important supplement to abstract propositions because they map the complex causal connections – direct and indirect effects, feedback loops, reciprocal effects, etc. – among the concepts in propositions. Without such models, it is difficult to know what processes and mechanisms are involved in creating the relations that are specified in a proposition.

In light of these considerations, then, positivistic theory must be abstract; it must denote generic properties of the universe; it must be testable or capable of generating testable propositions; and it cannot ignore causality, process, and operative mechanisms. The best approach to theory-building in sociology is thus a combination of sensitizing analytical schemes, abstract formal propositions, and analytical models (Turner 1986). This is where the most creative synergy is; and while various theorists tend to emphasize one over the other, it is the *simultaneous* use of all three approaches that offers the most potential for developing a "natural science of society." Such would be the nature of the positivism that I advocate and that I have sought to develop (Turner 1984, 1987a, b, 1988). Figure 1 portrays my position in schematic form.

As is evident, one way to begin theorizing is by constructing sensitizing analytical schemes that denote in a provisional manner key properties of the social universe. By itself such activity is unproductive, since the scheme cannot be tested. Rather, it can only be used to denote classes of important processes and, at best, to interpret specific empirical events. In my view, this is inadequate; it is also necessary to generate

Figure 1:   Strategies for building theory

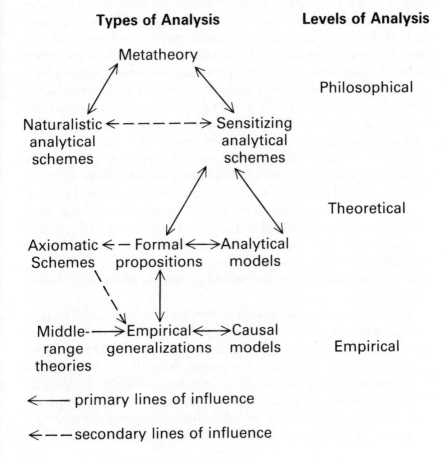

abstract and testable propositions and, at the same time, to model the processes that operate to connect the concepts in the propositions. This exercise itself, regardless of empirical tests, can force revision of the sensitizing scheme. Or, construction of an analytical model can encourage rethinking of a proposition. As is indicated in the diagram, the critical point here is that these three activities are mutually reinforcing; this is what I mean by "creative synergy."

In contrast, naturalistic analytical schemes and metatheorizing tend to be too philosophical and detached from the actual workings of the world. They become overly reified and either concerned with their architecture or obsessed with their scholastic capacity to "resolve" philosophical issues. Yet, I do not consider these to be unimportant activities but rather as being useful only *after* we have developed laws and models in which we have confidence. Then, more philosophical discussion is useful and can force re-examination of laws and propositions. But without these laws and propositions, naturalistic analytical schemes and metatheorizing become self-sustaining philosophical treatises. The vehicle for connecting propositions and models to more formal analytical schemes and metatheory is the sensitizing analytical scheme. These sensitizing schemes, when used to stimulate the formulation of propositions and when reassessed in light of tests of propositions, can provide empirically informed presuppositions for more complex naturalistic schemes and for metatheorizing. In turn, when metatheory and naturalistic schemes have been built from a propositional base, they can provide useful insights that force assessment of existing propositions and models. Yet without this attachment to testable theory, analytical schemes and metatheory float away into the reified and rarefied world of philosophical speculation and debate.

On the more empirical side of theory-building, middle-range propositions are, in essence, empirical generalizations for an entire substantive area. To be useful, however, they must be converted into abstract laws (most difficult to do) or into discrete empirical generalizations (much easier to do). Empirical-causal models can explicate the temporal processes that operate to connect variables, but to be useful in building theory, they need to be incorpoated into empirical generalizations. Then they can help to assess the plausibility of abstract propositions. Without the abstract laws and models, however, these more empirical approaches will not help to build theory. For if uninformed by abstract laws and formal models, then middle-range theories, causal models, and empirical generalizations are constructed *ad hoc*, without concern for whether or not they illustrate an underlying dynamic of the social universe. Only infrequently does one make inductions from these empirical formats and create theory, for the reality of theory-building is the other way around: theory first, then assessment with data. But the data have to be arranged in a way that makes them testable with an abstract proposition.

Such is my position on positivism. Start with sensitizing schemes, propositions, and models, and only then move on to the formal collection of data or to metatheorizing and scheme-building. In this way, it will be possible to generate scientific knowledge about the social universe, with the result that sociology can take its place among the natural sciences. If all this seems naive and idealized, such is no doubt the case. But my sense is most practicing scientists – that is, those who try to understand how things work – engage in a process, often implicitly, of using sensitizing schemes, analytical models, and propositions. Such should be the case for sociologists, especially theorists, who should start to theorize rather than merely proclaiming all of the difficulty involved, or retracing, once again, the history of ideas. In my view, the problems facing social science are no different than those in the natural sciences. Social theorists just think that they are and, as a result, rarely get around to actually theorizing.

CONCLUSIONS: PROSPECTS FOR GENERAL THEORY IN SOCIOLOGY

I think that the prospects for general and positivistic theory in sociology are not very bright. We seem to have lost the vision of Comte and the early masters (whose works we continue to summarize as if this, in itself, were theorizing). And with the invasion of so many new intellectual stances from Europe, as well as the fostering of those initiated in the United States, theoretical activity is partitioned into too many "camps," "orientations," "perspectives," or "paradigms" for any general theory, cutting across this diversity, to ever be possible. Such is especially likely to be the case in a field that will not even take itself seriously as a science, preferring instead to be a mixture of history, philosophy, social commentary, ideological advocacy, and empirical description.

Added to these intellectual partitions and barriers are profoundly important organizational forces in sociology. National sociological associations all over the world, but especially the American Sociological Association, are differentiating into "sections" which perpetuate specialization without intellectual (either theoretical or methodological) integration. Added to this node of differentiation is the proliferation, again particularly in the United States, of specialty associations for just about every substantive topic, further dividing sociologists into camps where specialists talk, and write for, each other rather than sociology in general. The end result, I have argued (Fuchs and Turner 1986; Turner and Turner, 1990), is to create a field composed of narrow practitioners who have little interest in theoretical issues, particularly those in the philosophy-laden theory practiced by contemporary sociologists.

Thus, while positivism offers great promise, as it did in Comte's time, I am agraid that this promise will never be realized. Such is inevitably the case when, as other contributors to this volume will make abundantly clear, most "theorists" in sociology do not believe that sociology can be a natural science.

REFERENCES

Alexander, Jeffrey C. 1982–3: *Theoretical Logic in Sociology*. 4 vols. Berkeley and Los Angeles: University of California Press.
Blalock, Hubert M. 1964: *Causal Inferences in Nonexperimental Research*. Chapel Hill: University of North Carolina Press.
Carnap, R. 1966: *Philosophical Foundations of Physics*. New York: Basic Books.
Collins, Randall 1975: *Conflict Sociology*. New York: Academic Press.

Comte, Auguste 1830–42: *A System of Positive Philosophy*, 3 vols. London: George Bell.

Duncan, Otis Dudley 1966: "Path analysis: sociological examples," *American Sociological Review*, 72: 1–16.

Durkheim, Emile [1933] 1893: *The Division of Labor in Society*. New York: Macmillan.

Emerson, Richard M. 1972a: "Exchange theory, part I: a psychological basis for social exchange," in J. Berger, M. Zelditch, and B. Anderson (eds), *Sociological Theories in Progress*, vol. 2. Boston: Houghton Mifflin.

Emerson, Richard M. 1972b: "Exchange theory, part II," in J. Berger, M. Zelditch, and B. Anderson (eds), *Sociological Theories in Progress*, vol. 2. Boston: Houghton Mifflin.

Freese, Lee 1980: "Formal theorizing," *Annual review of Sociology*, 6: 187–212.

Fuchs, Stephen 1986: "The social organization of scientific knowledge," *Sociological Theory*, 4/7: 126–42.

Fuchs, Stephen, and Jonathan H. Turner 1986: "What makes a science mature: organizational control in scientific production," *Sociological Theory*, 4/7: 143–50.

Giddens, Anthony 1977: *New Rules of Sociological Method*. New York: Basic Books.

Giddens, Anthony 1984: *The Constitution of Society: Outline of the Theory of Structuration*. Berkeley: University of California Press.

Habermas, Jürgen 1970: *Knowledge and Human Interests*. London: Heinemann.

Hempel, Carl G. 1965: *Aspects of Scientific Explanation*. New York: Free Press.

Homans, George C. 1974: *Social Behavior: Its Elementary Forms*, rev. edn. New York: Harcourt Brace Jovanovich.

Kuhn, Thomas S. 1970: *The Structure of Scientific Revolutions*, 2nd edn. Chicago: University of Chicago Press.

Lenski, Gerhard 1966: *Power and Privilege*. New York: McGraw-Hill.

Mann, Michael 1986: *The Social Sources of Power*, vol. 1. Cambridge: Cambridge University Press.

Merton, Robert K. 1957: *Social Theory and Social Structure*. New York: Free Press.

Münch, Richard 1982: *Theory of Action: Reconstructing the Contributions of Talcott Parsons, Emile Durkheim, and Max Weber*, 2 vols. Frankfurt: Suhrkamp.

Parsons, Talcott 1937: *The Structure of Social Action*. New York: Free Press.

Parsons, Talcott 1951: *The Social System*. New York: Free Press.

Popper, Karl R. 1959: *The Logic of Scientific Discovery*. London: Hutchinson.

Popper, Karl R. 1969: *Conjectures and Refutations*. London: Routledge.

Skinner, B. F. 1938: *The Behavior of Organisms: An Experimental Analysis*. New York: Appleton-Century-Crofts.

Thorndike, Edward Lee 1932: *The Fundamentals of Learning*. New York: Teachers College Press.

Turner, Jonathan H. 1984: *Societal Stratification: A Theoretical Analysis*. New York: Columbia University Press.

Turner, Jonathan H. 1985: "In defense of positivism," *Sociological Theory*, 4 (Fall): 32–44.

Turner, Jonathan H. 1986: *The Structure of Sociological Theory*, 4th edn. Chicago: Dorsey Press.

Turner, Jonathan H. 1987a: "Analytical theorizing," in A. Giddens and J. H. Turner (eds), *Social Theory Today*. Cambridge: Polity Press.

Turner, Jonathan H. 1987b: "Toward a sociological theory of motivation," *American Sociological Review*, 52/1: 15–27.

Turner, Jonathan H. 1988: *A Theory of Social Interaction*. Stanford: Stanford University Press.

Turner, Stephen P. and Jonathan H. Turner. 1990. *The Impossible Science: An Institutional Analysis of American Sociology*. Newbury Park, Calif.: Sage.

Turner, Ralph 1962: "Role-taking vs. conformity." in A. M. Rose (ed.), *Human Behavior and Social Processes*, Boston: Houghton Mifflin.

Wallerstein, Immanuel M. 1974: *The Modern World System: Capitalist Agriculture and the Origins of the European World Economy in the Sixteenth Century*. New York: Academic Press.

Whitley, Richard. 1984: *The Intellectual and Social Organization of the Sciences*. Oxford: Clarendon Press.

Willer, David, and Murray Webster, Jr 1970: "Theoretical concepts and observables," *American Sociological Review*, 35 (August): 748–57.

7

The Confusion of the Modes
of Sociology

Randall Collins

When future historians look back on the sociology of the late twentieth century, what will they say about us? Have we accomplished anything? Have we accumulated any knowledge that will carry over into the future and that might be called a science? Or will they say that the late twentieth century – not merely in sociology, but across the intellectual world generally – was dominated by a revival of philosophical idealism, an idealism without religion, based on the intellectual community turning inward upon itself? One might well say that the late twentieth century, with its massive university systems and tens of thousands of academic intellectuals, has gotten caught in a publication explosion. We are awash in a sea of texts; is it surprising that many intellectuals have come to the conclusion that there is no world behind the texts, that the world itself is nothing but a text or a discourse, endlessly being rewritten? And indeed this is true, if all that we see is the intellectual community itself, engaging in self-reflection in a time of informational overload.

Let us suppose that postmodernism is more than a passing mood. Let us suppose that in the coming years it wins out, not only in the humanities, not only in sociology, but that it even succeeds in vanquishing any science with a claim to having discovered objective knowledge about the world. One might imagine reading the following book review, written by an elated, early twenty-first-century sociologist:

REVIEW OF: *Multiple Paradigms in Modern Physics: An Introductory Text* by Juergen von Himmel.
Berkeley and Cambridge: Bootleg and Edens Fall, 2001. 149 pp.,
$299.95

Reviewed by Posthumous V. Empiricus, Jr.
Institute for Transcendental Sociology

It is unusual for a sociology journal to review a physics textbook,
but this case is so important for illustrating the growing importance
of sociology in the intellectual world that it is worth an exception. I
am happy to report that sociological sophistication has finally made
it into the "physical sciences," if that is the right word for them.
Remember when they used to be called just plain "science?" You
could tell they were getting defensive when they started calling
themselves "hard science" (as opposed to "soft"). Then we nailed
them as "positivists." The critique hit home; as a sign of victory
now there is even a physics textbook that could almost be mistaken
for a sociological theory book.

Gone are the old topical headings that physics books used to
have: motion, energy, gravity, electricity, magnetism, light, radio-
activity, and all the rest. Instead, we have a textbook that squarely
faces the fact that physics is a human construction. Hence we have a
textbook organized not around these alleged topics of the "objective
world," but around the human theorists themselves. The author
puts them into schools of thought, although (as in a good sociology
book) one can always quarrel with the labels. Newton is treated as a
"Structuralist," Galileo as a "Positivist." The chapter on Einstein
deals with the influential school of "Religious Physics," which has
become so dominant in the educational reforms of the late twentieth
century; it is based on Einstein's seminal text: "God does not play
dice with the Universe." It also shows how Einstein's liberating
ideas in physics derive entirely from his profound commitment to
Zionist praxis. The real meat of the book is in the chapter on
"Phenomenology" (especially Werner Heisenberg and his "uncertainty principle"). This book tries to be unbiased and not opt for
any particular theory, but it can hardly be doubted that the author
has done a great service in bringing physics intellectually up to date
by applying Heisenberg's uncertainty not merely to subatomic
participles, but to physical theories themselves.

There are also chapters on "Ethnophysicists," "Exchange Physicists," and "Conflict Physicists." The author is fair and unprejudiced,
and commits no Whiggish presentist fallacies. Not only is Kepler
just as contemporary as Einstein, but there is even a nice chapter on

phlogiston theory, and another on why nature abhors a vacuum and why the circle is the most perfect form of motion. The last nicely fits under the rubric of "Functionalist Physics," which also includes Aristotle, the Talcott Parsons of their field.

The book concludes with chapters on the two greatest contemporary physicists. One of these, on Thomas Kuhn, explains why there is so much more to contribute in writing the history of physics than in doing physics itself. The other chapter, on Fritzhof Capra, is particularly inspiring because it shows that not only is physics merely a rediscovery of what has always been known in the universal vision of ancient religions, but also that the same religious foundation holds in every other field of knowledge.

In criticism, I have to say that the textbook still has a tendency to let some empirical evidence creep in. Of course, it is true that a lot of these theorists thought they were discovering something called "laws" about a "world" that they believed existed "out there." But that is no excuse for letting their opinions carry over into a book on which the young minds of our world (oops! I mean of our inter-subjective sphere of communicative action) are going to be brought up. Fortunately, the author does follow good sociological practice and rarely tells us just what those "laws" were that the theorists thought they had "discovered." There is also a good discussion of experimental research methodology, which is kept well within bounds; it never tries to impose on us any results of such researches, but stays on the meta-level where all sophisticated minds work, and comments mostly on the narrow-mindedness and lack of philosophical grounding of people who actually try to base theory on empirical research.

All in all, this book shold make us all happy with the progress that has been made in spreading the message of the "sociological revolution" into the rest of the intellectual world. Well, I guess I shouldn't use the word "progress," since that's awfully Whiggish and presentist. But doesn't it seem fair to say that there is "progress" in discovering that there is no such thing as intellectual progress? Of course I'm just sounding like a provincial American, and there must be a good deconstructionist answer to that. Probably Anthony Giddens is having it translated from the French right now.

Now, that book so far is just a fantasy, but the following one really exists. It is called *The Word and the World: Explorations in the Form of Sociological Analysis*, and it was published by

Allen & Unwin in 1985. I am not going to tell you yet who the author is, for reasons that will become apparent. The author of this book proposes a new form of scientific communication. After studying the written and spoken communications of scientists, he has concluded (along with many other British sociologists of science) that scientists state their own positions in a language of objective empiricism. *My* views are founded on facts, on the objective evidence; *your* views, if you happen to disagree with me, are your subjective interpretations. But, in fact, everyone's position is based upon interpretations, socially contingent constructions, and there are an indefinite number of ways of interpreting anything. The reason scientists find it so hard to resolve disputes, especially when they exchange letters about their disagreements, is that each one claims the privileged position of letting the facts speak for him (or her), while it is one's opponent alone who is lodged in the realm of subjectivity and interpretation.

To remedy this, the author advocates that we should abandon monologue and institute dialogue. In a scientific publication, one voice hogs the floor; no other position gets to speak, no reader can ask questions. The monologue form is congruent with the objectivist stance; even the voice of the paper's author is hidden, and the illusion is given off that the facts are speaking for themselves. Even an exchange of letters on scientific issues is just an exchange of monologues. Since no true dialogue takes place, it is no wonder that opponents never come to agreement.

What we need, then, is genuine dialogue. If possible, it should be face to face.

If we still must indulge in written communications, even (perish the thought!) books and papers directed to an audience of people one hasn't personally met, at the least we ought to break out of the monologic, empiricist/objectivist form. We should introduce different voices, lay bare the one-sided interpretive work that is always going on, let multiple meanings emerge. And if the result looks more like fiction than scholarship, be consoled that *that* distinction too is only a simplistic interpretation, and that the two forms are really not so different after all. Indeed, the fictional form has at least this superiority, that it openly reminds us of the constructed nature of our text, instead of hiding it behind an objectivist message.

The Brits who are in on it call this practicing a New Literary Form.

In that spirit, I would like to abandon the usual style of scholarly writing and propose the following. This book is alleged to have been written by "Michael Mulkay." That's what it says on the title page, but I don't believe it. (But no, it wasn't written by Jürgen Habermas.) In my opinion, the book was actually written by Erving Goffman. In support of my interpretation, I could cite its similarity to the layers of analysis which Goffman employed in his earlier publication, *Frame Analysis*. Indeed, it follows up his lifetime concerns with the presentation of self in everyday life. As his last work, Erving simply turned to yet another area of ordinary reality, the one inhabited by academic intellectuals like himself, and proceeded to lay bare the backstage maneuvering that go into constructing frontstage scientific positions. The self of the scientist, the "genius discoverer" that Goffman analyzes in the pages of *The Word and the World*, is a mirage, a construction based on rituals such as the awarding of the Nobel Prize. And since Erving had been using the theatrical analogy throughout his writings, it is inevitable that he would actually organize his last book in the style of the stage script.

Moreover, I have personal reasons for believing that Goffman not only could have, but actually did write the book. (And personal reasons, especially when openly avowed, are superior to any other form of documentation, because they avoid the objectivist fallacy.) I met Erving in a hotel corridor once and told him that he ought to write a book, applying his methods to the maneuverings of the intellectual world. Of course, Erving – sly devil! – brushed off the suggestion, with the contemptuous remark that I was becoming a publisher's flack. Besides, he said, that's a job for a theorist; I'm just a plain-spoken, detail-scrounging empirical researcher.

Well, that of course is a dead give-away. Erving was playing one of his presentational games; if he said he was going to write the book I wouldn't have believed him. Also, he wouldn't want to come out openly and give away his tricks of intellectual impression-management. But he always did things behind your back. And lo and behold, when the book comes out, it is just as he said it should be done: full of careful empirical observation of just how scientists actually talk to each other, write letters, make Nobel speeches, and so forth. To top it off, in a typical Goffmanian move, Erving has managed to attribute the book to an Englishman named "Michael Mulkay" so no one would suspect he'd done it.

MICHAEL MULKAY: Now wait a minute. Don't you think that's a bit thick? After all, I did write the book. And Goffman has been dead since 1982, so he couldn't have done it.

ME: It is only your interpretation that you wrote the book instead of Goffman. Even you must agree with that, because that is what the book itself says. The fact that you don't agree proves that you didn't write the book. As for Goffman being dead all these years, what difference does that make? The condition of "being dead" is just a social construct. And even if I were to agree that he is dead (since I did write an obituary about him), that still doesn't rule out the interpretation that his ghost came back and wrote the book – maybe even by possessing your writing hand.

MICHAEL MULKAY: Are you saying you believe in ghosts?

ME: Why not? After all, Harry Collins does, and he is a respected British sociologist of science. (Harry is no relation of mine, by the way.)

HARRY COLLINS: I can't let that pass. I have never said that I believe in ghosts.

ME Well, you did say that on the basis of your research, people who study the occult use the same methods and forms of reasoning as scientists do, including scientists who try to disprove the existence of the occult. You put telekinesis on the same level as nuclear physics, and so I'm going to call on your support for the existence of ghosts.

HARRY COLLINS: But I don't give you my support.

ME: I don't think I'm going to let you talk any more. This is my paper, and you're just a fictional voice.

MICHAEL MULKAY: But what about me? I am real. You can find me in York, England, just like you can find Harry in Bath.

ME: That is one way of putting it. I will admit I've actually seen Mike Mulkay in the flesh, and even spoken to him; in fact, I complimented him on this very book. But that was just a frontstage ritual, a form of politeness. What was said on that occasion was merely a local interpretation, of no general significance. It is not a reason to disbelieve my present position, that the book was really written by Erving Goffman. Besides, how do I know you're the real Michael Mulkay? He never talks about things being empirically real; and he would never dispute whether one voice in a dialogue is superior to another. He would never try to claim intellectual property against someone else.

MICHAEL MULKAY: Okay, you're right. We are all cognitive equals. Yours is actually a perfectly valid interpretation. The book could well have been written by Erving Goffman.

ME: Oh-oh, now I'm beginning to get suspicious. This one does sound like the real Michael Mulkay, the champion of cognitive democracy. And his admission, that Goffman really could have written the book, actually is congruent with the message of the book itself. So maybe Mulkay did write the book after all.

MICHAEL MULKAY: I'll leave that to your sense of fairness.

ME: Let's take it from another angle. Does this book really look like it was written by Goffman? Despte the fact that he documented layers of reality-construction and deception, Goffman always criticized the ethnomethodologists for going too far and sending everything into reflexivity and unreality. His frames are ordered in a hierarchy; they are transformations built upon one another, but they are chain-linked back to the basic untransformed reality of human bodies in the physical world. Goffman's world was open-ended, in the sense that endless reflexive self-commentaries could be added at the "upper" end, but this hyper-intellectual world is just something that emerges out of the lower frames, and by a determinative process.

So I am going to conclude that Erving Goffman didn't write this book after all. Not for the superficial reason that he actually didn't write it; but for the more profound reason that Goffman was more serious. But wait. On the other hand, maybe Goffman wrote it as a parody of those who had misunderstood his position. In that case, Goffman did write the book . . .

Now let us ring down the curtain and turn on the lights in the theater. It is true that we can become involved in these elaborate games of what Goffman called framing and reframing; and if one sticks to those very specialized situations, mostly found among intellectuals, one can construct quite involuted situations which make us want to throw up our hands as to where reality lies. But the theater of the mind is grounded ultimately on real human action, and if we stick to the fundamentals at that level, there is much less cause to be pessimistic about the accumulation of sociological knowledge. It is the sociology of science that casts light on why we are in the intellectual situation of today; and the sociology of science is a strong example of a field which has accumulated generalized explanatory knowledge about some aspect of the world. There are many other areas in which sociology has accumulated knowledge about some of the core processes of the social world: micro-interaction, the structural properties of social networks, many of the generic features of stratification and especially of formal organizations. Out of these fundamental processes many particular phenomena can be explained.

Our problem today is not so much the lack of knowledge – although we clearly have much more to learn – but rather knowing what it is we do know. The huge numbers of sciologists have produced intellectual specialization to the point of fragmentation. We simply can't keep up with the literature. It is the job of theory to carry out the necessary abstraction and cumulation so that we don't lose what is valuable in this ever-rising sea of texts as we float on top of it. But theorists themselves have been fragmented, and many of us have turned our backs on the task. There are sociological reasons for this too; one reason is that we have gotten too big before we have gotten ourselves well organized, and we have developed vested interests in being fragmented.

Our fragmentation takes the following form; one might call it the form of the internal politics of our discipline. We disagree about the purposes of what we are doing, about what kind of intellectual enterprise we are constructing. Roughly speaking, there is division among three groups: those who want sociology to produce scientific knowledge, those who want it to be practical, and those whose aim is to be ideological. Although this last term sounds rather contentious, I want to characterize generically a stance that covers many varieties, including the political, the humanistic, the aesthetic, and the self-reflexive. You might wish to call it "evaluative" if you object to the term "ideological."

To head off misundestanding, let me emphasize two points. First: I am not equating scientific sociology with quantitative sociology. Qualitative, historical, and subjective versions of sociology all have contributed to the generalizable knowledge that I am calling scientific sociology, and will continue to contribute in the future. And second: the three categories scientific, practical, and ideological/evaluative are *analytical* categories: the same field, or even some particular publication, can combine any two of these orientations or even all three. For instance, the current upsurge of work in the sociology of sex and gender – or feminist sociology – includes all three stances.

One can see this already by looking at the controversies over what to call the field.

Our problem in the disciplinary politics of sociology is that the proponents of these different goals – scientific, practical, or ideological/evaluative – can be quite hostile to one another. We don't want to borrow, share, or cooperate; more often we want to drive the others from the field. This is one reason why many people think sociology doesn't know anything; many of us have a vested interest in ignorance, at least as a political stance. An even more serious problem is that we don't see what is involved in each of these areas, what they can or cannot do, or give them credit where it is due. Let me briefly consider some of these confusions.

PRACTICALITY AND ITS PROBLEMS

First of all: the scientific mode is often confused with the practical. This is most typically done by critics who dismiss their sociological opponents as "positivists"; but it is also done by the "political party" on the opposite side, sociologists who are closest to actually being traditional "positivists". It is an agreement of the extremes. Both sides get in trouble because of the way they compare sociology to the natural sciences. The successful sciences seem to have a close connection between basic science and practical applications. Physics is connected to mechanical and electrical engineering, chemistry to the manufacture of materials and drugs, biology and physiology to medicine and agriculture. The vulgar position is to equate science with its products, or at any rate to see the link between them as very tight, so that basic science always produces some practical benefit. Natural scientists themselves have not been above pushing this line, since they feel the public would not support pure science for its own sake. But the sociology of science and the historical sociology of technology shows that these are very different enterprises, although basic science and practicality have had varying links at various times.

What is the sociological difference between pure science and practical science? In the pure science end of the field, the relevant human interests are those of the intellectuals themselves

– intellectuals searching for knowledge and simultaneously for status within the competitive networks that make up the scientific community. In the practical field, the motivating interests are those of lay people, and of professionals confronting lay people: we leave the internal affairs of the scientific community and enter the realms of business, the state, social classes, and lay interest groups generally. I would suggest that, even though there are controversies in the practical side of natural science, these are nothing compared to the conflicts of interest that characterize practical sociology. The natural sciences have come in for some criticism for their practical work in the military and for adverse effects on the environment, but the vast majority of applied science products are smoothly appropriated by consumers as private ends. One simply buys one's refrigerator or VCR and puts it to personal use. It is other people's machines that are alienating, not our own.

Not so with the practical products of sociology. Sociology's products inevitably deal with human beings, so we cannot avoid conflicting interests over power and control that are inherent in all social arrangements. Someone might formulate a sociological program, for instance, to make people stop smoking marijuana or snorting cocaine. But the issue itself is formulated as the result of political pressures and emotional crusades; and any implementation of such a program involves some people attempting to control others, even if they mask this fact by being self-righteous about it. This is equally true for interventions in the area of racial or gender inequality, or any other social issue. It should not be surprising that practical sociology is not often very successful, for it is usually intervening in a morass of conflicting political forces, and not always on the side of the biggest battalions. This is of course especially true if one's vision of "praxis" is grandiose, such as carrying out a revolution or creating the emancipated society.

The fact that sociology deals directly with people, and people who have conflicting interests, makes the task of practical sociology much more difficult than the applied natural sciences. This is not particularly a problem for basic science in sociology, since we can explain people's behavior, including understanding their conflicts and ideologies, without having to control them. The practical sociology which has been most successful has set its sights lower: it collects information *describing* the condition of some particular social problem, while leaving it for lay policy makers to do something about it. We are competent at documenting the amount of school desegregation or the social mobility of disadvantaged groups, although this leaves many people with a feeling of dissatisfaction because they want practical sociology to be a more powerful force for change. The result is that they feel any all-out push for sociological praxis tends to be frustrated.

What does this do to the intellectual side of our discipline? The most narrowly positivist sociology is typically found in the descriptive side, amassing information about social problems; since there is no theory applied, the work doesn't cumulate much, and gives only local descriptions of particular times and places. This is to a certain extent inevitable; I think we should recognize what practical sociology can and cannot do, and stop confusing it with something else. Above all, the anti-positivist critics ought to recognize that they are mainly inveighing against a type of practical sociology and not against basic science.

There is another reason why sociology does not work as well as the applied natural sciences. Virtually all of the successes of applied natural science have come by constructing closed systems. Consider a refrigerator or an automobile engine. The engineer has constructed a closed system, a physical space within which only certain physical laws are allowed to operate. A few elementary principles of mechanics, electricity, and chemistry will do the job, because the machinery has walls which keep all other processes out. When a machine fails to function properly, it is typically because something external has breached the system, like leaving your refrigerator door open. The physical world is no simpler than the social world; certainly the realm of subatomic particles is as messy an arena of multiple causality as any sociologist could imagine. Practical success in natural science has come by reducing the complexity in a literal, physical sense: by creating physical barriers inside of which only certain processes are allowed to operate. (One might say too that this is what living organisms are: it is because a living body has a skin that a determinate, if rather complex, system can operate; medicine is successful insofar as it can intervene with some very specific agent, such as a drug, inside this closed system; medicine fails typically when it is unable to exclude unexpected environmental conditions.)

The ultimate problem with practical sociology is that we cannot build social machines. There are very few physically closed systems in the social world; even formal organizations, which are something like an effort to build a social machine, typically have major transactions with their environments. We can have some practical success if we do the following: we create a temporarily closed system, and we make it small enough so that it has relatively little complexity or hierarchy; and we recruit members for homogeneity, especially with respect to their motivations for belonging. Social psychologists know how to put together a structure of group pressure to get willing subjects to give up smoking. An encounter group works because it is a highly focused social machine for channeling emotions and giving its members emotional energy. The problem is that people's emotional batteries start running down after the group session ends, when the system is opened up again to all the myriad influences of the wider social environment. So the participant either has to keep coming back for a recharge, or decides that the cure didn't really work. This is unfair, since the expectation was unrealistic. The encounter group does its work, but only as long as it is a closed system. If members really want the payoff, they have acquired a sociological addiction, so to speak, to being in that group situation. This same phenomenon is what underlies the attraction of cultish religions for their members: they keep coming back for their "fix" of closed-system solidarity.

I should add that the natural sciences encounter the same problems whenever they try to have practical effects, or even to make good predictions, in their own arenas when these cannot be reduced to closed systems. Meteorology is not a very precise field, and its predictive power remains modest despite a great deal of research, because the system which produces the weather is an open system of very great complexity (Tribbia and Anthes 1987). Similarly, a great deal is known now in such areas as geology without our being able to control earthquakes, or even to predict them very precisely. In many areas, the natural sciences are in the same position as historical sociologists; a geologist or an evolutionary biologist understands many of the fundamental processes, but the particular combinations of these conditions which make up the sequences of the history of the earth, or of living species, are far too complex a system to have a predictable pattern. On a higher level of abstraction, this property of highly complex systems is recognized and formalized in physics as chaos theory (Crutchfield et al. 1986).

These are reasons why we should not have too negative a view of sociology's accomplishments. Our science has formulated a certain number of basic processes, which in combination, generate the myriad outcomes of the empirical world. That world is historically situated, permutating through an enormous variety of combinations of conditions. Hence the impossibility of reducing history to a simple pattern, much less of intervening practically in this morass to get a few isolated outcomes that some faction happens to desire. But in the realm of open systems, sociology and the natural sciences are more or less on an even footing. It just happens that the natural sciences can create systems which are more closed, physically, than we can – and, probably, than we would want to.

BASIC SCIENCE AS COMBINATIONS OF ANALYTICAL PRINCIPLES

The intellectual success of both the natural sciences and sociology is a different story, and it comes from isolating the basic processes on the analytical level, in basic science. The empirical world is generated out of combinations of these basic processes. My colleague Jonathan Turner, who has been working at assembling the analytical principles at this fundamental level, estimates that there may be about 40 such basic laws in sociology. This might seem at first glance to be totally inadequate to explain the myriad phenomena of social life. But if each of these basic processes has, let us say, 10 significant levels of variation in the dependent variable, then the number of possible empirical combinations of these processes is 10^{40}. That is 1 followed by 40 zeros, a number which is in the realm of the total number of molecules in the universe.

This is a very crude first approximation. Certain combinations will turn out not to be theoretically possible. Also, we should distinguish among processes on the micro- and on the macro-levels; these interact insofar as the macro- contain within them micro-entities (i.e. situations, individuals), and hence the macro- and micro-principles are mutually constraining in ways yet unformulated. Thus the number of combinations of principles which can operate simultaneously would be reduced below 10^{40}. On the other hand, the number of possible sequences in time would be a multiple of each cross-section of principles operating simultaneously, so that the number of possible sequences would be on the order of 10^{40} raised to yet another (rather large) power. But here again some sequences would not be possible; these constraints themselves would be very large-scale macro-principles, added to our list of approximately 40.

Whatever the actual number of basic sociological principles might turn out to be, their analytical recombination would certainly produce results on an order of magnitude sufficient to account for the enormous variety of human history, as well as for the fact that each individual person has certain unique features, even though each of us is the product of certain rather limited classes of social experience.

I believe we have already discovered about a dozen of these 40 principles, at a reasonable level of approximation. Others are lying scattered in the mass of existing research, though much work remains to be done to bring them to the most useful degree of abstraction, and relate them to more specialized variants. In the long perspective, sociological science has been making progress.[1]

EVALUATIVE/IDEOLOGICAL SOCIOLOGY

My first two categories were science and practicality. My third category is what I called ideology. I am using this very generally, to refer to any mode of analysis which is mainly concerned to show what is right or wrong. This is the arena of value judgments. There are various kinds of ideology. Political ideologies are the most familiar, whether defending the desirability of a given state of affairs, or critiquing it and crusading for a change. I want to be clear that despite the usual connotations of the term "ideology," I am not opposed to sociologists engaging in this kind of activity. My main concern is that we should be open and aware of what we are doing. What is debilitating is ideology masquerading as science: i.e. a description of what is considered desirable or undesirable is passed off as an analysis of why things are as they are. Critical ideology, mostly produced on the left, has been very useful in exposing the ideology in some positions that used to be prominent in sociology. A prime example is the functionalism of 30 years ago, which was not very good at explanation, precisely because what it took to be explanation was mainly justifying some arrangement as desirable for the functioning of the social system. But even turning this around into the analysis of dysfunctions does not make it a real explanation; it only substitutes negative value judgments for positive ones. The weakness of Marxian sociology comes when it operates as a kind of functionalism of evil.

Ideological analysis becomes debilitating when it declares that doing ideology is the only desirable or even the only possible thing that we can do. Unmasking ideologies is useful, but above all because it is a step towards better scientific theories. I suggest that an area in which unmasking is still to be done is in a type of ideology that is not explicitly political. There are a variety of positions that are humanistic, subjectivist, or interpretive. In many ways, these offer contributions to understanding what human beings are like, and in that sense they contribute elements to a scientific theory of the social world. These positions become ideological when they claim that their viewpoints show that science is impossible, and even pernicious, something to be destroyed.

For instance, we often hear it claimed that everything is a phenomenon of human consciousness (or of human discourse), and that no other way of understanding the social world has any validity. If this position is put forward as a claim to describe the way the world is, then it needs to be evaluated scientifically. The result of that, I would say briefly, is that human consciousness and discourse are only part of the social world – an important part, about which we can learn something from semiotics, symbolic interaction, or conversation analysis. But this part is embedded in social interactions on the physical and emotional level, in social networks and organizations, and in physical environments. I don't think this would be so much at issue if the subjectivist positions in sociology did not have a strong ideological thrust: often its advocates want to see the world a certain way because they believe that is morally desirable to see it that way, and they condemn positions which disagree with their vision because those alternative visions are regarded as dehumanizing.

One branch of subjectivistic interpretation stresses the role of the human agent. There must be a bedrock of human consciousness, human decisions, human free will; any other view of the world is an insult to the dignity of the human being. But is this a convincing argument about the way the world is? That question can only be decided scientifically, in the broadest sense: i.e. what theory works best at explaining the varieties of human social arrangements. This kind of subjectivistic ideology is a backward-looking movement. We do not want to go further ahead; we do not want to discover non-cognitive processes at the root of cognition, emotional processes which are not interpretive, or structural constraints on what interpretations we can make. We do not want a theory of when and how consciousness itself arises in various ways, or to explain when and to what extent people do feel that they have a sense of human agency, free will. Here we reach an unpassable frontier; we don't want sociology to go any farther forward. In this respect, sociologists in the subjectivist, interpretive camp tend to put themselves in the same position as the theologians of the Catholic Church who condemned Galileo for discovering things about the universe that upset traditionally valued conceptions.

This is the problem with an ideological stance generally. As long as ideology confines itself to crusading for action in the lay world, there is no problem. Often we ought to do this. But when ideology invades scientific terrain, then the issue becomes whether we have the right to go ahead and investigate the social world intellectually, to discover, come what may. The ideological stance, when it gets out of its own turf, becomes a set of blinders. Not only does it try to prevent us from understanding as deeply as we can; there are many things that we cannot even see unless we have some detachment.

Turner's 40 or so general principles, which in combination generate the empirical world, are not moral judgments, either positive or negative. They are on a deeper analytical level. Some of them concern cognition; some tell us the conditions under which people make certain kinds of moral judgments (Durkheimian theory about rituals and solidarity has already laid out some main lines here). Some of these principles surely include things that we learn from the subjectivist/interpretive schools, such as George Herbert Mead on the internalized conversation that constitutes mind, the ethnomethodologists on the limitations of cognition and the strategies people use to deal with cognitive ambiguities.

One of the discoveries that has emerged from the whole sweep of subjectivist and interpretive thought in the twentieth century (but also from logic, mathematics, and information science) is the multi-leveled character of human symbol systems. Erving Goffman put the point very usefully in his *Frame Analysis* (1974), showing how meaning on one level is typically built by putting a contextual frame around some other level of social action. The result is the hierarchy of frames in which we think; the frames are not free-floating, but are built up link by link from one another in sequence. I submit that this conception, whether in Goffman's version, or Gödel's, or Garfinkel's, is a scientific one, not an ideology. It tells us how the world is, not what is desirable or undesirable about it.

Science, practicality, and ideology are all frames through which we see the social world. The proponents of different frames can fight with one another, reformulate each other in their own terms, and attempt to negate or destroy each other. But they are not in equivalent structural positions in the hierarchy of frames. Insofar as they are all part of the intellectual world, the scientific frame is the largest frame for interpreting the others. We have already seen that the ideological frame, by its moralizing, reduces the focus; it allows us to see only what it wants to see (either as good or evil); that which doesn't fit its grid of categories it must assimilate to evil. The practical frame, too, is a limited one for intellectual purposes. It operates well only in one part of the world, the part that consists of physically closed systems; when it tries to deal with the open-system part of the world, it leaves us locked in particularistic descriptions, never rising to the generality of explanations.

The scientific frame, taken in its broadest sense, is the encompassing frame. The scientific frame can understand the practical frame, both when practicality works and when it doesn't. And science can both understand and empathize with the ideological frames, at whatever degree of nuance one wishes to pursue. The advantage of the scientific frame is that, by its detachment, it is able to encompass and analyze whatever it focuses upon, while relating it to the overall sphere of explanatory conceptions that is the storehouse of its knowledge. Science alone can turn back on itself without undermining itself; this is what the sociology of science does. Science is the one sphere that can operate without blinders; and for that reason, it is the one sphere in which we can expect to make progress as sociology.

The novelist Scott Fitzgerald, writing in an aesthetic mode, but with the eye of a sociologist, captured as well as anyone ever has the stance of our science. In *The Great Gatsby* his character looks out the window from a Manhattan skyscraper where a drunken party is going on, and thinks: "High over the city our line of yellow windows must have contributed their share of human secrecy to the casual watcher in the darkening streets, and I was him too, looking up and wondering. I was within and without, simultaneously enchanted and repelled by the inexhaustible variety of life."

NOTES

1 For an overview of the condition of our sociological knowledge on the analytical level, see Collins 1988 and, in a more specialized area, Turner 1988.

REFERENCES

Collins, Randall 1988: *Theoretical Sociology*. San Diego, Calif.: Harcourt Brace Jovanovich.

Crutchfield, James P., et al. 1986: "Chaos," *Scientific American*, 255: 46–57.

Goffman, E. 1974: *Frame Analysis*. New York: Harper & Row.

Mulkay, M. 1985: *The Word and the World: Explorations in the Form of Sociological Analysis*. London: Allen & Unwin.

Tribbia, Joseph J., and Richard A. Anthes 1987: "Scientific basis of modern weather prediction," *Science*, 237: 493–9.

Turner, Jonathan H. 1988: *A Theory of Social Interaction*. Stanford, Calif.: Stanford University Press.

8

Daring Modesty: On Metatheory, Observation, and Theory Growth

David G. Wagner

THE TWO INTELLECTUAL CULTURES OF SOCIOLOGY

There are, alas, a great many issues that divide contemporary sociologists. Are sociological phenomena primarily objective and material or subjective and symbolic (or perhaps some combination of both)? Should we focus our attention primarily on historical or generalizing social processes? Are quantitative or qualitative methods more appropriate for sociological analysis? Recently, the salient question has been: Are the most basic social processes macrosociological or microsociological in scale, and how do we translate the one into the other?

One can often infer quite a bit about a sociologist simply on the basis of his or her position with respect to any one of these issues. For example, a sociologist who believes that sociological phenomena are primarily subjective and symbolic is also very likely to be historical, qualtitative, and microsociological in orientation as well. There are, of course, exceptions, but in general we sociologists are a very predictable lot.

None of these issues so clearly – and so predictably – divides sociologists as does our assessment of the relative importance of theory and empirical research. For some of us, theoretical reflection is the primary concern; for others, empirical analysis is primary. As a result of this division, two radically different intellectual cultures have emerged in sociology. These cultures incorporate differing values, norms, and patterns of behavior, differing standards of success and means of attaining those standards, even differing basic conceptualizations of what the sociological enterprise is all about.

In theoretical sociology, for example, a great deal of emphasis is placed on the exegesis and interpretation of classic texts. The worth of a particular piece of work is defined in terms of its contribution to one of the classic debates raised in those texts. At the core of the discipline is a series of deep philosophical questions: What is the nature of human existence? What are the essential defining properties of society? What is the relationship between the moral commitment of the sociological investigator and the character of the knowledge gained in the investigation? And so on. Theoretical work is justified by the depth and orginality of its response to one or more of these questions.

In empirical sociology, by contrast, most of the emphasis is placed on the generation, analysis, and interpretation of data (and on methodological techniques useful in accomplishing these tasks). The work of a piece of empirical work is defined in terms of its contribution to the collection of empirical generalizations that can be made about a particular social phenomenon. At the core of the discipline are several bodies of well-supported generalizations, each of which constitutes a "theory" of the phenomenon upon which the generalizations focus. Empirical work is justified by the depth and orginality of its contribution to one or more of these bodies of generalizations.

The division between theoretical and empirical work permeates every aspect of our sociological lives. It affects our preferences in reading material. How many theorists have ever turned the pages of a *Sociological Methodology* annual? Indeed, how many read any of the research articles in the major sociology journals? In turn, how many empirical sociologists have read a page of *The Division of Labor* or *The Protestant Ethic* since their first year in graduate school?

The division also affects the training of graduate students. And it is not just a matter of the relative importance attached to learning LISREL or reading the *Grundrisse*. The analysis of theory and the development of methodological techniques are both relegated to courses devoted exclusively to those topics. The substance of sociological knowledge, however conceived, is treated as separate from the basic tools and conceptual apparatus to be used in generating and evaluating that substance. When we are fortunate, students become either methodologically literate or theoretically literate; they seldom become both.

One of the reasons the theroetical/empirical division is so basic and pervasive is that it crosscuts the other divisions I have mentioned. There does seem to be a general preference among theorists for qualitative sociology. However, sociologists of varying stripes on these issues can often interact, debate, even work together *as long as they are on the same side of the abyss* between theoretical and empirical work. Many of us attended a conference at the University of Maryland in 1988 where theoretical positions from network analysis to poststructuralism were discussed. Although there was plenty of disagreement, every topic was treated as an appropriate subject for intellectual discussion. Reports of research investigating any of the topics discussed, however, were rare. The same is true of the chapters in this volume.

As a consequence of the insularity of theoretical and empirical work from each other in the discipline, sociologists have become increasingly imperial regarding the division. The choice we have made, be it theoretical or empirical, is the right one; all others are simply wrong, or at least less central to the advancement of the discipline. Theorists often view empirical sociologists as narrow and largely unsophisticated about the broader framework of basic theoretical and philosophical issues that underpin their work. Empirical sociologists often view theorists as frustratingly vague and either unwilling or unable to bring observation to bear on their ideas.

It is ironic that the division between theoretical and empirical work should become so basic and pervasive in sociology. None of our most prominent intellectual ancestors treated the two as distinct. In fact, Marx, Weber, and Durkheim all became central to sociological work in large part because they so thoroughly integrated theoretical analysis with empirical investigation. Their theoretical insights remain valuable to us today because they reflect serious and intensive observations of the world around them. Their empirical and methodological insights remain valuable because they were closely tied to the resolution of important theoretical questions. We claim these people as our models, yet we do not follow the pattern of their work.

I regard all these manifestations of the division between theoretical and empirical work as unfortunate. However, for me none is as unfortunate as the effect the division has on the growth of sociological knowledge. I have argued elsewhere (Wagner 1984; Wagner and Berger 1985) that the cumulation of sociological knowledge is most evident in bodies of related theories and empirical investigations I call *theoretical research programs*. Obviously, when theorists do little or no empirical investigation and researchers do little or no theoretical analysis, fewer programs can emerge or develop; the cumulation of our knowledge is hindered. Perhaps less obvious but just as important, we are less aware of the programs that do exist and the progress that has occurred in them. We fail to recognize cumulation when it occurs because we see only empirical generalizations and basic philosophical issues, with nothing in between and no way of relating them to each other.

As long as the two intellectual cultures of sociology remain so radically at odds with one another, these problems will continue. The gap needs to be bridged. In the next section I review two previous attempts to bridge the gap and explain why I believe they failed. Then in the following sections I outline my own attempt to bridge the gap and what is required to make this attempt more successful than previous attempts. Along the way, my analysis will give me an opportunity to discuss the role that general theories of society may play in this project.

PREVIOUS ATTEMPTS TO INTEGRATE THE CULTURES

I am certainly not the first to note the separation of theoretical from empirical sociology. Nor am I the first to propose some way of integrating them. At least two other comparatively recent attempts are noteworthy: Merton's call for "theories of the middle range" (see primarily Merton 1968) and the brief surge of emphasis on issues of theory construction (see e.g. Blalock 1969; Hage 1972; Stinchcombe 1968; Wallace 1971; Zetterberg 1965).

Merton's call was a direct response to Parsons's attempt to develop a comprehensive conceptual framework within which all social phenomena could be analyzed. Such a general theory of society is, Merton argued, premature. Without a strong foundation of empirical work to support it, the scheme is bound to be sterile and fated to fall into "deserved disuse" (Merton 1968: 45).

Thus, for Merton empirical investigation is essential to the development of theoretical knowledge. It is not, however, sufficient. For without a strong theoretical foundation to organize and focus the research, empirical research is just as sterile and useless as an all-encompassing theory of society.

What is needed therefore is to make theoretical work empirically "relevant" and to make empirical work theoretically "relevant." When this occurs, the result is a middle-range theory: a specialized theoretical argument about a particular sociological phenomenon, grounded in and justified by a body of research about that phenomenon. Moreover, as work continues on a middle-range theory, the theoretical and empirical relevance enlarge its scope of application and increase the clarity of its account of the phenomena that fall within that scope; it becomes less specialized and more general. Eventually, then, a focus on middle-range theories yields a general theory of society.

Thus, Merton retained the goal of developing a general theory of society. He simply proposed a different method of achieving that goal. Parsons had assumed that a general theory could be generated directly and justified by the convergence of various theoretical analyses on the same basic elements. Merton substituted a method of incremental generation and justification of those elements, with each increment thoroughly grounded in empirical work. In terms of Merton's famous metaphor, we cannot have our Einstein (i.e. a general theory of society) until we find our Kepler (i.e. more specialized middle-range theories). However, if we have enough Keplers (and Newtons and Laplaces and . . .), we will eventually have our Einstein as well.

There are two primary virtues in Merton's call for middle-range theories. The first is his recognition that theoretical analysis and empirical investigation are implicated in each other. Any useful theoretical argument proposes something about the world that ought to be directly investigated. Any useful empirical investigation assumes a theoretical framework that ought to be explicitly analyzed.

The second is his awareness of the possibility of incremental improvement in our knowledge. Important theoretical ideas generally do not emerge full-blowm from the head of either Zeus or Talcott Parsons. Ideas emerge through a trial-and-error process; they may be improved as we gradually eliminate known errors and as we expand the domain within which such errors can be discovered. Specialized theories can become broader and clearer, in short more general, in their application.

There are, however, several defects in Merton's proposal. The most obvious ones result from the vagueness of the term "relevance." It is unclear just *how* theory is to be made relevant to research and vice versa. As a consequence, virtually any piece of work may be made to sound relevant. It is not uncommon for a rudimentary theoretical interpretation to be tacked on to the end of an empirical investigation after the data analysis is finished. This *ex post facto* theorizing is intended to establish the relevance of the research theory, even though the ideas discussed may have had little or nothing to do with the formulation of the research problem or the kind of empirical analysis performed. Nor is it unusual to find a literature review that refers to one or more theoretical arguments as legitimation for pursuit of the planned research with little or no effort made to incorporate an evaluation of those arguments in the investigation.

Another consequence of the unfortunate vagueness in Merton's prescription is the excessive concreteness of many of the theories developed. We have seen the proliferation of theories about various concrete populations of social objects and events, rather than about the abstract social structures and processes that are manifested in those populations. Thus, we develop "sociologies" of, say, the automotive industry, the one-parent family, or the 1988 presidential election. How we can develop abstract theories of organizational inertia, socialization, or leadership from this sort of middle-range theory is difficult to see. It is as though we attempted to develop a theory of propulsion by studying the physics of Fords and Chevys. Even making our investigation cross-cultural (say by studying Toyotas as well) or generalizing our argument to deal with other means of propulsion (say bicycles) is unlikely to yield much greater knowledge about the underlying theoretical process. Increasing the number and variety of concrete entities to which we apply our ideas does not make those ideas more abstract.

To be fair, Merton may not have intended middle-range theories to be used in the ways I have criticized. Nevertheless, the vagueness of his prescription of "relevance" encourages such usage.

There is another, very different kind of flaw in Merton's proposal. If we are to eschew general theory for middle-range theory, then a lot of theoretical work by some very highly respected sociologists is cast on the slag heap. At the very least, this represents bad intellectual politics (and helps to explain why empirically oriented sociologists have adopted middle-range theorizing much more readily than theoretically oriented sociologists). I would argue that it also reflects an inadequate appreciation of the variety of different theoretical activities that contribute to the growth of sociological knowledge. That general theory is not (in fact, ordinarily cannot be) subjected to empirical investigation does not mean it cannot contribute to the development of our knowledge; it means only that general theory contributes to our knowledge in a different way – as I shall outline in the next section.

The second recent attempt to bridge the gap between theoretical and empirical sociology emerged from a series of texts and other works on theory construction. This attempt was considerably less focused than Merton's attempt. First, many more people were involved in articulating the argument. Second, those who contributed often had dramatically different approaches to the substance of the discipline. Blalock (1969), Glaser and Strauss (1967), and Zetterberg (1965), for example, all have sharply differing views about what kinds of sociological problems are worth investigating and therefore what kinds of theories are worth constructing.

Nevertheless, these and other contributors shared a set of basic assumptions about the link between theoretical and empirical work. Specifically, most assumed theory ought to emerge from more or less systematic exploration of the empirical world. Theoretical analysis does not precede empirical investigation; it follows from it and is justified by it. The value of a theory is determined by its faithfulness to a particular set of observations.

Moreover, the greater the number and variety of observations to which a theory is faithful, the more general the theory. Ideally, the process of generalization continues until we arrive at a theory that is faithful to (at least a representative sample of) all possible observations of social phenomena, without constraint. Then, and only then, can we state a general theory of society.

The parallels with Merton here are striking. Both he and the contributors to the theory construction literature retained the goal of a general theory of society. Both assumed, however, that such a theory could not be directly constructed but must emerge from another kind of activity: middle-range theorizing for Merton, systematic observation for the theory construction contributors. Finally, both assumed that the incremental justification of our knowledge by empirical investigation would assure the validity of the general theory that eventually emerges.

The primary virtue of this second attempt to integrate theoretical and empirical sociology is the specificity of its recommendations for relating theoretical reasoning to empirical observation. Whether one chooses the grounded theorizing of Glaser and Strauss or the mathematical formalization of Blalock, a wealth of detailed information is available to guide our theory construction. Where Merton is inordinately vague, theory construction is admirably specific.

Unfortunately, this very specificity is largely responsible for one of the most telling defects in the theory construction project. When so much detailed information about techniques of empirical investigation is available, there is a tendency for the use of a particular technique to become its own justification. Some problems are investigated primarily because they are readily amenable to analysis using the technique, not because the investigation is likely to yield useful theoretical knowledge. Just as important, other problems are ignored because they are not amenable to use of the technique.

This "fetishism of the technique" has been most evident in quantitative empirical work. Tabular analysis, factor analysis, and causal modeling have all been used indiscriminately at one time or another. I suspect event history analysis will soon join the list. Qualitative work has not, however, been immune.

Participant observation, grounded theorizing, and unobtrusive measures have all been employed just as indiscriminately as any of the quantitative techniques.

Again, to be fair, the people who generated these techniques (e.g. Blalock) are often not the ones who abuse them. A technique is usually developed with a specific purpose in mind and the creator ordinarily adheres to that purpose. Otherwise, why go to the trouble of inventing a new technique? Unfortunately, once a new hammer becomes generally available, others are likely to turn everything else into nails to drive with it.

The other major flaw in the theory construction project is one it shares with Merton's project. Its emphasis on empirical generalizations yields knowledge that is excessively concrete. Empirical generalizations are *not* theoretical statements. Theoretical statements are abstract; empirical generalizations are summaries of concrete observational statements. Increasing the scope of an empirical generalization only adds to the number of concrete observations it summarizes. It does not make the generalization more abstract. If the goal is an *abstract* general theory of society, this path does not lead to it.

How then are we to proceed? I draw several lessons from these previous attempts to integrate theoretical and empirical sociology:

1 Theory need not be all-encompassing to be useful. A general theory of society may turn out to be a valuable addition to our knowledge. However, we can learn quite a bit about the social world without having one in hand. Other theories, more directly tied to empirical investigation, may always tell us more about any particular sociological phenomenon than a general theory ever could.

2 Nevertheless, general theory will always serve an integretative and directive purpose, no matter how well-developed an empirically evaluable theory becomes. Indeed, a variety of *different* kinds of theoretical activity may be of importance in developing our knowledge. The nature of each of these activities and the standards by which we evaluate their performance are bound to differ.

3 We need therefore to understand how each of these

activities is pursued and – perhaps even more importantly – how they are related to each other. In what ways do general theories and specific theories implicate each other? Do general theories in fact have any implications for empirical investigations (and vice versa), and what are the consequences if they do?

4 In answering such questions, we must do more than simply insist on the "relevance" of each kind of activity for the other. We must specify in detail how they are related. We cannot expect empirical investigators to be seriously concerned with either specific or general theories without showing exactly how their work yields important theoretical ideas. Similarly we cannot expect theorists to be seriously concerned with empirical investigation without showing exactly how their work implies specific and evaluable relationships in the empirical world.

5 It is a mistake to assume that particular techniques of empirical analysis – whether they involve participant observation or event history analysis – provide the detailed answers we seek. All such techniques, useful as they are, assume that the goal of inquiry is the generation and validation of empirical generalizations. But empirical generalizations are not theory. At best they may serve as the *explananda* for theory; they may not serve as *explanans*.

6 What is key to answering the questions is understanding the nature of abstraction and its role in relating theoretical analysis and empirical investigation. For abstraction is a double-edged sword. It challenges the imperialism of both cultures. It means, for example, that the observational validation of theoretical ideas sought by the empirical sociologist cannot be fully attained; one can never analyze all the observations relevant to an abstract idea. It also means that the comprehensiveness of theoretical scope sought by the theoretical sociologist cannot be fully attained; abstraction inherently narrows our focus, forces us to be selective in our choice of problems to investigate, and prevents us from ever being fully general. The first step in integrating the cultures of theoretical and empirical sociology may be increasing each one's awareness of the incompleteness of its own project.

A NEW ATTEMPT TO INTEGRATE THE TWO CULTURES

I have embarked on a project attempting to integrate the cultures of theoretical and empirical sociology based on these principles. An analysis of one part of that project – dealing almost exclusively with *theoretical research programs* – was presented in my 1984 book and in a somewhat more advanced form in Wagner and Berger (1985; 1986). A much more comprehensive (and much more developed) analysis, again in book form, is nearing completion. This new analysis deals with what I call *orienting strategies* and *unit theories*, as well as programs, and with the relationships among these theoretical activities and empirical investigation.

Obviously, I cannot lay out all the details of my analysis here. There simply is not enough room. I can, however, highlight certain aspects of the analysis that are particularly important in overcoming the barriers between theoretical and empirical sociology.

Perhaps most important to theorists is the role that general theory plays in the analysis. To me, general theory is almost always metatheoretical in character. Much like a Kuhnian paradigm (see Kuhn 1962; 1970) or a Lakatosian hard core (see Lakatos 1968, 1970), it provides a comprehensive frame of reference within which other more specific theoretical ideas may be generated. It provides directives for the selection of appropriate sociological problems for investigation, the formulation of specific theoretical accounts of those problems and the evaluation of the empirical sufficiency of those accounts. It defines the subject matter of the discipline, the goals of sociological inquiry, the nature of social reality. In my terms a general theory is an orienting strategy. Human ecology, Marxism, various neo- and post-Marxisms, critical theory, conflict sociology, exchange theory, behavioral sociology, functionalism, neofunctionalism, evolutionism, symbolic interactionism (both Chicago and Iowa school varieties), structuration theory, phenomenology, ethmethodology, structuralism, and poststructuralism (as well as others that simply do not come to mind at the moment) all have primarily the character of orienting strategies.

Several features of orienting strategies are useful to mention here. First is the absolute necessity of adopting such a frame of reference if one wishes to do sociological work. One must *presume* a general theory of society in order even to know what to theorize about, let alone how to formulate a plausible argument and evaluate it. All our knowledge is filtered through the lens of a perspective. We cannot see without it.

This does not mean, however, that a general theory of society must be fully explicated before we can see anything sociologically. One's strategy may be, at least initially, entirely implicit. This is certainly the case for most empirical sociologists. And, as Jonathan Turner (1986: 9) has pointed out, metatheoretical analysis in most disciplines occurs after the development of a body of accepted theoretical arguments. We often become aware of the strategic assumptions we have been making only through our continued employment of them in more specific theoretical and empirical work.

Whether we explicate our strategic assumptions before or after we use them is less important than that we be aware we are making them. No investigation is ever truly atheoretical or "objective." Even if we cannot presently specify our general theory of society, we should be conscious of the guidance it gives to our work.

The second critical feature of orienting strategies, in direct counterpoint to the first, is the absolute impossibility of demonstrating the truth or validity of such a frame of reference. Strategies are directive; they tell us how to approach the sociological world, not what is true about the world, given that approach. In fact, generally speaking, strategies are immune from direct empirical evaluation.

Often, our criticisms of one or another strategy stem from a misunderstanding of the untestable character of these directives. When we excoriate Parsons for tautology in his analysis of functional requisites (see e.g. Parsons 1951) we fall prey to this misunderstanding. Yes, the argument is tautological. Parsons claims that if functional requisites are not met, the survival of the social system is in danger; the way we determine whether functional requisites are being met is through the survival and stability of the system. Yes, this tautology does render at least this part of Parsons's analysis untestable. *But that is not the role the argument plays in Parsons's analysis.* Parsons is telling us what to look for when we study society: a social system and structures within it that appear to enhance its survival, stability, and integration. If the structure does not appear to have that effect, look elsewhere, for that is what it means for the structure to be functional.

Similarly, when we criticize Homans (1961; 1974) for tautology in the relationship between reward and performance, we misunderstand the role these ideas play in his analysis. (Note that I think Homans himself may even misunderstand the role they play.) When we study sociological phenomena, we are to look for behavior (i.e. performance). Moreover, we are to explain that behavior in terms of rewards. If the things we have identified as rewards are not associated with patterns of behavior, then we must look elsewhere, for reward means performance. We have not found what was rewarding to the actor *because* we have not revealed an association with behavior.

The misunderstanding is not limited to the role of tautologies in orienting strategies, either. When Marx (1977 [1848]) tells us that "the history of all hitherto existing society is the history of class struggle," he is not making an empirical claim about the universal character of conflict. Such a claim would obviously be false. Instead, he is telling us what is important to study if we wish to understand society. If we have not identified the centrality that class struggle plays in the phenomenon we are studying, then either we have not looked hard enough or the phenomenon we are studying is sociologically trivial.

Arguments like these are at the core of every orienting strategy. Their directive character renders them empirically untestable. It does not render them theoretically useless.

Orienting strategies *are* evaluated, both directly and indirectly. On the more direct level, we assess the originality, clarity, and internal consistency of the theorist's vision, among other things. And there can certainly be progress in our strategic knowledge on this direct level, particularly as it regards clarity and internal consistency.

More indirectly, we assess the fertility of the theorist's vision. Strategies direct the construction and evaluation of one or another kind of theoretical formulation in solving "worthwhile" sociological problems. Generally, the evaluation includes a comparison with some sort of empirical observation. The more successful a strategy is in generating solutions to these problems that satisfy its criteria for construction and evaluation, the more fertile or useful the strategy is perceived to be.

This, to me, is the most obvious way in which our theoretical knowledge grows. Strategies tell us how to answer sociological questions. When we answer them, we learn something. The more we answer, the more we learn. Thus, at least within the constraints of a particular orienting strategy, it is possible to have cumulative development of sociological knowledge.

Growth across strategies is a more complex subject, about which my thinking is much less well developed. Strategies (or more strictly speaking the theories that strategies direct us to construct) compete for dominance over various explanatory domains. The boundaries and characteristics of those domains are defined by the social, cultural, and historical environment, as well as by the competition itself. Strategies grow by generating theoretical accounts that either maintain an established explanatory dominance or challenge the dominance of another account. As long as a strategy continues to generate viable candidate theories in one or more domains, the strategy retains some level of utility. It continues to attract adherents and to generate theoretical and empirical work. However, if a strategy comes to be dominated through all the explanatory domains in which its theories compete, it is likely to become extinct rather quickly.

The strategies that remain continue to grow through their competition. If at some point a single strategy comes to dominate through all the extant explanatory domains, it becomes the "received view" regarding that subject matter. Note, however, that achieving this status does not establish a strategy as "true." First, other explanatory domains may become important. Second, other strategies may emerge to compete over some of the existing domains. Third, none of this success changes the directive character of the strategy. Its success depends on accepting its definition of what is important to investigate and how to investigate it.

Thus, growth at this level may be said to occur only in the sense that a strategy was better at accommodating the demands of various explanatory domains than its competitors. At this level I suspect a strategy is more likely to be successful by eliminating its competitors than by becoming integrated with them.

This has important consequences for our judgment of the viability of developing a single, overarching general theory of society. Note, to begin, that a truly *all*-encompassing general theory is not technically possible. By virtue of its nature as a directive framework, a general theory of society abstracts and selects certain features of the social world as important. Such a theory can come to incorporate more and more features. However, it cannot incorporate all conceivable features without becoming something other than a framework. An all-encompassing framework is a contradiction in terms.

But, of course, this is not what I believe most proponents of general theory are aiming for. The goal as I perceive it is a theory that encompasses all "important" or "relevant" sociological problems or phenomena. Such a theory is possible. However, its success is based on its ability to define the terms of the debate (i.e. what explanatory domains are to be considered important or relevant) and to generate specific theoretical arguments that outshine others on those terms (i.e. are more successfully adapted to the demands of those explanatory domains).

Success of this sort of general theory is built on shifting sands. Its "generality" lasts only as long as no viable competitor appears in the intellectual environment. It cannot provide a firm and lasting foundation for all future consideration of sociological issues. It is not, if you will, "true"; it is only the most successful theory currently available.

Suppose Jeffrey Alexander were successful in convincing us all that neofunctionalism was such a general theory (or at least the prototype for one). Now, in fact, I believe he and other neofunctionalists are a long way from accomplishing this. There is too little consensus over the importance of various explanatory domains and too much viable competition in most of those domains. Nevertheless, let us suppose. If neofunctionalism were to become our single, overarching general theory of society, its success would not be based on its inherent validity but on its ability to establish the importance of the explanatory domains it considers and to generate theoretical and empirical work that successfully (i.e. more successfully than any other general theory) accounts for problems in those domains.

This would be no small accomplishment. Nevertheless, the accomplishment would be only temporary, the foundation insecure. For as soon as the social, intellectual, or cultural environment identifies a new explanatory domain or a new and viable alternative general theory (call it "post-neofunctionalism") emerges, the hegemony dissolves and we must begin again.

Thus, to me general theor*ies* of society are important, indeed essential, elements of all sociological work. I regard the search for a single theory of society, however, as chimerical.

A consideration of the role of general theories of society – orienting strategies – is necessary if we are to integrate theoretical and empirical sociology. It is not sufficient. My analysis focuses equal attention on empirical observation and the role it plays in theoretical analysis.

My argument here parallels my argument for metatheoretical work. Empirical evaluation of our theoretical ideas is as absolutely necessary in studying social phenomena as is adopting a framework. No theorist ever states an argument without presuming some empirical evidence in support of the argument. And that evidence is almost always brought to bear when a defense of the argument is requested.

This claim holds not just for those theoretical positions that regard themselves as scientific but for others that often raise serious challenge to the project of science altogether. Consider first Marxism. I have had colleagues and students suggest to me that the nature of the Marxian dialectic rendered all empirical evidence supportive of one's class position; empirical truth therefore emerges only through synthesis of the contradictions in that evidence. But that is simply not consistent with Marx's use of the dialectic or with his use of empirical evidence. The dialectic for Marx is material; it refers to the *substance* of social structures, not to the form of intellectual argumentation one uses to demonstrate the character of that substance. It is the contradictions of capitalism, not of observations, that concerned Marx. This is all the more obvious when we consider Marx's use of observations. *Capital* especially is replete with empirical observations Marx clearly considered to be "objective" evidence for his characterization of capitalism. He intended us to be convinced by this evidence, not to contradict it, nor to create a synthesis that was in any way inconsistent with Marx's own conclusions.

A similar claim applies as well to areas of interactionism, phenomenology, and ethmethodology, though for somewhat different reasons. Presumably, the subjectivity (and therefore uniqueness) of each individual actor's construction of reality renders the analysis of "objective" empirical regularities meaning-less. Yet, to perform a breaching experiment (for example) requires the assumption of many such regularities. On a surface level, one assumes, say, that appliance salesmen will in fact bargain over price. On a more basic level, one assumes that the process by which actors construct reality is highly regular, even though the product generated by that process is unique. (In fact, all of the more subjectively oriented theoretical positions yield this sort of empirical regularity when one steps back from the concrete features of the constructed social world to the abstract process by which that world was constructed.)

Observation *is* analytically dependent on theory. One cannot even begin to observe without first establishing a frame of reference that tells one what to observe. This is not the same, however, as a determination of data by one's theoretical framework. In fact, one of the purposes of the directives of a strategy is to make certain kinds of evaluative decisions "objective" within the context of the strategy itself. The strategy dictates what sort of observations are to be considered relevant in evaluating theories based on the strategy. It dictates what criteria are to be used in performing that evaluation. It often dictates how one should respond to failures of the observations to support these theories based on the given criteria. However, it does not dictate that the relevant observations support the proposed theory. The former create a contextually objective frame of reference within which an evaluation of the latter can occur.

Particular techniques of observational analysis are part of that contextually objective frame of reference. There is no technique we can use, quantitative or qualitative, that can assure the validity or truth of our observations independent of the strategic assumptions we make. We still use the techniques, of course, but we use them at the behest of our strategy directives.

Finally, it is as futile to attempt to demonstrate the theoretical truth of our empirical generalizations as it is to attempt to demonstrate the empirical truth of our frames of reference. That is, summaries of our empirical observations do not inherently lead to valid theories. As I have noted, observation is theory-laden. We must presume a great deal theoretically before we can even begin to observe. Just as important, observations are concrete while theories are abstract. Abstraction implies application to an indefinite (and potentially infinite) number of times and places. No empirical generalization can ever encompass all (or even a representative sample) of that abstract population of applications.

What we are left with is consistency – the consistency of our observational techniques with the directives of our strategy and the consistency of our observations with the theories proposed by that strategy. As consistency increases, our knowledge accumulates. However, the truth of that knowledge is never guaranteed.

As I have outlined my analysis, several kinds of theoretical activities are involved. I have argued (Wagner 1984; Wagner and Berger 1985, 1986) that programs of theoretical research play a critical role in linking theoretical concerns with empirical concerns. Here I have attempted to show the equally critical role played by orienting strategies and by observations. Orienting strategies are essential guides to the construction, evaluation, and revision of theories. They do not, however, constitute such theories. They are as analytically distinct as the blueprints for a building and the structure one actually constructs using those blueprints. Similarly, observations are critical elements in our attempt to refine and improve our theories. However, they also do not constitute such theories (nor do they constitute the only means by which we evaluate such theories. Observations are as analytically distinct from theories as particular examples of buildings are from the principles one uses to design one's own structure.

All three – strategies, programs, and observations – are necessary to the development of sociological knowledge. None, however, assures the validity of that knowledge. There is no firm foundation.

A CALL FOR DARING AND MODESTY

This last point has implications for the integration of theoretical and empirical sociology that should be explored. I have mentioned several times in this chapter the imperialism evident in both cultures. Theoretical sociology manifests what I call the "imperialism of the perspective." Not only is theoretical work more important to the discipline than is empirical work, one's own particular brand of theorizing (i.e. one's own orienting strategy) is the only legitimate one. All others are fatally flawed; they are outdated, insufficiently comprehensive, or too unidimensional. Similarly, empirical sociology manifests what I call the "imperialism of the technique." Not only is empirical work more important to the discipline than is theoretical work, one's own particular brand of investigation (i.e. one's own observational technique) is the only legitimate one. All others are fatally flawed; they are outdated, too limiting, or too simple.

Strong antagonisms often develop between members of the two cultures because of these imperial claims. Antagonisms almost as strong sometimes develop among members of different camps within the same culture because of these claims. Ironically, despite the radical differences in the nature of the claims made, the *bases* for the claims are everywhere the same. All presume there is a more or less standardized, objective process by which we can justify our knowledge.

Theoretical sociologists assume that there is a firm foundation of key concepts and ideas (i.e. a general theory) upon which all of our knowledge can be based. If we can just uncover that foundation and frame all of our questions and answers in its terms, our knowledge will be inherently valid and therefore secure. Moreover, all others will eventually fall into line behind our foundational position because of its inherent validity and security.

Empirical sociologists assume that there is a firm foundation of key observations and observational techniques upon which all of our knowledge can be based. If we can just generate enough reliable observations and link the generalizations we use to summarize them, our knowledge will be inherently valid and therefore secure. Again, all others will eventually fall into line behind our codification because of its inherent validity and security.

It should be evident from my earlier arguments that I regard justificationism as irrelevant to the growth of our knowledge. Indeed, in many ways I see it as a hindrance to that growth. There is no epistemological privilege, no method we can use to guarantee sociological truth. Furthermore, no epistemological privilege is needed; we can and do proceed without it. To assume that it is both feasible and necessary is to perpetuate the imperial tendencies and unbridgeable divisions I have outlined.

Although several recent philosophers have developed similar positions (notably Rorty (1979), with whom I disagree strongly regarding the alternative to justificationism), the earliest, most cogent and probably still the most radical position is developed by Popper (see especially Popper 1971). In fact, although I understand the association Popper has with positivism for most sociologists, I have always found that representation inaccurate. Popper's challenge to justificationism (and therefore to quite a large body of philosophical thought, including most versions of positivism) is at the absolute core of his philosophy. Since there is not room here to fully develop my own critique of justificationism, I refer the reader to Popper for further discussion.

If there is no ultimate basis for justifying our theoretical claims (either foundationally or observationally), rather greater modesty in our ontological and epistemological claims is called for. If, as I have argued, we cannot avoid making metatheoretical assumptions about social reality, that does not mean these assumptions must constitute the only plausible reality. Several different positions may have something legitimate to say about the social world. We might even benefit from a periodic substitution of the lens of another perspective for the one we prefer, simply to see how different the world looks from that point of view.

But modesty is not enough. The problem is that the lack of a firm foundation leads many to refrain from specific theorizing about social phenomena altogether. The lack of a firm foundation does not mean we cannot theorize. More than a little daring is called for.

There is a certain "Nevertheless!" quality to theorizing we must cultivate. We can never be certain of the truth of our ideas, but we can conjecture and hypothesize. *What if* the social world operated in this particular way or that particular way? How would that affect other assumptions we make about the world?

Moreover, we can learn from these conjectures and hypotheses. Our knowledge can improve in the sense that it is less prone to error than our previous conjectures were. We simply cannot be sure that we are approaching sociological truth as an endpoint. In Kuhn's (1970: ch. 7) terms, progress is better described as "evolution from what we do know" (i.e. from the less articulated and more specialized theories of the past) than as "evolution toward what we wish to know" (i.e. toward some sort of ultimate truth).

Thus, I call for both greater modesty and greater daring in our sociological theorizing. They will certainly help to break down the imperial barriers currently separating theoretical work from empirical work in the discipline. However, I also make a stronger claim. Some daring modesty will also enhance the prospects for growth of our knowledge. With it, we will still never reach security or certainty in our understanding of the social world. But then again, without it, our knowledge may not cumulate much at all.

REFERENCES

Blalock, H. M., Jr. 1969: *Theory Construction*. Englewood Cliffs, NJ: Prentice-Hall.

Glaser, B. G., and A. S. Strauss 1967: *The Discovery of Grounded Theory*. Chicago: Aldine.

Hage, J. 1972: *Techniques and Problems of Theory Construction in Sociology*. New York: Wiley.

Homans, G. C. 1961; 2nd edn 1974: *Social Behavior: Its Elementary Forms*. New York: Harcourt Brace & World.

Kuhn, T. S. 1962; rev. enl. edn 1970: *The Structure of Scientific Revolutions*. Chicago: University of Chicago Press.

Lakatos, I. 1968: "Criticism and the methodology of scientific research programmes," *Proceedings of the Aristotelian Society*, 69: 149–86.

Lakatos, I. 1970: "Falsification and the methodology of scientific research programmes," in I. Lakatos and A. Musgrave (eds), *Criticism and the*

Growth of Knowledge. New York: Cambridge University Press, pp. 91–196.

Marx, K. 1977 [1848]: *The Communist Manifesto*, in D. McLellan (ed.), *Karl Marx: Selected Writings*. New York: Oxford University Press, pp. 221–47.

Merton, R. K. 1968: "On sociological theories of the middle range," in *Social Theory and Social Structure* 2nd enl. edn; 1st edn 1957). New York: Free Press, pp. 39–72.

Parsons, T. 1951: *The Social System*. New York: Free Press.

Popper, K. R. 1971: "Conjectural knowledge: my solution to the problem of induction," in *Objective Knowledge*. Oxford: Oxford University Press, pp. 1–31.

Rorty, R. 1979: *Philosophy and the Mirror of Nature*. Princeton, NJ: Princeton University Press.

Stinchcombe, A. L. 1968: *Constructing Social Theories*. New York: Harcourt Brace Jovanovich.

Turner, J. 1986: *The Structure of Sociological Theory*, 4th edn. Chicago: Dorsey Press.

Wagner, D. G. 1984: *The Growth of Sociological Theories*. Beverly Hills, Calif.: Sage.

Wagner, D. G., and J. Berger 1985: "Do sociological theories grow?" *American Journal of Sociology*, 90: 697–728.

Wagner, D. G., and J. Berger 1986: "Programs, theory and metatheory," *American Journal of Sociology*, 92: 168–81.

Wallace, W. L. 1971: *The Logic of Science in Sociology*. Chicago: Aldine.

Zetterberg, H. 1965: *On Theory and Verification in Sociology*. Totowa, NJ: Bedminster Press.

PART III

Between Modernism and
Postmodernism: Toward a
Contextualizing General Theory

PART III

Between Modernism and
Postmodernism: Towards a
Reconstructive Critical Theory

9

Social Science and Society as Discourse: Toward a Sociology for Civic Competence

Richard Harvey Brown

> So the real issue is not between people who think one
> view is as good as another and people who do not. It is
> between those who think our culture, or purpose, or
> institutions cannot be supported except conversationally,
> and people who still hope for other sorts of support.
> Richard Rorty, *Consequences of Pragmatism*

> As soon as there is a society, every usage is converted
> into a sign of itself.
> Roland Barthes, *Elements of Semiology*

Social science is a civic discourse and so its theories may be
properly judged by how they function in the larger polity. This
political function of theory is not independent of its intellectual
content. Social theories operate within, and implicitly project, a
basic image of the world, a root metaphor of the "nature" of the
person and of society. Positivist general theory elaborates the
metaphors of society as an organism or a machine. Since these root
metaphors do not provide a language for describing human agency,
contradictions arise whenever positivists seek to extend their
theories to include the lifeworlds of persons.

By contrast, I propose an alternative to positivist general theory
based on the metaphor of society as a discourse or language rather
than as an organism or machine. I outline such an approach and

then illustrate it by discussing general theorists, such as Mary Douglas, Pierre Bourdieu, and Ferruccio Rossi-Landi. I do not advance the discursive approach to advocate a new universal paradigm, but to relativize the positivist approach and thereby invite a broader pluralism of perspectives (Ford and Klumpp 1985).

Nonetheless, the root metaphor of society as discourse may be more adequate logically, morally, and politically. Logically, this metaphor can describe both social structure and personal consciousness, both *langue* and *parole*, in an integrated and consistent fashion. Morally, this approach begins and ends in the conception of personal agency and the human authorship of the world, thereby providing a theoretical resource for any possible ethics. Politically, it serves to reveal the ideological encoding of any discourse, thereby encouraging criticality and openness in public debate.

GENERAL THEORY AND THE TRAVAILS
OF CIVIC TRUTH

The crises of our culture, and the tasks for any general theory, manifest themselves on three levels: the philosophical, the theoretical, and the political. The *philosopher* is concerned with the nature of reality, how it can be known, and what it should become. The *theorist* is interested in describing that which is, its origins, causes, and functions, its scarcities and potentials. The *activist* focuses on how we are to move from the theorist's "is" to the philosopher's "ought."

At the *epistemological* level, having begun by disenchanting the world, sociologists have come to disenchant their own absolutist mystique, forcing upon themselves a new methodological self-consciousness as a prerequisite to any future inquiry. A sequel to the unmasking of sociology's positivistic presuppositions has been the emergence of alternative approaches for understanding social reality. Yet each of these competing paradigms appears to be rooted in conflicting ontological and epistemological assumptions. Each paradigm defines social reality differently. The paradigms not only have different techniques of research but different definitions of what it is they are researching, what constitutes sociological knowledge, and what are the logical procedures by which such knowledge can be gained. Hence, though the various approaches may be complementary in their results, each in some fashion giving us a piece of a puzzle that must be assembled, they appear contradictory in their underlying methods of logic. General theory thus becomes a hodge-podge of paradigms that are ontologically and epistemologically incommensurate.

Central to the *theoretical* criticisms of orthodox general theory is its unanalyzed assumptions about the social world it seeks to understand. Its entire edifice rests upon the analogy that society is like an organism, a machine, or, more recently, a cybernetic system. Yet to unreflectively posit such an analogy is to beg many questions that sociology seeks to answer. It not only prevents finding out how society is possible, but also posits a determinate world inhabited by creatures largely unaware of the forces that move them. Hence, the role of human agency in the constitution or transformation of society becomes elusive as a datum of analysis. The orthodox position also assumes *a priori* the interdependence of societal parts – that is, institutions, roles, and the like – each contributing to the dynamic equilibrium of the whole. Moreover, human cooperation – a basic element to be accounted for by sociology – is presumed to be the natural outcome of socialization within a common value system; yet the nature of values and socialization remain almost as much a mystery as the explanation of their effects on human sociation. Since socialized individuals are assumed to be actors unwittingly manipulated by invisible social forces, the positivist puts little stock in these actors' conceptions of meaning and conduct, preferring to rely on his or her own objective observations.

An inverted version in this orthodoxy is that of some Marxist theorists, for whom cooperation is explained in terms of ideology. Sociation, in this view, is largely a product of force or fraud. But here again the exact nature of these key processes is little understood, and actors are seen more as automatons than as agents.

By contrast, alternative approaches such as symbolic interaction, ethnomethodology, or existential sociology assume that persons are volitional actors in the social drama, or players in the social game. These approaches describe the lifeworlds of persons as negotiated, symbolically constructed realities. But they tend to provide a sociology of consciousness without a sociology of structure. Moreover, it is unclear how the root metaphors of the organism or machine could be conjoined with consistency to those of drama or game. Efforts to integrate these different paradigms have remained a congeries of fragile patchworks.

These epistemological and theoretical difficulties are matched by a third problem: the relationship of theory and *practice*. From its very beginnings and with few exceptions, liberal sociology in America and Marxian sociology in Europe assumed that causational knowledge leads to curative action. But there remain immense gaps between the theoretical explanation of causes, the articulation of moral purposes, and the practical politics of improvement. Indeed, the achievement of morally sensitive, self-reflective, critical, phenomenological, or dialectical knowledge would appear to preclude the establishment of predictive and prescriptive theory. To be true to itself and the nature of its subject matter, "general theory" in the social sciences may have to remain partial and retrospective. Conversely, to yield predictive theory, sociology may have to dehumanize its subject matter and eliminate personal agency.

Thus the relationship of orthodox social theory to personal dignity and civic action remains problematic. The positivist paradigm leaves both the investigator and the objects of investigation in a state of fatalistic determinism and proposes a sterile neutrality toward values. Insofar as they adhere to their ideal of knowledge without a point of view, however, positivist thinkers remain insensitive to the historically relative and inevitably partial character of their own theoretical practices. Thus policies derived from social scientific knowledge are conceived either as technical instruments to rationally facilitate a given system or, conversely, as "ideological" and hence scientifically unsound. Despite such difficulties, commitment to the possibility of moral agency and political responsibility seem necessary if general theory is to be made a humanizing resource for social structural change. But how can this be achieved without violating the canons of established methods and theories?

I think we can draw some implications from these conundrums. First, it seems that we can have either no general theory or several general theories, but that we cannot with consistency have only one general theory. The various dichotomies and contradictions of methods of logic, levels of analysis, and implications for practice sketched above emanate from the lingering Cartesianism that pervades most efforts at general theory. Cartesian bifurcations between mind and body, consciousness and world, or reason and experience continue to inhabit social thought. Thus efforts at a single general theory tend either to patch together basically different approaches, or to diminish a plurality of approaches to a single dominant one. The first strategy yields self-contradiction; the second is a reductive imperialism.

The alternative to these sterile choices is a plurality of general theories, each internally consistent, but each based on a different root metaphor; each expressing a different intellectual telos and, implicitly, each representing a different ideological interest. To illustrate this possibility I now outline some dimensions and examples of a general theory based on the metaphor of society as communicative action.

SOCIETY AS DISCOURSE: AN ALTERNATIVE METAPHOR FOR GENERAL THEORY

Discursive analysis of society reveals that social science is itself a discursive practice. Like all of human experience, science is a conversation that takes place over time, in which accounts of what is, what has occurred, and what is true of this past and present are negotiated through symbolic interaction. It may be correct, as Louis Mink (1987: 60) argued, that "stories are not lived but told." But it is also the case that most of living is itself a telling of stories, including both the retrospective construction of for-the-moment completed stories as well as the conspective and prospective projection of candidate versions of the present and the future.

The metaphor of society as discourse also suggests that social structures can be understood as structures of language and that these structures are invented through acts of speech. A number of theorists have taken up the challenge of analyzing structural determinism from the viewpoint of a phenomenonology of language or, conversely, of understanding the intentionality of speech as engendered through language-like social structures. By conceptualizing both *langue* and *parole* as emerging from discursive practices, such theorists have sought to overcome the reificiation of language, on the one hand, and the subjectification of speech, on the other. Basil Bernstein, for example, argued that speech performances express and embody different worlds of meaning that are ordered hierarchically in society. Such symbol systems are realizations and regulators not only of speech performances but also of the structure of social relationships. One might further say that social relations are themselves symbolic systems, in that society itself is a system of communicative action (see Bernstein 1971; Brown 1987; Harré 1979).

This perspective has been enlarged by Mary Douglas, who has sought to link structure to meaning in a model of society as language. In her work with Aaron Wildavsky (1982), for example, Douglas interpreted contemporary political behavior in terms of structuralist concepts of purity and pollution. Elsewhere (1972) she elaborated empirically the assumption that symbols can symbolize only within a structured framework. Meaning depends on distinction, and distinction is an essential dimension of structure. For example, the concept of a meal as a semantic unit requires a grammatical distinction between meals and other kinds of eatings. This binary structure of meal/non-meal is created by distinctions *within* eatings that are meals, distinctions which are absent or structured differently in non-meals. In the English-speaking world, the core of a proper meal consists of meat and two vegetables, preceded by soup and followed by dessert. Douglas also observed that the structural element "meat" in relation to "two vegetables" is homologous to the structure of a "proper meal" as a whole, with its main course and subsidiary soup and dessert. This triadic structure makes it possible to distinguish meals from other eatings, and so enables us to invest meals with semantic meanings. For example, a "meal" may mean "this is for family only," or "eating thus with us, you are now a friend." As Douglas (1972) said, "Drinks are for strangers, acquaintances, workmen, and family. Meals are for family, close friends, honoured guests. The grand operator of the system is the line between intimacy and distance." Those we know at meals we also know at drinks, but not the reverse. The semantics *of* the meal (closeness) is made possible by its syntactics (triadic structure) *as* a meal.

Perhaps the most successful attempt to integrate agency and structure in largely discursive terms is the work of Pierre Bourdieu. Bourdieu recognized the cognitive power of structuralist theories of objective economic and political relations that provide a framework for practice (1977: 3). Instead of protesting against scientific objectification in the name of lived experience and withdrawing into a naive humanism, however, Bourdieu urged us to put structuralism "back on its feet" (ibid.: 3–4). Structuralism is off its feet because it fails to recognize the practical mastery of members, who are able to evoke the structure and deploy it to their own needs, needs that usually involve the imposition or evasion of domination. Concerning kinship structures, for example, Bourdieu (ibid.: 39–40) qualified the formulation of Lévi-Strauss: "The genealogical relationship is never strong enough on its own to provide a complete determination of the relationship between the individuals which it united, and it has such predictive value only when it goes with the shared interests, produced by the common possession of a material and symbolic patrimony."

The genealogical charts defined by anthropologists as having lawlike regularities are in practice invoked strategically either to establish greater inclusion by finding a common ancestor further back in time, or to mark greater exclusion, by shortening the lineage to include only more recent descendants and kin. Similarly, legal codes are "enacted" not only in parliaments, but also through their performance – that is, through their strategic invocation or selective enforcement. As Garfinkel (1967) or Bourdieu (1977) might have said with Kafka, "The verdict doesn't come all at once. The proceedings gradually merge into the verdict" (Kafka 1956 [1925]). Those with sufficient authority and wit can solemnize an incident into a precedent. What would have been a private occurrence, say the affront of a woman named Helen, thus can become an official insult and a cause for war. Conversely, clever underlings may manipulate the formal structure for their own ends; for example, when employees "work to rule" they may subvert the intent of these regulations. In this sense, determinism and agency, or social structure and individual consciousness, both emerge from the same discursive practices.

Another example of this relation of semiotic structures and hermeneutic contents can be generated by comparing structuralist and phenomenological analyses of the exchange of gifts. Marcel Mauss, and later Claude Lévi-Strauss, insisted on a complete break with natives' experience and their theories of that experience, and urged instead that the exchange, and not the actions or intentions of the individual engaged in it, constitutes the primary object of study. But, as Pierre Bourdieu noted, counter-gifts must be *deferred* and *different* if they are not to be taken as an insult. Too hasty a discharge of one's obligations is a sign of mistrust and ingratitude, for it retrospectively redefines the initial gift as intended to put one under obligation. Similarly, a counter-gift that is identical to the initial gift retrospectively redefines the relationship as one of swapping or lending. Contrary to structuralists, then, the constitution of gift exchanges requires strategy and style, timing and tact. Gift exchanges are never simply a blind grammar that operates independently of the will or consciousness of members. At the same time, and contrary to a naive hermeneutics, this "subjective" dimension is not identical to the self-perceptions of members nor to their own vocabularies of motive. "If the system is to work," said Bourdieu (1977: 6 n. 7; 4 n. 5), "the agents must not be entirely unaware of the truth of their exchanges, which is made explicit in the anthropologist's model, while at the same time they must refuse to know and above all to recognize it."

LINGUISTICS AND ECONOMICS

One can also cast the net of a linguistic approach to general theory over the big fish of economics. One way to do this would be to expand Saussure's theory of linguistic value to include value in general. Stated slightly differently, one would create a Marxian semiotics that subsumed the political economy of commodities under a political economy of signs. To see how this might be done, we should first distinguish theories of language as a system of signification from theories of language as a system of communication. The discursive approach presupposes a conception of language as a system of signification rather than as a system of communication. In the view of language as a system of communication, objects, ideas, relationships, selves, or institutions exist independently from the language that is used to describe them. In this theory a message is formulated to convey (or disguise) the meaning of extralingusitic objects, intentions, or conditions. The speaker encodes this extralinguistic reality into words and sentences and transmits it to an audience in the form of a message, which the audience then decodes (Thompson 1989: 7).

By contrast, in the view of language as a system of signification, the crucial category is the sign. The sign is made up of two aspects – the signifier (the sound image) and the signified (the concept). In this Saussurean view of language,

> linguistic values do not involve any pre-existing ideas but emanate from the very system itself. The concepts (the signified) are purely differential and defined not by their positive content but negatively by their relations with other terms of the system. This means that in the case of the sign, the concept (the signified) openly symbolizes a value determined by its relations with other similar values.
>
> (Ahonen 1989b: 36)

Likewise, on the material side of signification (the signifier, the sound-image) only the difference between sounds is crucial, and the means by which signs are produced are therefore unimportant.

This "economy of signs" is not so different from a monetary economy. As Saussure himself noted, in linguistics "as in political economy we are confronted with the notion of *value*; both sciences are concerned with a *system for equating things of different orders* – labor and wages in one and signified and signifier in the other" (1982: 115; 1966: 79). And it is unimportant whether the signifier of value (the money-image) be coins, paper, cowrie shells, or computer bits.

If we push this conception further, we could say that the sign constructs its own adequate signified. In this formulation, the signifier dominates the signified, and our attention is thereby directed to the conditions of discourse in order to understand the origin of meaning and sense. Meaning is not something already formed prior to its articulation, for which language serves only as a mechanism of transmission. Instead, the "play" of meaning and sense is a consequence of the play of signification itself, as exemplified by the system of signs that make up those very means of signification (Thompson 1989: 8).

If we transfer this way of thinking to the case of money, we see that both neoclassical and Marxist economics assume the communication or representational theory of language, and thus treat money as a sign of something else. Both see money as a means of representing value, though they differ as to what the value is. For neoclassical theorists, "value" is given by the utility obtained from the use of the commodity.

> The amount of money consumers are prepared to pay for a commodity depends upon the utility they derive from it. Of course, that utility cannot be observed directly. It is represented by money as it remains hidden. In Marxist theories, money is a phenomenal form of value, where value is determined by the abstract labor power embodied in that commodity.
>
> *(Thompson 1989: 8)*

Here again, that value can never be seen directly. It is "transformed" into money and prices. In both neoclassical and Marxian conceptions, then, it is the representation of value that we observe – the realm of money and prices – and not the deeper reality of utility or labor that determines it.

This representational theory distinguishes appearance (representation) from reality (the deeper meaning, structure, etc.), and then decodes the reality as it is displayed through the appearance. The absent reality becomes present through its representation. It is both absent and present at the same time. If we strictly applied positivist canons to such thinking, it would appear to be a logical contradiction, even an example of mystical thought, as in the absent presence of Christ's blood and flesh in the wine and the wafer. In Marxist literature this is called the "transformation problem."

By contrast, if we take seriously the view of language as signification, we understand the signifier to "construct" the signified. Analogously, money does not represent anything in terms of an extralinguistic domain of utility or value. Instead, money "constructs" value, but value on the same semiotic "surface" as money itself. Thus "value" and "money" are synonymous.

This view of money and value as "appearance" or "surface" would become more plausible if it were understood in the context of a general theory of economic action as a significatory system. Such a theory is hinted at in some of the writings of Saussure and Marx. Saussure (1982: 33; 1966:16) held that

"A science that studies the life of signs within society is conceivable," and he understood economics to be part of society. In a somewhat parallel notion, Marx (1971: 17) compared the fetishism of language to the fetishism of money:

> It is no less false to compare money with language. It is not the case that ideas are transmuted in language in such a way that their particular nature disappears and their social character exists alongside them in language, as prices exist alongside goods. Ideas do not exist apart from language.

We could extend this point and say that the world does not form speech, but that speech forms the world, or gives form *to* the world (Roche 1973: 79–80; Mehan and Wood 1975: 218–224). Class, economic exchange, and value take their existence and form in their linguistic enactment. In *Capital* Marx followed the logico-empiricism of Feuerbach and so he conceived of the value of goods as an expression of the labor of those who produced them. But he also argued in the more Hegelian *Grundrisse* that, under capitalism, language becomes reified. Language becomes the "agent of divorce" (Marx 1971: 71). Like virtue, love, or conviction, which men had considered inalienable, language too becomes "an object of exchange, or traffic . . . [what] till then had been communicated, but never sold; acquired, but never bought . . . passed into commerce."
Rossi-Landi's *Linguistics and Economics* (1975), a Marxist semiotics of intellectual life.[1] For Marxism, the problem was whether language in the social totality is determined or determining, whether it is part of the base or the superstructure. In admitting that language is neither of these, Rossi-Landi also recognized that any rigid theoretical separation between base and superstructure was inadequate and that the analysis of language was not possible within this framework (Bodner 1987). Thus Rossi-Landi tried to provide a new theory of the relations between structure and superstructure. His working hypothesis is that what mediates between the two is the totality of sign systems that define any particular social formation.

Rossi-Landi (1975: 6) described the categories of social reproduction and language as a homology between material production and linguistic production: "One of the most important aspects of this theory is that everything that has value (and therefore, as we shall see, everything that has meaning) is always a product of human work; value is something that man has introduced and continues to introduce into the world."

The central feature of all social signs is that they have meaning that is produced by human work. Rossi-Landi assumed that there are two fundamental modes of social development: the production and circulation of goods (in the form of commodities); and the production and circulation of sentences (in the form of messages). These two modes are essentially homologous. To describe their coinciding properties, Rossi-Landi transcoded into semiotic terms such basic concepts of Marxist economics as work, material production, exchange, and consumption. These economic phenomena are akin to linguistic activities. Goods and words are both artifacts. The material production of goods and the linguistic production of sounds, words, or sentences are forms of human work. "We sustain, then, the Vichian and Marxian thesis that the notion of artifact is in principle applicable to language" (Rossi-Landi, 1975: 33).[2]

Following Marx's political economic theory, Rossi-Landi (1975: 155) distinguished production, exchange, and consumption, and then applied these concepts to linguistic production as well: "The operation of total linguistic capital, i.e., of a language as constant linguistic capital together with its speakers as variable linguistic capital, is communication: [communication is the] production, circulation and accumulation of messages within a linguistic community, in a communicative market."

Rossi-Landi (1975: 183) also attempted to discover private ownership and exploitation of signs as a logical extension of his homology: "The major misunderstanding as regards linguistic private property is that the supra-individual, public, social character of the language is considered sufficient to exclude the possibility of the language itself being subject to private ownership." For example, in advanced capitalist societies, the game of economic semiosis is stacked in favor of oligopolistic owners. The capitalists' discourse may overwhelm the consumers' ability to effectively respond. Even if they do protest, *as consumers* they reinforce the dominant capitalist discourse. In more primal societies there also may be an elite ownership of customary or historical discourse. Thus Hocart's informant in Fiji (quoted in Sahlins 1985: 49) "was said to know little because he had been brought up among the common people and not the nobles"; likewise, Freeley-Harnick (1978: 402) in Madagascar found that "History is not evenly distributed because to have it is a sign of politico-religious power and authority."

Rossi-Landi's Marxist semiotics does not have a strong hermeneutic moment. There is much more structure of language than enactment of speech. Thus communicative agents are not seen to have much freedom; instead, their behavior is preprogrammed by the deep grammar of the semiotic system. "Semiotics finds its proper place, its significance, and its foundation alongside the study of modes of production and of ideologies, within the sphere of the social programming of all behavior" (Rossi-Landi 1975: 203).

Seen linguistically, economics becomes a subject of semiotics. As objects have become commodities and relationships have become ones of commodity exchange, the use value of things or people is subordinated to their exchange value. This exchange value is stated in terms of money, the purest of signs since it now stands for virtually anything (Marx 1946; Simmel 1978; Lukács 1971; Kelemen 1982). As Baudrillard (1981 [1976]: 63) said, "The object is *nothing* . . . but the different types of relations and significations that converge, contradict themselves, and twist around it." This semiotic critique of the political economy of the sign parallels the earlier Marxist critique of the political economy of the commodity. Indeed, in a Marxian semiotics, they become the same critique, since commodities are now seen as signs *par excellence*. The commodity combines use and exchange value, whereas "the sign . . . combines the signifier and the signified. A Marxian semiotics merges these two structures into a single structure that may be called the *signified commodity*" (ibid.; see also Baudrillard 1975, 1981; Denzin 1987).

In such a view, economic concepts such as "poverty" or "wealth" are themselves the outcome of human communicative actions that alter the horizons of experience and knowledge. "Goods acquire apparently necessary significances, much as language *seems* to lose its arbitrariness, because of a social context in which those goods are read as defining one's social availability" (Herzfeld 1985: 170). Once the semiotic properties of economic exchanges are recognized, they cease to be an isolated facet of human experience. Instead, "the meanings of goods are viewed as construed within a fluid social environment that is itself negotiated. Production and consumption are active process[es] in which all the social categories are being continually redefined" (Douglas and Isherwood 1978: 68). This is true of local firms and markets as well as of national and international economic processes, since ultimately producers and consumers alike remain actors in the creation of significance.

SOCIAL THEORY AND CIVIC DISCOURSE

These brief reflections are intended to suggest the possibility of an alternative general theory, one based on the metaphor of society as discourse or language rather than as organism or machine. Hence, I make no pretense that my examples are complete or that authors I cite are fully correct.[3] As a relatively new paradigm, or rather a Renaissance paradigm only recently revived, the discursive approach to general theory has not been elaborated nearly as much as the normal science of positivism. But my point is not that a linguistic orientation will or should become the new, single, unifying one. On the contrary, my arguments are those of a systematic pluralist. Hence, I advance the discursive metaphor not to overthrow positivism, but only to limit its sometimes absolutist and imperious claims.

   Nonetheless, I believe that the metaphor of society as discourse has certain logical and moral-political advantages over organistic and mechanistic ways of thinking. First, general social theory on the linguistic model can encompass micro-social phenomena such as meals, mezo-level phenomena such as gift exchanges, and macro-social phenomena such as economic structures. In the discursive approach, language is not a natural fact of daily life nor a mere epiphenomenon of forces and relations of production. Instead it expresses a social covenant. As Saussure (1982: 14, 113, 109) put it, this covenant is "the social side of language, outside the individual who can never create or modify it by himself; it exists only by virtue of a sort of contract signed by the members of the community. The community is necessary . . . by himself the individual cannot fix a single value. Each time I say [a] word I renew its substance."

The dichotomy of base and superstructure or structure and agency is mediated by discourse. The structure, envisioned as language, is both a constraint and a resource for enactments, envisioned as speech. The semiotic moment of the linguistic metaphor deals well with structure; its hermeneutic moment treats well of meaning and action. Both these dimensions – syntactics and grammatics, on the one hand, and semantics and pragmatics, on the other – are contained and logically consistent within the metaphor of society as discourse. In effect, this metaphor combines in linguistic terms Durkheim's conception of constraining structures with Marx's idea that the system of exchanges is the source of values (Lemert 1990). But it also incorporates Mead's and Garfinkel's conceptions of social reality as constructed through symbolic interaction.

Second, on a moral-political level, the discursive approach is reflexive. It sees the social sciences as providing *logoi* by which members generate their own social texts. Thus general theory on the metaphor of discourse explicitly recognizes its moral and political functions. That is, it acknowledges that its discourse *about* society reflects and engenders discourse *within* society. It thus sees social science as value-soaked civic talk about our common life.

The discursive approach to general theory also abandons the distorting notion of disciplines as well as positivist and hermeneutic dichotomies within these disciplines. Instead, it enables us to slice up modes of argumentation differently and understand "theory construction" in terms of various linguistic and textual strategies. Such an approach highlights the presuppositions and meta-logics of all the social sciences and thus brings values back to the fore. The devices of discovery and judgment, or invention and legitimation, are of course rhetorical terms; under the aegis of the language metaphor of society they now can be used to develop general social theories as discourses for reasoned civic judgment.

In abandoning the anti-rhetorical rhetoric of positivism, the discursive approach recovers the ancient function of social thought as a moral and political practice. In this critical rhetorical view, in constructing general theory we attend not only to logical propositions and empirical contents, but also to linguistic methods and existential functions. From this perspective, the linguistic dimension of social theory is an integral part of its truth or falsity to social life. This is for two reasons. First, truth and validity are themselves rhetorically constructed (Brown 1987, 1989a, b, 1990). Second, as rhetorical interventions, social scientific theories convey an existential as well as a propositional truth. Scientific truth about society is a truth of facts or meanings, an appeal to the telos of elegance and precision, predictability or comprehension. But seen discursively or rhetorically, such truth is also an implicit call to action. Its existential telos is self-understanding, critique, and emancipation. Positivists have sought to silence this existential dimension by treating general theory as an external object that makes no personal moral claim upon us. But social theories do convey an existential truth. And, unlike propositional truth, existential truth is not merely to be cross-examined. Instead, when it speaks we ourselves become its "object," and we must examine ourselves, for it is we who are addressed.

Thus, different approaches to general theory are not merely competing or complementary language games. Instead, each of them implies a different moral affirmation. For a purely language analytic philosophy, all interpretations are equally valid within the limits of the theory that provides their given rules of reading. But each such set of rules also has its own existential function (Ricoeur 1980: 107). The telos of psychoanalysis, for example, is an archaeology of the subject, the telos of positivist social science is technical direction of society. The telos of a discursive analysis of society is the human authorship of the world.

CODA

With reference to the theme of this volume, my conclusion is that the search for a single, unified theory in the social sciences is misguided, since it assumes that integration of general theories based on different root metaphors is both feasible and desirable. But as I have tried to show, such an integration is not logically feasible even within the positivist paradigm as long as it remains wedded to a Cartesian epistemology or its intaglios. And it is even less feasible when one tries to conjoin theories based on the imagery of the organism or machine with others based on metaphors of the theatre, ritual, game, or language.

Moreover, to the extent that various theoretical approaches articulate the visions and interests of different social groups, a single general theory of society is not desirable. Indeed, the hegemony of general theory from a mechanistic, organistic, or cybernetic perspective is suspicious, since it tends to legitimate a new class of technicians, managers, and experts, and to depower ordinary citizens in their efforts to rationally govern their lives. Conversely, general theories based on metaphors of human intentionality are weak at identifying causal interdependencies or rule-governed regularities in complex social orders; hence such theories are inadequate as discourses for the guidance of late modern social-technical systems.

While the discursive approach goes far in overcoming such dualisms, we should not claim for it an absolute privileged status. Indeed, even the discursive approach would be undesirable as an absolutist and hegemonic general theory. As long as we remain committed to some form of democratic pluralism and open public discourse, as long as we require efficient systems management for survival, and as long as we seek self-understanding and dignity in our life worlds, we will need alternative general theories to fully articulate these different practical interests. The key question, then, is not how to create a single integrated theory, but how various integrated theoretical discourses can contribute to a civic culture of citizens shaping their collective fate.

A discursive view of society does help us in this project. By affirming authorial agency through its use, we encourage ethical responsibility and provide cultural support for the telos of human emancipation within a democratic polity. And by simultaneously addressing both structure and agency as emerging from discursive practices, we also can unmask overdetermined encodings and begin to develop practical definitions of morally and politically competent speech. Discursive analysis of society thus is central to what Habermas (1970) and Stanley (1981) regard as the next stage in the moral evolution of Reason: the development of a rational ethic of civic communication.

NOTES

1 My comments on Rossi-Landi draw heavily on the work of Judith Bodner, whom I happily thank. For other interesting attempts at a linguistic analysis of economics see Ahonen 1989a, b; Amariglio 1988; Goux 1973, 1984; Irvine 1987; and Thompson 1989. For relevant general works see Bilmes 1986; Lemert 1979; MacCannell and Flower MacCannell 1986; Perinbanayagam 1985; and Rossi 1983.

2 There are interesting parallels between Rossi-Landi's ideas and those of Pierre Bourdieu. As Axel Honneth (1986: 56) noted, "Bourdieu offers a theory of action which analytically puts symbolic practices on the same level as economic practices, so that the former can be interpreted as strategies in the competition for prestige or standing in the social hierarchy. Both forms of activity, symbolic representations as well as economic accumulation, serve as means by which the social groups can improve their social position." In Bourdieu's idea of an "economy of practices . . . all actions, even those understood as disinterested or non-purposive, and thus freed from economic motives, are to be conceived economically as actions aimed at the maximization of material or symbolic gain" (Bourdieu 1977: 235). Like Rossi-Landi, Bourdieu has been accused of reducing the symbolic order to a materialistic or utilitarian one. Mary Douglas (with Baron Isherwood) also has developed a symbolic economics. For example, see their *World of Goods* (1978).

3 For example, Rossi-Landi's concept of "homology" implies that the similarity between work and language is so deeply rooted that these two phenomena no longer need to be distinguished. He also elaborates the homology in only one direction – language or communication is seen as work, but the idea of work as language or communication is less developed. Rossi-Landi's view of the exchange of commodities as a semiotic system could be enhanced by more discussion of the universal equivalent, money, as described in Marx's chapter in *Capital* on value, use value, and exchange value, or in Simmel's *Philosophy of Money* (1978). Yet Rossi-Landi seems to miss these points. Further, Rossi-Landi fails to adequately distinguish language as communication and language as signification. Thus, his promising approach has the "infantile disorders" of an early Marxist semiology.

REFERENCES

Ahonen, Pertti 1989a: "The meaning of money: comparing a Peircean and de Saussurean perspective." Unpublished manuscript. University of Tampere, Finland.

Ahonen, Pertti 1989b: "Tracing the meaning of money." Unpublished manuscript. University of Tampere, Finland.

Amariglio, J. L. 1988: "The body, economic discourse, and power: an economist's introduction to Foucault," *History of Political Economy*, 20/4: 583–614.

Barthes, Roland 1967: *Elements of Semiology*. New York: Hill & Wang.

Baudrillard, Jean 1975: *The Mirror of Production*. St Louis: Telos Press.

Baudrillard, Jean 1981: *For a Critique of the Political Economy of the Sign*. St Louis: Telos Press.

Bernstein, Basil 1971: *Class, Codes, and Control*, 3 vols. London: Routledge.

Bilmes, Jack 1986: *Discourse and Behavior*. New York: Plenum.

Bodner, Judith 1987: "Another approach to semiotics." Unpublished manuscript. Department of Sociology, Johns Hopkins University.

Bourdieu, Pierre 1977: *Outline for a Theory of Practice*. New York: Cambridge University Press.

Bourdieu, Pierre 1984: *Distinction: A Social Critique of the Judgment of Taste*. Cambridge, Mass.: Harvard University Press.

Brown, Richard Harvey 1987: *Society as Text: Essays on Rhetoric, Reason, and Reality*. Chicago: University of Chicago Press.

Brown, Richard H. 1989a [1977]: *A Poetic for Sociology: Toward a Logic of Discovery for the Human Sciences*. Chicago: University of Chicago Press.

Brown, Richard H. 1989b: *Social Science as Civic Discourse: Essays on the Invention, Legitimation, and Uses of Social Theory*. Chicago: University of Chicago Press.

Brown, Richard H. 1990: "Narrative in scientific knowledge and civic discourse," *Current Perspectives in Social Theory*, 11: 313–329.

Denzin, Norman K. 1987: "On semiotics and symbolic interactionism," *Symbolic Interaction*, 10/1: 1–19.

Douglas, Mary 1972: "Deciphering a meal," in *Implicit Meanings: Essays in Anthropology*. London: Routledge, pp. 249–75.

Douglas, Mary, and Baron Isherwood 1978: *The World of Goods*. New York: Basic Books.

Douglas, Mary, and Aaron Wildavsky 1982: *Risk and Culture: An Essay* on the Selection of Technological and Environmental Dangers. Berkeley: University of California Press.

Ford, James E., and James F. Klumpp 1985: "Systematic pluralism: an inquiry into the bases of communication research," *Critical Studies in Mass Communication*, 2 (December): 407–34.

Foucault, Michel 1970 [1966]: *The Order of Things: An Archaeology of the Human Sciences*. New York: Pantheon.

Foucault, Michel 1980: *Power/Knowledge: Selected Interviews and Other Writings, 1972–1977*, ed. Colin Gordon. New York: Pantheon.

Freeley-Harnik, Gillian 1978: "Divine kingship and the meaning of history among the Sakalava of Madagascar," *Man*, n.s. 13/2: 402–17.

Garfinkel, Harold 1967: *Studies in Ethnomethodology*. Englewood Cliffs, NJ: Prentice-Hall.

Goux, Jean-Joseph 1973: *Economie et symbolique*. Paris: Seuil.

Goux, Jean-Joseph 1984: *Les monnayeurs du language*. Paris: Galilée.

Habermas, Jürgen 1970: "Toward a theory of communicative competence," in Hans Peter Dreitzel (ed.), *Recent Sociology, No. 2: Patterns of Communicative Behavior*. New York: Macmillan, pp. 115–48.

Harré, Rom 1979: "Architectonic man: on the structuring of lived experience," in Richard Harvey Brown and Stanford M. Lyman (eds), *Structure, Consciousness, and History*. New York and London: Cambridge University Press, pp. 139–72.

Herzfeld, Michael 1985: "Converging paths in semiotics and anthropology?" *Semiotica*, 56/1 and 2: 153–77.

Honneth, Axel 1986: "The fragmented world of symbolic forms: reflections on Pierre Bourdieu's sociology of culture," *Theory, Culture, and Society*, 3/3: 55–66.

Irvine, Judith T. 1987: "The division of labor in language and society," *Working Papers and Proceedings of the Center for Psychosocial Studies*, 7.

Kafka, Franz 1956 [1925]: *The Trial*. New York: Modern Library.

Kelemen, Janos 1982: "Lukács's ideas on language," in Ferenc Kiefer (ed.), *Hungarian Linguistics*. The Hague: Mouton, pp. 245–68.

Lemert, Charles 1979: *Sociology and the Twilight of Man: Homocentrism and Discourse in Sociological Theory*. Carbondale: Southern Illinois University Press.

Lukács, Gyorg 1971 [1922]: *History and Class Consciousness: Studies in Marxist Dialectics*. Cambridge, Mass.: MIT Press.

MacCannell, Dean, and Juliet Flower MacCannell 1986: *The Time of the Sign*. Bloomington: Indiana University Press.

Marx, Karl 1946 [1848]: *Capital*. New York: Everyman's Library.

Marx, Karl 1971 [1857–8]: *Marx's Grundrisse*, ed. D. McLellan. London: Macmillan.

Mauss, Marcel 1967: *The Gift: Forms and Functions of Exchange in Archaic Societies*. New York: Norton.

Mehan, Hugh, and Houston Wood 1975: *The Reality of Ethnomethodology*. New York: John Wiley.

Mink, Louis 1987: in Brian Fay, Eugene O. Golob, and Richard T. Vann (eds), *Historical Understanding*. Ithaca, NY: Cornell University Press.

Perinbanayagam, R. S. 1985: *Signifying Acts: Structure and meaning in Everyday Life*. Carbondale: Southern Illinois University Press.

Ricoeur, Paul 1980: "Existence and hermeneutics," in Josef Bleicher (ed.), *Contemporary Hermeneutics: Hermeneutics as Method, Philosophy, and Critique*. London: Routledge, pp. 236–56.

Roche, Maurice 1973: "Class analysis and the showing of dichotomy," in Paul Filmer, Michael Phillipson, Maurice Roche, Barry Sandywell, and David Silverman, "Stratifying Practices." Unpublished manuscript. Goldsmiths' College, London.

Rorty, Richard 1982: *Consequences of Pragmatism*. Minneapolis: University of Minnesota Press.

Rossi, Ino 1983: *From the Sociology of Symbols to the Sociology of Signs: Toward a Dialectical Sociology*. New York: Columbia University Press.

Rossi-Landi, Ferruccio 1975: *Linguistics and Economics*. The Hague: Mouton.

Rossi-Landi, Ferruccio 1983: *Language as Work and Trade: A Semiotic Homology of Linguistics and Economics*, tr. Martha Adams et al. South Hadley, Mass.: Bergin & Garvey.

Sahlins, Marshall 1985: *Islands of History*. Chicago: University of Chicago Press.

Saussure, Ferdinand de 1982 [1945]: *Cours de linguistique générale*, ed. Tullio de Mauro. Paris: Payot. Eng. tr. by Wade Baskin: *Course in General Linguistics*. New York: McGraw-Hill, 1966.

Simmel, Georg 1978 [1900]: *The Philosophy of Money*, tr. Tom Bottomore and David Frisby. London: Routledge.

Stanley, Manfred 1981 [1978]: *The Technological Conscience: Survival and Dignity in an Age of Expertise*. Chicago: University of Chicago Press.

Thompson, Grahame 1989: "Homo Rhetoricus: economics and the social sciences discover the linguistic model and postmodernism, or do they?" Unpublished manuscript. Faculty of Social Sciences, The Open University, Milton Keynes, England.

10

Culture, History, and the Problem of Specificity in Social Theory

Craig Calhoun

Two different approaches have been involved in the project of developing "general" theory in sociology. The first of these seeks breadth, richness, or far-reaching application. The theories of Marx, Weber, and Durkheim, for example, are said to be general because they can be applied to so many areas or dimensions of social life. They are thus contrasted both with theories of the middle range (*pace* Merton 1968) and with the very local theories which are proposed and tested in most sociological research (e.g. the "theory" of the demographic transition, or even more the basic building blocks in Stinch-combe's 1968 conception of sociological theory). In the second approach theory is held to be general on more positivist grounds, because of its relative success in producing universally applicable, preferably lawlike statements.

The first of these understandings points to a virtue of the classical tradition of sociological theory, the attempt to build theories adequate to the understanding of social life in its full richness. It accepts rather too easily, however, the claims of the classical theorists – or at least most of them, most of the time – to be able to grasp with a single theory the sum total of instances of "society" or "social life." Even more, this understanding follows Parsons in exaggerating the extent to which the classical theorists were developing theory which was independent of specific historical and cultural contexts, and which was about a similarly abstracted notion of social life. In fact, Marx especially and in many ways Weber were quite attentive to the historical (if not always the cultural) specificity of social theory. This is one reason why their conceptual frameworks, although very broad in reach, were always developed in close relationship to specific empirical historical accounts; their abstractions were not free-floating but historically specific and determinate.

The second understanding of general theory derives from a widespread modern notion of science as discovery of universal truths. Durkheim was its main expositor among classical social theorists.[1] This second understanding of generality does not have to do with reach so much as with universal validity, certainty, positivity. It shapes not only debates over general theory but sociologists' folk imaginings of what physical scientists do: (1) theorizing about universal phenomena, (2) making universally valid statements about restricted scopes of phenomena, (3) attempting to make specific empirical or abstract propositions add up to maximally general ones, and (4) attempting to deduce specific subsidiary theories as special cases of more general ones.

This project has been challenged in a variety of ways. It has been shown, for example, that putatively universal laws were either false or applicable only within a very narrow empirical scope (e.g. innumerable claims about "human nature" have been shown to apply only or primarily to the American college students of the 1950s or 1960s who formed the population from which research subjects were drawn). This challenge, of course, strikes only at particular theories; though it complicates the inductive dimension of positivist theory-building, it does not in itself invalidate it. Similarly, the argument that sociology shows few, if any, cases of either the deduction of successful local theories from more general ones, or of the combination of tested propositions and/or local theories into more general ones does not demonstrate that the discipline cannot in principle do better in the future. In some ways, epistemological critiques are more damaging. The hermeneutic argument against the easy assumption of the pure facticity of observations (let alone survey or interview responses) suggests the fundamental impossibility of a theory pure in its empirical as well as its logical positivism. This challenge is often presented in such a radical way, however, as to make all research seem pointless because no secure grounds can be given for comparative evaluation of results. Paradoxically, perhaps, this tends to lead researchers to feel justified in ignoring the critique. In any case, theory of the sort challenged thrives, even where the challenges would seem on philosophical grounds to have been fatal. At least the beginning of an explanation for why lies in the very separation of "abstracted empiricism" from "grand [read, in part, general] theory" which Mills (1959) critiqued two generations ago.

I want to turn my attention in this chapter not towards further epistemological critique, but to the question of what sort of work should be offered as an alternative to both abstracted empiricism and positivist grand theory. One of the problems of many epistemological critiques is that they have seemed to endorse or entail a relativism so thoroughgoing as to make empirical research – and most scholarly discourse – meaningless. I want to argue not only for the importance of empirical work, but for the essential mutual implication of theoretical and empirical work. Specifically, my claim is that most good sociological theories – especially those which attempt to grasp social life in something of its fullness – need to be culturally sensitive and historically specific. My argument is not just for the virtues of history and ethnography, but for the virtues of a theory which can take both of them seriously. Yet, let me stress in advance, this is an argument for theory – including both empirical and normative theory, and theory of very broad reach – and against extreme relativism. It offers two cheers for particularism, but suggests that though theoretical groundings are always by nature incomplete, they are nonetheless achievable in some proportion and worth pursuing. The kind of theory I advocate would be continuous with cross-cultural and historical description, but not identical to them because the explanations the theory proposes would purport to anticipate or account for cases beyond those for which they were developed (*pace* Lakatos 1970 and, in passing, Stephen Turner's essay in chapter 4 of this volume).

Four sections follow. In the first, I shall elaborate on what I mean in my statement of theoretical desiderata by "culturally sensitive." In the second I shall similarly explore the notion of historical specificity. The third section will take as given my claim that social theory should be culturally sensitive and historically specific, and ask just what such theories should look like. The final section will discuss briefly the relationship of the project suggested here to some aspects of so-called postmodernism.

CULTURAL SENSITIVITY

By advocating cultural sensitivity, I mean that we should be attentive to problems of difference in a way social theorists seldom have been. Social theorists are too fully the heirs of the Enlightenment when they accept an ideology of science based on decontextualized truth claims, and when in both empirical and normative ways they join forces too uncritically with Enlightenment universalism. Though the latter in particular has certain normative virtues, grounding aspects of liberalism which have not outlived their usefulness, it also poses serious problems.

The very scientistic attempt to sever empirical theory from normative theory has contributed to normative theory's problematic over-commitment to a culturally insensitive Enlightenment universalism. Normative theory has continued to adopt an eighteenth-century view of human beings as essentially interchangeable individuals. Both the individualism and its usual corollary that individuals are or should be essentially similar are problematic and ethnocentric. This is somewhat ironic, since critiques of Western ethnocentrism are often couched in the language of liberal individualism; they are in essence arguments that the underlying similarities of individuals are more important than the apparent cultural (and other) differences among them. There are even cases where extreme relativism and strong universalism actually meet in a shared individualism. On the one hand, assertions that there are no generally defensible grounds for normative judgment make this individualism into a declaration of the inevitability of arbitrary subjectivity; on the other hand assertions that certain moral injunctions (like the Kantian categorical imperative) must apply everywhere make an alternative individualism the basis for claiming to discover implicitly universal grounds for morality. In this sense, both that branch of modernity which has lately traveled under the name of postmodernism and the explicit Enlightenment modernism proclaimed for example by Habermas suffer from weaknesses of cross-cultural sensibility. The former strain of thought is apt to make cultural difference into an insuperable barrier to both general discourse and normative critique. The latter is apt to reduce cultural difference to mere positions in a developmental scheme or grant it no theoretical significance whatsoever.[2]

Enlightenment universalism with its impoverishment of cross-cultural outlook informs not only the normative theories directly in its lineage but the bulk of universalizing empirical theoretical discourse. The idea that we can make significant general statements true of all human action, or human beings, or society at large is its heir. Such a notion is not false, I might add, for I believe there are some such statements to be made. Rather, problems arise when theorists try to make such statements beyond a very narrow range of minimal and generally highly formal and highly qualified propositions. There is a long-standing critique of this sort of ethnocentric positivism, which is not worth reproducing here.

The recent struggles between self-proclaimed postmodernists, poststructuralists, and similar thinkers, on the one hand, and adherents of the Enlightenment project of modernity as rationalization on the other, however, suggest that the normative dimension requires more comment. One of the virtues of the work of Foucault, Derrida, and a number of other fellow travelers has been to thematize the importance of difference. Here I will only point schematically to two lessons to be learned.[3]

The first I would call the importance of fundamental differences of value. Universalist thought tends towards the position that there can only be one set of fundamental values; others can be justified to the extent that they are derivative from these. These are not generally concrete norms, as they might be in Aristotelian thought, but categorical or procedural injunctions. For Habermas (1984), famously, these are held to be implicit in the validity claims of all speech (to intelligibility, truthfulness, rightness or appropriateness, and sincerity). Since any responsible participation in communicative action must be open to redemption of these implicit validity claims, Habermas can claim an empirical basis for his normative theory, and indeed for expecting its developmental advancement. The relevant catch, for present purposes, comes with his decontextualized treatment of the giving of reasons. He combines a neo-Kantian philosophical groundwork with speech act theory and Kohlberg's account of moral reasoning as a hierarchical sequence of stages in which justice is conceptualized in progressively more abstract and general ways. As the now famous Kohlberg–Gilligan debate makes clear, however, this understanding of moral reasoning privileges one mode over others.[4] It grants greater validity and rationality to "post-conventional" moral reasoning (that which is maximally universalistic and in which the giving of reasons for moral judgments is oriented to a decontextualized discussion of formal, general "rights" or other principles of decision). So, generally, do the courts and most philosophers and other arbiters of moral judgment in the West. But do Kohlberg or Habermas offer an adequate basis for denying that a partially particularistic, situated moral reasoning based on ideas of care rather than abstract justice should not be considered comparably "advanced"? I think not. Though Habermas does stress the importance of conceiving human beings intersubjectively rather than individualistically, he does not advance this approach to a fully social understanding of morality. Rather, he returns moral judgment to a Kantian realm of decontextualized individuals. He does not consider whether the best moral judgment might not begin with relationships rather than individual persons, for example. Indeed, if (as seems true) the very notion of individual is culturally and historically specific, this affects normative statements incorporating it. And human individuals may be non-equivalent in varying ways internal to cultural formations or historical epochs. The non-equivalence, non-interchangeability of men and women in our own and nearly every other culture is of major import for moral theory (see Young 1987, on the problems built into the assumption that justice must rest on impartiality). More to the point of the present discussion, Habermas never questions that moral theory requires that all moral questions be rationally decidable, at least in principle, and that there be a clear and singular hierarchy of procedures and reasons for moral judgments. In other words, within the scope of Habermas's theory (and not just where he bases his work on Kohlberg) there is no room for recognition of a plurality of orientations to reason or action as equally meritorious.

Secondly, we should appreciate not only differences of value but the positive value of difference. In other words, contrary again to Habermas's vision, cultural difference among human societies and differences among people within societies or communicative communities is in itself desirable. Like the inherent desirability of a multiplicity of species in the biological world, there is an intrinsic advantage to the production of cultural variation. This is, of course, not an unlimited advantage; like most others it can reach points of diminishing return and must be hemmed in by other fundamental values. Nonetheless, difference is good. Freedom entails difference, it seems to me, and creativity may well depend on diversity. Moreover, social integration and reproduction both depend on at least some sorts of difference. Habermas does grant solidarity a place alongside justice in his account of basic social goods, and recognizes Durkheim's arguments for the possibility of solidarity based directly on reciprocal need (and hence difference). Yet social integration based on communication would seem to depend at least on a full respect for difference, if not an actual value on it, since it depends on a mutually empowering discourse across lines of difference (Calhoun 1988). Empirical social theory which does not fully address cultural and interpersonal difference at the most fundamental levels reinforces the tendency of normative theory to devalue difference. Here we confront the complicity of theory in the normalizing process to which Foucault (e.g. 1965, 1977a) has drawn our attention.

Related to these two points is the need for social theory to recognize the cultural construction (rather than autonomy) of putatively general categories. Race and gender, for example, need to be seen as sociocultural organizations of roles and identities, not simple derivations from the alleged facts of biology. This much has been a staple of sociological wisdom for generations. The step which many sociologists do not take is to recognize the fundamental significance of such categories. Even many self-declared feminist sociologists, for example, address issues of gender only by adding the variable of sex to established research paradigms like status attainment. They do not consider how the cultural construction of a categorical opposition between male and female shapes the very way in which we conceptualize society. Nor do they reflexively evaluate the place of gender in scientific practice as more than a problem of material opportunities for female graduate students and scientists (cf. Harding 1986). A genuinely culturally sensitive social theory has to analyze and ask about the implications of the fact that we live in a deeply gendered world. Similarly, such a theory must go beyond the opposition between seeing race as a biologically given category and, by deconstructing its biological foundation, acceding to a claim that it exists only in the eyes of the biased observer. The latter sort of liberal critique of racism returns to the Enlightenment notion of essentially similar individuals. Just as a really serious feminism is about rethinking the categories of gender, not just getting women to wear business suits, so a really serious approach to race must begin with the cultural production and reproduction of race as a socially salient category and involve basic categorial rethinking, not merely reduction in objective consequences of racial sorting. We must recognize the assimilationist bias built into the liberal critique of racism.

One of the implications of trying to take difference seriously is that theory must be contentful, not purely and exclusively formal. There is certainly room for purely formal theory, but it must be recognized that it cannot and does not stand alone as an enterprise.[5] Social theory can only be constructed on the basis of some explicitly or implicitly induced knowledge of the world. The categories used in declaredly purely formal theory – categories like gender, race, class, individual – are always at some level culturally specific inductions. This is not simply a flaw which is to be avoided or mimimized by maximally abstract and artificial definitions of the phenomena under study, but rather the occasion for making clear the immanent relationship of any theory to its own empirical context and history. Making this relationship clear is not simply a prolegomenon to theory construction, but the primary means of establishing connection between the most fundamental categories of a theory and the empirical world on which they purport to have purchase.[6] The place of empirical content in theory, and especially the assertion that basic categories are always linked to such content, raises the problem of theoretical generality in a particularly provocative way. We can approach this by looking at the problem of translation and evaluation across cultural boundaries.

Peter Winch's *Idea of a Social Science* (1958) set off a controversy about cross-cultural imputations of rationality which poses fundamental questions for the notion of general social theory. Winch argued that it was irrevocably the case that different cultures had different standards of judgment, and that it was therefore necessary to admit of a plurality of standards of rationality. This much I think has to be granted. Winch also argued, however, that it was impossible to translate among and compare these standards of rationality in a way that did justice to the internal meaning of each, or justified treating any one of them as superior to the others. Our preference for our own must be seen as purely arbitrary and accidental. It is primarily around these latter points that debate has raged (see the collections edited by Wilson, 1970, and Hollis and Lukes, 1982), foreshadowing in some ways aspects of "postmodernism." Most claims that there is a single universal standard of rationality are really claims for the absolute superiority of one standard, and are compatible with recognition that other people may act on other standards, though arguers may wish to deny the label of rationality to those standards.[7] The fundamental questions are: can we translate among very different cultures (or, at the extreme, among any differing discourses), and on what grounds can we claim superiority for one standard of judgment? These are very hard questions and I do not propose to attempt an answer here. Rather, I want simply to raise certain implications of the debate for the practice of social theory.

The problem of translation arises at two levels. The first is the difficulty of rendering observations, interpretations, or propositions in language which is neutral and equivalent across cultural contexts. In other words, to take a simple example, sociologists are apt to use a single term like "family" or "monastery" to refer to a range of concrete instances which are designated by varying and not entirely synonymous terms in different languages. This may be inevitable and even necessary, but we need continually to remind ourselves of its problematic nature. There is no self-evident warrant for treating a Buddhist "monastery" as a token of the same type as a Catholic monastery. Rather, our use of a single term to refer to both is an assertion about their commonality. The type is our construct; it does not inhere in some external reality, and like any construct it is language- as well as referent-dependent. We modern Western (and especially English-language) sociologists are remarkably prone to treat extensions of terms defined within our linguistic and institutional universes as though they were transparent, neutral and able to fit precisely in culturally variant contexts. But the problems which arise from the fact that "monastery" may not mean precisely the same thing as the terms from other languages which we gloss with it, or indeed that "class" and its putative synonyms may not refer to the same categorical constructs in all Western (let alone non-Western) settings are ultimately the easier of the two sorts of problems of translation. The problems of translation in this sense begin with the potential looseness of fit in any linguistic exchange, even in conversation between competent speakers of the same language. Each speaker may refer to slightly different things by the same term, fix the term slightly differently in the web of intra-linguistic associations, and intend or experience slightly different emotional feelings or perlocutionary effects. Ordinary conversation allows a good deal of redundancy, as well as opportunities for checking and exploring understandings, as ways of dealing with this. The problem is similar, though much more complex, when cross-linguistic understanding is sought.

The second level for the problem of translation arises when we seek to understand linguistic meanings which are not simply different from our own, but involve incommensurable practices. It is one thing, for example, to learn that dozens of shades and hues of blue have different names, and that recognition of the phenomenal differences may depend in part on learning the categories by which they are labeled. The misunderstanding which might have come from translating terms for azure, faience and turquoise all simply as blue can be remedied fairly straightforwardly. Indeed English has a great many color terms which are familiar to artists and not common in ordinary discourse; these may allow for progressively better translation. The situation is made simple by the fact that the English speaker and the speaker of the other language are engaged in similar practices when using names for colors. It becomes a great deal more complicated when translation is attempted among practices which are fundamentally different, and especially so when those different practices are incommensurable with our own. Practices are incommensurable, Charles Taylor (1982) suggests, when they are incompatible in principle, when they cannot be carried on simultaneously. Rugby football and soccer are thus incommensurable, because each is organized according to a different set of rules, and the rules conflict in fundamental ways (e.g. with regard to whether carrying the ball is a legitimate tactic or a foul). As this example suggests, we may know about and have the capacity to participate in a multitude of incommensurable activities within our own daily lives and cultural contexts. This does not mean, however, that we can easily translate among them. How would we make rugby understandable in terms of soccer (literally, in terms of, not simply in relation to or to a player of soccer)? The challenge becomes more complex and more theoretically salient when we take up the issue of translating between incommensurable practices in very different cultures – say, comparing traditional Chinese and modern Western medicine.[8]

In this case, the two sorts of practices are different in form and content, in mode of reasoning and material prescription, but they make competing claims to something of the same practical efficacy. When they are brought into relationship with each other, they are naturally apt to become competitors. It is, moreover, nearly unavoidable that some judgments of their relative efficacy will be made (at the very least by consumers, if not by "disinterested observers"). This is so precisely because they are incommensurable and not simply different. Chinese traditional medicine is also at least as much different from Western architectural practices as from Western medicine, but it is not incommensurable with the former in the same sense, and indeed Chinese traditional medicine is happily practiced in Western-style buildings.

The point of all this is to suggest that overcoming ethnocentrism in social theory involves not just appreciating differences but coming to terms with incommensurable practices. The implications of this are somewhat surprising. It is commonly assumed that the appropriate approach to cross-cultural understanding, the antidote to ethnocentrism, is simply to suspend critical judgment. This is sometimes made into a ground for thoroughgoing relativism. The importance of understanding incommensurable practices, however, challenges this relativism.

To be sure, a first principle for understanding the practices of people very different from oneself is to suspend the sort of critical judgment one might apply to apparently similar practices in one's own culture. One should first attempt to understand just what the practice is, not categorize it immediately on the basis of its surface similarity to practices with which one is familiar. Unfortunately, too many sociologists do not take seriously the difficulty of this first step. As Taylor says (1982: 93): "The very nature of human action requires that we understand it, at least initially, in its own terms; that means that we understand the descriptions that it bears for the agents. It is only because we have failed to do that that we can fall into the fatal error of assimilating foreign practices to our own familiar ones." But generally, at least as researchers and social theorists, we do not wish to stop with this effort to understand an action in its own terms. Indeed, where investigators claim that such an understanding is the sole object of their investigation, they are generally disingenuous. They are engaged in an investigation which is itself outside of the practice they are investigating; they try to render practical knowledge discursive; they write articles and books aimed at audiences not composed of participants in the practice (or else urging participants to take a somewhat distanced stance towards their own practice). More generally, researchers usually are quite explicit in their intention to achieve, minimally, a translation of the practice into a form understandable in some discourse outside of that practice – usually that of the researcher's scholarly associates. Anthropologists do not go to New Guinea simply to become Papuans, or Ilongat, or what-have-you, they go in order to return and reveal something of what it means to be Papuan, or Ilongat, or what-have-you. Translation is thus a vital part of achieving social knowledge.

But is translation *per se* a good description of how the anthropologist or other investigator first achieves understanding? Largely, especially for the best fieldwork, I think not. In the first place, the knowledge of a practice is in many cases itself a largely practical, intuitive, even embodied *sense* (cf. Bourdieu 1976, 1977) not objectified in discourse. Even for purely discursive knowledge, however, the process of achieving understanding across lines of cultural difference does not seem to be one of translation as such but of a richer, more complex discourse. Interlocuters – anthropologist and informant, say – engage each other in a process of gradually improving understanding, which must be conceived in dynamic terms. Both the anthropologist and the informant are changed by it. They achieve the understanding precisely because they change into people who can understand each other, not because one translates the static fully formed knowledge of the other into a form which he or she can appropriate without becoming a significantly different person. Since knowing is an action constitutive of the person, not a mechanical storing up of data, gaining in knowledge always means changing somewhat. But specifically where there are basic incompatibilities in practices (and accordingly in practical knowledge and sensibilities), achieving understanding involves becoming a person who in principle can play two different games which cannot be played simultaneously and which cannot be translated directly into the terms of each other. The anthropologist may thus construct an ethnography of the Nuer, revealing a good deal of what it means to be Nuer, but doing so is not simply translating Nuer life into Western anthropological (or ordinary) language.[9] Moreover, the anthropologist is doing something which stands not only outside of but in a hierarchical relationship to what Nuer generally do (since, for example, Nuer do not send anthropologists to Britain).[10] The transformations which are entailed by mutual understanding need not be symmetrical.

Earlier I chose the example of Chinese traditional medicine confronting Western "scientific" medicine precisely because this is not as starkly hierarchical a contrast as the one commonly used in the literature on cross-cultural translation and evaluation of rationality: that of witchcraft vs. modern science.[11] While we do not imagine the participants in Zande discourse on witchcraft attempt to comprehend Western science in Zande terms (though something of this might in principle be imaginable), there clearly is some such effort on the part of traditional Chinese medical practitioners. These not only attempt to understand Western medicine, they have appropriated aspects of it – both specific treatments and especially a quasi-experimental mode of research into and discussion of traditional medicine.[12] Nonetheless, the existence of incommensurable practices forces on us the necessity of evaluation. Where two activities are simply different, we may (disregarding opportunity and resource costs) say, "let a hundred flowers bloom," and enjoy the diversity without pretending to evaluation. Indeed, where difference is complete, comparative evaluation may be either impossible or a purely subjective, rationally arbitrary matter. But incommensurable activities are precisely linked by certain similarities; though they may be radically different, they pose related claims on the attention of observers – and, in the case of medicine, of potential clients. Possibly neither Chinese nor Western medicine is "better" in some overall way, but within certain domains where both claim efficacy, they are bound to be the subject of comparative evaluations. Moreover, it is not the case that such evaluations are merely arbitrary exercises of subjectivity or the will to power (as post-Foucaultian discourse might lead one to believe). Western medicine reveals sufficient technical effectiveness that it demands some combination of acceptance, explanation, or suppression (as, indeed, did Western science when it first began to achieve notable technical success in the West). Practitioners of Chinese medicine are, in fact, forced onto the defensive whenever they are put into direct competition with Western-style medicine on one of the latter's strong points. But of course Western-style medicine has weak points as well, and there is at least room for Chinese specialists to advance compelling practical claims of their own in these areas. Thus acupuncture and certain herbal remedies travel to the West, where an attempt is made to appropriate them – an attempt which will continue to make Western specialists uneasy until their efficacy is fully explained on grounds internal to the Western scientific medical discourse.

A full understanding of each discourse from within the other, however, is impossible. If the respective groups of practitioners were to achieve a full understanding of each other, it could only be by creating some new form of medical practice which incorporated elements of each tradition but was not reducible to either. Then, of course, the groups would have changed. The same, I would contend, is true of all the sorts of cross-cultural discourses in which we engage and on which our theories' claims to generality rest. The doing of theory is itself a form of discourse which grows as it is transformed in changing historical circumstances and cultural contexts. It cannot achieve true generality simply by subsuming or being tested against data from a wide range of cultural settings and historical periods. Nor can it be translated transparently across cultures in a way which does not in some combination change the original, impose the original as an alien, dominating form, or simply fail to communicate. As a result, it will always be incumbent on social theorists – the more so as they increasingly attempt to grasp fundamental social categories – both to situate themselves in their cultural context, and to open themselves to reformation by confrontation with other cultural contexts.

I have already introduced the issue of historical specificity by talking about processes of theoretical change; I could also say about historical context everything said about cultural context in the previous sentence. Indeed, many of the issues posed by historical change are similar to those posed by cross-cultural variation – with the added difficulty of the impossibility of engaging in a proper dialogue to achieve mutual understanding. Cultural and historical specificity are thus inextricably linked, but there are some specific points to be made about the latter.

HISTORICAL SPECIFICITY

In advocating "historically specific" theory, I mean not merely "taking history into account," and still less claiming to explain all of history. Rather, I mean recognizing that (1) the production of theories is a historical phenomenon, (2) the categories used in theoretical discourse are adequate only to specific historical epochs (partly because they are inevitably contentful as suggested above), and (3) theories exist in discursive fields, in relation to other theories, and are not self-sufficient statements of their meaning.

That the production of theories is itself a historical problem is now widely, though hardly universally, recognized. At least within the discourse of critical theory, the need to ground a theoretical statement with an account of its own production (or the potential for such an account without performative contradiction) is generally accepted. This idea of grounding is more or less distinctive to critical theory, however; it does not figure significantly at all in "mainstream" social theory.[13] Most self-proclaimed positivist theory is constructed without any attempt to make the act of theory construction itself intelligible within the theory.

The historical specificity of theoretical categories themselves is much less widely accepted. This is somewhat surprising inasmuch as both Weber and Marx worked in large part through historically specific conceptualisation. Even devout followers of each, however, have often tended to ignore their (admittedly sometimes ambiguous) historical specifications and treat their concepts and theories as transhistorical, timeless truths. Consider the use of the term "labor" in Marxist theory.[14] Most readings of Marx take labor to be a transhistorical category applying to all epochs and cultures. Others argue – correctly, in my view – that as a category in Marx's fully developed theory, "labor" should be treated as specific to capitalism. To be sure, work – in some general sense – may be understood to occur more broadly, but this is precisely because it is an untheorized term. The notion of labor is central to the mature Marx because labor as a form of abstract value is theoretically constitutive of capitalism, and it is a concept adequate and specific to a society in which capitalism as a set of cultural categories as well as material relationships can be said to exist.[15]

The historical specificity and contentfulness of all complex theoretical categories cannot be eliminated by analytic reformulation. It constitutes a reason why theoretical work cannot be strictly cumulative, in the positivist sense, and why deductive formulations are always limited and parasitic on inductive accounts. The hope for a theoretical millennium of deductive/cumulative theory is misleading at best (see also Stephen Turner's essay in chapter 4 of this volume). Among the effects of pursuing this chimera, I would contend, is a necessary impoverishment of theoretical categories and consequently theories. No effort to specify the "scope statements" (cf. Walker and Cohen 1985) for a theory solves (or even really addresses) this problem, for it presumes the adequacy of the accounts of the basic categories across the lines of contexts in which the theory's propositions are found to hold or not to hold.

The need for historical specificity is not simply the difficulty an omniscient author has of indicating which of his or her equally true statements apply at what moment in a narrative of dramatic changes. Rather, it is the need to recognize (1) the limited vantage points provided by the historical perspective of each and every theorist, and (2) the immanence of theoretical categories in the world of practice. With regard to the latter, I mean first off and quite simply that it is not imaginable that Marx would have developed his theory of capitalism had he lived in the ninth and not the nineteenth century. More specifically, even theoretical concerns which run through the whole history of social thought – the attempt to understand and specify what a person is, for example – are always only thinkable in ways which are inextricably tied to the nature of society (and hence of persons) within the realm of experience and learning of a given thinker. Learning, scholarship, in this context, may help to overcome the limits imposed by the reach of one's own experience; it may make one less ethnocentric and less historically naive. Nonetheless, personal experience must be assigned a central role in accounting for the understandability (and particular reference) of theoretical categories and concepts, and of the theories into which they are woven.

The issue of historical specificity arises at all levels of analysis. It also concerns all time periods. Thus, there are historical changes which distinguish the context of theory production from one generation to the next. But the most important application of this point comes in the demarcation of epochs in human history, and the construction of conceptual frameworks adequate to epochal changes. Thus historical specificity comes to be of special significance for debates about whether modernity is giving way to postmodernity, whether theories based on the economic strategies of individual capitalists explain much about contemporary captialism, or whether normalization of power is a social process of distinctive significance to modern societies or more general application. To reiterate, the issue is not simply one of scope statements. It is more fundamentally a matter of how the conceptual construction of these basic historical demarcations determines what sorts of categories will be appropriate to the analysis of phenomena internal to them. This is particularly important for a theory which proposes to take a critical stance towards existing social arrangements. It is essential that such a theory be able to show that it stands in an immanent relationship to such social arrangements in order for its critique to avoid being merely an arbitrary subjective expression on the one hand, or an only slightly less arbitrary imposition of universalistic values.

The importance of the fact that theories exist in historically and culturally limited discursive fields has partly to do with the impossibility of separating the evaluation of any theory from the range of possible alternatives to it. Choices are made with regard to epistemic gain, not absolute truth; political advantage, not political certainty; and so forth.[16] Such choices are always part of a process of projection and examination of possible future paths, thus, and inevitably of communication concerning the range of options. Such theoretical communication presents itself as being able to rise above the ordinary problems of communication, to offer not only greater clarity and precision, but in Habermas's terms to offer readier redemption of validity claims. There is, I think, some truth to this self-presentation of theory. Among discourses about society, theoretical ones have particular advantages in enabling communication across lines of cultural difference. They have these advantages, generally, because even where theory does not thematize reflexivity it nonetheless involves it. But the advantages are greatest where the theory can be clear about its historical grounding and application.

Under the best of circumstances, however, communication is never perfect. Because theory sets up a higher standard for its own internal discourse, it makes an easy target for critique. In particular, it is easy to show that theory presenting itself as politically and otherwise neutral, is strongly biased, and that theory claiming objective clarity and certainty can do so only by presupposing a foundation in the habitus of its practitioners and the tacit assumptions of their culture – "that which can be left unsaid." The answer to this, I am suggesting, lies in increasing the grounding of theories in the self-reflexivity of theorists, in cultural sensitivity and historical specificity, not in suggesting that because theoretical discourse cannot live up to its own ideals we must forfeit those ideals as regulative constructs. We must make choices among available theoretical options or abandon a gret deal of contemporary scholarly, political, and ethical discourse. The path of avoiding such choices, of letting the inadequacy of all available theories be a license for dismissing them all, is far more radical and problematic than many of its seeming advocates suppose. In this connection, I think that so-called postmodernists are misleading to claim that the presence of ambiguity and ethnocentrism in all previous means proposed for overcoming breakdowns in communications constitutes grounds for their dismissal or radical relativization.[17] One of the key problems with the postmodernist position is that its critique is not accompanied by an alternative social theory offering epistemic gain. Of course, this is not to say that such a theory could not be elaborated drawing on insights from so-called postmodernist thinkers, but generally speaking this has not occurred; indeed Foucault (1980) spoke prominently against the impulse to theorize. The effort to develop a postmodernist social theory (and in fact much of the postmodernist empirical literature) is prone to performative contradictions: asserting claims to rhetorical persuasiveness as more true or more adequate while denying the meaningfulness, legitimacy, utility, or interpersonal adjudicability of the notions of truth or adequacy.

IMPLICATIONS

If theory is truly historically grounded and sensitive to cultural variation, then the project of developing maximally general social theory cannot take some of the forms which have been proposed for it, or in which it has been proposed. To begin with, theory must be a polyphonic discourse, not a monological statement (Taylor 1985a: ch. 10). That is, for the most part theory will not be a matter just of right answers. It will not be cumulative in any simple sense and it will not be possible for it to be "completed." More specifically, the achievements of theory will appear in the form of a discourse in which many voices shed light on a problem from different vantage points.[18] Indeed, internal to the best theories, there will be some play of different voices, a dialectic which does not attempt to reduce the world to a set of surface descriptions.[19] In this sense, the notion of polyphony shares much with the structuralist insight that aggregation of empirical instances of a phenomenon may be misleading as to the underlying structures generating a range of objective possibilities, and with the dialectical understanding that what exists at any one point in time is not necessarily the most fundamentally real and certainly not the limit of the real. A good theory of the more "general" sort must not pretend to closure, but open itself internally to the play of contending tendencies and possibilities.[20] Even more, it must be recognized that individual theories derive their meaning largely from the field of theoretical discourse in which they are developed and presented; they are not self-sufficient.

Relatedly, we need to recognize that the strong versions of claims for deductive theorizing and aggregation of tested hypotheses into theories are unreachable (claims 3 and 4 of the list of claims about theoretical generality presented in the introduction to this chapter). Local theories do not add up to middle-range ones; these do not add up to general theory. Each level of theory may encompass lower levels, or receive guidance from more general ones. It is not, however, possible to produce or understand a middle-range theory, say, simply by enumerating a series of local theories – still less a series of successfully tested propositions – in its domain. There is separate theoretical work which must be done, not least of all in establishing the historical grounding of the theory and in clarifying the cultural context of its concepts, as well as in relating different, more local theories to each other. Local theories in any case cannot altogether escape implication in cultural outlooks and historical processes which cannot be grasped internally to them. Such cultural and historical dimensions can, of course, be left naively unspecified. This may mask an implicit reliance on a more general theory – as much local theory in sociology today relies on a loose mixture of functionalism and positivism without serious intellectual attention to either. And non-specification of cultural and historical situation removes the grounding for a critical relationship between a theory and the social context of its production.

Local theory thus cannot escape dependence on more general theory. Either it will be directly dependent on a specific line of more general theory or it will be dependent on an untheorized set of cultural factors which could only be theorized at a more general level. Conversely, however, complete deduction of local and middle-range theories from more general ones is no more plausible an ideal.[21] It is certainly possible to construct a deductive theory, and such efforts have some value in restricted areas, but they do not indicate a plausible path for theoretical development overall. An entirely (or even mainly) deductive theory cannot be very culturally sensitive or very well historically grounded. It must be overwhelmingly formal and minimally contentful.[22]

Such deductive theories (e.g. rational choice theory, Blau's macrosocial structuralism) are often taken as models for general theory. In the sense of my argument here, however, this "generality" is highly restricted. Universal (or nearly universal) application is bought at the expense of cultural sensitivity and historical specificity such that the theory cannot ground itself in any rich way in concrete social life. Putatively universal propositions or structures of propositions about relatively narrow ranges of phenomena, or highly abstract aspects of phenomena are in this sense not "general theory" but variants of local theory. Rational choice theory, for example, consists of a highly general set of procedures or guidelines for constructing highly local theories; it does not offer much of a general theory *per se*.[23] Whether we call it "general" or something else, the best social theory (in the sense of most adequate to accounting for social life in all its multidimensionality and cultural and historical variation) is empirically rich. It combines comparative and historical substantive (empirical) discourse with reflection on and development of categories.[24] Marx, Weber, and to a large extent Durkheim thus remain exemplars in ways which Parsons and Habermas do not quite achieve.

The best of the "general" theories in the sense of universalizing, especially deductive theories are not strictly speaking theories of social life. Rather, they theorize certain of the conditions of social life. This is true of a good part of Simmel's work, and in this it has a modern heir in Peter Blau's macrostructural theory of inequality and heterogeneity (Blau 1977; Blau and Schwartz 1982). Theories of social life must always be historical because social life is always a historical process, and contentful because social life is always culturally particular. While a formal theory like Blau's can be very wide in its application, perhaps even universal (and in that sense general), it cannot be concretized or become in any way empirical without becoming to some extent particular, in both historical and cultural terms (see Calhoun and Scott 1989). This is something Simmel recognized rather more, or at least more explicitly, than Blau. Even the simplest or most "obvious" concrete categories with which Blau illustrates his formal theory – e.g. those of race and class – must be at least implicit and *ad hoc* introductions of the historically and culturally particular into the theory.[25]

The importance of cultural and historical particularity within good theories, however, does not preclude cross-cultural and cross-time generalization or comparison. I suggested some reasons for this in the first section above. It is worth mentioning again, however, as we turn to considering – very briefly and from an arbitrary range of sources – how the postmodern project might preclude both such generalization and meaningful comparison (perhaps despite the intentions of some of its proponents).

"POSTMODERNISM"

Self-styled postmodernists are often happy relativists – perfectly prepared to acknowledge that there are no certain truths and perhaps even no ways to be sure of meaningful communication across intellectual traditions or cultures, untroubled by the lack of grounding this leaves them for normative judgments and scholarly disputes. A good many eschew the gloom which the prospect of radical relativism suggests to Enlightenment thinkers and adopt instead a Rabelaisian carnival attitude, playful before the intellectual abyss.[26] Some try to avoid the ungrounded judgments, others proffer them anyway, as simple assertions or some of the infinity of possible disseminations of life's text. While most postmodernists, thus, remain unconcerned by the central charge that "modernists" (e.g. Habermas 1988a) levy at them, a few have argued that abandoning the Enlightenment project of general theory and adopting a postmodern stance entail neither relativism nor the impossibility of a strong politics (see e.g. Linda Nicholson's chapter 3 in this volume). I am sympathetic, but have my doubts.

Nicholson shares the widespread contemporary rejection of

foundationalism. One of the central claims of postmodernist thought is that the search for ultimate philosophical foundations for knowledge is (1) an impossible quest, and (2) part of an intellectual imperialism which does violence to the necessary multivocality of intellectual and political discourse. In such arguments, as Stephen Turner has suggested (in chapter 4 of this volume), the proponents of critical "postpositivist" programs rely on notions of fundamental proof which have all too much similarity to those found in positivism. This tends rhetorically to eliminate the possibility of a middle position between foundationalism and extreme relativism (happy or not). Nicholson claims, somewhat more surprisingly, that the postmodern abandonment of foundationalism does not entail the impossibility of general theories (or values, or categories), though she does not specify the basis (if any) on which they will rest their persuasiveness. As she sees it, relativism is not so much a theoretical position (or failing) as a "life possibility . . . the situation which results when communication breaks down" (p. 86). Conversely, she does not go so far in condemnation of general truth claims as many postmodernists (who regard all such claims as arbitrary exercises of the will to power).[27] Such truth claims have only to be seen as internal to historical traditions to be acceptable:

> the postmodernist need not abandon the distinction between legitimate and illegitimate claims to power as she or he need not abandon the more encompassing idea of criteria of truth. The difference between the postmodernist and the modernist on these issues is rather that the former and not the latter denies the possibility of such criteria external to any specific historical tradition. (p. 87 above)[28]

By implication, since communicative conflicts are to be solved by finding a common belief or value, the more "historical tradition" people share the better, and the less the worse. If this is so, then any grounding of theory only in cultural traditions (*pace* Rorty) confronts serious problems. Such an account recognizes difference, but does not grant it a positive place (which is, in particular, a serious problem for feminism).[29] In most postmodernist accounts, the coming together of people from different traditions, or those abiding by different rules from within the same tradition, seems primarily an occasion for communication to break down, not for the kind of mutual learning and growth discussed above. Obviously modernist thought has shared historically in the imperialist drive of modern politics, economics, and culture generally. But the postmodernists make a stronger claim than historical connection, joint culpability, or tendency. They see no basis other than power for relations among people of very different traditions.

At this point it is necessary to stop talking about post-modernism in general and recognize the different and contending voices within that movement. Of course, I cannot pretend to review the range of positions here, and will only note the connections of a few, arbitrarily selected but important to the present argument.

It is Foucault, above all, who has taught the inevitable mutuality of knowledge and power. In his view, all ways of knowing are exercises of power: "Truth is a thing of this world; it is produced only by virtue of multiple forms of constraint" (1980: 73). This power is not reducible to interpersonal domination, but is constitutive of social life and culture generally.

> If power were never anything but repressive, if it never did anything but to say no, do you really think one would be brought to obey it? What makes power hold good, what makes it accepted, is simply the fact that it doesn't only weigh on us as a force that says no, but that it traverses and produces things, it induces pleasure, forms knowledge, produces discourse.
>
> (*Rabinow 1977: 61*)

Power is, in this sense, "decentered," not the property of any subject. Power is normalized, rendered into discipline, practiced routinely by subjects upon themselves insofar as they re-enact the premises of their culture. This seems to grasp a dimension of the modern experience of power, but at the same time it obscures the specifically modern increase in occasions and resources for people to distinguish between what power is and ought to be. One of the central problematics of power disappears in this formulation: there are no criteria for distinguishing legitimate from illegitimate power. Foucault's theory, indeed, may actually make such criteria internally impossible.

A fundamental challenge for any postmodernist theory is to offer bases for making critical judgments. I have argued above that such bases need ideally to be grounded in strong recognition of their cultural and historical specificity, and preferably to stand in an immanent relationship to the context of their development. Nonetheless, to be meaningful – both politically and theoretically – such bases need to allow for critical judgments to be arguable, defensible, in discourse *across* lines of cultural and other difference. A position which cannot give reasons for why it should be persuasive to those who are not already a part of its "tradition" is a severely problematic political as well as scientific tool. Agreement must then be arbitrary, or imposed; if people are moved, there is no internal account of why. At the same time as discourse among people different from each other is vital to democracy and public life, so it is crucial that people within any one tradition (and for that matter individuals within their own lives) be able to give accounts simultaneously of how they have come to be who they are and how they want to become better in the future. That is, a critical historical consciousness implies an ability to express and defend not only one's interests but the project of developing better interests, wanting to have better desires (cf. Taylor 1985a, chs. 1 and 2; 1985b, ch. 3). Foucault does offer social criticism, certainly through his tone and choices of descriptive content, but also sometimes explicitly. It is not clear, however, that he could ground such criticism without performative contradiction. The potential for doing so within his theory is weakened especially when it loses its historical specificity.

In his early and middle works, up through *Discipline and Punish* (1977a [1975]), Foucault emphasizes deep ruptures between historical epochs and focuses his attention on the birth of modern power in the reformation of institutions of carceral control in the seventeenth and eighteenth centuries. But in his later work on sexuality, and in some interviews and essays, he implies that the mutuality of power and knowledge is universal, not distinctive to modernity, and that similar analyses can be developed for all cultures and historical periods. Foucault does enunciate something of the distinctiveness of the power/

knowledge implication in modernity, even as late as the 1970s: "It's not a matter of emancipating truth from every system of power (which would be a chimera, for truth is already power), but of detaching the power of truth from the forms of hegemony, social, economic, and cultural, within which it operates at the present time" (1980: 75). Foucault holds out the option of specific criticisms of the modern forms of hegemony, but he does not suggest any direction for criticism to move in. Like most other "postmodernists," he can advocate only resistance, not emancipation. At extremes, he seems to imply that anything would be better than what obtains now. But this sort of account is in an odd tension with the historical approach he developed earlier. There he argued for recognizing the centrality of epochal transformations which made sense of many small changes (but made historically specific sense, within the context of a specific epochal transformation, not the sense which comes from imposing a single transhistorical narrative or set of categories on historically specific events):

> In order to analyse such events [e.g. the introduction of a new form of positivity or other epochal shifts in consciousness], it is not enough simply to indicate changes, and to relate them immediately to the theological, aesthetic model of creation . . . or to the psychological model of the act of consciousness . . . or to the biological model of evolution. We must define precisely what these changes consist of: that is, substitute for an undifferentiated reference to *change* – which is both a general container for all events and the abstract principle of their succession – the analysis of *transformations.*
>
> (*Foucault 1972: 172*)

It is curious that the advice informing the history (though less so, perhaps, Foucault's earlier formulation, the archaeology) of forms of power/knowledge should not provide a different outlook, one with a normative direction, for the analysis of contemporary questions. Such a normative direction need not involve a "supernarrative" of history, a single moral to all stories. It could consist, rather, of suggestions for the direction in which we should move from where we are, recognizing that new considerations will inform decisions about the appropriate directions to be followed thereafter. It seems to me that the nature of practical involvement in the world, especially political involvement, calls necessarily for confronting such questions of directionality. Moreover, seeking understanding across lines of important cultural differences necessarily involves confronting contrasting normative directions because these produce incommensurable practices of the sort (discussed above) which cannot coexist without posing competing claims for adherence.

At this point, where it cannot achieve historical specificity or confront the incommensurable practices of different cultures, Foucault's analytics of power loses any potential critical edge. Ironically enough, fashionable anthropologists have followed the lead of the later Foucault and begin to unravel ubiquitous subjectless power in all settings, while combining this with a self declared critical orientation and affirmation of cultural difference.[30] It seems to me that the postmodernist claim to historical grounding – indeed, even to historicity – is in important aspects spurious. The history which is introduced is often remarkably unsystematic.[31] Like postmodernist architecture, its historical side consists of incomplete and decontextualized borrowings. Even in the hands of an extraordinary historical scholar like Foucault, postmodernist historical writing is often a bit like an orientalism of the past – an appropriation of history for purposes of debating the contemporary condition directly, not an inquiry into the fullest possible understanding of another way of life which might indirectly or in later comparison shed light on our own. It is partly for this reason that Foucault, the great theorist of historical ruptures, in his later work began to find the same mechanisms of power/knowledge at work in ancient Greece, China, and modern France, and everywhere else he looked. Most importantly of all, the postmodernist position is not historically or culturally *specific*, either in grounding or in analytic purchase.

Foucault, of course, did emphasize the poststructuralist, postmodernist theme of difference: "What is found at the historical beginning of things is not the inviolable identity of their origin; it is the dissension of other things. It is disparity" (1977b: 79). This theme, however, is especially associated with Derrida, for whom it has remained enduringly central. Derrida's *différance* is a "primordial nonself-presence" (Derrida 1973: 81). It is transcendental, even prior to presence and the transcendental reduction (Dews 1987: 19); it is "not something which occurs to a transcendental subject. It is what produces it" (Derrida 1973: 86). The structuralist and poststructuralist displacement of the subject from modernity's and philosophy's center is thus basic to Derrida; it is not the self which we presuppose in all thought and action, but *différance*. In Dews's words, "in the majority of his work, Derrida bases his analyses on the concept of absolute difference: of an essential *logical priority* of non-identity over identity" (1987: 27).[32] It is this which orients the deconstructionist project to the discovery of internal incoherences within texts, rather than reading them more conventionally by "constructing" from them a meaningful whole (Derrida 1978).

Not only the unity of a text, but subjectivity itself, the originating unity of consciousness, is merely a thought, a fiction (Dews 1987: 31). This is the basis for viewing the world as a textual or discursive structure to be deconstructed, its incoherencies exposed. Derrida's opposition is to the notion of speech as transparent, self-sufficient presentation of truth, and for the priority of textuality understood as always embodying tensions and hence making deconstruction possible (or perhaps even inevitable). This is what he means by challenging the "logocentrism" of Western thought. But left to itself this offers only a critical moment. It is a very problematic basis for social or political analysis. Even Derrida is unwilling to regard social institutions as merely textual or discursive structures (though some of his followers have not balked at this). Derrida insists on retaining the option of social and political criticism, but falls back on Heideggerian grounds for it. His own theory cannot ground a critical account of political antagonisms insofar as these cannot be reduced to logical antagonisms. Deconstruction can offer a certain sort of constant vigilance and attempt to escape mere positivity, but it cannot offer a political or ethical program, or a properly explanatory analysis.

Deconstructionism is also a seriously deficient approach to developing a culturally sensitive and historically specific social theory – despite the fact that it has helped to call attention to the importance of difference. In the first place, deconstruction must remain a wholly negative technique. Secondly, though Derrida attempts to avoid the radical relativism some of his followers embrace, he does not succeed in explaining theoretically why he should do so. His very attempt to absolutize *différance* produces incoherencies in his theory. More specifically, the theory offers no openings to sociality or to material factors in history and social relations. It severs cultural from social and political-economic analysis. The deconstruction of a text plays infinitely on its internal capacities for dissemination; it neither needs nor addresses other sources of meaning. Unlike some other approaches influenced by phenomenology (e.g. hermeneutics), deconstruction offers no approach to historical or even cultural specificity. All texts have a life free from specific contexts; they cannot be grounded within them. There is, thus, no satisfactory basis for comparison. This, by the way, is part of the attraction of Derrida for those who regard all canons as *mere* exercises of power, rather the combinations of power with more satisfactorily grounded judgments.

What is for Derrida the absence of an approach to the social becomes for Baudrillard (1975, 1977, 1981) an explicit devaluation of the social. Modernity has been ruptured, he asserts, by the collapse of normalizing power, expanding material productivity, and the possibility of grasping social life as a relation among subjects. The modern sense of the social had been dominated by the centralization and deterritorialization of power (by implication the effect of the growth of the state), and the production of commodities which gained their value from abstract human labor and whose pattern of circulation could be criticized from the standpoint of concrete use value and concrete labor. In other words, modernity was the era of power and the production of commodities. Postmodernity is the era of the sign and the seduction of consumers. The structure of relations which now matters is among signs. People are "exteriorized" into a techno-culture of "hyperreality" where significance replaces reification and we know only the simulacra of mass existence. Baudrillard's vision is basically a tragic account of the completion of the abstraction of power suggested by the Weberian notion of rationalization, and of production (reconstituted as seduction) by the Marxian commodity-based system of capitalism. But it takes him far from those masters theoretically. And it leaves him facing nihilism squarely and advocating an attitude simply of "ironic detachment." Baudrillard almost celebrates the fear of mass culture which helped make Adorno and Horkheimer into such pessimists. As he asks: "Are the mass media on the side of power in the manipulation of the masses, or are they on the side of the masses in the liquidation of meaning, and in the fascination which results? Is it the media which induce fascination in the masses, or is it the masses which divert the media into spectacles?" (1983: 105).

At one level, Baudrillard regains within his tragic vision some sense of historical specificity: we face the abyss; our ancestors did not. A key reason is because he ties his vision of postmodernist culture to a more general view of postmodern society; he does mot make postmodernism something free-floating, purely within the realm of ideas. But his theses of the implosion of meaning and the out-of-control production of signification suggest the impossibility of any theoretical grounding, and of cross-cultural evaluation. And Baudrillard radicalizes Barthes's (1982) vision of the destruction of cultural difference by the media. His theory thus has an enormous amount in common with the views of mass society, mass culture, or the revolt of the masses which have been endemic to modernity. We might question, however, whether there is not a great deal of internal differentiation among "the masses" which might be addressed by an empirical theory more focused on cultural variation, and which might be valorized by a normative theory more respectful of differences.

The very distinction between modernism and postmodernism is also problematic. I would suggest that postmodernism is an internal product of modernity, not its true opponent. It is a counterpoint to the modernist project, but one generated from within modernity, a recurrent modern form of challenge to Enlightenment universalism and foundationalism (and thus not, as Habermas (1988a) implies, simply a sort of throwback to the pre-modern resistance to modernity). Lyotard is distinctive in recognizing that "postmodernity is undoubtedly a part of the modern" (1984a: 79). Postmodernists are quite modern, for example, in style, not least of all in constantly searching for the new, suspecting that which has been received. "A work [of art] can become modern only if it is first postmodern. Postmodernism thus understood is not modernism at its end but in the nascent state, and this state is constant" (ibid.). In nearly all material ways the modern tendencies continue: centralization of power, demand for economic productivity. Even the exploding and fragmenting of once more integrated cultural systems or communities is not "after" modern. It is, rather, something modernity has done throughout its existence.[33]

Elsewhere, unfortunately, Lyotard (1984a) does tend to treat postmodernity as a historical period and postmodernism as a separable project. Such treatments, which are common in the postmodernist rhetoric, force us to ask the question: when did the postmodern era begin? There are a number of possible answers implied by various writings within the postmodern tradition (this very vagueness is testimony to the non-specificity of the theories):

- With "poststructuralism" in the late 1960s. Derrida might be taken as marking this break most strikingly with his publication of three books in 1967.[34]
- With "postindustrial society," computerization, and/or other socio-technical changes taken to undermine the privileging of labor as the source of value. This is an idea put forward by Lyotard especially.
- With the ascendancy of consumption/seduction over production/power, an argument launched by Baudrillard.
- With non-traditional critics of modernity from Nietzsche (emphasizing the will to power) to Simmel (the fragmentation of society) to Musil (who in *The Man without Qualities* put forward a notion of the self as insufficient to bear the weight of "modernist" subjectivity).

Underlying this concern is the problem of how to relate the intellectual current of "postmodernism" to change in social life. Identification of a new-age "postmodernity" is postmodernism's main possibility for claiming a historical grounding.

Lyotard suggests that the core difference between modernist and postmodernist thought be seen in the tendency of the former to impose suprahistorical narratives on the concrete and ultimately directionless flux of history:

> I will use the term *modern* to designate any science that legitimates itself with reference to a metadiscourse of this kind making an explicit appeal to some grand narrative,

such as the dialectics of Spirit, the hermeneutics of
meaning, the emancipation of the rational or working
subject, or the creation of wealth . . . Simplifying to the
extreme, I define *postmodern* as incredulity toward metanarratives.

(1984: xxiii–xxiv)

Lyotard thus argues that neither of the "modern" views of
society – functional, systemic unity and conflictual division held
together by power – is acceptable, and the very division is
representative of a form of thought out of step simultaneously
with postmodern forms of knowledge and patterns of social
change. These changes are fundamental: "the old poles of
attraction represented by nation-states, parties, professions,
institutions, and historical traditions are losing their attraction.
And it does not look as though they will be replaced, at least not
on their former scale" (ibid.: 14). As a result, if Lyotard is right,
sociological analysis focused on these institutions or "poles
of attraction" can no longer grasp the social condition very well.
Instead we must look at the flow of communication through a
social grid in the form of endless language games. "[T]he
observable social bond is composed of language 'moves'"
(ibid.: 11). Because these are competitive moves in language
games, they cannot be grasped by a purely cybernetic theory,
but must be seen in terms of their agonistic aspect. Society,
then, has become "atomized" into flexible networks of language
games (ibid.: 17); Lyotard claims that the prominence of
bureaucratic and other institutional constraints or control
mechanisms does not seriously challenge this view; these limits
are merely the stakes and provisional results of language
strategies.[35]

At the same time, we have seen the displacement of narrative
forms of customary knowledge: "Lamenting the 'loss of
meaning' in postmodernity boils down to mourning the fact
that knowledge is no longer principally narrative" (ibid.: 26).
Science is the principal antagonist of narrative and thus of the
sort of language game which combines to form the social bond.
But note here that the postmodern condition seems to describe a
"loss of meaning" which has been lamented for at least a century
in very similar terms, and that science as the antagonist of

narrative must be seen to have played a role in nearly the whole history of *modern* culture. In other words, the "postmodern" critique grasps something of contemporary life because it grasps something of a modernity which continues, not because it calls attention to something new.

Historically, grand narratives pursued (and to some extent achieved) legitimation of the social order, either as the metanarrative of an ideal subject (spirit, knowledge actualizing itself) or of a practical subject (humanity liberating itself) (Lyotard 1984: 35). But in postmodern culture, such grand narratives have lost their credibility. Science seeks its own internal and external legitimation, sometimes in terms of old narratives of knowledge and emancipation. Other times it offers up simply its "performativity" – achieving the best input/output equation for its sponsors (ibid.: 40). But increasingly, science appears simply as playing its own language game, and therefore incapable of legitimating itself or other language games (ibid.). Faced with this, one may become pessimistic, become nostalgic for the old narratives, or – if one is a good postmodernist – simply accept that legitimation can only spring from people's own linguistic practice and communicative interaction (ibid.: 41).

For Lyotard (ibid.: 81–2) the most important result of such acceptance is rejection of the "transcendental illusion" – the fantasy of putting all the heterogeneous language games of the world together in a single whole. Totalization of this sort breeds terror (especially, we might add, the historically specific sorts of terrors of the nineteenth and twentieth centuries, like genocide). Such material terrors are the counterparts of intellectual and aesthetic violence done by attempts to impose a single vision of reality or set of standards on the diverse experimenters of art, thought, and life.

CONCLUSION

Here we come to a critique of Enlightenment universalism with substantial similarities to that developed in the first parts of this chapter. What then are the crucial distinctions to be drawn?

First, there is the matter of cultural and historical specificity.

Even for Foucault, with his historically rich scholarship – let alone for the deconstructionists – their very particularism produces a decontextualization which loses or even denies the importance of temporal and cultural situation to the interpretation of meaning.[36] The pursuit of cultural and historical specificity challenges universalism but can give only two cheers to particularism. The postmodernist decontextualization of referents is held to mirror various contemporary social and cultural processes: mediatization, internalization, mobility, etc. I think there is a great deal to this, but the question is how to respond. Seeing only a choice between totalizing power and free play of thought at the expense of relativism, postmodernists have generally opted for the latter. But I have tried to show in this chapter that other paths are open – particularly a culturally sensitive and historically specific sort of theory which must be highly contentful and aim at epistemic gain, not final truth.[37] One can respond to diversity by attempting to find relationships, not just by embracing or eradicating difference.

Second, there is the question of whether "postmodernism" points to, draws on, or provides for any termination or transcendence of modernity. I argue elsewhere (Calhoun, 1991) that in terms of the basic material trends in modern society – centralization of power, extension of geographical incorporation, and accumulation of capital – modernity must be seen as continuing. This is obscured by the rhetoric of postmodernism. I agree with Lyotard that so-called postmodernism is coeval with and even a part of modernity – so it is mislabeled. Beyond mislabeling, this points to the virtue of a theory which can be clear about its own historical groundings. Critical theorists within the Marxist tradition have developed substantial and sometimes brilliant arguments as to how capitalism contributed to – provided for – crucial developments of modern Western intellectual history (e.g. Lukács 1922).[38] Building on those, we can provide a better historical basis for Lyotard's critique of the totalizing nature of modern thought. Totalizing thought embodies the experience of totalizing capitalism and centralizing state power; the question is how to grasp this totalization and at the same time recognize it as reification. Rejecting the transcendental illusion which Lukács embraces, we can use this historical grounding to situate and use theories which are neither universalistic nor radically particularistic and relativistic.

Third, I have suggested that postmodernist thinkers generally are unable to provide grounds for their normative judgments which can serve as the basis for discourse with those who do not already share their orientations. This transmutes particularism into relativism. It limits the central stance of postmodernists to Foucault's sophisticated version of the slogan "resist authority," Derrida's eternal vigilance for incoherencies, Baudrillard's ironic detachment, and Lyotard's encouragement of experimentation. In varying degrees these may be worthy, but they are not sufficient normative bases for living an ordinary human life, let alone taking on a political project of any significance. I have argued that taking seriously other cultures and in general practices different from our own requires us to respond to their claims of technical efficacy and normative rightness – at least where these practices are incommensurable with our own. We cannot escape normative judgments and simply to refuse to provide discursively addressable grounds for them is to make them arbitrary.[39] If they are arbitrary, any attempt to commend them to others must be an explicit attempt at power through illocutionary means, or a performative contradiction.

Finally, there is the issue of comparison. The postmodernist approaches allow for, even encourage, the recognition of a multitude of voices in history.[40] They sharpen our awareness of difference, but they provide no basis for comparison and in some cases make it seem impossible from within the approach. The reasons are somewhat similar to those producing a strong normative relativism. Ironically, in this way postmodernists are often the mirror image of the Enlightenment universalists they challenge, making of difference – especially Derrida's *différance* – an absolute as rigid as unitary identity or universalism is to their enemies. And if positive, unitary identity is a form of violence against difference, so absolutized difference is a form of violence against intersubjectivity or, more specifically, the human will to bridge the gap between people, traditions, cultures.

What is called for must be a *processual* approach to understanding. It will require a form of communicative action (*pace* Habermas 1984, 1988b) which allows for discourse in which intersubjectivity grows. It will expect that mutual understanding itself will be achieved not simply by translation but by a historical process of change on both sides. It will situate comparative scholarship within such a historical process, seeking epistemic gain through highly contentful theories which must be subject to a continual play of reinterpretation. It will attempt to make clear the historical and cultural frames of reference which make it possible, not losing sight of the finitude and limited generalizability of those frames.

In short, doing social and political theory and doing historical and cross-cultural comparison must be continuous, mutually involved enterprises.

NOTES

I am grateful for comments from Pamela DeLargy

1 Though not without some ambivalence, as Alexander (1982) has shown. Parsons (1937) attempted to overcome the division between this positivist notion of science and the approach of Weber and the other classical theorists whom he accepted into the sociological canon. Sica (1988) has shown how far Parsons's reading was from the hermeneutic dimension of Weber's theory.

2 "Orientalism" of the sort epitomized by Montesquieu and prominently critiqued by Said (1976) is a variant of this problematic treatment of cross-cultural variation. While difference is made theoretically salient by the orientalist, his or her project is not the understanding of the other but rather the use of accounts of the other to inform ethnocentric self-understanding. Such accounts may be positive ("see what we can learn even from the noble savage or the heathen Chinese") or negative ("we may lack full democracy but thank God we don't live under Kadi, pasha or some other form of oriental despot") in their view of the other. The other may be given a more schematic or more richly detailed description. Nonetheless, in such accounts, the other is understood only externally and as a marked rather than primary or independent category.

3 These are lessons which Habermas at least seems inclined to take seriously in his recent lectures on Foucault (Habermas 1988a), though they have not yet resulted in any major theoretical reformulation.

4 In addition to the original contributions of Kohlberg (1981, 1984) and Gilligan (1982) see Benhabib's (1985) insightful commentary and theorization of the controversy.

5 For a sympathetic methodological critique of Blau's formal theory of social structure following this same direction, see Calhoun and Scott (1990).

6 We shall see something more of what this means in considering the historical specificity of theoretical categories in the next section.

7 Theories of economizing or utilitarian rational choice may constitute exceptions to this. To the extent that they involve empirical claims rather than hypothetical constructs, they do seem to claim that actors do in fact always or almost always behave according to a single universal standard of rationality.

8 Culture is not, it should perhaps be stressed, the static collection of norms, values, and beliefs which introductory sociology textbooks present it as. It is a dynamic dimension of social practice. In the present context, simply being a member of a culture is being engaged in a variety of practices which are incommensurable with those of other cultures, from ways of eating to religion and family life. To be both an American (of any specific sort) and a Nuer, say, is to be engaged in many incommensurable practices; in a sense, to be American and to be Nuer *are* incommensurable practices. This is the source of the fundamental challenge in reporting anthropological fieldwork.

9 Indeed, as Steiner (1975) has famously argued and modern semiotics generally would suggest, all translation is in some part construction, not mere rendering of equivalences.

10 Of course, third world anthropologists have worked (albeit rarely) in Western settings, but this is not quite as reciprocal as it sounds. Such anthropologists are still participants in a discourse which had its origins not in their traditional culture, and not in the national cultural or international third world culture to which that traditional culture may have partially given way, but in the West. By becoming anthropologists these people, even if of Nuer or other traditional ancestry, and even if highly committed to an alternative third world view, nonetheless leave the realm of practices internal to traditional culture. This does not mean that such practices are not internal to their own current culture – anthropology is now an internal part of Sudanese culture, say, and much more so of Indian. But though internal, it is not altogether indigenous and is not the product primarily of traditional practices.

11 See Winch 1964, and the essays in Wilson 1970 and Hollis and Lukes 1982.

12 As I learned in observation of and discussions with traditional medical practitioners in Chengdu in 1984. I say "quasi-experimental" both because the experiments most commonly conducted involve "tests" of the remedies prescribed in the classical texts which always result in their confirmation, and because the link between causal reasoning and experimentation in the Western scientific sense is commonly absent.

13 In fact, this notion of grounding is one of the key distinguishing features of critical theory, which I take to be considerably broader than the Frankfurt School itself. Pierre Bourdieu, for example, has made this sort of self-reflexivity and grounding a central part of his sociological enterprise. See especially *Homo Academicus* (1988) and *Leçon sur la Leçon* (1982).

14 On this, compare Nicholson's assumption in ch. 3 of this volume that Marxism simply *is* transhistorical; she does not even recognize the ambiguity in Marx or the different lines of interpretation among his followers.

15 See Postone 1983 and, one hopes, his eventual book for an excellent statement of the view that labor should be treated as a historically specific category.

16 On the notion of epistemic gain as an alternative to complete relativism and absolute truth claims, see several of the essays in Charles Taylor 1985a, b). See also Gadamer 1975: esp. 280ff) on the essential orientation to action which is a part of the knowledge of the human sciences, and which limits both absolute truth claims and relativistic failure to decide on approximate truths.

17 In the immediately following discussion I shall accept the premise that there is some scholarly position of sufficient coherence to warrant the single label "postmodernism." In fact, it is not at all clear that this is so. In France, Foucault, Derrida, Lacan, and other thinkers commonly grouped together in American discourse appear largely as rivals; their differences are much more strongly accented. "Postmodernism" is associated less with them than with its self-declared apostles like Lyotard. Questions could also be raised about the meaningfulness of the label postmodernism, which seems to me unfortunate at best. Its implied historical frame seems especially misleading.

18 The writings of Pierre Bourdieu and Jacques Derrida have gone further in this direction than those of any other major contemporary theorist, sometimes frustrating those who wish to read them monologically by their continuous playing of perspectives against each other. Both, but especially Derrida, have experimented with novel presentations of text on the page. Foucault and Lyotard, by contrast, tend to write more or less monologically even when their writings are meant to critique the monological normalization imposed by modern society and culture.

So do most of the "American deconstructionists" who half-follow and half-distort Derrida (Norris 1987) and other postmodernists who declare but often fail to evidence commitment to a plurality of voices.

19 Though current popular usage extends the term "polyphonic" very widely, it was introduced by Bakhtin specifically to refer to the internal play of voices within a certain sort of novel. The same novels of Dostoevsky were seized upon by Freud as exemplifications of psychoanalytic insight before the invention of psychoanalysis. This connection warrants the observation that polyphonic discourse ought not to refer simply to a toleration for the voices of many individuals each speaking monologically, but rather to a capacity for internal speech, a tolerance for the internal complexity which suggests that the singular human being is not altogether monological, and accordingly is not strictly speaking *individual* – an irreducible whole – at least not in all senses.

20 This is an advantage of many of the uses of the textual metaphor for society (advocated for example by Richard Brown in chapter 9 of this volume). It is crucial that such a metaphor always be used in a clearly polyphonic or dialogical way, to describe a "text" of many contending voices, and not allowed to encourage a notion of monologically "reading" society. At the same time, the textual metaphor does have serious drawbacks, not least a tendency to treat society only or mainly as a symbol system and not as a material historical process.

21 See also Stephen Turner (1986 and ch. 4 of this volume) for other reasons bearing on the same point.

22 More specifically, this is true of deductive theories which claim considerable autonomy from induction. It does not apply equally to the place of deductive, formal reasoning as a moment in a more contentful theory. Formalization may serve a useful role of codification, rigorous self-checking and suggestion of new hypotheses in the latter sort of case.

23 See also critical discussion in Wacquant and Calhoun (1989).

24 I am thus sympathetic both to Nicholson's call for use of narratives and Brown's pluralism and suggestion that multiple and overlapping accounts are necessarily involved (as presented in chs. 3 and 9 of this volume), though I have some difficulty with specifics of each proposal.

25 In this theory, Blau never addresses gender in any very substantial way. Ironically, his main exemplification of how groups can be defined by the prevalence of in-group over out-group association is intermarriage rates. Needless to say, he does not show homosexual marriages outnumbering heterosexual, yet gender remains a salient category. This suggests some problems for his contention that there is

no significance to culturally defined membership categories which are not charactrized by such prevalence of in-group association on all or most important dimensions.

26 This is at least as reasonable as gloom, of course. There was no rational reason why Weber's Calvinists, believing in predestination, faced with the prospect of likely damnation and a distant God unwilling to reveal the elect, chose to seek the simulacra of salvation through hard work and worldy asceticism; an attitude of "eat, drink, and be merry" would have followed just as logically from their predicament.

27 Nicholson correctly notes that the observation that truth contains a dimension of power does not entitle us to deduce that truth *is* power, a faulty deduction too often made by those fighting on the postmodern barricades. Nonetheless, Nicholson does set up a false opposition between potentially authoritarian claims to adjudicate universal truths and her postmodern tradition. She neglects to consider arguments (such as that in Charles Taylor's work) that all real choices are among imperfect alternatives and made according to criteria of epistemic (or ethical, or political) *gain*, not perfection.

28 Presumably these claims can be seen as general in their proposed scope of application, rather than other senses.

29 Nicholson states the excellent general goal of retaining continuity between feminist politics and feminist theory. This is not only sensible, it speaks to a real contemporary problem. But, as the text suggests, although postmodernist authors tend to share an apparent value on differences of all sorts, it is hard to see how on Nicholson's or any other postmodernist account we are to *ground* a positive value on gender (or other) differences. It is not clear whether she sees gender-based biases and limits to knowledge as potentially rectified by mere addition of knowledge or as requiring more fundamental categorial reconstruction of social theory. I assume the latter, but to my view again that would be hard to ground in any very extreme postmodernist account.

30 It seems a widespread anthropological neurosis at present to combine, despite their logical incompatibility, a highly critical stance towards "first world" depredations and often towards the play of power in all settings with a radical relativism and a cultural survivalism.

31 It is worth noting, however (since sociologists are often confused on this issue), that though Foucault was firmly anti-positivist, he was very much an empiricist, and one able to command a masterful range of sources, even if his deployment of data was disturbingly decontextualized, his willingness to generalize on the basis of highly particular evidence sometimes misleading, and his manner of citing sources sometimes cavalier.

32 Dews in fact argues that "despite all appearances, *différance* is itself a powerful principle of unity," an absolute (1987: 43).

33 Thus Simmel raises a number of the themes characteristic of today's postmodernists, including especially that of the fragmentation of culture, yet he emphatically must be considered a theorist of modernity (Frisby 1985a, b). Of course, both Simmel and Weber share with many of the postmodernists the stamp of Nietzsche's influence.

34 Poststructuralism itself is a move visible only retrospectively in the careers of former structuralists who decided they could decenter the subject and still reflect critically on the categories of thought, and thus could give up structuralism's denial of epistemology which was based on the belief that it could be pursued only in terms of a philosophy of the subject.

35 Like many other postmodernist theorists, Lyotard here turns the social almost entirely into the linguistic – a radical reduction of even social relations in which communication plays a part, let alone of material factors in social life. Where for structuralists like Lévi-Strauss linguistic phenomena provided an instructive heurisitc example of social phenomena, perhaps even a privileged and pre-eminent one, for many postmodernists – Derrida more extremely than Lyotard, for example – the linguistic becomes the only form of the social to which their theory gives them access.

36 Most of Foucault's followers among historians do more or less conventional investigations which recognize the importance of situation while exploring Foucaltian themes, like how structures of medical knowledge are implicated in control over the body. Some, however, also head down the path of historical decontextualization, interpreting ideas or events with no attempt to relate them to a more general understanding of their epoch.

37 Western scientific discourse has been typical of modern culture in its monologicality, especially its tendency monophonically to declare itself as self-sufficient. Not only do theories frequently present themselves as containing the whole of the truth on some matter, or at least at some level of analysis, even more basically, they nearly always put themselves forward as self-sufficient statements of their own meaning. But this they never are. Theories, as I observed earlier, always exist in discursive fields, in relation to other theories; their meaning is graspable and their epistemic contributions are made only within this larger discursive field (cf. Bourdieu's various writings on academic fields (esp. 1988) where not only other theorists but the practical struggles of theorists help to define not only the success but the actual content and meaning of theoretical work). While "postmodernist"

work directs our attention to this aspect of discursive fields generally, postmodernists themselves often write as though their discourse could be self-sufficient, as though it were not comprehensible in some substantial part only as a reaction to more conventional modernist discourse. More specifically, so-called postmodernist contributions offer a very inadequate and highly partial grasp of social phenomena on their own. It is not as separate modes of understanding that they make their contribution to the enterprise of social knowledge, but as moments – particularly but not exclusively moments of negative critique – in a more general modern discourse of social understanding.

38 It is high time, by the way, that more work of this kind be done in non-Western and/or third world settings.

39 In fact, it seems to me that at least as much danger of intellectual violence or "totalitarianism" lies in such a refusal to engage in a process of discursive justification as in the foundationalist project against which postmodernists levy those charges.

40 This, for example, is perhaps the most important critical counterweight which they offer to Habermas's highly universalistic theory.

REFERENCES

Alexander, Jeffrey 1982: *Theoretical Logic in Sociology*, vol 2: *The Antinomies of Classical Social Thought: Marx and Durkheim*. Berkeley: University of California Press.

Barthes, Roland 1982: *Empire of Signs*. New York: Hill & Wang.

Baudrillard, Jean 1975: *The Mirror of Production*. St Louis: Telos Press.

Baudrillard, Jean 1977: *Oublier Foucault*. New York: Semiotext(e).

Baudrillard, Jean 1981: *For a Critique of the Political Economy of the Sign*. St Louis: Telos Press.

Baudrillard, Jean 1983: *In the Shadow of the Silent Majorities*. New York: Semiotext(e).

Benhabib, Seyla 1985: "The generalized and the concrete Other: the Kohlberg–Gilligan controversy and feminist theory," in S. Benhabib and D. Cornell (eds), *Feminism as Critique*. Minneapolis: University of Minnesota Press.

Blau, Peter 1977: *Inequality and Heterogeneity*. New York: Free Press.

Blau, Peter, and Joseph Schwartz 1982: *Cross-Cutting Social Circles*. New York: Academic Press.

Bourdieu, Pierre 1976: *Outline of a Theory of Practice*. Cambridge: Cambridge University Press.

Bourdieu, Pierre 1977: *Le Sens Pratique*. Paris: Editions de Minuit.

Bourdieu, Pierre 1982: *Leçon sur la Leçon*. Paris: Editions de Minuit.

Bourdieu, Pierre 1988: *Homo Academicus*. Stanford, Calif.: Stanford University Press.

Calhoun, Craig 1988: "Populist politics, communications media, and large scale social integration," *Sociological Theory*, vol. 6/2: 219–41.

Calhoun, Craig 1991: "The infrastructure of modernity: indirect relationships, information technology, and social integration," in Neil Smelser and Hans Haferkamp (eds), *Social Change and Modernity*. Berkeley: University of California Press, (pp. 205–236).

Calhoun, Craig, and W. Richard Scott 1990: "Peter Blau's sociological structuralism," in C. Calhoun, M. Meyer, and W. R. Scott (eds), *Structures of Power and Constraint*. Cambridge: Cambridge University Press pp. 1–33.

Derrida, Jacques 1973: *Speech and Phenomena*. Evanston, Ill.: Northwestern University Press.

Derrida, Jacques 1978: *Writing and Difference*. Chicago: University of Chicago Press.

Dews, Peter 1987: *Logics of Disintegration*. London: Verso.

Foucault, Michel 1965: *Madness and Civilization*. New York: Random House.

Foucault, Michel 1972 [1969] *The Archaeology of Knowledge*. New York: Harper Torchbooks.

Foucault, Michel 1977a: *Discipline and Punish: The Birth of the Prison*. New York: Pantheon.

Foucault, Michel 1977b: "Nietzsche, Geneaology and History," in Rabinow (ed.), *The Foucault Reader*, pp. 76–100.

Foucault, Michel 1980: *Power/Knowledge: Selected Interviews and Other Writings, 1972–1977*, ed. Colin Gordon. New York: Pantheon.

Frisby, David 1985a: *Fragments of Modernity*. New York: Basil Blackwell.

Frisby, David 1985b: "Georg Simmel, first sociologist of modernity," *Theory, Culture and Society*, 2/3: 49–68.

Gadamer, Hans-Georg 1975: *Truth and Method*. New York: Seabury Press.

Gilligan, Carol 1982: *In a Different Voice: Psychological Theory and Women's Development*. Cambridge, Mass.: Harvard University Press.

Habermas, Jürgen 1979: *Communication and the Evolution of Society*. Boston: Beacon Press.

Habermas, Jürgen 1984: *The Theory of Communicative Action*, vol. 1: *Reason and the Rationalization of Society*. Boston: Beacon Press.

Habermas, Jürgen 1988a: *The Philosophical Discourse of Modernity*. Cambridge, Mass.: MIT Press.

Habermas, Jürgen 1988b: *The Theory of Communicative Action*, vol. 2: *Lifeworld and System: A Critique of Functionalist Reason*. Boston: Beacon Press.

Harding, Sandra 1986: *The Science Question in Feminism*. Ithaca, NY: Cornell University Press.

Hollis, Martin and Steven Lukes (eds) 1982: *Rationality and Relativism*. Cambridge, Mass.: MIT Press.

Kohlberg, Lawrence 1981: *Essays on Moral Development*, vol. 1: *The Philosophy of Moral Development*. New York: Harper & Row.

Kohlberg, Lawrence 1984: *Essays on Moral Development*, vol. 2: *The Psychology of Moral Development*. San Francisco: Jossey-Bass.

Lakatos, Imre 1970: "Falsification and the methodology of scientific research programmes," in I. Lakatos and A. Musgrave (eds), *Criticism and the Growth of Knowledge*. Cambridge: Cambridge University Press, pp. 91–196.

Lukács, Georg 1971 [1922]: *History and Class Consciousness*. Cambridge, Mass.: MIT Press.

Lyotard, Jean-François 1984a [1979]: *The Postmodern Condition: A Report on Knowledge*, tr. G. Bennington and B. Massumi. Minneapolis: University of Minnesota Press.

Lyotard, Jean-François 1984 [1982]: "Answering the question: what is postmodernism?" Appendix to *The Postmodern Condition*. Minneapolis: University of Minnesota Press.

Merton, Robert 1968 (2nd enl. edn; 1st edn 1957): *Social Theory and Social Structure*. New York: Free Press.

Mills, C. Wright 1959: *The Sociological Imagination*. Harmondsworth: Penguin.

Norris, Christopher 1987: *Derrida*. Cambridge, Mass.: Harvard University Press.

Parsons, Talcott 1937: *The Structure of Social Action*. Glencoe, Ill.: Free Press.

Postone, Moishe 1983: *The Present as Necessity: Towards a Reinterpretation of the Marxian Critique of Labor and Time*. Inaugural dissertation, Goethe-Universität, Frankfurt a. M.

Rabinow, P. (ed.) 1977: *The Foucault Reader*. New York: Pantheon.

Said, Edward 1976: *The End of Orientalism*. New York: Pantheon.

Sica, Alan 1988: *Max Weber on Rationality and Social Order*. Berkeley: University of California Press.

Steiner, George 1975: *After Babel*. Oxford: Oxford University Press.

Stinchcombe, Arthur 1968: *Constructing Sociological Theories*. New York: Harcourt Brace Jovanovich.

Taylor, Charles 1982: "Rationality," in M. Hollis and S. Lukes (eds), *Rationality and Relativism*. Cambridge, Mass.: MIT Press.

Taylor, Charles 1985a: *Human Agency and Language: Philosophical Papers, I Cambridge: Cambridge University Press.*

Taylor, Charles 1985b: *Philosophy and the Human Sciences: Philosophical Papers, II.* Cambridge: Cambridge University Press.

Turner, Stephen 1986: *The Search for a Methodology of Social Science: Durkheim, Weber, and the Nineteenth-Century Problem of Cause, Probability and Action.* Boston Studies in the Philosophy of Science, 92. Dordrecht: Reidel.

Wacquant, Loïc, and Craig Calhoun 1989: "Intérêt, rationalité, et histoire: apropos d'un débat americain sur la theorie d'action," *Actes de la Recherche en Sciences Sociales,* 78 (June): 41–60.

Walker, Henry, and Bernard P. Cohen 1985: "Scope statements: imperatives for evaluating theory," *American Sociological Review,* 50/3: 288–301.

Wilson, Bryan (ed.) 1970: *Rationality.* Oxford: Basil Blackwell.

Winch, Peter 1958: *The Idea of a Social Science and Its Relation to Philosophy.* London: Routledge.

Winch, Peter 1964: "Understanding a primitive society," *American Philosophical Quarterly,* 1: 307–24; reprinted in B. Wilson (ed.), *Rationality.* Oxford: Basil Blackwell, 1970, pp. 78–111.

Young, Iris 1987: "Impartiality and civic virtue," in S. Benhabib and D. Cornell (eds), *Feminism as Critique.* Minneapolis: University of Minnesota Press.

11

The Tensions of Critical Theory: Is Negative Dialectics All There Is?

Stanley Aronowitz

I

The learned essay,[1] not the treatise, is the authentic genre of critical theory, the term adopted by scholars at the Frankfurt Institute for Social Research to encompass both their philosophy and their social theory. The term connotes an intention to oppose general social theory which in its classical exemplars generates positive categories from which the propositions of social science may derive. Thus, in contrast to the treatise which, typically, sets forth definitions from which a series of empirical hypotheses may be tested, the essay form, which is both more discursive and more speculative, is employed because critical theory is suspicious of the application of norms of physical and biological sciences to human relations.

In the first place, true to its Marxist roots, the leading exponents of critical social theory (CST), Theodor Adorno, Max Horkheimer, and Herbert Marcuse, were urgently concerned with history, not only that of society but also, perhaps predominantly, the break between natural and human history as regulative of relations within the social order. For the Frankfurt School, the domination of nature was a defining event in human history. With Weber, Horkheimer and Adorno understand the history of capitalism as a disruption of the relatively stable social order marked by a low level of technological development and a moral order in which nature was accorded substantial respect. An agrarian-based ethic is displaced by a new ethic in which nature becomes an antagonistic "Other" to society and ethics are defined by the degree to which mankind devotes itself to exploiting its natural environment to meet historically defined human wants or needs (Horkheimer and Adorno 1972; Marcuse 1978).

However, while Weber privileges self-denial and work as the content of this spiritual upheaval, CST focuses on the changed relationship between humans and nature made possible by science and technology. On the one hand, biological science places "man" at the apex of natural history; on the other, science becomes a metaphor for dominion of the new capitalist social order over the natural order, the laws of which, having been discovered by experiment, become the foundation of human intervention (Horkheimer and Adorno 1972: 3–42). Scientific ideology postulates that we are no longer bound to our biological givens. As Parsons argues, fully consonantly with this tradition, society is governed by norms, by the cultural system. The organism constitutes only a boundary condition for other systems, but does not control human destiny (Parsons 1951: ch. 1; Parsons 1955: 627–33). In fact, after Weber, whose later investigations constitute a tacit critique of his earlier historical preoccupations, social theory loses its historical dimension as time is taken itself as merely a framework for the structural and function relations between system and subsystem of the social and cultural order (Parsons 1951: 11). General social theory, true to Durkheim's rule to treat the social as a fact sui generis, generates hierarchically arranged categories of (social) Being (Durkheim 1966 [1938]).[2] The lower forms are, ineluctibly, functionally linked to the higher forms and thereby retain only a relative autonomy from the system of which they are a contingent part; they owe their existence to the "control" by the higher system. Thus, while the biological organism is a condition for the personality, social and cultural systems, in Talcott Parsons's theory the cultural system embodies the norms by which society retains equilibrium.

Parsons models his sociology on classical mechanics with its categories of inertia and equilibrium, and borrows from biology a systems approach according to which change, indeed any notion of temporality results from external influences that disrupt the natural inertia of society. He follows Pareto in holding only the personality, which determines the organism's goals (within the framework of a relatively fixed normative order), to be subject to significant variation and appears, at least until Parsons's later years to be the wild card in an otherwise coherent system (see Pareto 1963 [1935]). This coherence is spatially arranged in a series of relations which are relatively fixed. What has become the fundamental departure of relativity and quantum physics from the classical Newtonian framework is assiduously ignored in Parsons's schema – the question of the space/time continuum and, more profoundly, the whole scaffolding of causality in the Newtonian system:

> Time relations present what, for us, is a simpler problem. All the empirical sciences take it for inexorable fact that certain events have occurred at given times and in given time sequence. Given certain antecedent time determinations other time determinations can be deduced by theoretical reasoning; this is what we mean by prediction in its temporal aspect. But time is never a manipulable variable; time is a frame of reference within which one can state and interpret the assumptions about and the consequences of the operations of manipulable variables . . . time is one fundamental aspect of the givenness of the empirical world which provides the empirical base from which any deduction or prediction can be carried out.
>
> *(Parsons 1955: 638)*

Of course, Parsons allows for "exigencies" between system and subsystem, but these are relegated to "deflections" in an otherwise invariate structure within which internal relations are fixed by determinations of hierarchy (ibid.: 632).[3]

In the current revival of the philosophy and social theory of the Frankfurt School two distinct modes of appraisal can be discerned: by far the most prevalent is critical theory as a somewhat iconoclastic social theory that accounts for historical changes: the problem of technological domination in late capitalist societies; considerations in the cultural and political history of fascism and especially the rise of the authoritarian state; the problem of mass culture and consumer society as subversions of democracy; the relevance of psychoanalytic theory to understanding social life. Some of these themes were taken up by others, although in a different way. For example, Parsons himself openly invokes Freud's categories of cathexis and the unconscious to explain disruptions in system maintenance. Like Horkheimer, but with a different political perspective, Hannah Arendt (1956) derives the fascist moral and political order from some aspects of the Enlightenment, refusing the liberal view of the Holocaust as an astonishing mutation from the norms of Western culture. And Ortega y Gasset (1932 [1929]) sees the decline of the West as a consequence of the rise of mass culture, but from a deeply conservative standpoint which nevertheless postulates an integrated past in which high culture flourished, a position not far from that of the Frankfurt School. Despite the many political differences among these writers, they share a common bond of humanism and, Parsons excepted, a penchant for negative philosophical assumptions. That is, their concern is to account for disruption as more than contingent, but rather as the mode of being of contemporary life. In this mode such categories as equilibrium and inertia are exceptional, rather than regulative of social relations, at least in the twentieth century.[4]

The second line of discussion concerns the problem of what might commonly be called "method." Of course, CST has no method if by that term we mean a theory of object relations from which one may derive a series of algorithms to guide research and experiment about the empirical world. Hence its characteristic discourse is reflexive and hermeneutic rather than scientific in the eighteenth-century meaning of the term. For above all, critical theory (the general philosophical position underlying CST) is a discourse about the relation of subject and object exemplified in the texts of philosophy, literature, and social and cultural theory and criticism. In this sense it approximates, however unwittingly, the collective biography of intellectuals situated in a concrete historical moment, the period between the two world wars when nearly all the old assumptions about the equilibrium conditions appeared to have collapsed or were in the process of disintegration. Just as the Weimar environment gave rise to a new physics which built upon the classical orientation of relativity physics, if only to radicalize it, so, following Lukács's revision of Marx, the Frankfurt School insisted upon the relevance of subjectively meaningful action to the constitution of social relations. Lukács, influenced by Simmel's theory of reification, situated the reversal of capitalism's collapse in the power of the commodity form over human consciousness and restricted his inquiry to the level of philosophic and literaty discourse. The Frankfurt School, however, having rejected metaphysical speculation as a vestige of bourgeois ideology, turned to performing relentless criticism of contemporary fashions in German philosophy, and in addition to the practice of sociology.[5] In the 1930s its studies of the institutional frameworks of advanced capitalist social life, particularly the family and mass culture; the historical legacy of science and technology; and finally its studies of that great absence in historical materialism, the state, were in their totality efforts to break from the economistic bias of Marxist social theory.[6]

In effect, the first major contribution of CST was to explain the failure of the Western working class in the interwar period to reverse the rise of totalitarian and authoritarian states in advanced capitalist societies. They sought answers in the psychosocial deformations of mass consciousness. Thus the central category of explanation for the rise of fascism was not, at the root, the laws of economic life, it was the transformation of mass psychology on the one hand and, on the other, the transformation of science and technology from forms of subordinate knowledge – tools of human purposes to a new normative order.[7]

These ruminations are shaped, but by no means determined, by contemporary intellectual influences (see Horkheimer and Adorno 1972; Adorno et al. 1950).[8] Besides Marx and Freud, each of whom influenced the scaffolding of critical theory, providing the key orientations, we must add that of German phenomenology, particularly Heidegger and Spengler, whose different though closely linked critiques of the scientific Enlightenment and its philosophical underpinnings stunned the postwar intellectual communities, including scientists themselves.[9] We must of course also include Hegel, who, as Foucault (1972) has said, prowls through the twentieth century reminding us of the price we have paid for our anti-foundationalism, especially our refusal of the totality. By this Foucault means the possibility of a historical process of emerging self-consciousness whose outcome is the identical subject/object. With Hegel, critical theory insists that the subject/object dialectic constitutes the structuration of society, the starting point of which is the part played by labor in the formation of humans and whose key category is that of domination. In contrast to the Marxist concept of labor exploitation as the foundation of social structure, CST borrows from both the early Marx and from Weber the more general term "domination" because it encompasses a wider sphere of social relations, it thereby refuses to locate the determination of social divisions in economic life (see esp. Marcuse 1964). Consequently, the subject is not identical with itself. It is fractured not only by class relations (the unequal division of the product of labor) but also by civilization's greatest achievements, science and technology. In effect, Horkheimer and Adorno argue, we have subordinated ends to means: the power of our tools of dominion over nature have penetrated our social unconscious, so that the self in both individual and collective terms has become little more than an instrument of its own domination by technology and technology's most egregious form, administration (Horkheimer and Adorno 1972; Horkheimer 1947). In modern industrial societies executive authorities rule persons in the model of the administration of things, since the reflexive self is inimical to the achievement of a conformist social order which requires an other-directed character structure (Horkheimer 1947). And, because the rewards of the awesome industrial machine mankind has constructed on its knowledge achievements are so seductive, we can no longer critically reflect on domination as a generalized social form because we have lost the capacity to distance ourselves from the world we have constructed on the basis of science. The subject is object-dominated even as it, in turn, dominates its natural environment.

These constructed objects now constitute our second nature. Reason, which became the religion of the bourgeois Enlightenment, had through its permutations within science become thoroughly instrumentalized and could no longer provide the way to any truth beyond the propositions of science and their technological application in the work of dominting nature and humans. In effect, ethical and philosophical inquiry, now subordinated to science, had lost their critical character (critical in the sense of transcending the conditions of the given, empirical world). People in advanced industrial societies are capable of solving technical problems associated with social, political, and economic development, but we can longer see the larger transformations that have delivered us into a new kind of political and moral slavery. Long before the rise of the current ecological movement, the dialectic of the Enlightenment presaged the imminent revolt of nature against its masters. Having completely subordinated the external environment to fulfill human needs as configured by capitalist social relations, humans were themselves in danger of extinction. Taking nature as pure, instrumentally mediated object was itself the product of our blind evolutionary ideology. According to this all "lower" organic and inorganic forms are subordinate to our will and inorganic nature is taken as inert "matter," a passive receptacle of human intervention. Precisely what Parsons posits, the control by the cultural system over all human relations, produces not equilibrium but crisis. Although the crisis has not fulfilled the letter of Marx's fateful prediction of proletarian revolution, but has been displaced into what C. Wright Mills (1951) calls "private troubles," ecological disasters and permanent wars, for the Frankfurt School there is no question of characterizing our social world by terms such as inertia.[10] Thus, the historical sociology of the Frankfurt School conducted its research on the basis of a philosophical anthropology that became the surrogate for method. Accordingly, the starting point of CST was to define the problematic of human sociation in terms of the need to secure human existence against a vicious and recalcitrant nature (Horkheimer and Adorno 1972; Marcuse 1978).[11] This ontological need is mediated by historical needs which are ever-changing according to the development of our collective powers over nature, but remained the irreversible element, both the boundary condition of the social order and the content of its social unconscious. Where Parsons holds time constant to enable sociology to predict human action, critical theory problematizes the goals of prediction and control, since these are the stuff of domination. Parsons posits adaptation of actors and the integration of the action situation into the larger system of control as a natural event subject only to exigencies; critical theory views the project of system maintenance as a system of domination, as inimical to freedom. Freedom consists in the capacity of actors to make themselves subjects, that is, beings capable of reflexivity and, consequently, self-management. Therefore critical theory must negate science as conventionally understood as unimpeachable knowledge. Its negative philosophy is premised on the requirement that we need to be jolted from the ideology of inertia and equilibrium. The categories of general social theory cannot be taken at face value, but must be subjected, in the interest of emancipation from positive science, to critical reflection (Adorno et al. 1976).[12]

From the perspective of the contemporary worship of natural techno-sciences as the model for all knowledge, Critical Theory appears, on the one hand, as a legatee to the Romantic movement in German philosophy for which science had become one of the obstacles to freedom and, on the other, a throwback to metaphysics, which science supposedly consigns to the past (see esp. Schelling 1988). Critical theory refuses the radical distinction between science and ideology but claims, to the contrary, that the goals of science – prediction and control – are forms of "interest."[13] To this I would add that the claims of science to value-neutrality, by means of the scientific method, presuppose the efficacy of the laboratory situation, that is, abstraction of the object or processes from the natural context.[14]

To the reductionism characteristic of idealist dialectics, in which the object is reduced to a form which permits contradiction, Adorno counterposes the notion that "dialectics is the consistent sense of nonidentity" (Adorno 1973: 5). This view contrasts with that of Hegel and Marx, for whom contradiction and totality are inextricably linked by the requirement that difference be resolved by a synthesis in which the elements of opposition are simultaneously preserved and transformed on a higher level. The negative dialectic asserts only the ineluctability of difference, and, in Gaston Bachelard's somewhat differently rooted version (1984 [1934]) argues that new knowledge can be generated only by an epistemological break between past and future. In Bachelard's *Philosophy of No* (1968 [1940]) critical exploration of the foundations of knowledge replaces method. Bachelard distinguishes his conception of the dialectic from an effort to follow in Hegel's footsteps. "What Bachelard calls dialectic is the inductive movement which reorganizes knowledge and enlarges its base, where the negation of concepts and of axioms is only an aspect of their generalization" (Canguillhem 1983: 196; my tr.). By dialectic Bachelard means difference – not difference as pure negation but as a determinate complementarity. His major concern is to oppose monologism as an impediment to the further development and enrichment of science. Nor does the notion of a synthetic dialectic appear in Bachelard, for synthesis implies reconciliation of opposites on a higher level of identical being. Bachelard's theory of the development of scientific knowledge as a series of epistemological "breaks" prefigures by a quarter-century the perspectives of Thomas Kuhn (if not Paul Feyerabend), which have become virtually canonical for the philosophy of science since the 1960s. Bachelard's best-known works, *The New Scientific Spirit* and *The Philosophy of No*, were really readings of the philosophical implications of developments in modern physics which may be taken as an unintended effort to bring the "subject" back into considerations of scientific knowledge. As a consequence of the "crisis" of representation, the reflection theory of knowledge and the correspondence theory of truth have been overthrown; because acts of measurement are part of the "field" of inquiry, all knowledge is relative to its frame of reference and its truth value, is at best probabilistic. These changes have only begun to call into question social scientific knowledge, which appears firmly ensconced in eighteenth-century assumptions.

Thus in place of determinate categories of which positive science is so fond, negative theory in its quest for the sources of transformation is caught between a critique of categories as fulfilling an ontological need, and its own will to explanation, a program which requires positive, unhistorically mediated, categories (see esp. Adorno 1973a). Bachelard addresses this difficulty by relying on categories of physical sciences to trace the transformations in their meaning. For example, the opening chapters of his *Philosophy of No* is largely a historical exploration of the varieties of the use of the concept of "mass" within different theoretical frameworks in modern physics. By rigorously adhering to the actual movement of science, he is able to show the remarkable degree to which this so-called empirical category is suffused with philosophical, metatheoretical presuppositions. From this style of theorizing, Bachelard powerfully influenced not only French philosophy but also social theory. Like critical theory, however, Bachelard has had only marginal influence in Anglo-American social sciences.

A similar strategy is adopted by critical theory, with the important difference that the death of the subject is not made axiomatic at the theoretical level but is traced as the outcome of distinctive historical developments. At the most philosophical level, Adorno's work is an extensive metacritique of the Hegelian categories, showing that, intentions notwithstanding, they remain profoundly anti-dialectical by affirming the positive as the outcome of negation and synthesis. But its concrete critical objects are the categories of sociology. As a consequence of its disdain for system-building, critical sociology becomes a critique of sociology's own categories – society, group, social agents, culture, science and technology, politics, and the state, considered as forms of social knowledge and social practices.

In their short volume *Aspects of Sociology* (1972) the Frankfurt Institute for Social Research (intellectually and administratively directed by Horkheimer and Adorno at the time of its original publication in the mid-1950s), announces its critical intention from the outset: Sociology "is a child of positivism," which, although commendably founded to "free knowledge from religious beliefs and metaphysical speculation," surrenders, in its quest for scientific accuracy, the sense of the totality and condemns itself to partial knowledge. Sociology is charged with having sought not the specifically social or human relations but the "natural laws" governing human action in order to modify or control them. The tacit claim in this critique of sociology is that it is concerned not merely with discerning the "facts," however they are construed, but with modifying and otherwise controlling human action. In effect, social science can study humans with the methods of natural science because it takes social relations as objective relations and at a distance. That is, the process of investigation is abstracted from the object of knowledge. Further, by slicing up society into a series of domains the investigator is able to better grasp the date and make (partial) generalizations. But these domains are conventionally defined and do not possess the status of "natural" fact. After the critique of the epistemology of sociology, it is to the sources of conventional categorical construction that critical theory devotes its attention, except where, in the case of prejudice, a solution serves the interest of general emancipation. The critique of categories becomes, for critical theory, an alternative to the artificial positivities of mainstream sociology.

Yet, the Frankfurt School recognizes the legitimacy of the specific domain of sociology – to discern the "laws of sociation; that is of social formation and integration." If this is the case, then the sociological investigation of the individual given an understanding of society as a mere aggregation of indivduals, is faced with severe epistemologial and historical difficulties. Should sociology accept the liberal evocation of the autonomous, thinking individual as the foundation for social investigation? If, as critical theory claims, the basis of a satisfactory relation of individual to society is a healthy, humane social order, it follows that the individual fate is linked to that of society and the liberal assumption of individual autonomy (whether as an ontological or a methodological concept) is put into question. Further, is the individual an irreducible unit or is the individual nothing other than "an ensemble of social relations," as Marx claims? The presumption of methodological individualism which forms the basis of much contemporary sociological research becomes untenable if either of these propositions is accepted. *Aspects of Sociology* argues that the individual is itself a historically constituted category and presupposes the emergence of civil society in the late medieval period when market relations – with their concomitant characteristics-competition between independent producers and other owners of property – dominated economic, social, and ideological relations and, as Habermas argues, the separation of the public from the private spheres constructs new conditions for human interaction. By denaturalizing the individual and other categories of sociology, critical theory tries to show that, abstracted from its frame of reference, sociological knowledge becomes ideological in the sense of interested inquiry. In its characteristic American form (against which Parsons was the most outstanding exception), sociology puts the idea of society itself as a social fact in question and with it structuring concepts such as system and classes as historical actors.

Thus, critical theory joins sociology's criticis such as Robert Lynde, C. Wright Mills, and Alvin Gouldner in asking the fundamental question: "Knowledge for what?" (Mills 1964;

Merton 1957).[15] However, science is not irrevocably debunked and philosophy installed as the arbiter of all knowledge claims, in which the criterion of the historical frame of reference mediates truth claims. Instead, this historical frame of reference constitutes a series of categories which, taken together, may be construed as a general social theory. It is to this social theory that I now turn.

II

Contemporary social theory is deeply enmeshed in a debate about the relation between social structure and social agency. All of the canonical figures of social theory (Marx, Weber, Simmel, Durkheim) and their later twentieth-century successors have puzzled over the question because of its saliency to the problem of historical determination. None of the major theorists can avoid dealing with structure and agency but their emphasis usually focuses on one or another side. For example, Marx is alternately labeled an economic or historical determinist or a voluntarist. But it is plain that as a thinker influenced by nineteenth-century science as well as by its economics and philosophy, he was obliged to name historical subjects – classes – but placed strong emphasis on naturalized social "forces" which propelled classes, groups, and individuals to engage in action of historical consequence. Conversely, Weber's strong sense of the influence of economic structure on the course of ancient history was tempered by his investigation of the transition from feudalism to capitalism where the role of subjectively meaningful ideas (in the Kantian, not the Hegelian sense) in producing social change is accorded primacy. Similarly, at the pinnacle of Parsons's structured social totality stand values which powerfully influence action; the cultural system, really the internalized values of any society, controls relatively variable subsystems. Indeterminacy is produced by external and internal variability, but Parsons is constrained to insist upon the objectivity of belief systems and their controlling power.

Critical theory, which itself rejects the artificial totalizations of classical Marxism, criticizes sociology's rejection of the totality but refuses, equally, a conception in which society is conceived as the sum of its parts, whether constituted by differentiated systems, by Durkheimian categories of solidarity and other equilibria, or by a single hypostasized structure such as Simmel's money economy. Even more, as we have seen, does critical theory attack the positivistic penchant, following writers such as Robert Merton, to divide the field of social investigation into a series of social problems. The only unity of these problems is provided by methodological inscriptions the dominant values of which are observation and quantification.

The empirical referent of critical sociology is the history of societies. Its crucial "method" is immanent critique, if by that phrase is connoted a close analysis of texts – historical, literary, philosophical – even, as in the atypical case of Adorno's magisterial study *The Authoritarian Personality*, survey forms. For each of the examined texts, the object of reading is to disassemble, and otherwise disrupt apparently seamless narratives to show the hidden text, particularly its linkages with knowledge, power, and action. This investigation takes the form of ideology-critique, showing that knowledges that purport to be neutral observation – value-free theory, empirically "verified" fact – are a veiled discourse of domination. Beneath this mode of inquiry is the assumption that narratives, scientific texts, "information" typically conceal their content, which can only be revealed by interrogation as to underlying motives and values – regardless of whether they are consciously held. This "procedure" presupposes a sociological community which has freed itself of scientism, the doctrine according to which scientific facts can be established by rigorous methods of empirical research whose fundamental feature is the apodictic status of knowledge gained through the senses supplemented by rational calculation.

Perhaps two texts, Horkheimer and Adorno's *Dialectic of the Enlightenment* (1972 [1944]) and Herbert Marcuse's *One Dimensional Man* (1964) exemplify best how critical sociology unwittingly generates new, one might say positive, categories – not in the course of constructing analytic categories such as system and structure, but as a concomitant (not the outcome) of historically and hermeneutically based inquiry. *Dialectic of the Enlightenment* problematizes the rupture between myth and science and thereby begins an investigation of the Enlightenment by subverting one of its underlying claims: to have freed knowledge (and therefore humanity) of the thrall of superstition. This is accomplished by choosing, as a starting point, the viewpoint of its most articulate tribune, Francis Bacon. Following Weber's notion that the Enlightenment signals the disenchantment of nature, Horkheimer and Adorno show Bacon as a key ideologist of the domination of nature:

> Despite his lack of mathematics, Bacon's view was appropriate to the scientific attitude that prevailed after him. The concordance between mind of man and the nature of things that he had in mind was patriarchal: the human mind, which overcomes superstition, is to hold sway over a disenchanted nature. Knowledge, which is power, knows no obstacles: neither in the enslavement of men nor in compliance with the world's rulers . . . What men want to learn from nature is how to use it in order to wholly dominate it and other men. That is the only aim. Ruthlessly the Enlightenment has extinguished any trace of its own self-consciousness.
>
> (*Horkheimer and Adorno 1972 [1944]: 4*)

In Bacon's own words, the acquisition of knowledge is not undertaken for the purposes of "satisfaction" but to achieve "the better endowment and help of man's life." The old mysteries are to be laid aside, the old rituals abandoned, and our relation to nature is conceived as purely instrumental. In the process by which knowledge is subordinated to the specific ends, all social relations are instrumentalized, that is, made subordinate to the imperatives of production. In turn, the development of science and technology becomes the key to such commercial activities as navigation, mining, and trade. While the aim of Enlightenment thought and practice is to facilitate the return of the subject to the social process in which "men" make their own history against a feudal order which subordinated individuals to the dictates of ecclesiastical law (which was identical, in many instances, with civil law), its long-term effects have been to raise technology to the level of social principle. In the service of "endowing" human life, nature has been subdued, but so has mankind itself. "Scientific" evidence becomes the arbiter of human affairs. Following a certain reading of

Darwin's theory, Herbert Spencer, Francis Galton, and others offered biologically based views of human intelligence and, more broadly, social fate. Although these ideas were temporarily eclipsed in the wake of the Holocaust which employed racial difference to justify Jewish, gay, and gypsy extermination, they have made their way back to public opinion in the 1970s and 1980s, if not (yet) to public policy. After a prolonged period during which Freud's critical and hermeneutic theory of the unconscious powerfully influenced clinical psychology as well as sociology, biologically based theories of the brain, the new eugenics, genetic engineering, and Edward O. Wilson's sociobiology signal the return of the repressed. Quantitative social science has formed the backdrop of social policy's legitimation and has, in proportion as state economic and social intervention increased, become a technological value orientation in itself. What Marcuse calls the "technological imperative" replaces religion or, to be more precise, becomes the new religion.

Marcuse argues from the premise that social relations have become near-identical with this imperative. Speaking in historical materialist terms, the critique of technology is, in the late twentieth century, descriptive of practices in both the infrastructure and the superstructure, so that the distinction between them has collapsed. We may no longer speak of ideology in the nineteenth-century sense, since this term implies a relation between relative truths to statements in which "interest" predominates. Now, we have seen the merger of ideology and science such that knowledge's validity can only be considered as a local case; for the system as a whole, all ideas, including scientific knowledge, religion, ethical judgments, derive their validation from the degree to which they are instrumental to achieving specific ends. For Marcuse, the existence of the individual, let alone the historical subject, is in grave danger; for we may have reached the end of history, if by that term we mean the possibility of control by self-conscious subjects over their own social fate. Horkheimer and Adorno try to show the wide gulf between the objective of Enlightenment thought to free humans from the shackles of superstition and the reality of science and technology as the new superstition. Marcuse is primarily concerned with the problem of agents. If we live in a technological society where critical thought itself is occluded by the progressive narrowing of public discourse to problems soluble within a technocratic framework, where systemic alternatives have been marginalized to the point of extinction; if our language has lost its capacity for the eloquence associated with negation, and consciousness can no longer take itself as its own object because the Other-directed self is overwhelmed by the object-world; if everyday life is suffused with buying and getting and our work relations have dissolved in a solitary relation with machines in which the old factory system is displaced by homework and other isolating environments, what possibilities are there for history, or for collective action in the interest of emancipation?

Marcuse and Mills (whose social theory owed as much to pragmatism and Merton's understanding of it as it did to CST) derived little solace from the early signs of "postindustrial" culture. The new automated workplace failed to address alienation and may have exacerbated its main features. Suburban life merely reproduced the forms of white-collar alienation and displaced them to living situations. Consumerism, practiced in suburban and ex-urban shopping centers, may tap libidinal desire, but sap community life which once flourished, albeit under sometimes impoverished conditions, in the huge industrial cities. In the absence of the historic conditions for collective action – culturally diverse large cities, heavily concentrated workplaces, vital radical political traditions, and a public sphere where politcal discourse was part of everyday existence – the emergence of new subjects was highly unlikely. Although, at the end of his life, Marcuse began to see such possibilities in feminism and ecological movements, he never fully reconciled this changed perspective with the negative dialectic; nor could he completely free his theory of agency from the fundamental premise of socialist and Marxist thought grounded in the problematic of the proletarian revolution. To have recognized in the new social movements genuine moral and political agents would have entailed radical revision of the dialectic of labor as the core of human existence. In Marcuse's thought mode, heavily influenced by Heiddegger's *Dasein*, labor is an ontological as well as historical activity – the predominant form of life. Hence, the entire scaffolding of technological domination and its consequence – one-dimensionality.

III

Beyond the negative dialectic's metacritique of scientific sociology, critical sociology investigates the social world with
categories derived from historical materialism's negation of
Hegel's philosophy of history and dialectic of the spirit. It
presupposes Marx's theory of social formations if not his stage
theory, but does not privilege the categories of political
economy to account for historical transformation. Rather, with
Weber, the concept of instrumental rationality becomes the
driving force of modern civilizations. However, rather than
accepting, as did Weber, its institutional forms – bureaucracy,
science and technology, and mass culture – as egregious but
necessary compromises on the road to progress, critical
sociology raises the stakes of general theory. We must scrutinize
the transformation of reason entailed by the Enlightenment and
examine its consequences in the course of world history.
Horkheimer, in perhaps his most radical article (1950), argues
that the authoritarian states of the 1930s were direct outgrowths
of the dark side of the logic of capitalist development and not, as
the liberals and communists contended, horrific mutations in a
seriously impaired liberal social order. Recall that, at the
outbreak of the war, predominant contemporary leftist thought
still believed that bourgeois democracy was endemic to capitalism;
the rise of fascism represented a political, not a systemic
transformation.[16] Horkheimer, following Spengler's prescient
observations in the second volume of his *Decline of the West* as
well as the Institute's own sociological investigations into the
state and social institutions of Weimar Germany, especially its
families and culture, concluded that genuine democracy had
never taken root, that the structures of patriarchal authority,
reproduced in the workplace as managerial power, militated
against whatever political democracy had been codified in the
Constitution. Further, the growing power of executive authorities,
corresponding to the requirements of capital for state intervention
to cushion the effects of the profound international economic
crisis, strengthened authoritarian tendencies even before the rise
of Hitler to power. Mass culture, condemned but also dismissed
by Marxist and liberal theory, as little more than the latest outlet

for capital investment – whose audience, the masses, has always thrived on bread and circuses – is now understood as part of the long-term consequences of the penetration of the commodity form and technological thought to all forms of the social world. Where Marxism, in this framework, consonant with the assumptions of liberal thought, retains its optimism that social engineering can cure all or at least most of capitalist-wrought ills, critical theorists, under the influence of Nietszche and especially Spengler, are haunted by the dystopian vision of the West's decline amidst a surfeit of honey. The masses, once heralded by socialists and radical democrats as the hope of humanity, are, under this new regime, its willing victims even as they benefit from the pleasures of a technologically wrought affluence. By the 1960s Marcuse in *One Dimensional Man* can cite only the world's poor, systematically deprived of even a small share in what Mills called the Great Celebration of capitalist progress, and intellectuals' Great (moral) Refusal as potential agents. Yet this invocation remains, in his discourse, more speculative and poetic than analytic. In the hands of CST historical agency has collapsed into an ethical ideal, since virtually all people in advanced industrial societies are more or less well off. Surely there is still considerable poverty in the US but, if the poor protest and revolt, technologically rich societies are capable of coopting nearly all economic demands by modification of the system of redistributive justice. Critical sociology does not predict the end of social conflict or of agency. It foresees the end of historical change in the sense that the fundamental power relations are likely to remain unchanged, not only in political society but, more important, in civil society, the sphere of lived experience. In the darkest formulation, the negative dialectic exists but only as a simulation, as "artificial" negativity. Even a society of total administration requires some kind of agent to provide the dynamism without which the system cannot reproduce itself, much less grow. Jean Baudrillard developed the theory of the simulacra as a postmodernist intellectual game, but Philip K. Dick's novels develop the possibilities for a new morality from the agonies of the simulacra.

The many concrete sociological studies of culture which Adorno performed seem to reproduce the fundamental thesis that technology and its concomitant proliferation of products has enabled advanced capitalist societies to offer to the underlying population both bread and roses (the familiar slogan of the turn-of-the-century socialist movement); but even as these societies appear more tolerant of dissent, the content of democratic participation is, more and more, repressed in a veritable orgy of consumption. Or, in Marcuse's notorious formulation of the theory of repressive tolerance, dissent remains more or less uninhibited in Western societies, but the stakes have been lowered (Marcuse 1965). Radical ideas are largely unfettered in their utterance but are typically unheard. Even in that dissent which is provided by the corporate-controlled media some voice must be shaped and therefore neutralized to fit into prevailing discourses. The opposition itself becomes an essential component of the prevailing order; its existence is tolerated to legitimate the democratic claims of the political and economic system. We get conflicts but no systemic contradictions. The American critical theorist Paul Piccone calls this phenomenon artificial negativity.

This paradox is nowhere more evident than in spread of the culture industry to what had formerly been considered "high" art – especially classical music and painting. Adorno's pioneering work on the sociology of music (1988 [1962]) focuses on the ubiquity of the middle-brow audience that has become the soul of high art concert performances. The large symphony orchestra organization has become subordinated to the patrons and the audience for top 40 classics – almost all of Mozart and Haydn, the Beethoven symphonies and concertos, the works of Chopin, Tchaikovsky, and Brahms and a sprinkling of the twentieth-century music: the neoclassical Stravinsky and works influenced by the late Romantic era or the nationalist phase of American music of the thirties and forties. At the publication of Adorno's book on the sociology of music in 1962, the works of Schoenberg, Berg, and Webern and their followers were virtually absent in the classical repertoire, certainly among major US and European orchestras. Adorno took this fact to be one more empirical validation of the thesis that the fashion process penetrates all forms of the social world, an insight borrowed from Simmel but documented by him, with mixed results. The commodification of high culture has been amply demonstrated by world cultural history since the end of the Second World War; but Adorno's claim (1967) that jazz is merely a "perennial fashion" possessing little or no intrinsic aesthetic value (an Adorno preoccupation in the forties and fifties) demonstrated the ultimate limits of the sociological understanding and indeed the artistic judgment of the Frankfurt School.

For critical theory genuine high art was the last refuge of critical practice in a world completely dominated by total administration. Society was marked by a wizened lifeworld in which entertainment replaced a vital public sphere where citizens are competent to fully debate political issues and can really control their own affairs. The degradation of art consisted in its subordination to the technological colossus which controlled nearly every aspect of social life except that of the artistic avant garde, whose subversive content was virtually assured by its distance from art forms consonant with popular taste. Expressionist and surrealist painting in the 1920s, the novels of Joyce, and the poetry of Pound were as dissonant in relation to mainstream aesthetic standards as Schoenberg's seriality was oppositional to the sonorities of Romantic and classical music. It was precisely at the margins of official art that the critical spirit stayed alive. For Adorno (1973b), Schoenberg's project in the 1920s, with its fairly daunting rules, to systematize dissonance in terms of a "system" of atonality marked the end of his specifically critical intervention. In other words, when Schoenberg succumbed to the positivities of method his art was dead. Schoenberg has never been fully integrated into the symphonic repertoire, except through his late Romantic works such as *Transfigured Night* and *Pelleas and Melisande*. But in academic precincts in the United States in the period after the Second World War his method became *de rigueur*. Nearly all of the more important "serious music" composers, even the folk-and jazz-influenced Aaron Copland, were obliged to adopt variations of serial music by the late 1950s. On the other hand, performances of their works were confined, almost entirely, to small, university-sponsored concerts. The large orchestras, dominated by the alliance of the corporate patrons and middle-class subscribers, tolerated this music only to forestall embarrassment.

As for "society," critical theory appears to have been hoist by its own petard. The very weapons the Frankfurt School used to convict advanced industrial society as "total administration" in which state, economy, and culture were integrated by technology (and, in turn, integrated the underlying population by means of every cooptation other than coercion) left it with an account resembling that of conventional general social theory. For critical theory, the dynamic dimension of society, more specifically its internal capacity for generating change, had yielded to repressive inertia, masked by ever-changing fashion and the appearance of opposition, and made particularly powerful by the reduction of all conflict to a series of problems subject to managerial solutions. These solutions were possible within the framework of system maintenance precisely because of the instrumentalization of nature and social life made possible by the repression of the critical function of reason. Now reason had become attached to the apparatus of domination. Change was possible only from without – from those excluded from partaking in the benefits and processes of the system. In any case, this possibility is time-limited, and is constrained by the great powers of the apparatus under appropriate political pressure, to make even poverty, hunger, and disease subject to administrative solutions.

The subject-less discourse of late critical theory was predicated on the collapse of the working-class movement between the two world wars, the calamitous rise of totalitarian states, especially in those societies where Enlightenment ideology had sunk the deepest roots, and the virtual disappearance of the traditional intellectuals, that is, those still in contact with eighteenth- and nineteenth-century Western critical philosophy. The displacement of all but scientific philosophy by social and natural sciences, what Horkheimer termed the "eclipse of reason" in the wake of instrumental rationality, produced in critical theory a curious account of contemporary society as one of stasis. Notwithstanding its insistence on the ineluctability of difference, its refusal of *a priori* categories of Marxism or systematic sociology, CCT reproduced contemporary sociology garbed in Hegelian rhetoric. Of course, as Adorno has argued (1973a: 54–6), rhetoric is not merely a question of style or a formal device; persuasion is, in the hands of dialectics, a content. This is true because language is not merely the means of expression but configures thought itself. Thus, close attention to the use of words, phrases, aphorisms, metaphors, and the presence of moral passion in CCT signifies; and this signification cannot be separated from the so-called content. Yet, one cannot avoid noticing the powerful parallels between Parsonian sociology and critical theory despite these differences. From the perspective of critical theory Parsons lacks history (except in his wonderful account of intellectuals, where the object is its history, even as he retains the notion of social definition as social role).

I claim that the core category for critical theory as sociology is what Parsons calls the cultural system, whose normative specifications surely differ from those named by Parsons. While Parsons assumes the religiously based value systems of the classical Enlightenment – parsimony, hard work, scientific reason – are still regulative of social action and can, therefore, produce equilibrium subject to the exigencies of the social and personality systems, CCS castigates industrial societies for elevating means to ends. Neither conventional bourgeois values nor coercion constitute the essential condition for the stability of modernized society. For critical theory it is the conflation of reason with the technological requirement which permits the attainment of a soul-less material affluence, which becomes a framework of social domination. Here we might compare Daniel Bell's generally joyous announcement of the coming of postindustrial society (1973), in which politics is largely collapsed into the quiet, computer-based process of technocratic decision-making, with the outcome of critical theory. What for Bell, a pioneer ideologist of technology as power, is a social forecast deprived of any critical content becomes the dystopia of the alienated traditional intellectual.

IV

Negative Dialectics, just like *The Philosophy of No*, was offered as a corrective to the tendency of knowledge to reproduce itself dogmatically in the wake of epochal changes in society. They are intellectual responses to both the new scientific and technological revolutions which had visibly transformed the social landscape in the twentieth century and the concomitant changes in the nature of power relations. In both cases, although in somewhat different ways, the question asked was: what are the sources and contours of historical changes? But critical theory as a sociology found itself, perhaps against its will, obliged to explain the radical departures from the Marxist script exhibited in all Western capitalist societies as well as the existing socialist countries. As a consequence of the crisis of socialism and the socialist movement which had by the 1950s become manifest, the category of dialectics underwent a profound shift that prefigured poststructuralisms of the 1960s to the present. Having rejected the Hegelian/Marxist schema according to which the subject and object are transformed by a series of double negations and become identical after a long series, Adorno seeks recourse for the dialectic in Walter Benjamin's category of "constellation," in which "ideas are to objects as constellations are to stars. This means in the first place that they are neither their concepts nor their laws. They do not contribute to the knowledge of phenomena and in no way can the latter be criteria for which to judge the existence of ideas" (Benjamin 1977: 34). Therefore ideas cannot represent things. Adorno remarks that constellations as groups of ideas are the "more" pushed out by objects and unrepresented by concepts and can be likened to Weber's ideal types.[17] Representation of the empirically actual is replaced by placing the object in constellation. Weber "explicitly rejected the delimiting procedure of definition, the adherence to the *schema proximum differentia specifica*, and asked instead that sociological concepts be 'gradually composed' from 'individual parts taken from historical reality. The place of definitive conceptual comprehension cannot, therefore, be the beginning of the inquiry, only the end.'" (Adorno 1973a: 165). These compositions are analogous to the notion of constellations which, despite their origin in fragments of social reality, are really ideas whose correspondence with any empirical object is problematic by virtue of the assemblage method itself. Adorno criticizes Weber's penchant in his last works for definition and argues that the ideal-type succumbs to neither idealism nor positivism but is a critical category precisely because of its explicit admission of non-correspondence. This is Adorno's most explicit attempt to appropriate Weber for a non-positivist social science. Benjamin had transmuted Goethe's elective affinity to explain the unity of ideas and its objects, but only speculatively. Constellation infers the elective affinity of non-identical objects/ideas whose relation must, thereby, remain unstable. The separation of the objects from which the constellation is composed opens up to the possibility for the formation of new constellations. Hence, rather than positing the social world as a system of necessary, relatively invariant relations, critical theory in this most promising moment retains Heraclitian flux, even as its description of the contemporary world provides little hope that the prevailing constellation at the level of the social totality will obey this "law." Yet, since the affinities are "composed" and are not the outcome of inevitable synthetic processes, indeterminacy is preserved.

Adorno's critique of Spengler (1967) reveals the ambiguity of the negative dialectic. Despite the prescience of Spengler's major work – his prediction of the coming of a new Caesarism in Europe, his penetrating critique of the hypocritical actions of democratic states, his pioneering critique of scientism and especially positivism – Adorno finds fatal flaws in Spengler's own immanent positivism, his glorification of facts, of technolgy, and especially his anti-intellectual attacks on culture. Above all, Spengler's prognostications and the assumption that society is a closed system leave little or no room for agency, nor can he truly grasp the part played by the domination of nature in the cultural decline he so accurately chronicles. In the last analysis Spengler is, according to Adorno, a "metaphysical positivist . . . in [his] hatred of all thought that takes the possible seriously in its opposition to the actual." At the conclusion of this essay, Adorno delivers the ultimate blow against an unrelenting pessimism that makes no room for those rendered most powerless by a progressively decaying society: "The powerless, who at Spengler's command are to be thrown aside and annihilated by history, are the negative embodiment within the negativity of this culture of everything which promises, however feebly, to break the dictatorship of culture and put an end to the horror of pre-history. In their protest lies the only hope that fate and power will not have the last word. What can oppose the decline of the west is not a resurrected culture but

the utopia that is silently contained in the image of its decline"
(Adorno 1967: 72).

The silently contained utopia consists in protest that refuses
"fate and power" the last word. But this eloquent comment in
the interest of emancipation, Adorno's stubborn insistence
upon philosophy and social theory that, having no specific
standpoint rooted in concrete historical actors, addresses its
enunciations in the name of the nameless "powerless" matches
Benjamin's rueful "it is only for the sake of those without hope
that hope is given us." Thus does aphorism replace social
theory. Marcuse: "The critical theory of society possesses no
concepts which could bridge the gap between the present and its
[civilization's] future; holding no promise and showing no
success, it remains negative. Thus, it wants to remain loyal to
those who, without hope, have given their life to the Great
Refusal" (1964: 257). But the problem with this Refusal is that it
resembles an exigency, since CST provides us with no specific
theory that can account for the appearance of Refusal, protest,
or revolt. Indeed in *One Dimensional Man* Marcuse argues:

> The totalitarian tendencies of the one-dimensional society
> render the traditional ways and means of protest ineffective
> – perhaps even dangerous because they preserve the
> illusion of popular sovereignty. Social transformation
> remains a utopian hope without a contemporary base in
> the actual social life; in fact, social life is counter factual to
> any hope for change unless we are somehow able to
> compose a constellation of differentiated elements.
>
> *(Marcuse 1964: 256)*

But this entails concrete social research for these are drawn from
"fragments" of historical reality. For example, one would have to
imagine the conditions under which disparate social movements
–ecology, feminists, movements for gay liberation, squatters,
even sectors of the working class – could collectively constitute
an alternative culture and an alternative political power. This
level of specificity was beyond CST's purview since such an
eventuality implies that the closed discursive universe so central
to its historical judgment had somehow been pried open. And in
this "somehow" lie the contours of a new social theory, one that

would have to preserve the negativity of CST, but would also be obliged to abandon its unintended Spenglerian legacy.

By way of conclusion, I argue that no critical theory, including that of the Frankfurt School, can dispense with either categories or metacategories from which to make historical and empirical judgments. Surely, ideas such as the totally administered society, domination of nature, and one-dimensionality are "synthetic" categories upon which critical social theory depends. In turn, these are really constellations constructed from such abstractions as domination, bureaucracy, reason, ideology, nature and, in a different register, class, labor, the state, and so on.[18] Similarly, when Adorno writes on the "Culture Industry" or the Enlightenment, he is invoking capitalism, culture, science, and technology as basic categories from which the concatenation is made. In short, just as doing science entails making judgments in the sense that its axiomatic structures may be interrogated, so those who would interrogate social life cannot avoid "science," if by this constellation we mean positing a hierarchy of existents without which empirical judgment is arbitrary.

When we seek to explain social relations, we must go beyond negative dialectics. From critical theory's own perspective, what lies beyond must necessarily be historically and practically situated. I believe that just as Foucault is right to point out that intellectuals no longer work in categories of the "universal" truths but theorize and do practical research in situated locations (either professional or within "their conditions of life"), so the categories of social knowledge must also be specific. We can no longer characterize entire societies by divisions into sectors, orders, or invariant relations of determination such as economic infrastructure or Great Ideas. One possible explanation for this perspective is the historically conditioned disaggregation of social totalities such as "organized" capitalism, socialism, the third world, and other constellations from which these universals were crafted. On the other hand, poststructuralist historiography has maintained that the past was never constituted as more than unstable totalities of incommensurable discourses, the most powerful of which are underdetermined by the economic infrastructure. Rather, they may be considered the resultant of a conjuncture, particularly of the power/knowledge constellation.

Nevertheless, the intention to be specific, to avoid large abstractions, has not spared even the most meticulous of local histories from being generalized. Foucault's work has been shamelessly appropriated by his universalizing disciples who, nudged by academic environments, are prone to overtheorization. Foucault's fecund use of categories such as discourse, discursive formation, power/knowledge, produced the rudiments of an alternative social-theoretical paradigm from which history has been rewritten. As Derrida once readily acknowledged, we are not able to avoid logocentric Western culture among whose leading themes is the high value placed upon intellectual knowledge and its core of abstract universals. It was, after all, in consideration of the dangers entailed by such a use of science that schools of social inquiry, including Marxism as well as positivist social science, bid us return to the concrete.

Although we need not return to what C. Wright Mills once called "abstracted empiricism" to grasp the concrete, neither can we avoid general theory. I am persuaded that these debates will not end; a final solution will not be found.

NOTES

1 I owe this insight to Jonathan Lang and to Fredric Jameson, who is among our best essayists in this tradition.

2 As Talcott Parsons comments (1955: 631): "As an essential point of reference for defining the four functional exigencies or dimensions of the systems, we assume one law, or postulate according to the way it is viewed. Thus, we call the law of inertia, on the analogy (or more than that) of the use of the term in classical mechanics. The law may be stated as the proposition that a process of action (as part of the system of action) will tend to continue with its direction and potency . . . unchanged unless it is deflected or otherwise changed by the impingement of some other process (in the system or its situation)." In this extract, the influence of Pareto's analogy between mechanical phenomena and social phenomena is striking. See Pareto 1966: 106–7.

3 "We define the 'tendency to seek goals' not in terms of any specific propensity of organism or personality or social system, but in terms of the concepts of inertia and equilibrium as applied to a system. From

the concept of cathectic orientation it follows that an actor-unit or system will develop differential evaluations of different objects, and of different relations to the same object (or category of objects) in its situation in different circumstances" (Parsons 1955: 632). In turn, cathexis is the "optimum relation" to a given object "an approximation to which we may call the 'consummatory' or 'maximum-gratification state.'" To this Parsons hastens to add that it is not a "static" relation because it varies with "rates of inputs and outputs to the object."

4 Given their collective antipathy for science, the physical analogy is rarely, if ever, invoked by these writers. However, one cannot avoid, at the discursive level, the articulation between their collective reading of the twentieth century as a massive break with the past and Einstein's comment that Relativity physics does not "surpass" the Newtonian model; instead, it relegates classical mechanics to a special case in the general theory. If mass society, new information and communications technologies, the rapid pace of scientific discoveries, economic restructuring can be grouped under the indefinite rubric "postmodernism," conservative and radical critics of contemporary culture, even if they differ about modernity (democracy, industrial-ization, the emergence of the mass "subject"), surely converge in their hostility to "technological" society and culture.

5 In Lukács 1971 [1922], Marcuse 1968, and other works, the concept of ideology is linked either with the vicissitudes of the commodity form or the transformations of rationality from traditional to instrumental forms. In both formulations domination of nature and of humans is the objective, but Marcuse retains the dialectical relation of "interest" and the construction of technological domination: "The very concept of technical reason is perhaps ideological. Not only the application of technology but technology itself is domination (of nature and men) – methodical, scientific, calculated, calculating control. Specific purposes and interests of domination are not foisted upon technology 'subsequently' and from the outside; they enter the very construction of the technical apparatus. Technology is always a historical-social project: in it is projected what a society and its ruling interests intend to do with men and things. Such a 'purpose' of domination is 'substantive' and to this extent belongs to the very form of technical reasons" (Marcuse 1968: 223–4).

In contrast, Weber leaves little room for this sense of the concept of ideology because, like most social theorists, he considers explorations of "intention" a teleological fallacy or, worse, an example of psychologism.

6 These studies began in the early thirties with Studies in Authority and the Family, a research project directed by Horkheimer. During this

period, the Institute actively sought contact with psychoanalytical theory and recruited Erich Fromm, who until the late thirties was among those who tried to link Marx and Freud, and Otto Fenichel. Of course, critical theory was profoundly influenced by Wilhelm Reich's *Mass Psychology of Fascism* (1970 [1946]) and other works of his Marxist period. The struggle to develop a mass social psychology runs like a red thread through critical theory into the 1960s.

7 Of course, I refer here to "really existing" Marxism of the socialist and communist internationals, which heavily emphasized the study of political economy as the pre-eminent paradigm for understanding politics, culture, and ideology.

8 Adorno and his colleagues specifically acknowledge the influences on their views of authoritarianism: Fromm, Erik Erikson, A. Maslow, M. Chisholm and Reich (Adorno et al. 1950: 231n). Of these, it is Reich's monumental work *Character Analysis* (1972 [19]), which elaborated the authoritarian character structure, was, after Freud, the fundamental theoretical work on the transformation of the subject in our century.

9 For a thorough description of Spengler's influence on Weimar science, see Forman 1971; on Heidegger's influence, see Friedman 1981: ch. 5. For a direct example of this, see Marcuse 1973; and for a perhaps more convincing case, Marcuse 1987 (first published in 1932). Marcuse's effort here is to reconcile Heidegger's ontology with history, a synthesis rejected by Heidegger, with whom Marcuse had studied for the five years just prior to Hitler's assumption of power in 1933. In the Introduction to her translation of this work, Seyla Benhabib suggests that the general interpretation that Heidegger rejected the book because of political differences should be tempered on Marcuse's own authority.

10 *White Collar* (1951), together with Mills's *Power Elite* (1956), were to have profound impact on Marcuse's subsequent social theory. I would argue that, having been influenced by mass society theory, in which critical theory played an important part, Mills provided both the "empirical" demonstration for its crucial conclusions and contributed to critical theory by linking bureaucratic rationality to questions of work and power.

11 These were written in the same period, the late thirties and early forties, when the shift from studies of authority to studies of science and technology is evident.

12 In this symposium, whose contributions were made, at various times, in the 1960s, Karl Popper and Hans Albert extensively debate the "logic" of the social sciences with Adorno and Jürgen Habermas. It is perhaps the fullest statement from the standpoint of CST on the

presuppositions of social theory. This is not the place to exhaustively mine its riches. For our purpose it is enough to quote Adorno's comment on Parsons: "The harmonistic tendency of science, which makes the antagonisms of reality disappear through its methodical processing, lies in the classificatory method which is devoid of the intention of those who utilize it. It reduces to the same concept what is not fundamentally homonymous, what is mutually opposed, through the selection of the conceptual apparatus, and in the service of its unanimity. In recent years, an example of this tendency has been provided by Talcott Parsons's well-known attempt to create a unified science of man. His system of categories subsumes individual and society, psychology and sociology or at least places them in a continuum. The ideal of continuity current since Descartes and Leibnitz, especially, has become dubious, though not merely as a result of recent scientific development. In society the ideal conceals the rift between the general and the particular, in which the continuing antagonism expresses itself. The unity of science represses the contradictory nature of its object" (Adorno et al. 1976: 16–17).

13 For a succinct statement of critical theory's position on science, see Habermas 1976.

14 For a discussion of this point, see Aronowitz 1988.

15 Their reading of pragmatism as well as the history of the physical and biological sciences warned both Mills and Merton against large generalizations, even general theory. Merton's famous argument that science develops by empirically verifiable hypotheses, which inevitably can only be of the middle range, became the basis for Mills's celebrated but misunderstood *Sociological Imagination* (1959). In this essay, Mills takes both Parsons and his antimonies the empiricists of dominant American sociology to task for failing to observe both the critical and the middle-range routes to knowledge.

16 For a classic example, see Dimitrov 1935. This is the main report to the seventh world congress of the Communist International, in which its general secretary "refutes" the leftist argument that fascism is continuous with capitalism and argues, to the contrary, that it is the rule of a fraction of capital, "its most openly terroristic" imperialist wing.

17 In *Negative Dialectics* (1973a), Adorno cites this formulation by Benjamin only to signify the superiority of Weber's category of Ideal Type for its avoidance of a mystical element. Nevertheless, the possibility of acquiring knowledge through non-correspondence, in which the idea exceeds its object, is clearly rooted in one strain of Kantian as well as Hegelian thought, which appears systematically expunged by empirical science.

18 Among the sadder aspects of the legacy of critical theory is the fate of its epigones. Despite all, Adorno and Marcuse kept watch for social agents whose "protest and revolt" could mitigate, if not disprove, their political prognostications. But the watch is today kept by others. Russell Jacoby dismisses the intellectuals associated with the new social movements as "specialized" and in no way does their appearance contradict the finding in his *Last Intellectuals* (1987) that the game of social transformation is up since the incorporation of intellectuals into the academic system after the sixties. As we have seen, Piccone labels these movements merely recent examples of "artificial negativity" within the totally administered society. Although little has been said in *Telos*, the American journal of critical theory, about the upheavals in eastern Europe, Africa, and the US – movements particularly concerning sexuality – we can imagine how easily they can be discounted by intellectuals cathexted to Berlin, 1923.

REFERENCES

Adorno, Theodor W. 1967 [1955]: "Jazz: perennial fashion" and "Spengler after the decline," in *Prisms*, tr. Samuel and Sherry Weber. London: Neville Spearman.

Adorno, Theodor W. 1973a [1966]: *Negative Dialectics*. New York: Seabury Press.

Adorno, Theodor W. 1973b [1949]: *Philosophy of Modern Music*. New York: Seabury Press.

Adorno, Theodor W. 1988 [1962]: *An Introduction to the Sociology of Music*. New York: Continuum Books.

Adorno, Theodor W., et al. 1950: *The Authoritarian Personality*. New York: Norton.

Adorno, Theodor W., et al. 1976: *The Positivist Dispute in German Sociology*. New York: Harper & Row.

Arendt, Hannah 1956: *The Origins of Totalitarianism*. Glencoe, Ill.: Free Press.

Aronowitz, Stanley 1988: *Science as Power*. Minneapolis: University of Minnesota Press.

Bachelard, Gaston 1968 [1940]: *The Philosophy of No*. New York: Orion Press.

Bachelard, Gaston 1984 [1934]: *The New Scientific Spirit*. Boston: Beacon Press.

Bell, Daniel 1973: *The Coming of Post-Industrial Society*. New York: Basic Books.

Benjamin, Walter 1977: *The Origin of German Tragic Drama*. London: New Left Books.

Canguillhem, Georges 1983: *Etudes d'histoire et de philosophie des sciences*. Paris: Vrin.

Dimitrov, George 1935: *The United Front against Fascism*. New York: International.

Durkheim, Emile 1966 [1938]: *Rules of Sociological Method*. Glencoe, Ill.: Free Press.

Forman, Paul 1971: "Weimar culture, causality and quantum theory," in *Historical Studies in the Physical Sciences*. Philadelphia: University of Pennsylvania Press.

Foucault, Michel 1972: "Discourse on language," in *The Archaeology of Knowledge*, tr. A. M. Sheridan Smith. New York: Pantheon.

Frankfurt Institute for Social Research 1972: *Aspects of Sociology*. Boston: Beacon Press.

Friedman, George 1981: *The Political Philosophy of the Frankfurt School*. Ithaca, NY: Cornell University Press.

Habermas, Jürgen 1976: "The analytic theory of science and dialectics," in Adorno et al. 1976.

Horkheimer, Max 1947: *Eclipse of Reason*. New York: Oxford University Press.

Horkheimer, Max 1950: "The authoritarian state," in Adorno et al. 1950.

Horkheimer, Max, and Theodor Adorno 1972 [1944]: *Dialectic of the Enlightenment*, tr. John Cumming. New York: Seabury Press.

Jacoby, Russell 1987: *The Last Intellectuals*. New York: Basic Books.

Lukács, Georg 1971 [1922]: *History and Class Consciousness*, tr. Rodney Livingstone. Cambridge, Mass.: MIT Press.

Marcuse, Herbert 1964: *One Dimensional Man*. Boston: Beacon Press.

Marcuse, Herbert 1965: "Repressive tolerance," in Herbert Marcuse, Robert Paul Wolff, and Barrington Moore, *A Critique of Pure Tolerance*. Boston: Beacon Press.

Marcuse, Herbert 1968: "Industrialism and capitalism in the work of Max Weber," in *Negations: Essays in Critical Theory*. Boston: Beacon Press.

Marcuse, Herbert 1973: "Foundations of historical materialism" (1932), in *Studies in Critical Philosophy*. Boston: Beacon Press.

Marcuse, Herbert 1978: "Some social implications of modern technology," in Andrew Arato and Eike Gebhardt (eds), *The Essential Frankfurt School Reader*. New York: Urizen Books.

Marcuse, Herbert 1987 [1932]: *Ontology and the Theory of Historicity*, tr. Seyla Benhabib. Cambridge, Mass.: MIT Press.

Merton, Robert 1957; 2nd edn 1968: *Social Theory and Social Structure.* New York: Free Press.

Mills, C. Wright 1951: *White Collar: The American Middle Classes.* New York: Oxford University Press.

Mills, C. Wright 1956: *The Power Elite.* New York: Oxford University Press.

Mills, C. Wright 1959: *Sociological Imagination.* New York: Oxford University Press.

Mills, C. Wright 1964: *Sociology and Pragmatism.* New York: Oxford University Press.

Ortega y Gasset, José 1932 [1929]: *The Revolt of the Masses.* New York: Norton.

Pareto, Vilfredo 1963 [1935]: *The Mind and Society*, tr. A. Livingston and A. Bongiorno. 4 vols. New York and London:

Pareto, Vilfredo 1963 [1935]: *The Mind and Society*, tr. A. Livingston and A. Bongiorno. 4 vols. New York and London: Harcourt Brace Jovanovich.

Parsons, Talcott 1951: *The Social System.* Glencoe, Ill.: Free Press.

Parsons, Talcott 1955: "An approach to psychological theory in terms of the theory of action," in Simon Koch (ed.), *Psychology: A Study of Science*, vol. 3. New York: McGraw-Hill.

Reich, Wilhelm 1972: *Character Analysis.* New York: Farrar, Straus & Giroux.

Reich, Wilhelm 1970 [1946]: *Mass Psychology of Fascism.* New York: Farrar, Straus & Giroux.

Schelling, F. 1988: *Ideas for a Philosophy of Nature.* Cambridge and New York: Cambridge University Press.

12

General Theory in the Postpositivist Mode: The "Epistemological Dilemma" and the Search for Present Reason

Jeffrey Alexander

In the postwar period, general sociological theory has been associated with the search for nomothetic knowledge. It has been viewed, by its proponents and critics alike, as the crowning glory of the positive science of society. As the positivist conviction has weakened, the attractiveness of pursuing general theories in social science has waned; indeed, the very viability of the project has come to be seriously questioned. If subjective frameworks inevitably mediate scientific observations, it is reasoned, then efforts at generalization from these observations must themselves have a particularist component. Once the pristine universal status of theory has been undermined in this way, it has seemed only logical to many that social science should not just acknowledge the personal but embrace it. Increasingly, there have been calls for social science to give up its one-dimensional quest for cognitive truth; social science as praxis or moral inquiry (Haan et al. 1983; Wardell and Turner 1986), or as a hermeneutics of the concrete (ibid.; Rabinow and Sullivan 1979; Gibbons 1987) have been offered as alternatives.

On such intellectual grounds, and for historical and political reasons as well, non-empirical discourse in the social sciences has become more relativist than ever before. Some intellectuals have embraced this relativism enthusiastically; others have adopted it in a spirit of resignation, believing that no other alternative to positivism can be defended. My point in this chapter is that this *simpliste* choice between scientistic theory and anti-theoretical relativism represents not only a false dichotomy but a dangerous one.

I will call the presentation of these alternatives the "epistemological dilemma," for it presents the fate of general theory as dependent upon an epistemological choice alone. Either knowledge of the world is unrelated to the social position and intellectual interests of the knower, in which case general theory and universal knowledge are viable, or knowledge is affected by its relation to the knower, in which case relativistic and particularistic knowledge can be the only result. This is a true dilemma because it presents a choice between two equally unpalatable alternatives. I argue that neither pole of this dilemma should be accepted. The alternative to positivist theory is not resigned relativism; the alternative to relativism is not positivist theory. Theoretical knowledge can never be anything other than the socially rooted efforts of historical agents. But this social character does not negate the possibility for developing either generalized categories or increasingly disciplined, impersonal, and critical modes of evaluation (cf. Will 1985).

To acknowledge relativism is not necessarily to imply that actors impose on knowledge personal and idiosyncratic imprints. Actors can be bound – by their societies and themselves – to standards that are rooted within, and after a manner are reflections of, broader and more inclusive social institutions and groups. They may also be bound by traditions that have a distinctively rational, impersonal bent. One must differentiate, then, within the category "relativist." Evaluative criteria, while contextually relative, can be both more universalistic and less so. The search for truth can be fused with the search for other kinds of knowledge – with the search for beauty and moral purity – or it can be separated from them and controlled in specialized and more impersonal ways. It is possible, in other words, to defend the search for universal truth, and the possibility of gaining valuable approximations to it, in a manner that does not reflect positivist credulity.

In the course of this chapter I seek to overcome the

epistemological dilemma in a variety of ways. In the section immediately following I present the argument that universalistic standards of evaluation, and impersonal conceptual constructs, are products of millenia-long development in human civilization. Because the effort to gain distance from objects outside of the self – to separate the knower from the known – did not begin with the positivism of the seventeenth-century scientific revolution, the quest for universalism cannot be evaluated on the grounds of a simple objection to philosophical positivism as such. In the course of this discussion I introduce the counterpoint to universalization that, in different guises, is the critical object throughout much of this chapter. I suggest that the demand for a turning away from universalism has been intrinsic to cultural history and, in the section following, that this dialectic can be seen throughout the modern history of social thought.

After these general considerations, my focus becomes narrower and more detailed. I show how the epistemological dilemma was reproduced with debilitating consequences in the postwar debate between scientism and theoreticism on the one hand and neo-romantic contextualism on the other. After discussing the deepening skepticism about theory and "truth" which has marked a range of intellectual movements over the last two decades, I develop a detailed criticism of Richard Rorty's brief for anti-foundational relativism. Only after these critical and hermeneutic discussions are completed do I offer, in the concluding section of this chapter, a relatively systematic defense of the possibility for general theorizing within a postpositivist frame.

THE DIALECTIC OF UNIVERSAL AND CONCRETE
IN CULTURAL HISTORY

Social science theory is one important manifestation of the search for universalism, for fair and principled standards of evaluation, that has been one of the principal ambitions of civilizational development. The contemporary debate between general theory and its critics can be seen, therefore, as one version of the conflict between the universal and the concrete that has marked cultural history itself.

To advocate the necessity for general theory is to uphold the possibility of universal thought. Universalism rests upon the capacity for actors to decenter themselves, to understand that the world does not revolve around them, that they are not its creators, that they can study "it" in a relatively impersonal way. As Nagel writes in his important argument about the paradoxical pursuit of objective knowledge,

> The aim of such understanding is to go beyond the distinction between appearance and reality by including the existence of appearances in an elaborated reality. But this expanded reality, like physical reality, is centerless. Though the subjective features of our own minds are at the center of *our* world, we must try to conceive of them as just one manifestation of the mental in a world that is not given especially to the human point of view.
>
> *(Nagel 1986: 18; original italic)*[1]

Yet, paradoxically, this decentered world is at the same time a world view, and the human view of it a human creation. When this agency is forgotten, universalism becomes an objectification that seems not just to decenter human beings but to deny them. Objectivity is viewed not as world mastery but as alienation. The consequence is the return to the concrete.

The process of decentering actors from their world is the process upon which the claims of civilization rest. The earlier the human society, the more its members experience centeredness. The world is whole, it is our world, it is experienced in its subjective immediacy. Actors live in the dreaming, in circular narrative time, in myth, conventions, parables, stories.[2] As Weber first demonstrated, and as many others have substantiated since, as societies become larger and more complex, experience becomes more fragmented. Reality is posited more as something that exists outside the actor, that is removed from immediate experience and the concrete. As it becomes more universal, time flattens out; reflection and self-consciously constructed recipes, maps, and hypotheses take their place alongside myths as organized orientations for social action.[3]

With the great monotheistic religions – particularly with Judaism and Christianity – but also with Buddhism, Hinduism, and Confucianism, this reality is expressed as a higher truth that not only stands completely outside of subjectively experienced time and place but that actually creates them. This reality, expressed as God, is so universal that in Judaism it could not even be personalized through a name, so abstract it could not be worshipped through any concrete form.[4] The same kind of decentering and objectifying process occurred in ancient Greece (Voegelin 1957; Jaeger 1965), where nature assumed the status of an impersonal force, challenging the pantheon of personal divinities. For both secular and religious society, the universal forces that decenter men and women are at the same time sources for the exercise of their reason. If it is men and women who have created the universal, then they must, after all, have the capacity to understand it.

For the Greeks, the connection between impersonal nature and the exercise of reason is easy to see. It is perhaps more difficult in the case of religion. It is easier when we understand that the will and motives of the impersonal religious force are also conceived by believers as forms of reason. God's reasons are presented to believers not only through the deep order of the natural and social worlds but through his laws. As radically decentered beings, men and women strive to emulate the abstract model of divinity in order to understand its order and submit to its laws. For the ancient Jews, to submit to this universal personalization was to gain salvation. Salvation can be called religious "truth," for it is based on understanding rather than on immediate experience. For the Greeks, effacing oneself before impersonal nature gained access to truth in a more secular and obviously rational way.

This interplay between expanding religious abstraction and secular universalism continued to develop in the modern world. Depersonalization brings individuation, not simply domination.[5] It was the great world religions that gave birth to the very conception of autobiography.[6] Cosmic abstraction brings metaphysical dualism; such dualism is the key to the experience of the separated "self." Thus, even while the world is increasingly experienced as objective and impersonal – as rational and rationalized – actors can experience an intimate connection to the objective forces from which they have become estranged. Insofar as this experience can be sustained, there exists what I will call present reason.

The experience of present reason is difficult to maintain. In the course of its progress, impersonal reason is continually negated by the demand for the concrete. As soon as the existence of the universal is posited, it is denied. This negation is generated because depersonalization is experienced as having caused reason to be absent. Actors experience the fear of obliteration from the forces that they have themselves created, from the isolated and demanding self, from the impersonally organized society, from an omnipotent God, from the rationally reorganized forces of nature.

This is not a deception, but rather another form of truth. The dialectic of present and absent reason forms the main topic of Hegel's *Phenomenology*. Insofar as human beings posit reason as outside of themselves, they create the conditions for the alienation of reason from its human origins. Religion becomes an orthodoxy in which the faithful lose touch with their own spiritual life. Philosophy becomes a dogma that is casuistic, obfuscatory, elitist, and merely abstract. When decentered reason becomes objectified in colossal weapons of death that obliterate human beings, the alienation of reason assumes more than a metaphysical form (Alexander 1990). Because reason appears to be absent from the objects created by rational human beings, people deny its very existence. In response to this alienation of reason, truth is sought within, not without, in the concrete rather than the abstract. Reason is abandoned for experience, rationality for the irrational. This countermovement is expressed by cabalistic movements in Judaism, by Gnosticism in Christianity, by antinomianism in Puritanism, and by sophistry, skepticism, and idealism in philosophy.

UNIVERSAL AND CONCRETE IN SOCIAL THOUGHT

In the realm of thought this dialectic has been conceptualized as the relation of the knower to the known. The scientific revolution of the early modern period decentered the human being, the knower, in a particularly dramatic way. Social thought followed in its wake, as thinkers from Hobbes to the French philosophers strove to find the social physics corresponding to Newton's heavenly ones. These decentering movements of thought were experienced as liberating but also as forms of alienation. Romanticism created a countermovement that continues to inform reactions against universalism today. Fichte, Hegel, and the early Marx were not the only thinkers who believed that self and world division were only necessary steps on the way to a higher experience of unity.[7] Romantic literary and theoretical protests against objectification were also firmly rooted in English thought, as M. H. Abrams (1971) has shown in his discussions of Wordsworth, Coleridge, and Blake.

Still, it was British thinkers who produced political economy and utilitarian social science and Germans who created hermeneutics, the great intellectual countermovement whose call for the recentering of the knower within the known has become increasingly influential in recent times. While I will suggest later that Dilthey, at least, did not intend to give up on scientific generalization, his program for *Geisteswissenschaft* clearly emphasizes intuition and experience over reason and abstraction. It places activities governed by impersonal laws – including much of political, economic, and geopolitical life – outside the bounds of interpretive social thought.

When Nietzsche condemned abstract reason as the invention of monotheism and the Greeks, he was not wrong; however, in his feverish effort to get behind (and beyond) reason to the sensate and concrete, to embrace particularism at any cost, he pushed Romanticism into a radically destructive form. When it takes less nihilistic forms, its anti-epistemological message is much the same. When he rejected Husserl's transcendental phenomenology for existentialism, Heidegger was insisting on the disaster of depersonalization. Following Husserl led only to understanding how impersonality is rationally constructed, not to the demand for its abolition. Heidegger wanted philosophy to be more personal and direct, an ontology of "being there" (*Dasein*).

Following Heidegger and Hegel, Sartre called for a radical recentering of existence and questioned the very reality of the depersonalized world. In his early work he described what was outside the individual as nothingness; in his later work he called it the concrete inert. Both are conceptions of the world in which abstractions have no meaning, in which it is impossible to experience the world outside of the self in a real and satisfying way. In this critical respect, the later Wittgenstein is no different. Words do not refer to things outside of consciousness but to other words. When we speak of the world as red we speak not of redness as such, of the world out there, but rather we refer to a linguistic concept whose referent we accept because convention relates the word to other concepts with similar objects. Chained within the subjective though not private world of our language games, we do not have any access to the impersonal world itself.

It is not my intention in this essay to deny the intellectual significance, much less the moral importance, of this Romantic and idealistic movement in modern thought and culture. There is a pathology inherent in the universalism that civilization upholds, and it is precisely that reason itself is often experienced as absent. To "treat" this pathology, rational actors must be reminded that they are the creators of the world view that allows them to comprehend nature, self, and society in a universalistic and impersonal way. Romanticism in its various forms has been the teacher of this lesson, for every generation fortunate enough to experience its tutelage.

I do wish to maintain, however, that in important respects the world outside of the self can, in fact, be comprehended. Human beings create the world view that allows them to conceive of this world, but they do not create this world as such. Nor do they invent the society whose regularities this decentering allows them to see, regularities which if not lawful in the same sense as physical laws, exhibit powerful and consistent patterning. The countermovement against impersonal rationality allows us not to forget that it is we who are seeing this society and world; it is not seeing itself through us. This is the achievement of Romantic social thought in its modern guise. Yet, we can decenter ourselves from this personal process of objective knowing in turn. Insofar as we do so, we can understand and explain what this process of constructing rational perception involves. This understanding, however, does not threaten the universality of perception. To the contrary, it can become another, equally universalistic theory – a theory of knowledge and perception – in its own right.

SCIENTISM AND THEORETICISM
IN THE POSTWAR PERIOD

These broad considerations are central to the problem of general theory and its critics. One can argue about what exactly "theory" is, whether it is a model, a set of interlinked propositions that produces testable hypotheses, a frame of reference, a set of classifications, a conceptual scheme. One cannot argue, however, with the notion that, no matter how defined, theory implies an abstraction from the concrete. The more general the theory – the greater its interpretive and explanatory reach – the more general the abstraction. Theory is the quintessence of the decentering process that distinguishes the modern world.

The universalism of general theory cannot be justified if this universalism is understood, and experienced, as a decentering that demands the alienation of reason. General theory is not something that simply reflects the objective out there. Positivism and empiricism reduce theory in just this way, viewing it merely as the studied reflection of the natural world. For this reason, their justification for theory have been particularly vulnerable in the contemporary period, for in this recent period the agentic contribution to our perception of the objective world has become increasingly well understood. In the present context, general theory can be justified only in a postpositivist way, as the case for present reason.

Positivism and empiricism take their warrant for universal theorizing from the role it seems to play in the sciences of nature. I say "seems to play," for in the practice of natural science the exercise of reason is camouflaged in a particularly effective way. In its natural science form, the practice of general theory has become, at least in its normal science mode, a process of absent reason. Scientists experience themselves as mirroring nature.[8] Their own exercise in rationality – the manner in which it is this rationality itself whch has allowed perceptual access to a world which mathematics and scientific method can model – is forgotten. For many decades absent reason also characterized the philosophy of natural science. Effacement, abnegation, objectivity, transparency – when these terms describe the relation of scientists to nature their agentic construction of the natural world is ignored. Theories are held to be proven or falsified by exposing their human-made tenets to the force of non-human empirical facts.

This perspective on natural science practice, articulated philosophically by logical positivism, carried forcefully into the heyday of positive social science in the decades that followed the Second World War. The unified science movement, a position articulated by Neurath but shared by virtually the entire social scientific community, suggested no significant difference between natural and social science. The increasing technical efficiency of statistical methods made it appear that access to the social equivalent of unadorned nature would soon be approximated. With these methods, social scientists would not have to construct generalizations on the basis of their interpretive insights, intellectual power, and wit; on the basis simply of their commitment to the ironclad experimental codes of science, generalizations would emerge out of the data themselves.

This vision of absent reason can be found even in the work of sophisticated theorists like Talcott Parsons. While Parsons appreciated Weber's search for a universalistic version of the *Geisteswissenschaften*, presenting a subtle and powerful interpretation of it in his first major work (Parsons 1937: 579–639), he conceived his own theorizing on the model of Newtonian mechanics. He was not troubled by the possibility, which he himself recognized, that general theory placed the constructions of the knower onto the very perception of the known. To the contrary, Parsons confidently presented his action theory as a powerful reflection of "the real," even if a reflection that had been mediated in an analytic, *a priori* way.[9] This utopian rationalism was not the product of Parsons's functionalism. Writing at the high point of French communist ascendancy in the early 1960s, Louis Althusser (1969) confidently separated his own version of Marxist social science theory from mere bourgeois ideology. Postwar semiotics agreed to the idea that truth was accessible without the intervention of subjective frames. In "Myth today," Roland Barthes (1959) illustrated how social structural pressures distorted merely denotative analogies into redolent myths, without giving any thought to the question of how his own thought could have escaped the same mythic fate.[10]

It is not surprising that in the course of the 1960s there emerged in reaction against such absent reason an extraordinary neo-romantic critique. Optimism about the objectively progressive course of the postwar world had begun to fade; renewed racial, ethnic, and class conflicts, and the emergence of newly strengthened pimordial attachments, made the unthinking commitment to universal and social and intellectual structures more difficult. When they protested against "meaningless abstraction" in their newly expanded universities, college students were experiencing the absence of reason in the very heart of intellectual life; they viewed the university not as the expression of human creativity and imagination but as an objectified machine. They indicted science for its reification in weapons of war.

The classical embodiments of rational social theory also were challenged in an antinomian way. Against the reconstruction of Weber by Parsons and Bendix as the embodiment of rational sobriety, Mitzman (1970) claimed that charisma, pathos, and eros formed the revealing underside to Weber's rationalizing theme. Against Rieff's (1961) moralist Freud and Jones's (1963) scientific one, Norman O. Brown (1966) created a Freud of play and joy, while Russel Jacoby (1975) indicted American revisionists for ignoring the critical and erotic Freud that Marcuse (1954) had earlier unearthed. Garfinkel (1967) became dissatisfied with Husserl's epistemological stance, fearing that it too easily endorsed the existence of impersonal forms; inspired by Heidegger and Wittgenstein, he pushed ethnomethodology into a more radically anti-normative mode, away from the belief in, and the hope for, consensual normative constraints as they were embodied in theorizing of a Parsonian form (see Alexander 1987a: 257–80).

By the end of the 1960s, an antitheoretical orientation had begun to emerge throughout Western intellectual life.[11] I will call this broad movement contextualism. Thus, in what became an extraordinarily influential quarrel with functionalist theory, Clifford Geertz (1973a [1964]) attacked the notion that cognitive truth was relevant to the study of ideology, arguing against Parsons for an interpretive and relativist approach that emphasized the close link between political action and the rhetorical creation of meaning. Thomas Kuhn (1970 [1962]) rebelled against absent reason in natural science in an equally constructivist and contextualist way. While not denying the possibility of doing natural science, he identified the decentered scientist as a kind of "normal science" idiot while describing creative and revolutionary science in a subjective and recentered way. Also beginning to get serious attention was the work of Peter Winch (1958), which in questioning the very possibility of a social science went further than either Geertz or Kuhn. Following Wittgenstein, Winch argued that social scientists were imprisoned by linguistic-conceptual worlds that made it impossible to create even relatively independent knowledge about the actions and intentions of those outside one's cultural group.

THE DEEPENING SKEPTICISM ABOUT THEORY AND "TRUTH"

With the exception of Winch, these early contextualist reactions did not reject the possibility of universalism or the value of general theory. They had not, in other words, become fully confined by the epistemological dilemma. Those who followed them did, and were.

In the 1970s and 1980s the neo-romantic reaction deepened. What are taken to be the epistemological implications of contextualism – conventionalism and skepticism – have been explicitly formulated; in many quarters, theory has given way to the investigation of the concrete. Arguing from the mere existence of context, social scientists and philosophers have concluded that universalistic modes of argument are impossible. The facile and ultimately false dichotomy between positivism and relativism has thus inserted itself as a principal rubric in contemporary debate. The possibility that the context within which we operate is itself the very tradition of objective reason has been ignored.

This movement from the acknowledgment of context to the embrace of relativism and the abandonment of theory is nowhere more clear than in the intellectual odyssey of Clifford Geertz. In his 1960s essays on ideology and religion, Geertz had emphasized interpretative over scientific reason in order to avoid the sociological reductionism so prevalent in the social sciences of that day. Ideology and religion could be viewed as cultural systems only if their relation to social actors was evaluated by some criterion other than scientific truth. Ideological and religious actors, in other words, should not be mistaken for scientific ones. By the time he collected these earlier essays in his enormously influential *Interpretation of Cultures*, however, Geertz was arguing that scientific theorising should not be the goal of analysts themselves. Not universalistic theory but "thick description" of concrete behavior should be the goal of the human studies (Geertz 1973c).

The essays that appeared subsequent to this publication contain intriguing interpretations of cultural life, but they manifest virtually none of the theoretical ambitions, or the conceptual precision, of Geertz's earlier work. When he introduced his second collection of essays, *Local Knowledge*, published one decade after the first, Geertz (1983: 3–6) averred that in this latter set of essays he had, indeed, simply taken to their logical conclusion the implications of the first: "In anthropology, too, it so turns out, he who says A must say B, and I have spent much of my time since [that first collection] trying to say it." Employing the logic of the epistemological dilemma, Geertz identifies the social scientific search for theoretical generalization with the pretensions of the natural sciences. Citing the "growing recognition that [this] established approach . . . was not producing the triumphs of prediction, control, and testability that had for so long been promised," he condemns such efforts at "laws-and-causes social physics," as reflecting "a technological conception of those [human] sciences." One must choose either positivism or particularistic relativism: Geertz is condemning not simply empiricist social science but any attempt to theorize about society as such. "Calls for 'a general theory' of just about anything social," he asserts, "sound increasingly hollow." General theory "has never seemed further away, harder to imagine, or less certainly desirable than it does right now."

Once positivist and theoretical social science have been rejected, the only alternative Geertz can foresee is a return to the concrete. Social analysis must "turn from trying to explain social phenomena by weaving them into grand textures of cause and effect to trying to explain them by placing them in local frames of awareness." Ethnography, not generalizing social science, is the discipline best suited to this particularist task. "To an ethnographer, sorting through the machinery of distant ideas, the shapes of knowledge are always ineluctably local, indivisible from their instruments and their encasements. One may veil this fact with ecumenical rhetoric or blur it with strenuous theory, but one cannot really make it go away." Geertz concludes by warning his readers that, while his approach is a hermeneutic one, "one will not find very much in the way of 'the theory and methodology of interpretation' . . . in what follows." Nor surprisingly, Geertz believes that "there are enough general principles in the world already." He does not wish to see hermeneutics "reified into a parascience." What the essays in *Local Knowledge* offer instead of theorizing are "actual inter-pretations of something." In this relativizing task, Geertz aligns himself with "the views of such philosophers as Heidegger, Wittgenstein, Gadamer, or Ricoeur, such critics as Burke, Frye, Jameson, or Fish, and such all-purpose subversives as Foucault, Habermas, Barthes, or Kuhn." These are, of course, precisely the figures I have earlier identified as central to the contextual reaction against universalist thought (cf. Friedman 1987).

It is revealing, in this regard, that later developments in Thomas Kuhn's intellectual career manifest the epistemological dilemma in strikingly similar ways as those in Geertz's. Despite his quite legitimate protests that he had not intended to produce an irrationalist theory, Kuhn's revision of his paradigm concept (1970) made it impossible to identify it with theoretical presuppositions of a universal bent (see Alexander 1982b). Neophytes learn to exercise their scientific skills not by understanding intellectual frameworks but by mimicking the plots of specific problem solutions, which Kuhn calls "exemplars." Scientific results are controlled not, in the first instance, by universalistic theories or impersonal methods but by a "disciplinary matrix," which Kuhn is careful to define not as a set of ideas but as a social network of situated human relations. In his most recent monographic work Kuhn (1978) seems to have given up on efforts at theoretical clarification altogether. Eschewing even the claim to exemplify his theory of scientific revolution, he has returned to detailed historical description of a specific scientific case.

Equally revealing of the increasingly radical implications of contextualism is the poststructural movement beyond semiotics and structuralism. Since Saussure set forth semiotic philosophy in his general theory of linguistics, its key stipulation has been the arbitrary relation of sign and referent: there can be found no "rational reason," no force or correspondence in the outside world, for the particular signs that actors have chosen to represent their world. As I briefly indicated in my discussion of Barthes, early elaborations of the semiotic position exempted from this critique of objective reference semioticians themselves. It should not be surprising, perhaps, that the founder of the American pragmatic tradition of semiotics, Charles Peirce, was confident that practical experience eventually aligned scientific symbols with objective truth. What is striking, however, is that the same assurance of universalism marked the French semiotic school. Saussure showed no anxiety about his ability to perceive linguistic systems in a realistic way. Lévi-Strauss triumphantly described his structuralist interpretations as exemplifying the science of myth.

Contemporary inheritors of this semiotic and structuralist tradition were disappointed with the fate of what they conceived to be truth and reason in the 1960s. In addition to their experience of absent reason, they had well justified concerns with the epistemological naivety of their theoretical predecessors. In accord with the logic of the epistemological dilemma, poststructuralists moved to extend the arbitrary relativism of the semiotic field to the semioticians themselves. Acknowledging the arbitrary reference of "reality," they felt compelled to reject out of hand the very concept of an objectively differentiated world exercising an independent influence on the knower. Experience replaces reason, relativism and the embrace of hypercontextualism displace the search for universalistic truth. Emancipation is a logical impossibility, domination a condition that cannot logically be overcome.

Baudrillard's (1983) concept of the simulcrum represents the *reductio ad absurdum* of the poststructuralist position, the inevitable conclusion of an insistence not only on the referential arbitrariness but the particularism of symbolic codes. Where the early Barthes saw myth as the corruption of realistic reference at the hands of objective social power, Baudrillard sees the play of signifier and signified as a closed circuit into which the reality of social needs can never intrude. The contrast between Lévi-Strauss and Bourdieu can be seen in much the same way. Lévi-Strauss's overweening rationalism led him to cut symbolic thought short before the entry of the modern world. The *bricoleur* was replaced by the scientist. With Bourdieu, we can see, once again, how a latter-day follower of structuralism responds to the earlier faith in objectivity with cynical disappointment. Denying the very possibility of reference to critical universalism, the perceptual structures of bourgeois and proletarian actors alike are for Bourdieu (1984) mere particularistic reflections, primitive codes from which there is no escape.

Derrida and Foucault supply the deep justification for such poststructural argument. Whereas Bourdieu seems blithely to exempt himself from his own relativizing strictures, Derrida (1981) has insisted that the knower is simply a literate *bricoleur*. Reality, in turn, can be nothing other than a text, a symbolic construction that is itself related to other texts – not to history or social structure – in arbitrary ways. Indeed, texts cannot themselves be accepted as representations, even of arbitrarily signified referents. Composed not just of presences but of absences, texts do not exist as complete wholes.

To this reconstruction of the epistemological dilemma in its most nihilistic form, Foucault adds a history and sociology. Against the possibility of contemporary universalism, he makes a double critique. First, there is his substantive historical demonstration of absent reason. The rationalization of modern society, as manifest particularly in the thought and activity of the scientifically trained professions, is a fraud (e.g. Foucault 1977, 1978). Professionals actually engage in the manipulation of reason; their ministrations are forms of surveillance, their goal technical control. Enlightenment universalism amounts to the particularism of power; it results in the suppression of subjectivity, not in the exercise of present reason.

Foucault's second critique is an analytical one. In his later work he insists on the virtually complete identity of knowledge, or discourse, with power. In doing so, the very possibility of decentered experience is denied. The subject, Foucault is fond of repeating, is completely constituted by discourse. In this way, discourse becomes both the basis for power and merely its manifestation in another form. Because truth is relative to discourse, it is impossible to appeal to universalizing standards against worldly power: "Truth isn't outside power, or lacking in power . . . Each society has its regime of truth, its 'general politics' of truth: that is, the types of discourse which it accepts and makes function as true" (Foucault 1980: 131). To set about rationally to evaluate the logical consistency, theoretical implications, or explanatory value of a given discourse is obviously a waste of time.

The simple and dangerous dichotomy is firmly set. The only alternative to the fallacy of absent reason, to positivism, is a thoroughly relativist sociology of knowledge, an archaeology of the historical conditions of discourse.[12]

THE APOTHEOSIS OF ANTITHEORETICAL RELATIVISM: THE PHILOSOPHY OF RICHARD RORTY AND ITS POSTMODERN REPRISE

Nietzsche based his own genealogy of morals on his contempt for advocates of a belief in truth and the ascetic ideal. In their place, he "enthrones taste . . . as the sole organ of knowledge beyond Truth and Falsity, beyond Good and Evil," as Habermas puts it in his brilliant exploration of the disturbing underside of critical theory. Richard Rorty, while on his own account a good "postmodern bourgeois liberal" (1985a), reluctantly embraces this Nietzschean frame. He does so because, like Nietzsche, he experiences the history of Western ratiocination not as the radically imperfect expression of present reason but as the alienation of subjectivity from itself. When Rorty describes the scientific revolution, it is the pathology of absent reason of which he writes.

This is reality conceived as somehow represented by representations which are not merely ours but its own, as it looks to itself, as it would describe itself if it could . . . This fantasy of discovering, and somehow knowing that one has discovered, Nature's Own Vocabulary *seemed* to become more concrete when Galileo and Newton formulated a comprehensive set of predictively useful universal generalizations, written in suitably "cold," "inhuman," mathematical terms.

(1982a: 194; italics added)

This perception of absent reason leads Rorty to embrace the dichotomy between scientism and relativism. "The urge to tell stories of progress, maturation and synthesis might be overcome," he writes (1986: 48; italics added), "if we once took seriously the notion that we only know the world and ourselves *under a description*." Rorty is caught on the horns of the epistemological dilemma. If we acknowledge context, he believes, there is no possibility of evaluating the worth of various perspectives in a universalistic way.

If we once could feel the full force of the claim that our present discursive practices were given neither by God, nor by intuition of essence nor by the cunning of reason, but *only* by chance, then we would have a culture which lacked not only a theory of knowledge, not only a sense of progress, but *any* source of what Nietzsche called "metaphysical comfort."

(ibid.: italics added)

To embrace fully such relativism, indeed, one must avoid not only progressive theories but theorizing as such. "A Nietzschean must not want any substitute for theories," Rorty explains (ibid.). To theorize is to imply the possibility of at least partly circumventing the particularism of context. This is impossible, for a Nietzschean "views the very idea of 'theory' as tainted with the notion that there is something there to be contemplated, to be accurately represented in thought." The possibility of accurate representation is what Rorty wants to avoid. He succeeds remarkably well.

Rorty sees the history of philosophy as directed to "the

relation between universals and particulars" (1979: 149).[13] Because *Philosophy and the Mirror of Nature* is an argument against the possible existence of the concrete, it is necessarily an argument against the history of philosophy as well. The problem began long ago, with the Greeks. Plato's and Aristotle's search for universal categories and impersonal knowledge did not mark the beginning of human emancipation from an anthropomorphically distorted world; this search, rather, simply produced another kind of equally magical and distorted myth. "The metaphor of knowing general truths by internalizing universals," Rorty suggests (p. 42), became "the intellectual's substitute for the peasant's belief in life among the shades."

One of the peculiarities of Rorty's book is that this key proposition – that universal properties do not exist – is taken more as the basis upon which to draw other conclusions than as a point that needs to be demonstrated in and of itself. Rorty demonstrates that, after 2,500 years, philosophers still have not agreed about what such universals are, or about how they can be proved. He also discusses recent discoveries in the postpositivist philosophy and history of science and points to the skeptical conclusions of such contextualist philosophers as Wittgenstein, Heidegger and, more questionably, Dewey. Finally, Rorty argues that the split between mind and body cannot exist. He introduces a long parable about the visit to earth of Antipodeans, a mythical people from the other side of the galaxy whose vast knowledge of micro-neurology has demonstrated exactly how thoughts are produced by electrical impulse and physical laws. "Now that they have taught us micro-neurology," Rorty (p. 81) has his backward friends on earth suggest, "cannot we see that talk of mental states was merely a place-holder for talk of neurons?" Because we have bodies, in other words, there is no need for the concept of mind or for the theories they produce. "To suggest that the mind is the brain," Rorty insists, "is to suggest that we secrete theorems and symphonies as our spleen secretes dark humors" (pp. 43–4). Rorty's parable is amusing but ultimately terrifying in its anti-rationalist implications.

It might be argued that Rorty's failure to justify his assumption that universals do not exist places the intellectual edifice he is constructing on rather flimsy foundations. We will see that Rorty himself would offer to this fundamental objection the most skeptical of replies. Because universals do not exist, an effort to construct intellectual foundations is a hopeless enterprise from the start. At any rate, it is the implication that Rorty draws from this assumption against universals that makes his work interesting.

Because there are no universals, we can talk in good faith only about experience, not abstract norms; we can refer only "to common sense and common practice for details about what counts as justification" (p. 151). The real problem, as Rorty sees it, is "not to abjure such hypostatized universals but to explain why anyone had taken them seriously" (pp. 68–9). He laments (p. 38) the passing of the traditional world – "there would not have been thought to be a problem about the nature of reason had our race confined itself to pointing out particular states of affairs – warning of cliffs and rain, celebrating individual births and deaths." Unfortunately, for "no particular reason," some philosophers – but not many normal human beings – got it into their heads that "knowledge of universals" held the key to personhood and freedom. With the entrance of the Greeks, the slide down the slippery slope began. Among philosophers at least, it has come to the point that "to suggest that there are no universals . . . is to endanger our uniqueness" (p. 43).

The conclusion Rorty draws from the non-existence of universals is that foundational arguments – general theoretical ones, in the language of social science – are impossible to make. It is revealing that, despite his explicit condemnation of epistemology as such, this anti-foundational argument is made precisely in epistemological terms. Philosophers who espouse universals have justified their importance by describing them as objective entities. Against this, Rorty insists over and over again that it is impossible to have "pre-linguistic awareness" (p. 181). His (epistemological) point is that there is "no transcendental standpoint of our present set of representations from which we can inspect the relation between these representations and their object" (p. 293). He concludes that the " 'epistemological' quest for a way of refuting the skeptic and underwriting our claim to be talking about nonfictions [is] hopeless." The epistemological claim is hopeless because it is empiricist. It reflects the absence of reason. Rorty points to the coercive implications that flow from this loss. Such philosophers, he writes, believe that "knowing a proposition to be true is to be identified with being caused to do something by an object" (p. 157). According to this view "the object which the proposition is about *imposes* the proposition's truth" (original italics).

Rorty's claim is that philosophers seeking objectivity see themselves as reflectors, or mirrors, of reality; hence, they set out to establish the "foundations of knowledge." Foundational arguments are universals that establish the grounds for truth in what are conceived of as objectively rational ways, "truths which are certain because of their causes rather than because of the arguments given for them" (p. 159). Because they move "beyond argument to compulsion from the object known," foundational arguments are inhuman; they claim that "anyone gripped by the object in the required way will be *unable* to doubt or to see an alternative" (italics added). Foundationalism, Rorty insists (p. 163), is "the end-product of an original wish to substitute *confrontation* for *conversation* as the determinant of our belief."

Rorty is right to demand that reason be present, and he is also right that this can be achieved only if a hermeneutic rather than mechanistic stance is achieved.

> If the study of science's search for truth about the physical universe is viewed hermeneutically it will be viewed as the activity of spirit – the faculty which *makes* – rather than as the application of the mirroring faculties, those which *find* what nature has already made.
>
> (*p. 344; italics added*)

Rorty is wrong, however, to think that this can be accomplished only by abandoning the search for universals as such. The problem lies with his conviction that every argument against skepticism and for universalism is an "epistemological quest," that it is based upon reflection theory and the absence of reason. Philosophers who seek truthful foundations may perceive themselves as mirroring reality, but the interest and power of their arguments do not stand or fall on whether this claim can itself be true. These philosophers can be seen, rather, as rational agents who create frameworks within which to interpret a world whose objectivity and impersonality they take on faith. To the degree that they succeed, they falsify Rorty's espistemological syllogism, his claim (p. 181) that the proposition, "there is no neutral ground on which to stand," follows logically from the notion, "there is no such thing as pre-linguistic awareness."

Rorty says that when foundationalists make their arguments they are playing the language game of "philosophy-as-epistemology." But surely he is himself playing the same game from the other side of the net. Rorty characterizes (p. 293) foundationalism as the demand for "some transcendental standpoint outside our present set of representations from which we can inspect the relations between those representations and their objects." He believes that to deny the transparency of reality is to deny the interest and importance of universalistic ambition. Because he is caught within the epistemological dilemma, he cannot differentiate the levels and complexity of present reason in an appropriate way. Acknowledging representational subjectivity does not mean abandoning the possibility of differentiating our representations from objects in the outside world. The possibility for so comparing "objective" and "subjective" is produced by the development of human culture itself, which can be seen as progress because it has allowed an increasingly decentered construction of nature and social life. Reason can be exercised in a present way.

Because Rorty cannot conceptualize this fine-grained alternative to positivist credulity, he can only recommend that we return to the concrete. Rather than evaluating knowledge, he recommends, we should explore its social origins. Rather than criticizing society in light of universalist norms, we should criticize universalist norms in light of their social base. Because "justification is a matter of social practice" (p. 186), we must explain "rationality and epistemic authority by reference to what society lets us say, rather than the latter by the former" (p. 147). Rorty's recommendation that philosophy be abandoned for intellectual and cultural history – "the division of labor between the historian and philosopher no longer made sense" (p. 272) – is only the logical, Wittgensteinian conclusion. Because "the way people talk can 'create objects,'" it follows that "when we want to know how we know about such objects as these, we do and should turn not to the epistemologist but to the intellectual historian" (1986: 42).

The historian can make the shift from the old scheme to the new intelligible, and make one see why one would have been led from the one to the other if one had been an intellectual of that day. There is nothing the philosopher can add to what the historian has already done to show that this intelligible and plausible course is a "rational" one.

(1979: 272).

It is an either/or choice, ironically dictated by Rorty's location within the epistemological straitjacket from which he is trying to escape. This logic is particularly clear in his attack on anything other than a historical approach to science. If a non-historical, objectivistic reference for scientific concepts is impossible, then the effort to evaluate the truth of this concept must be abandoned. "We have the following dilemma: either the theory of reference is called upon to underwrite the success of contemporary science, or else it is simply a decision about how to write the history of science (rather than the provision of a 'philosophical foundation' for such historiography)" (pp. 287–8). "Once we understand (as historians of knowledge do) when and why various beliefs have been adopted or discarded," Rorty (p. 178) insists, there is simply nothing "called 'the relation of knowledge to reality' left over to be understood."

Once the problem of the relation of thought to reality is abandoned (cf. Rorty 1982b: 15), there is nothing much left for philosophers in the traditional sense, or for theorists in general, to do. Having given up on the traditional conception of truth-telling, Rorty suggests, the philosopher should become an "informed dilettante," the "polypragmatic" who can spread a little understanding by providing what are destined to be personal translations between discourses whose relative truth can never be compared (p. 317). In this way, philosophy can become an "edifying" profession, even a "poetic" one (p. 360), which follows from the belief that "our culture should become one in which the demand for constraint and confrontation is no longer felt" (p. 315). Compromise is possible because no principled positions are at stake – "edifying philosophers have to decry the very notion of having a view, while avoiding having a view about having views" (p. 371). Once the trappings of rationality are avoided – things like "inquiry" and notions like an "exchange of views" – a return to intimacy, love, and real community will result. "One way to see edifying philosophy as the love of wisdom is to see it as the attempt to prevent conversation from degenerating into inquiry, into an exchange of views. Edifying philosophers can never end philosophy, but they help prevent it from attaining the secure path of a science."[14]

This aestheticized and anti-theoretical vision, which believes itself incapable of distinguishing between telling stories and telling the truth, provides an analytic-philosophical rationale for the poststructuralist theory I described above (see Rorty 1985b). This connection surfaces most clearly in the postmodernism of Jean-François Lyotard. Lyotard contends that the age of the great "metanarratives" is past; the beliefs that such abstractions as science, education, democracy, and revolution would provide emancipation are myths that are no longer believed. Whereas modernism is defined as the search after such abstract will of the wisps, postmodernism marks a return to the concrete. In place of abstracting and transcendence, there is "heterogeneity" and "local determinism" (Lyotard 1984: xxiv). Rather than metanarratives, which through abstraction promote the mythical ideal of rational self-reflection, there remain only local narratives, from within which recourse to an extra-discursive principle is impossible.

Lyotard, too, is caught by the epistemological dilemma. Arguing from Hegel's relativizing of rational scientific thought in the *Phenomenology*, he moves from the simple existence of context to the impossibility of knowing as such.

> The speculative apparatus maintains an ambiguous relation to knowledge. It shows that knowledge is only worthy of that name up to the extent that it reduplicates itself ("lifts itself up," *hebt sich auf*; is sublated) by citing its own statements in a second-level discourse . . . that functions to legitimate them. This is as much as to say that . . . denotative discourse bearing on a certain referent (a living organism, a chemical property, a physical phenomenon, etc.) does not really know what it thinks it knows. Positive science is not a form of knowledge.
> (*Lyotard 1984: 38*)

Lyotard draws a sharp distinction between science – defined in its positivist mode as the knowledge that "does not really know what it thinks it knows" – and narrative, or centered knowledge. The positivist scientist dismisses narratives because, confidently assessing validity, he "concludes that they are never subject to argumentation or proof" (ibid.: 27). With the end of metanarratives, this demand for abstract legitimation has ceased. "Because narrative knowledge does not give priority to the question of its own legitimation, [it] certifies itself in the pragmatics of its own transmission without having recourse to argumentation and proof." What is left for the postmodern theorist to do? "All we can do," Lyotard concludes, "is gaze in wonderment at the diversity of discursive species" (ibid.: 26). At this juncture, Huyssen's lament about "the list of 'no longer possibles'" (1986: 288) seems very much to the point.

THE POSTPOSITIVIST CASE FOR THEORY

When Rorty puts hermeneutics forward as the alternative to theory and foundationalism, he emphasizes that he is not suggesting it as a "successor subject" to fill the vacancy left by foundationalist philosophy. Indeed, "hermeneutics is an expression of hope that the cultural space left by the demise of epistemology [e.g. foundationalism] will not be filled" (1979: p. 315). According to Rorty, in other words, hermeneutics is not a more sensitive or interpetive approach to universalism or rational understanding; it is the very opposite, the type case of an immersion in the sensuous concrete. With hermeneutics, Rorty believes, "the demand for constraint and confrontation is no longer felt." This understanding of hermeneutics, however, like Rorty's understanding of science, is distorted by the epistemological dilemma that confines his thought. We have seen how this condition makes it impossible to defend objectivity in even a conditional way, to defend the search for universal grounds and the possibility that some approximation of them can be achieved. It is the ambition of this final section to suggest, this time in a positive rather than in a critical form, how such a search can proceed and how this possibility of proximate universality can be understood.

I will introduce this discussion by examining a recent development within hermeneutical social theory itself (cf.

Ingram 1985). The possibility that hermeneutical understanding may not, after all, be the antithesis of reason has recently been recognized by even some of the most severe critics of "mainstream" social science. Shifts can be traced, for example, in the critical and hermeneutic philosophy of Richard Bernstein, which exemplify this recognition in the most vivid way. The central ambition of Bernstein's earlier work, which culminated in *The Restructuring of Social and Political Theory*, published in 1978, was to question the very possibility of a social science (see Alexander 1981). Attacking confidence in explanatory theorizing as profoundly misplaced, Bernstein issued a call for practical theory and contextual interpretation. In his most recent book, *Beyond Objectivism and Relativism*, Bernstein's ambition is very different. He wants to demonstrate that hermeneutics is antithetical neither to social science nor to the search for universals.

In his earlier work, Bernstein presents Kuhn's incommensurability thesis in a sympathetic way, urging his readers to agree that "the differences among competing paradigms are as radical as Kuhn suggests" and that "there is no set of standards for proving the superiority of one paradigm over another" (1978: 87). He goes on to praise the novelty of Kuhn's description of paradigm change as a conversion experience depending upon techniques of persuasion, an anti-rationalist position that surely confused the psychology of science with the normative structure within which scientific interaction proceeds. In his later work, however, Bernstein treats Kuhn's notion of incommensurability in a dramatically different way. He insists not only that the concept must be carefully distinguished from "incompatibility" and "incomparability," but that the claim that Kuhn himself conflates these terms "is not only mistaken but perverse" (1983: 82). Not only does Kuhn make these distinctions, but he does so, Bernstein would now have us believe, in order to demonstrate the manner in which "rational debate and argumentation between proponents of rival paradigms" is possible (1983: 85).

Whatever its merits as interpretation, these revisions demonstrate the new movement to defend rationality that characterizes Bernstein's recent work.[15] His intention is to escape the epistemological dilemma. Thus, whenever he contrasts rationality and contextualism, he qualifies his characterization of the former in a manner that points to a new, third term. While apparently paraphrasing Kuhn and Feyerabend on the decision-making process by which one scientific statement is judged to be more "logical and rational" than another, Bernstein writes that it is not "*free-floating* standards of rationality *detached from actual historical practices* to which we can appeal" (1983: 67; italics added). In such judgments, he continues, "we are not appealing to *permanent, atemporal* standards of rationality," to "a permanent set of *ahistorical* standards of rationality" (ibid.; italics added). After making these careful qualifications, Bernstein impatiently rejects what he calls a "false dichotomy" – "either permanent standards of rationality (objectivism) or arbitrary acceptance of one set of standards or practices over against its rival (relativism)" (ibid.: 68).

Bernstein now introduces the missing third term – "reasons embedded in . . . social practices." Rather than free-floating, reason is a practice imbedded in science; when scientists argue about truth, they refer not to some supra-social reality but to this imbedded reason – to "the best possible scientific reasons that can be given." To suggest that it is institutionalized, however, does not suggest that science is irrational. To the contrary, "a scientist is always under the obligation to give a rational account of what is right and wrong in the theory that is being displaced and to explain how his or her theory can account for what is 'true' in the preceding theory." By this point, it is clear that Bernstein's target is not positivism but skepticism. Indeed, he ends up by defending the possibility of social science theory against hermeneutics itself. "However much one recognizes the importance of the hermeneutical dimension of the social sciences," he warns, "one must also forthrightly confront those aspects of these disciplines that seek to develop theoretical and causal explanations of social phenomena" (ibid.: 160). Bernstein even chides Gadamer, the heroic figure of his book, for what he takes to be Gadamer's hermeneutic rejection of scientific method, insisting that "method is more like hermeneutic understanding than Gadamer frequently acknowledges" (ibid.: 169).

The third term that Bernstein inserts into the debate over science is the notion of present reason, the alternative to the epistemological dilemma which I have explored in a variety of ways above. My argument has been that, even while rationality is acknowledged to be an agentic accomplishment, objectivity can also be seen as an eminently worthy goal. To achieve grounded rationality, social actors promote a decentered understanding of the social and natural world, establish norms and frameworks that sanction personalization and that reward not only the ability to see the world as "out there" but the willingness to "subordinate" one's personal desires to that world's exploration.

It is time now to establish some general criteria for just how such a hermeneutically rooted version of universality can be established.

While present reason establishes the framework for understanding this world, it does not create this world itself. As Frederick Will (1985: 131) puts it in his modified brief for realism, action is "affected by, controlled by, or more exactly, constituted in part by determinants external to, independent of, the individuals engaged in them." For this reason, correspondence between framework and reality must ultimately be conceived of as the criterion governing every validity claim. Obviously, I am not myself proposing here a realist program. Since the world, in the brute pre-Kantian sense, cannot be seen as such, correspondence can be nothing other than the relationship between "reason-created" conceptual structures and reasonable "observational statements" about the world. Whether this differentiation can be confidently made is, then, the first criterion of whether universality, and some conditional conception of objectivity, can be achieved.

Has this criterion been met in contemporary natural and social science? The answer must certainly be yes. It has been one of the clearest achievements of Western and more recently modern intellectual life to create a world of observational statements which most practitioners at any given point in the development of their disciplines recognize as having an impersonal status. Scheffler (1976: 39) expresses this perspective in the following: "We simply have a false dichotomy in the notion that observation must be either a pure confrontation with an undifferentiated given, or else so conceptually contaminated that it must render circular any observational test of a hypothesis." The fact that Rorty (1979: 276n.) himself approvingly quotes this very passage to declare his own departure from idealism indicates the extent of consensus on this criterion. In social science, of course, there is a smaller body of agreed-upon observational statements than in natural science. Agreement about observations, however, is different from acknowledging that they exist in an impersonal realm which is conceived as separate from theoretical claims. This latter conception, even in social science, commands near unanimous consent. It is inscribed in, and sustained by, practical prohibitions against contaminating empirical data and by support for the experimental method broadly understood, whereby it is agreed that empirical variations can be compared with an experimenter's personal expectations. Observational tests of preconceptions – whether explicitly or implicitly "experimentally controlled" – are omnipresent in the practice of virtually every social scientist.

Whether impersonal worlds are acknowledged to exist is the first criterion for universality. Whether practitioners feel themselves bound to these frameworks points to the second. Insofar as scientists do not agree about the nature of their worlds – either about observations or the differentiated rules that interpret, document, model, and explain them – they will be unable to consider one another's claims as reasonable. Not only will they appear, instead, as particularistic and personal arguments, but they will in part be so. The more individuals share conceptions of their impersonal worlds, by contrast, the more individual practice can be subject to extra-personal control, the more it submits itself to universal criteria of evaluation. The more shared ground, the more neutral this ground not only seems but is in fact. The ground is not neutral in the sense of absent reason, but in the sense of a historical practice that neither party feels it can either own or control.[16]

The possibility of reaching consensus, then, is the second criterion of scientific objectivity. It was Merton's insight into the intrinsic connection between impersonality and consensus (1973 [1942]) that led him to identify universalism, communism, disinterestedness, and organized skepticism in his classic definition of the scientific ethos half a century ago. If Merton ignored the process by which interpretation allows the construction of reality, he clearly understood that the socially generated framework for this construction has to assume an impersonal form if the consensus and objectivity that are such distinctive characteristics of modern science are to be achieved.[17] In *Theoretical Logic in Sociology* I paid much more careful attention than Merton had to the interpretive process of reality construction. The criteria for evaluating these constructions, however, remained for me a central concern. With the notions of consensus and universality, I am telescoping the criteria for "postpositivist objectivity" I offered in that earlier work (Alexander 1982: 113–26).

In what remains of this discussion, I want to suggest that social science succeeds in developing the conditions for consensus, and therefore meets this second criterion of objectivity, more often than its relativist critics realize. Ultimately, I will argue that it does so because of the existence of "theories," multilayered impersonal worlds that create the conditions of agreement. Within theories, social scientists share broad traditions and research programs; moreover, in the context of contemporary social science, even competing theories crosscut one another in important ways. I will begin, however, by pursuing the notion that these impersonal worlds are not theories but lifeworlds. I will show that, contrary to the radical relativism implied by the epistemological dilemma, hermeneutical philosophy is premised on the notion that these lifeworlds are not only impersonal but that they typically assume a universal and consensual form.

Since Dilthey defined the *Geisteswissenschaften*, hermeneutics has taken as given the existence of an impersonal natural world. For Dilthey natural science did not seem to involve the exercise of reason. By contrast, he was extremely sensitive to the subjectivity of the social world and to the impact of this subjectivity on the methods of the human studies. "Though experience presents us with the reality of life in its many ramifications," he writes (1976: 186), "we only seem to know one particular thing, namely our own life." Since Dilthey posits a "direct relationship between life and the human studies," the subjective personalism he places at the center of life makes relativism a critical issue for the human sciences. As he puts it, there is "a conflict between the tendencies of life and the goal of science" (ibid.: 183).

Because historians, economists, teachers of law and students of religion are involved in life they want to influence it. They subject historical personages, mass movements and trends to their judgment, which is conditioned by their individuality, the nation to which they belong and the age in which they live. Even when they think they are being objective they are determined by their horizon, for every analysis of the concepts of a former generation reveals constituents in them which derive from the presuppositions of that generation.

(ibid.)

It is not well understood that, while Dilthey begins with a powerful insight into the inevitable personalization of data and methods in the human studies, he does not think that methodological depersonalization or shared and binding universal understandings are impossible. He immediately follows the statement quoted above, for example, by insisting: "Yet every science implies a claim to validity," and he wishes to apply these goals to the relativistic human sciences themselves: "If there are to be strictly scientific human studies they must aim more consciously and critically at validity" (ibid.). At least in the latter part of his career, Dilthey took as his task to demonstrate how the very personalization of human life made depersonalization and binding norms one of its central features.

Dilthey believed that it was precisely the ineluctable centrality of experience that made the supersession of particularism a continuous human project. Because experience is personal, mutual understanding becomes problematic and hence of ultimate importance. Precisely because we are primarily experiencing the world, we are always trying to understand others and not only ourselves. This leads us to strive for common knowledge and to construct categories. Thus, Dilthey can insist, in what would otherwise seem an enigmatic passage, that "understanding alone surmounts the limitation of the individual experience." It does so because "extending over several people, mental creations, and communities, it widens the horizon of the individual life and, in the human studies, opens up the path which leads from the common to the general" (ibid.). Because human understandings "possess an independent existence and development of their own," individual actors are bound by universals, by generalized "judgments of value, rules of conduct, definitions of goals and of what is good" (ibid.: 179). Not only does the universal "objective mind" exist, but, Dilthey insists, it is accessible to hermeneutic understanding. In their role of social and cultural analysts, individuals exercise the same sure sense of understanding as when they are lay participants. "Because we are at home everywhere in this historical and understood world," Dilthey writes, "we understand the sense and meaning of it all" (ibid.: 191). It is the existence of generals – contextually universalistic understandings – that allows Dilthey to argue for the possibility that, even within hermeneutics, validity claims can have an objective reference.

> What persons have in common is the starting-point for all the relations between the particular and the general in the human studies. A basic experience of what men have in common permeates the whole conception of the mind-constructed world . . . This is the presupposition for understanding . . . The degree of methodological uncertainty achieved by understanding depends on the development of the general truths on which the understanding of this relationship is based.
>
> (*ibid.: 187*)

This same confidence that subjectivity and contextuality actually create shared and binding norms – commensurability in the science studies phrase – rather than detract from them is at the heart of Gadamer's existential hermeneutics, which owes much more to Dilthey than Gadamer seems inclined to admit. Universal, depersonalized norms are possible – in life as well as in method – because on the level of social life there is openness and community between individuals, who relate to one another more in the mode of "I and thou" than "I and it."

> In human relations the important thing is, as we have seen, to experience the 'Thou' truly as a 'Thou,' i.e., not to overlook his claim and to listen to what he has to say to us. To this end, openness is necessary . . . Anyone who listens is fundamentally open. Without this kind of openness to one another there is no genuine human relationship.

> Belonging together always also means being able to listen
> to one another.
>
> *(Gadamer 1975 [1965]: 325)*

Because individuals are open to each other, they have a chance of mutual understanding. This act of understanding means acknowledging the decenteredness of human reality and accepting some at least of its impersonal claims: "Openness to the other, then, includes the acknowledgement that I must accept some things that are against myself, even though there is no one else who asks this of me."

This is where tradition enters in, but for Gadamer it is not the source of the unexamined, hence arbitrary reference that the contextual reaction to positivism suggests. Where these recent contextualists seem almost eager to embrace skeptical implications – with the implication, for example, that the project of justifying democracy is impossible – for Gadamer this was hardly the case. Half a century after Dilthey and one German Reich later, Gadamer is far more sensitive than the founder of hermeneutic philosophy to the possible arbitrariness of binding norms. Dilthey demonstrates that there is commensurability and assumes that this provides the context for sustaining critical evaluation. Gadamer demonstrates in detail how it is that shared bonds become standards for the exercise of critical reason. He argues that common norms are accepted as binding – hence become "traditional" – not simply because actors wish to be understood but because they recognize their validity claims. Actors are open to tradition in the same way that they are open to other persons, and with often the same results: "I must allow the validity of the claim made by tradition, not in the sense of simply acknowledging the past in its otherness, but in such a way that it has something to say to me" (Gadamer 1975 [1965]: 324). If I decide it has something to say, it is because I recognize that traditions can "be a source of truth," that there are "justified prejudices productive of knowledge" (ibid.: 247).

> The authority of persons is based ultimately, not on the subjection and abdication of reason, but on recognition and knowledge – knowledge, namely, that the other is superior to oneself in judgment and insight and that for this reason his judgment takes precedence . . . Authority

cannot actually be bestowed, but . . . must be acquired, if someone is to lay claim to it. It rests on recognition and hence on an act of reason itself.

(*ibid.: 248*)

In these passages, the language of hermeneutics echoes with the sounds of the Enlightenment. Authority is a "claim" that makes implicit "validity demands." Authority is recognized if these claims – in "an act of freedom and reason" – can "be seen in principle, to be true" (ibid.: 248–9). Even the preservation of tradition is "act of reason, though an inconspicuous one" (ibid.: 250). Indeed, "preservation is as much a freely-chosen action as revolution and renewal."

There could be no more relevant argument against the epistemological dilemma than this. Gadamer's hermeneutics has been taken – not just by Rorty but by most of the contextualists I have discussed – as the quintessence of the concrete and personal against the abstract and universal. Yet Gadamer himself argues that this cannot be the case. "It seems to me," he writes, "that there is no such unconditional antithesis between tradition and reason" (ibid.: 250). The reason that is exercised vis-à-vis tradition in everyday life is exercised by the interpreter of society as well. Universalism and objectivity are intrinsic to the exercise of the modern human sciences; they mark its coming of age. "At the beginning of all historical hermeneutics," Gadamer insists, "the abstract antithesis between tradition and historical research, between history and knowledge, must be discarded" (ibid.: 251). Interpretive understanding is not simply personal and empathic; it necessarily involves an impersonal reference that allows a critical and universalistic response.

This placing of ourselves is not the empathy of one individual for another, nor is it the application to another person of our own criteria, but it always involves the attainment of a higher universality that overcomes, not only our own particularity, but also that of the other . . . We have continually to test all our prejudices.

(*ibid.: 272–3*)

In light of this forcefully expressed self-understanding of hermeneutics, it seems clear that the distance Habermas has traveled with his theory of communicative action is not quite so great as he (1977 [1970]) and others have represented. The notion of immanent validity claims is already there in Dilthey; it became explicit in the notion of understanding and interpretive method developed by Gadamer.

What Habermas has done to hermeneutic philosophy is important nonetheless. He suggests that it has overemphasized the likelihood of fully mutual and consensual understanding of the spontaneous exercise of rational control. Actors are imbedded in social arrangements that systematically distort communication in ways of which they cannot be fully aware. On these grounds, Habermas argues that rational understanding must also be exercised, and often is, in a more self-conscious and less spontaneous way than through the exercise of understanding alone. This leads Habermas from hermeneutics as such – even when it is rightly understood – to a historically grounded advocacy of social science theory. In pursuit of theory, Habermas rephrases Gadamer's approach to traditional rationality in a manner that emphasizes its impersonality. Because "reflexivity and objectivity are fundamental traits of language," he writes, hermeneutics is actually suggesting that "pre-understanding can be thematized." Through self-reflection, "interpretive schemes . . . are formulated in everyday language . . . which both enable and pre-judge the making of experiences." Self-reflection, thematization, and interpretive schematization are interpretive practices that will at some point be applied to themselves: "The rational reconstruction of a system of linguistic rules . . . is undertaken with the aim of explaining linguistic competence   (1987 [1980]: 177–9).

Rationally reconstructed linguistic rules are one form of general knowledge – they are theories of language. In making this transition from the objectivity of commonsense communication to thematization of the rules for communicative understanding, we have moved from hermeneutics to social science. We can see that this has not been a leap but a logical step. The movement toward universalism is inherent in contextual interpretation itself, for actors make efforts to understand their own understanding in increasingly general ways. The universalistic result of each interpretive effort might be conceived of as a deposit of rationality. If these deposits are taken up by future efforts, they may become rational traditions; eventually, upon further reconstruction, they may become abstract theories.

Theories are couched at verious levels of generality. For this reason, "theories" present themselves in a variety of forms (Alexander 1982a), as arguments about presuppositional logic, as schematic interactive models, ideological prescriptions, methodological predictions, causal hypotheses. These theories do not reflect absent reason; they do not exist "out there" and impose themselves on credulous human beings. They do reflect thoughtful efforts, sometimes generations and centuries long, to understand and develop approximations of the society that surrounds human life. It is not only moral or aesthetic edification that prompts this effort but the desire for objective understanding itself.

Indeed, it is a simple thing to demonstrate that moral and aesthetic arguments – so often taken by contextualists as the very paradigms of anti-universalist, grounded discourse – have themselves aimed at developing general theories and have been guided by earlier theorizing in turn. One could illustrate this with even the most vulgar and popular of the arts. When French New Wave film critics developed their director-centered evaluative standards in the postwar era, they advanced what they called the "auteur theory" and the relied on André Bazin's (1967) ontological theories about cinema in turn. In the film criticism that followed, auteur theory was treated as a generalization and guided the practice and interpretation of film-making for decades (see e.g. Sarris 1968), despite the efforts of critics like Pauline Kael to refute it by offering falsifying data. In more sophisticated aesthetic domains, the generalizing references and the objective force of what is taken to be "true argument" are much more explicit. When William Empson (1935) helped to launch "New Criticism" in *Seven Types of Ambiguity*, he did not rely simply on textual intuition but on Freud's theories about ambivalence, and the claims he made for the universal validity of his new theory appeared to be sustained for several decades thereafter. When Harold Bloom (1973) made his influential riposte in *The Anxiety of Influence*, he rested his case upon other Freudian tenets and a more historical theory of knowledge production, but he aimed at producing a conceptual scheme that was just as generalizing and ambitious.

For moral argument, of course, it is that much easier to demonstrate the significance of general theory. Does John Rawls (1971) forsake propositions, models, and abstract conceptions simply because his concern in *A Theory of Justice* is practical and prescriptive? It could be argued, of course, that the theoretical abstraction of Rawls's argument is produced by his mistaken sense of the transcendental – in current moral philosophical language, "externalist" – nature of his project. Yet while he has subsequently acknowledged (Rawls et al. 1987) the historically specific moral underpinnings of his project, his central propositions look much the same. Michael Walzer (1983) has offered the most forceful hermeneutical alternative to Rawls. Despite the groundedness of Walzer's moral reasoning, however, *Spheres of Justice* presents an attempt to build a systematic, empirically documented, and highly general moral theory.

Neither aesthetic nor "practical" theory can or actually wishes to avoid strenuous references to validity claims; nor can they or wish they to avoid the effort to substantiate these claims by building arguments of the most generalized sort. In giving such reasons and making such arguments, they reflect their deep entrenchment within a depersonalized and decentered world. This universalistic mode is abandoned, indeed, only when there is a change in genre. Here we have the famous "imitative fallacy," that form should resemble substance. When the analysis of morality becomes an exercise in moral jeremiad, or when the argument for erotic and aesthetic freedom becomes an exemplification of poetic playfulness, moral or aesthetic argument may be edifying or satisfying but it certainly will not have the same claim to be true.[18]

While the centrality of general theorizing can be demonstrated even in such paradigmatically interpretive works, such theoretical reference does not create a comforting sense of objectivity. "Theories" may create, or crystallize, the impersonal worlds that are the necessary conditions for agreement, but within the social and humanistic sciences, at least, fully satisfying agreement rarely occurs. The disciplines of the human sciences are organized theoretically around broad and competing traditions and empirically around competing research programs (Alexander and Colomy 1991). These traditions and programs originate in the charismatic reason of figures who at some later point have been accorded classical status (Alexander 1987b). In periods of fission, the existence of such cleavages often leads to skepticism and discouragement. This, indeed, has been one of the principal reasons for the deepening movement toward contextualism of the present day.

Two responses can be made. The first follows directly from the argument thus far. These traditions and programs are not just sources of disagreement but powerful means of intertwining impersonal theoretical controls with disciplinary practice. While there is dissensus between programs and traditions, there is relative agreement within them. It is for this reason that, within the parameters of a school, practitioners can sometimes reach remarkable levels of mutual theoretical understanding and conceptual, even empirical precision. The objectivity of such practices is conditional but not ephemeral. Dominant and mature research programs often create entirely new realms of observational statements; they also set standards of explanatory scope and internal coherence that competing programs must meet. In the competition between such programs and traditions is found whatever progress the human sciences can provide (Alexander and Colomy 1992).

The second response to the prospect of continual disagreement is to suggest that these groups are neither as internally coherent nor as externally hermetic as the model of theoretical cleavage suggests. Kuhn exaggerated the incommensurability of paradigms because he viewed scientific orientations as expressive totalities, emphasizing the consistency between the different components of science. Yet the components of science – the different kinds and levels of theory – are relatively autonomous (Alexander 1982a); even within a single theorist's own work, let alone a particular school, commitments at different levels of the scientific continuum do not tightly cohere. While this variability reduces the possibility of objective controls over practices within a school, it increases the likelihood that there will be universal and shared references between schools.

In the history of natural-scientific thought (Alexander 1982a: 25ff), scientists of similar metaphysical orientations have often diverged radically over issues on the more empirically oriented side of the scientific continuum, such as proper models or correct propositions. On the other hand, scientists have agreed about empirical observations while disagreeing fundamentally about general presuppositional issues. If such crosscutting commitments, or "weak ties," occur even within the relatively controlled settings of the physical sciences, they are that much more frequent in the social. In both the natural and social sciences, moreover, powerful cross-cleavage agreements emanate from the methodological level, where common commitments to rationalist notions of evidence and logic can usually be found. These and other historically grounded yet deeply institutionalized agreements – which range from intellectual ambitions to topic selection procedures – form the shared disciplinary matrices (Toulmin 1972) within which theoretical traditions and research programs must find their place. In his slashing attack on Louis Althusser's contention that empirical historical research can be reduced to mere ideological particularities, E. P. Thompson demonstrates the controlling power of these broader disciplinary universals. "His comments," Thompson writes about Althusser, "display throughout no acquaintance with, nor understanding of, historical procedures; that is, procedures which make a 'history' a *discipline* and not a babble of alternating ideological assertions: procedures which provide for their own relevant discourse [about] proof" (1978: 205–6; original italics).[19]

These final considerations bring us back, fittingly, to the question of "foundations." To engage in foundationalism is to put forward general theoretical arguments, to create criteria for truthfulness that are so universally compelling that they produce agreement about validity claims between practitioners in a field. Rorty, we have seen, rejects foundational argument on the grounds that, because theory cannot mirror reality in an epistemological sense, there is no possibility of permanently uncontested truth. But surely this misses the point. It is precisely the perspectival quality of social science that makes its own version of foundationalism, its more or less continuous strain of general theorizing, so necessary and often so compelling. It is natural science that does not exhibit foundationalism, for the very reason that its access to external truth has become increasingly secure. Commensurability and realism delegitimate foundationalism, not increase its plausibility. In natural science, attention can plausibly be focused on the empirical side of the continuum. In social science, by contrast, practitioners cannot so easily accept "the evidence of their senses."

Discourse becomes as important a disciplinary activity as explanation. Discourse is general and foundational. It aims at thematizing the standards of validity that are immanent in the very practice of social science. Responding to the lack of disciplinary confidence in empirical mirroring, theoretical discourse aims to gain provisional acceptance on the basis of universal argument. It is, therefore, the very impossibility of establishing permanent foundations that makes foundationalism in the social sciences so critical. This is the postpositivist case for general theory. It is also the case for present reason.

NOTES

1 For a developmental perspective on the concept of decentering, see Piaget 1972. For the historical framing of societal generalization and depersonalization and their relation to human freedom, see the evolutionary theory of Parsons (1966, 1973) and Bellah (1964), which carries through on certain key themes in Weber and Durkheim and is pushed further and formalized by Habermas (e.g. 1984).

2 For Weber's understanding of civilization and dualism, see particularly Parsons's (1963) classic Introduction to Weber's *Sociology of Religion*. For civilization as an evolving, increasingly abstract and ascetic construct, see Elias 1975 [1939]. For Aboriginal consciousness as a fused and interpenetrated "dreaming," see Bellah 1970. For the interpenetration of levels in primitive thought, see Lévi-Strauss 1967.

3 I stress "organized social action" because the subjective, phenomenological dimension remains central to the construction of action and order in modern societies, just as, in earlier and more simple societies, actors had to sustain a strong sense of the objectivity of the world outside them. Indeed, to demonstrate this necessary interrelation of objectivity and subjectivity is the very point of phenomenological theory. Such a demonstration is also one of the main ambitions of Wittgenstein, at once the most influential relativist in modern thought and one of the most forceful critics of the notion of private language, e.g. Wittgenstein 1953, para. 272. Neither for Husserl nor for Wittgenstein is there the philosophical possibility of seeing the world out there as it really is. To recognize this possibility social theory and

philosophy must develop a historical conception of the human capacity for perception, one which emphasizes its cultural and social organization.

4 This is one of the principal themes of Weber's comparative religion.

5 This theme is developed in Alexander 1986.

6 For this hypothesis and some fascinating historical documentation, see Georg Misch 1973 [1907].

7 For this argument, see Hegel's *Phenomenology of Mind* and Marx's *Early Philosophical Manuscripts*. For a broad and important discussion of Romantic idealism as a countermovement, see Charles Taylor 1975.

8 I use Rorty's (1979) phrase ironically, to emphasize that it is the practitioners, not the philosophers of science, who are compelled to understand objectivity in a mirroring, subject-less stance.

9 For this position, see particularly Parsons 1954 [1945] and Parsons and Shils 1951. In his earlier work, Parsons (1937) developed the concept of analytic realism, which recognized the agentic contribution of the scientist but insisted (in a Kantian fashion) that the world could be mirrored nonetheless. Rather then transcending the dichotomy, however, this concept finesses it. A more Hegelian, less Kantian conception is needed.

10 After all, if the pressure of a particular historical conjuncture leads a popular audience to attach a new connotatively social "signified" to what had initially been merely a denotated referent, why should Barthes's environment not affect him in the same way? Can he really distance himself from the history that mythologizes other semiotic patterns in an objective way? Is he not merely reading in his own anti-bourgeois sentiment? Barthes's implicit response (1959: 156–9) is that he is the "scientific" student of myth. It is this unthought-out, implicit scientism of early semiotics that detonated later poststructural considerations.

11 It was not visible at that time, however, because of the continuing influence of critical theory, which insisted on the reality, if not the desirability, of the external world.

12 For a powerful critique of the political and epistemological implications of Foucault's work, which takes it as the archetype of an anti-humanism, see Taylor 1986.

13 Unless otherwise indicated, all following page references are to Rorty 1979.

14 It is probably not fair, then, for Cornell West (1985: 267) to call Rorty's philosophy "a form of ethnocentric posthumanism." Not fair, at least, in the sense that Rorty's aim is to create the basis for universal community and love. However, Rorty's rejection of universalism and embrace of the concrete make it impossible for him to respond in

principle to West's charge that "for Rorty . . . we are North Atlantic ethnocentrists in solidarity with a civilization (or set of contemporary tribal practices) – and possibly a decaying and declining one – which has no philosophical defense."

15 Nor is Bernstein alone in this shifting emphasis. As the contextualist movement has gained acceptance, the full ramifications of its relativism are beginning to lead to reconsiderations in different quarters of the social sciences. Cf. the important critique of deconstructive history in Grossman (1989).

16 This connection between the possibility for conditional objectivity and the ability for those engaged in a knowledge practice to sustain agreement about the frameworks for knowing is emphasized by Goldstein (1976), in a work on historiography that is highly pertinent to the present argument.

17 In the drive to personalize and relativize science, this dimension of Merton's contribution has been almost completely neglected, as, of course, has virtually the entire issue of scientific universalism as such. It is an incredible paradox that in an age when scientific technology has put the entire human world at fatal risk, the philosophy, history, and sociology of science have focused increasingly on relativistic idiography. Surely some attention must be paid to the opposite question, however: How has impersonal knowledge succeeded in so successfully exploring the objective world that it has learned to mimic it through humanly constructed machines?

18 Compare, in this latter regard, Marcuse's *Eros and Civilization* (1954) with Brown's *Love's Body* (1966).

19 In his essay on historiography, Grossman (1989: 49–50, 57) similarly emphasizes the critical role of the emergence of the disciplinary, professional organization in promoting the rational dimension of historical debate.

REFERENCES

Abrams, M. H. 1971: *Natural Supernaturalism*. New York: Norton.

Alexander, Jeffrey 1981: "Looking for theory: 'facts' and 'values' as the intellectual legacy of the 1970s," *Theory and Society*, 10: 279–92.

Alexander, Jeffrey 1982a: *Theoretical Logic in Sociology*, vol. 1: *Positivism, Presuppositions, and Current Controversies*, Berkeley and Los Angeles: University of California Press.

Alexander, Jeffrey 1982b: "Kuhn's unsuccessful revisionism: a rejoinder to Selby," *Canadian Journal of Sociology*, 7/2:

Alexander, Jeffrey 1986: "The dialectic of individuation and domination: Max Weber's rationalization theory and beyond," in Whimpster and Lash (eds), *Max Weber, Rationality and Modernity*. London: Allen & Unwin, pp. 185–206.

Alexander, Jeffrey 1987a: *Twenty Lectures: Sociological Theory since World War Two*. New York: Columbia University Press.

Alexander, Jeffrey 1987b: "On the centrality of the classics," in Anthony Giddens and Jonathan Turner (eds), *Social Theory Today*, Cambridge: Polity Press, pp. 11–57.

Alexander, Jeffrey 1990: "Between progress and apocalypse: social theory and the dream of reason in the twentieth century," in Alexander and Piotr Sztompka (eds), *Progress and Social Theory: Movement, Forces, and Ideas at the End of the Twentieth Century*. London: Unwin & Hyman, pp. 5–38.

Alexander, Jeffrey, and Paul Colomy 1991: "Neofunctionalism today: reconstructing a theoretical tradition," in George Ritzer (ed.), *Frontiers of Social Theory*. New York: Columbia University Press.

Alexander, Jeffrey, and Paul Colomy 1992: "Traditions and competition: preface to a postpositivist approach to knowledge accumulation," in George Ritzer (ed), *Metatheory in Sociology*. Newbury Park, Calif.: Sage.

Althusser, Louis 1969: *For Marx*. Harmondsworth: Penguin; New York: Vintage Books.

Barthes, Roland 1959: "Myth today," in *Mythologies*. New York: Hill & Wang, pp. 109–59.

Baudrillard, Jean 1983: *Simulations*. New York: Semiotext (e).

Bazin, André 1967: *What is Cinema?* Berkeley: University of California Press.

Bellah, Robert N. 1970: "Religious evolution," in *Beyond Belief*. New York: Random House, pp. 20–50.

Bernstein, Richard J. 1978: *The Restructuring of Social and Political Theory*. Philadelphia: University of Pennsylvania Press.

Bernstein, Richard J. 1983: *Beyond Objectivism and Relativism*. Philadelphia: University of Pennsylvania Press.

Bloom, Harold 1973: *The Anxiety of Influence*. New York: Oxford University Press.

Bourdieu, Pierre 1984: *Distinctions*. London: Routledge.

Brown, Norman O. 1966: *Love's Body*. New York: Vintage.

Derrida, Jacques 1981: *Positions*. Chicago: University of Chicago Press.

Dilthey, Wilhelm 1976: "The construction of the historical world in the human studies," in Dilthey, *Selected Writings*. New York and Cambridge: Cambridge University Press, pp. 168–245.

Elias, Norbert 1975 [1939]: *The Civilizing Process*. New York: Urizen Books.

Empson, William 1935: *Seven Types of Ambiguity*. London: Chatto and Windus.

Foucault, Michel 1977: *Discipline and Punish: The Birth of the Prison*. New York: Pantheon.

Foucault, Michel 1978: *The History of Sexuality*, vol. 1: *An Introduction*. New York: Pantheon.

Foucault, Michel 1980: *Power/Knowledge: Selected Interviews and Other Writings, 1972–1977*. New York: Pantheon.

Friedman, Jonathan 1987: "Beyond otherness or: the spectacularization of anthropology," *Telos*, 20/1: 161–70.

Gadamer, Hans-Georg 1975 [1965]: *Truth and Method*. New York: Seabury.

Garfinkle, Harold 1967: *Studies in Ethnomethodology*. Englewood Cliffs, N. J.: Prentice–Hall.

Geertz, Clifford 1973a (1964]: "Ideology as a cultural system," in Geertz, *The Interpretation of Cultures*. New York: Basic Books, pp. 193–233.

Geertz, Clifford 1973b [1966]: "Religion as a cultural system," in *The Interpretation of Cultures*. New York: Basic Books, pp. 87–125.

Geertz, Clifford 1973c: "Thick description: toward an interpretive theory of culture," in *The Interpretation of Cultures*. New York: Basic Books, pp. 3–32.

Geertz, Clifford 1983: "Introduction" in Geertz, *Local Knowledge*. New York: Basic Books, pp. 3–16.

Gibbons, Michael T. 1987: *Interpreting Politics*. London and New York: Basil Blackwell.

Goldstein, Leon J. 1976: *Historical Knowing*. Austin: University of Texas Press.

Grossman, Lionel 1989: "Toward a rational historiography," *Transactions of the American Philosophical Society* 79, 3.

Haan, Norma, Robert N. Bellah, Paul Rabinow, and William N. Sullivan (eds) 1983: *Social Science as Moral Inquiry*. New York: Columbia University Press.

Habermas, Jürgen 1977 [1970]: "A review of Gadamer's *Truth and Method*," in Fred R. Dallmayr and Thomas A. McCarthy (eds), *Understanding and Social Inquiry*. Notre Dame: University of Notre Dame Press, pp. 335–63.

Habermas, Jürgen 1982: "The entwinement of myth and Enlightenment: rereading the dialectic of Enlightenment," *New German Critique*, 26: 14–30.

Habermas, Jürgen 1984: *The Theory of Communicative Action*, vol. 1: *Reason and the Rationalization of Society*. Boston: Beacon Press.

Habermas, Jürgen 1987 [1980]: "The hermeneutic claim to universality," in Gibbons 1987, pp. 175–202.

Huyssen, Andreas 1986: "Mapping the postmodern," in *After the Great Divide*, Bloomington, Ind.: Indiana University Press, pp. 178–240.

Ingram, David 1985: "Hermeneutics and truth," in Robert Hollinger (ed.), *Hermeneutics and Praxis*. Notre Dame: Notre Dame University Press, pp. 32–53.

Jacoby, Russell 1975: *Social Amnesia*. Boston: Beacon Press.

Jaeger, Werner 1965: *Paideia: The Ideals of Greek Culture*. New York: Oxford University Press.

Jones, Ernest 1963: *The Life and Work of Sigmund Freud*. New York: Doubleday.

Kuhn, Thomas 1970 [1962]: *The Structure of Scientific Revolutions*. Chicago: University of Chicago Press.

Kuhn, Thomas 1978: *Black-Body Theory and the Quantum Discontinuity, 1894–1912*. New York: Oxford University Press.

Lévi-Stauss, Claude 1967 [1962]: *The Savage Mind*. Chicago: University of Chicago Press.

Lyotard, Jean-François 1984 [1979]: *The Postmodern Condition: A Report on Knowledge*, tr. G. Bennington and B. Massumi. Minneapolis: University of Minnesota Press.

Marcuse, Herbert 1954: *Eros and Civilization*. Boston: Beacon Press.

Merton, Robert K. 1973 [1942]: "The normative structure of science," in Merton, *The Sociology Science*, ed. Norman W. Storer, Chicago: University of Chicago Press, pp. 267–78.

Misch, Georg 1973 [1907]: *The History of Autobiography in Antiquity*. London: Routledge.

Mitzman, Arthur 1970: *The Iron Cage*. New York: Knopf.

Nagel, Thomas 1986: *The View from Nowhere*. New York: Oxford University Press.

Parsons, Talcott 1937: *The Structure of Social Action*. New York: Free Press.

Parsons, Talcott 1954 [1945]: "The present position and prospects of systematic theory in sociology," in *Essays in Sociological Theory*. New York: Free Press, pp. 212–37.

Parsons, Talcott 1963: Introduction to Max Weber, *Sociology of Religion*. Boston: Beacon Press.

Parsons, Talcott 1966: *Societies: Evolutionary and Comparative Perspectives*. Englewood Cliffs, NJ: Prentice-Hall.

Parsons, Talcott 1973: *The System of Modern Societies*. Englewood Cliffs, NJ: Prentice-Hall.

Parsons, Talcott, and Edward Shils (eds) 1951: *Towards a General Theory of Action*. Cambridge, Mass.: Harvard University Press.

Piaget, Jean 1972: *The Principles of Genetic Epistemology*. London: Routledge.

Rabinow, Paul, and William Sullivan (eds) 1979: *Interpretive Social Science: A Reader*. Berkeley and Los Angeles: University of California Press.

Rawls, John 1971: *A Theory of Justice*. Cambridge, Mass.: Harvard University Press.

Rawls, John, et al. 1987: *Liberty, Equality, and Law: Selected Tanner Lectures on Moral Philosophy*. Salt Lake City, Utah: University of Utah Press.

Rieff, Philip 1961: *Freud: The Mind of the Moralist*. New York: Doubleday.

Rorty, Richard 1979: *Philosophy and the Mirror of Nature*. Princeton, NJ: Princeton University Press.

Rorty, Richard 1982a: "Method, social science, social hope," in *Consequences of Pragmatism*. Minneapolis: University of Minneapolis Press, pp. 191–210.

Rorty, Richard 1982b: "The world well lost," in *Consequences of Pragmatism*. Minneapolis: University of Minneapolis Press, pp. 3–18.

Rorty, Richard 1985a: "Postmodernist bourgeois liberalism," in Robert Hollinger (ed.), *Hermeneutics and Praxis*. Notre dame: Notre Dame University Press, pp. 214–21.

Rorty, Richard 1985b: "Habermas and Lyotard on postmodernity," in Richard J. Bernstein (ed.), *Habermas and Modernity*. Cambridge, Mass.: MIT Press, pp. 161–75.

Rorty, Richard 1986: "Foucault and epistemology," in David Couzens Hoy (ed.), *Foucault: A Critical Reader*. Oxford and New York: Basil Blackwell.

Sarris, Andrew 1968: "Toward a theory of film history," in *The American Cinema: Directors and Directions 1929–1968*. New York: Dutton, pp. 19–37

Scheffler, Israel 1976: *Science and Subjectivity*. Indianapolis: Bobbs-Merril.

Taylor, Charles 1975: *Hegel*. Cambridge: Cambridge University Press.

Taylor, Charles 1986: "Foucault on freedom and truth," in David Couzens Hoy (ed.), *Foucault: A Critical Reader*. Oxford and New York: Basil Blackwell, pp. 69–102.

Thompson, E. P. 1978: *The Poverty of Theory and Other Essays*. London: Merlin.

Toulmin, Stephen 1972: *Human Understanding*, vol. 1. Princeton, NJ: Princeton University Press.

Voegelin, Eric 1957: *The World of the Polis*. New Orleans: Louisiana State University Press.

Walzer, Michael 1983: *Spheres of Justice*. New York: Basic Books.

Wardell, Mark L., and Stephen P. Turner (eds), 1986: *Sociological Theory in Transition*. Boston: Allen & Unwin.

West, Cornell 1985: "The politics of American neo-pragmatism," in John Rajchman and Cornell West (eds), *Post-Analytic Philosophy*. New York: Columbia University Press, pp. 259–72.

Will, Frederick L. 1985: "Reason, social practice, and scientific realism," in Robert Hollinger (ed.), *Hermeneutics and Praxis*. Notre Dame: Notre Dame University Press, pp. 122–42.

Winch, Peter 1958: *The Idea of a Social Science and Its Relation to Philosophy*. London: Routledge.

Wittgenstein, Ludwig 1953: *Philosophical Investigations*. New York: Macmillan.

Name Index

Subject Index